796.0973 BES 2007 **MPL**

The best American sports
writing 2007   AUG   08

D1506633

The Best American Sports Writing 2007

GUEST EDITORS OF
THE BEST AMERICAN SPORTS WRITING

1991 DAVID HALBERSTAM
1992 THOMAS MCGUANE
1993 FRANK DEFORD
1994 TOM BOSWELL
1995 DAN JENKINS
1996 JOHN FEINSTEIN
1997 GEORGE PLIMPTON
1998 BILL LITTLEFIELD
1999 RICHARD FORD
2000 DICK SCHAAP
2001 BUD COLLINS
2002 RICK REILLY
2003 BUZZ BISSINGER
2004 RICHARD BEN CRAMER
2005 MIKE LUPICA
2006 MICHAEL LEWIS
2007 DAVID MARANISS

The Best AMERICAN SPORTS WRITING™ 2007

Edited and with an Introduction
by David Maraniss

Glenn Stout, *Series Editor*

HOUGHTON MIFFLIN COMPANY
BOSTON • NEW YORK   2007

www.houghtonmifflinbooks.com

ISSN 1056-8034
ISBN-10: 0-618-75115-7   ISBN-13: 978-0-618-75115-0
ISBN-10: 0-618-75116-5 (pbk.)   ISBN-13: 978-0-618-75116-7 (pbk.)

Printed in the United States of America

MP 10 9 8 7 6 5 4 3 2 1

Contents

Foreword

I HAVE FRIENDS — really, I'm not *quite* as isolated as many imagine — who work as writers for newspapers and magazines and similar venues. Some are sportswriters, and others write in other genres, yet beyond their shared love of the written word they are all united by something else. Most believe they are too often being edited into monotony.

This is a relatively new phenomenon. The impact that changes in technology have had on writing over the last two decades has been both profound and, because the technology is so transparent and was so quickly adopted, nearly invisible. It amazes me that the effect this has had on the whole process of writing is never even mentioned. It is as if the way things used to be is an embarrassment.

At the risk of dating myself, I have recently passed the twenty-year mark in my career as a professional writer. I still remember when, before typing my first published story for *Big City Magazine*, I first had to write it in longhand time and time again. Even then, the final, handwritten draft contained several additional pages of inserts, arrows, and other scrawled changes.

Only then did I dare approach the typewriter, tapping each character with almost archaeological precision, as if one mis-strike would make dust of the entire story. I was certain that a single strikeover or other error caused by the accumulation of Wite-out fumes in an enclosed space would cause my career to lurch to a halt before it had even started.

This fear was made even worse by the fact that, owing to a mild neuropathy in my hands that sends several of my fingers flailing away on vacation alone, I cannot touch-type, at least not in a recognizable language. Typing on a typewriter was a physical challenge more difficult than hitting a baseball. Even after I discovered correcting ribbons and started sneaking into my workplace early to use the IBM Selectric, a two- or three-thousand-word story took me hours to type. Only when it was perfect would I even think of turning in the manuscript, delivering it to the front desk by hand.

But this was not altogether bad. As arduous as was the physical process of writing, editing was not much easier. *Big City Magazine* generally gave my copy two edits, one for content and creative issues and the other purely for grammar and spelling. This was all so labor-intensive and time-consuming that the story that appeared in print was very much the story I originally wrote. Significant changes were too damn hard to make and took too long. In general, my editor only tweaked the lead and the end, so I always tried to leave him something in each place that he could fix, thereby satisfying his need to fulfill his title yet leave the rest of my masterpiece alone. Then, after I signed off, the story was sent to some typing-wiz underling to be prepared for composition and printing.

Two decades later nothing is the same. Word processing and computers allow even bad typists to work on a piece for as long and as often as we wish. Errors of all kinds can be fixed, changed, and corrected in a matter of seconds. Every single element of every bit of writing is fully malleable. Even in a brief essay like this, I have been able to change it thousands of times, ranging from purely mechanical modifications to moving entire sentences and paragraphs around and back and forth, shuffling and reshuffling until I am, if not satisfied, at least pretty sure that further mucking around will only screw things up. Then I send it off to my editor in an e-mail as an attached file, and it's happy hour here at BASW world headquarters.

I have been fortunate that — with one egregious exception I have since self-medicated from my memory — most of the editors I have worked with either like the way I write or are lazy, because they rarely make dramatic changes to my copy. While this may be a mistake on their part, my pharmacist and I are deeply appreciative. At least I know that when my writing sucks, it is my fault.

My aforementioned friends are not so fortunate.

One writer I know recently left one high-profile writing job for another. In this person's former position, I usually knew within a sentence or two who I was reading. But now, in the new job, each story reads just like every other story in the same publication. The writer's style — presumably one of the reasons this person was hired in the first place — is nowhere to be found.

I have since learned why. Many stories my acquaintance files are edited, not just once or twice by one or two people, but up to five or six times by a like number of editors. Machine-readable text is so easily manipulated that each editor makes change upon change upon change upon change. And each time the story is passed down the assembly line it becomes a little less distinctive and a little safer and a little more bland, until it is finally spit out upon the published page the precise same shade of gray as everything else that goes through that process. On occasion my friend shows me the original copy. It is often just that, *original.* After comparing the original to the final product, I have sometimes wondered why the publication even bothers to include my friend's byline. A more accurate attribution would read simply "By Just About Anybody."

As anyone in the newspaper or magazine industry knows, these are perilous times. Print circulation is shrinking as more and more readers dive en masse into the great online sea. While reading online is, in a sense, cheaper and easier, I don't think that's the only reason more and more readers are doing it. I think some of it has to do with the fact that, at least to my eyes and ears, much of the material online isn't over-edited like so much print-based writing is. Yes, lack of editing can and does result in writing that is awkward, sloppy, fatuous, and indulgent — the verbal equivalent of an *American Idol* tryout — but sometimes it is also more lively, distinctive, and ambitious.

I am not arguing that there should be no editors (well, I do know of *one* the world could do without), but in the wrong hands a word processor can be a dangerous, dangerous thing. If I were in charge, there would certainly be fewer editors, and most would be encouraged to take a lot of time off. Editing done for any reason other than space, accuracy, and basic clarity is pretty much guaranteed to kill any chance of authentic communication. As I prepare this book each year I read hundreds of stories that I suspect may once have been memorable but were edited into paste.

In this editing climate, style is an enemy. Today a writer as talented and original as Ring Lardner, for instance, would have absolutely no chance of making it into print. One can well imagine what the contemporary editorial factory would do with something like Lardner's classic novel of letters from rookie ballplayer Jack Keefe, *You Know Me, Al.* The title certainly would have been changed, first to something like *I Know Al,* then perhaps to *Al and I,* then *Dear Al,* and, finally perhaps, to *Alan and Jack: A Love Story.* God knows what they would do to Lardner's text — probably force him to abandon his epistolary in favor of an e-mail exchange, then strip the vernacular in favor of :(s, :)s, ;)s, and other notated atrocities.

Many writers find the editing experience so castrating that, increasingly, some of the most talented leave print work as soon as they have the opportunity, and others don't aspire to it at all. A measure of creative freedom exists both online and in larger formats such as books that is rapidly disappearing in newspapers and magazines. Many publications would do well to admit as much and simply add the phrase "Individuals Not Valued" on the masthead.

Editing just because one can is no reason to do so. When I first made the headlong leap into writing on a word-processing program, one of the first things I had to learn was when to stop. I ruined several stories because once I got going moving and copying and inserting and pasting and deleting and spell-checking and the-saurus-ing, all I had was a series of words occasionally separated by periods and commas that looked like and read like but in the end did not feel or sound like writing.

I trust that the stories in this book each year avoid the problems I've just described, and I think they do. If there is one thing I try to avoid during my annual quest, it is the safe story that has been scrubbed clean of any sharp edges, for the story easily swallowed is just as easily forgotten. Fortunately, time and time again, there are still plenty of writers — and some editors — who seem to realize that.

Every season I read every issue of hundreds of general interest and sports magazines in search of writing that might merit inclusion in *The Best American Sports Writing.* I also contact the sports editors of some three hundred newspapers and hundreds of magazine editors and request their submissions, and I actively scour the online world myself.

Readers, writers, and any other interested parties are encouraged to send me stories they've written or read in the past year that they would like to see reprinted in *The Best American Sports Writing 2008.* Each story

- must be column length or longer;
- must have been published in 2007;
- must not be a reprint or book excerpt;
- must have been published in the United States or Canada; and
- must be received by me by February 1, 2008.

All submissions must include the name of the author, the date of publication, and the publication name and address. The number of stories I receive each year that lack this basic information is staggering, so pay attention. Photocopies, tear sheets, or clean copies are fine. Readable reductions to 8½-by-11 are preferred. Submissions from online publications must be made in hard copy, and those who submit stories from newspapers should submit the story in hard copy as published. Since newsprint generally suffers in transit, newspaper stories are best copied and then mounted on 8½-by-11 paper, with the appropriate URL attached if the story also appeared online. There is no limit to the number of submissions either an individual or a publication may make, but please use common sense. Owing to the volume of material I receive, no submission can be returned or acknowledged. I also believe it is inappropriate for me to comment on or critique any individual submission. Publications that want to be absolutely certain their contributions are considered are advised to provide a complimentary subscription to the address listed below. Those that already do so should make sure to extend the subscription.

No e-mail submissions will be accepted. All submissions should be made by U.S. mail — midwinter weather conditions being what they are in Vermont, I often can't receive submissions delivered by UPS or FedEx. In the event that a story is selected for publication, your publication will be contacted concerning rights and permissions.

Please submit either an original or a clear paper copy of each story, with the publication name, author, and date the story appeared, to:

Glenn Stout
P.O. Box 549
Alburgh, VT 05440

Those with questions or comments may contact me at basweditor@yahoo.com. Copies of previous editions of this book can be ordered through most bookstores or online book dealers. An index of stories that have appeared in this series can be found at glennstout.net.

Thanks again go out to Houghton Mifflin for allowing me to continue to work on such a gratifying project, particularly my editor, Susan Canavan, and Will Vincent, who does the heavy lifting on his end. Guest editor David Maraniss did his duty with enthusiasm, and I appreciate the time and care he put into making his selections. Thanks also to the website sportsjournalists.com for posting submission guidelines. My ten-year-old daughter Saorla deserves special recognition for her first appearance as my editorial assistant, and she and her mother both deserve thanks for sharing in both the hard work and harvest of this word farm. It may be just sports, but the writers in this book know better.

GLENN STOUT
Alburgh, Vermont

Introduction

ONE OF THE JOYS of visiting my parents at their apartment in Milwaukee during the final years of their lives was rummaging through the wide-ranging collection of magazines and newspapers that piled up on their couch and spilled over to the floor below. *The Nation* and the *Packer Report*. *The New Yorker* and *The Sporting News*. The *New York Review of Books* and *ESPN The Magazine*. *The Progressive* and *Packer Plus*. *The American Prospect* and *Baseball America*. The *Capital Times* and *Sports Illustrated*. The *Washington Post National Weekly Edition* and *Baseball Weekly*. If you wanted to know about my dad, Elliott Maraniss, his reading tastes told much of the story.

A lifelong newspaperman, he was always interested in history and politics. The books he checked out from the local library and stacked near the magazine pile tended to be about European writers, Civil War generals, American presidents, British diplomats. But what satisfied him as much or more, I think, was reading about a rookie defensive tackle showing promise in training camp with the Green Bay Packers or another phenom left fielder out in El Paso (when the Diablos were in the Brewers farm system) who was knocking the stuffing off the ball. Earl Warren, the former chief justice of the Supreme Court, was known, among his other greater accomplishments, for saying that when he got the newspaper in the morning he turned to the sports section before the front page. I'm not sure whether sports came first with my dad, but he certainly turned to it most often.

He was not a statistics guy. He had little interest in the Sabermetrics approach to baseball analysis in which everything is reduced to numbers. He loved baseball more as a story with characters and some drama. It didn't have to be elegiac, or melodramatic, or even particularly elegant. Maybe that's because he spent his adolescence in Coney Island rooting for the Brooklyn Dodgers when they were the "Lovable Bums." His baseball was the sort described by Mark Harris in *Bang the Drum Slowly* and *The Southpaw.* Just salt-of-the-earth kids, some dumb, some smart, making their way through the vagaries of baseball life. He was from the Ring Lardner school. I had a tendency to make things up when I was a kid and had an excuse for every wrong thing I did. My dad called me Alibi Ike long before I realized that he was at once chewing me out and letting me know that he loved me. In my family, where my mother and siblings were scholars, "The sun got in my eyes" held as much literary merit as any quotation from Shakespeare.

I was a bit surprised when my dad joined my brother as owner of a team in the baseball rotisserie league formed by a bunch of my friends at the *Washington Post* in 1984. The Washington Ghost League, as we called it, was one of the early leagues formed after the statistical game was invented a few years earlier by some writers and editors in New York. As I said, Elliott was not interested in statistics, so why would he take part in a game of statistics? Because it really wasn't about the numbers back then before the entire sporting nation got caught up in what later became fantasy baseball, and fantasy football, and fantasy basketball, and even fantasy NASCAR.

It was about the yearly drafts held at Tom Lippman's house on McKinley Street and the little dramas and characters of our league. How Lippman and his Tom-Toms had an obsession with catchers. How Ben Weiser of the Weiser Owls could almost persuade you that giving up Roger Clemens for Pete Ladd was a good deal. How Neil Henry, in his love for all things Mariner, could not discern the talent gap between Mickey Brantley and Ken Griffey Jr. How Bill Hamilton's team was lousy every year except the one when he disappeared to Europe for the entire summer and won the whole thing thanks to a monster season from Bo Jackson. How Mike Hill would sit snickering in the back and not say a word until Vince Coleman's name came up. How the Potts boys would argue excitedly over Mets farm hands never heard from again. And the assertiveness with which Peter Behr of the Archibald Behrisols delivered his immortal preemptive opening bid for a hack second baseman: "Jerry Remy for a dollar." (In our league, Remy would go for ten cents.)

In the lore of the Ghost League, Elliott uttered the first line at the first draft, and to this day his words have the resonance of Melville's "Call me Ishmael." The name of the team formed by my dad and brother Jim would be familiar to track fans of a certain era — the Jim-Elliott Jumbos. From the end of the long oval table, his voice as gruff and determined as if he were barking out an order for copy from his city editor days, Elliott opened the first draft by declaring, "The Jumbos want Jim Rice." I can't adequately describe what those few words convey to my brother and me. All I can say is that Jim uttered that phrase again at our father's funeral in May 2004. In the entire crowd that had gathered for the memorial service at the Unitarian church in Madison, maybe only Jim and I and my son Andrew had the slightest clue what he was talking about, but it had me in tears. It was all in the back story.

There were some apparent contradictions in my dad's view of sports.

As a tough-minded journalist, he was fearless in pushing reporters to challenge the traditional wisdom of coaches. He was always skeptical, questioning whether universities were running honest programs and whether sports icons were all they proclaimed to be. He took pride in the fact that one of his reporters at the *Madison Capital Times* broke a story that Bob Knight was leaving West Point to coach at the University of Wisconsin, and that Knight got so upset by the scoop — it was supposed to be kept secret for two days — that he backed away from the deal. Untold thousands of Badger fans who endured decades of losing seasons at the UW Field House in the ensuing decades might have felt the story wasn't worth all that suffering, but in fact the wound-tight Knight never would have fit in Madison anyway. Elliott also hired the first woman sportswriter at his newspaper, and the first African-American sportswriter, and he was constantly pushing at the traditions of the profession. Even though he was born in Boston, he taught me never to root for the Red Sox because they were the last major league team to integrate. His preference for the National League in the 1950s and 1960s was due in large part to the league's more progressive recruitment of black and Latino players, from Jackie Robinson to Hank Aaron to Roberto Clemente to Rico Carty and Felipe Alou, two of his favorite hitters from the last days of the Milwaukee Braves.

Yet in his personal tastes, when he was on the side porch in his boxer shorts and T-shirt listening to a ball game on the radio on a summer's night, his preferences ran completely to the babbling, incoherent, lovable homers. The newfangled announcers were either too bland or narrow-mindedly aggressive, from his perspective. He even had the temerity to criticize Vin Scully, who was one notch too glib for him. To be completely honest, his disdain for Scully might also have had to do with the fact that Scully sashayed out of Brooklyn with Walter O'Malley and made his name with the new Dodgers in Los Angeles, and that marked him as a traitor, but I still think my dad would rather hear Harry Caray or Jack Brickhouse obliterate the English language than listen to Scully recite a perfectly literate paragraph without so much as an "er" or an "uh." He felt that announcers like Caray and Brickhouse and Lou Boudreau weren't making more out of the game than what it was; they were closer to Ring Lardner and Mark Harris.

Which brings me to the balm of Ron Santo.

Many people, even some Cubs fans I know, might make the reasonable argument that Ron Santo, the old third baseman, ranks among the least articulate announcers ever to call a game. He made Caray, even in his drunken dotage, seem erudite. My dad would agree, but could not care less. He loved Ron Santo, first as an underrated ballplayer, but even more as the voice of Cubs radio with his partner Pat Hughes. Anyone can call balls and strikes, or offer an astute observation on the erratic play of the second baseman during a road trip in June, or coin some distinctive way of calling a home run, but who besides Santo can produce so many central European guttural sounds of agony as his team is on its way to blowing another game? Ahhhhhhhrrrggguuuuuhhhhhgggoooooh.

For most of his life, Elliott lived by the motto: it could be worse. That was in the real world. In the world of baseball his sensibility was that it is going to get worse, no matter how good things seem right now, and Santo was his favorite poet of imminent demise. From homer to Homer.

I'll never forget what Santo did for my dad one July day in 2001 when Elliott was starting to show his own first signs of mortality. He and my mother had taken the Badger Bus from Milwaukee to visit my wife and me in Madison, where we were spending the summer researching a book on the Vietnam era. As my dad stepped down off the bus, he said, "Dave, I'm sick. I've got to get to bed right away." We drove across town to the house and put my dad on a cot with a radio. The Cubs were playing a day game. I can't remember anymore who they were playing, either the Phillies or the Cards, I think. I do remember that the Cubs were leading 10–1 in the third or fourth inning. And as soon as my dad heard the score, he muttered, "Uh-oh. The Cubs are gonna blow it." For the next two hours, Elliott and Santo were on the same wavelength, Santo moaning, my dad laughing, as the Cubs did what they were destined to do and relinquished a nine-run lead. I was as into the game as either of them, but didn't care about the score or the final result. What made me deliriously happy was how much joy Santo was unwittingly bringing to my ailing dad. What drug, what surgical operation, what wisdom from what physician, what felicitous phrase from the Santo antipode Vin Scully, could have been better treatment for a sick old baseball guy? The answer is absolutely none. Two hours of joy and laughter, and he was up and ready for dinner.

None of this is to say that Elliott did not appreciate the well-spoken or well-written sentence. A baseball scholarship brought him to the University of Michigan in the late 1930s, but he stopped playing in his freshman year and started writing. Michigan had a world-class English department then; fellow students included the playwright Arthur Miller and the poet and critic John Ciardi. Dad was a fine writer himself, clear and clean, with an intelligent vernacular style that captured you in the first sentence and led you all the way to the end. And he gobbled up the best writers from the golden era of *Sports Illustrated* and anything written by Roger Angell. He was thrilled when writers like John Updike, Gay Talese, Norman Mailer, David Halberstam, John Wideman, George Plimpton, and Joyce Carol Oates turned their attention to sports. The best writers, he said, no matter how famous they were, never wrote down to their readers, and they invested the same amount of research and thought in any subject. He had written sports himself once, long ago, during a difficult period in his career when he was working at a labor newspaper in Bettendorf, Iowa. He used two pseudonyms: one was Jimmy Moran, taken in homage to my brother, and the other was Sal LaBarba, a takeoff on Sal "the Barber" Maglie, the old Dodger. The story I remember most vividly was a column blasting the Dodgers for callously trading Jackie Robinson to the Giants.

When I showed an interest in writing and could not decide between sports and politics, my dad gently nudged me toward politics, but said that one only fed off the other. I remember how often he pointed out that James Reston, the premier political columnist for the _New York Times_, got his start as a sportswriter. I happened to stumble across some of Reston's sports writing decades later when I was researching a book on Vince Lombardi. It was in a scrapbook up at the library archives at Fordham University, where Lombardi had played as an undersized lineman, one of the famed "Seven Blocks of Granite." In 1936, writing under the byline Scotty Reston, the cub reporter for the AP assessed the Fordham team's prospects. He wrote, accurately as it turned out, that they had "the biggest, fastest and most promising squad in years."

As I read through the impressive collection of submissions this year for the _Best American Sports Writing_ anthology, I tried to channel my father as much as possible in picking out the final twenty-eight selections. I'm not sure he would have gone with Paul Cullum's piece on the Mexican Midget Rodeo, though. My dad was modern and profane and hated the whole concept of political correctness as it was used by the righteous and manipulated by the bigots, but he was just plain respectful in ways that would have made him argue that this particular story could insult someone. Maybe he would be right, but I liked it. When he was proofreading the manuscripts of my books, I would make the vast majority of changes he suggested, but not every one. I remember the biggest dispute we got into was over whether I could write that one of Bill Clinton's stepfathers ran a hair salon where they dyed the hair of prostitutes in more places than on their heads. He said no, I said yes.

He had attained basic computer literacy by the time he died, but I'm certain he never weaved his way through the Internet to find the U.S.S. Mariner website that published the inimitable story by Derek Zumsteg on an iconic cartoon where Bugs Bunny plays all nine positions in a baseball game — not like Bert Campaneris or Cesar Tovar, one position per inning, but all nine at once. I can't remember ever seeing him watch a cartoon, but I know he would have enjoyed this story and probably would have called the sports editor at his old paper and, again reverting to his city editor days, shouted something like, "Jesus Christ, why can't you guys think of innovative stuff like that Bugs Bunny story!"

The question of what is sport and what is not seems to be provoked every year by these best-of selections. I kept my dad in mind when thinking about that too. He never hunted in his life, or fished, or went surfing, or played soccer, or raced a bike, or got behind the wheel of a Formula One racecar, or went looking for wild turkeys — but I know he could have devoured a story about any one of those subjects if it was deeply reported and well written, and that he would have ignored any stick-in-the-muds who would limit the definition of sports to the old baseball, football, basketball, hockey, boxing, track and field, tennis tradition. To him, that was like arguing over whether there should be a college football playoff, or how many teams should be in the basketball tournament, or whether a team was ranked too high or low in the midseason polls, or any number of so-called sports-related issues that he considered a foolish waste of time. Who the hell cares? he would ask. Why be narrow about it? Who knows what people will be playing a hundred years from now?

Although he spent most of his newspaper career dealing with other issues — politics, war and peace, civil rights, the environment, poverty, crime and corruption, the role of a great public university — Elliott never adopted a dismissive attitude toward sports. He believed that the substance was in the reporting, and the telling. Politics could be as trivial as sports, and sports as meaningful as politics, depending on the time and place and characters and themes. It was all in knowing what to take seriously and what not to worry about. Part of the beauty of sports, he thought, was the wide canvas it offered, as vast as the world itself — from Larry Brown's account of a white raccoon to L. Jon Wertheim's story on Kwame James, the basketball journeyman who fought off the terrorist shoe bomber; from Bill Buford off in search of wild turkeys to Bruce Wallace retracing the final living moments of Munar Mudhafar, who died playing soccer in Baghdad. In essence, the world of sports is as wonderfully eclectic as the pile of magazines and newspapers that cluttered my parents' couch and spilled onto the floor.

When my mother died last year, some of their old periodicals started coming to our mail slot in Washington. We now get *The Nation* and *ESPN The Magazine.*

DAVID MARANISS

The Best American
Sports Writing
2007

LARRY BROWN

The White Coon

FROM FIELD & STREAM

What better way to begin an anthology of 2006 sports writing than with
a piece about a white raccoon published last year but written in 1982 by
an author who died in 2004?
  — D.M.

THE DOGS WERE just about to lose their track, and Mr. Richard
was losing his patience fast. I shifted my weight from side to side
and tried to kick some feeling back into my numb toes. In February, when the clock gets close to midnight, the wind that comes
whistling through the hardwood timber sends a shiver down a
man's back. We were standing on the edge of Muckaloon Creek,
a small tendril of water that travels slowly through canebrakes and
cypress on its way to the Yocona River, the biggest body of water
around Tula, Mississippi, and the bank where we stood was slip-
pery with frozen mud. Ice crystals had been forced out of the
ground by the freezing and thawing turns that the water had taken.
After three hours of bumping and splashing in and out of the
creek, we were convinced that our three experienced hounds had
jumped something besides a coon. There was nothing we could do
but wait.

"They must be running a cat, Larry," Mr. Richard said.

"Yes sir," I answered with another shiver. "They must be. Something's sure got 'em messed up."

We were tired from fighting our way through wicked patches of
briers and buckvine that tore at our hands and faces. The only way
to get through the worst places was to back in, letting our thick
coats take the thorns. Mr. Richard's waders had a hole punched in
the right knee and had already been in water higher than that sev-

eral times. I could hear ice water squishing between his toes every time he took a step, but he didn't complain.

The year was 1968, and as a high school junior, I had to attend school the next day. Richard Grimes had to be on his job at the state highway department at seven o'clock sharp. Old Rock, Mr. Richard's white-footed redbone, was having a hard time following the track. Whenever his voice rolled through the big timber, it sounded unsure and questioning. Red, his littermate, and Smokey, my young bluetick, were chiming in and helping when they could.

"Boy," he said, "your mama's liable to skin my head for keeping you out this late on a school night."

"Aw, she won't say nothing," I said, even though I knew she probably would. My English grades were directly affected by the number of times we took the dogs out during the week. They dropped low enough during my senior year that my teachers denied me a diploma, but at that point in my life, I honestly believe I loved coonhunting as much as any man could. The voices of the dogs as they tore through a cotton patch or creek bottom, going all out, so close you could hear their bodies crashing through the brush, filled me with a thrill like no other endeavor, certainly not homework or school.

The dogs were running a little better now and moving away, so we walked on down in the bottom to get closer. They finally got it straightened out and got a pretty good race going, and we just stood and listened for a while. I knew it had to be past midnight by now, but I didn't say anything. I'd learned a long time before that when you went coon-hunting, there were no set hours. You might catch one in an hour and you might stay out until daylight. It all depended on the dogs.

The trees around us were tall and dark. Their naked branches were outlined against the blanket of stars above them. The dogs suddenly stopped running and the woods were quiet for a few seconds. Then Old Rock opened up with a steady, hammering chop that said, *Treed!*

"That's it, Larry," Mr. Richard said.

"Yes sir, I believe it is. Old Smokey's even barking a little."

"Let's get to 'em," he said, and we headed that way.

Our six-volt lanterns picked out a narrow trail of light through the frozen woods. In places, the mud was hard as rocks. The dogs' voices got louder as we got closer, and they started barking harder when they saw our lights coming through the darkness. Rock was treed solid with his two white feet up on the trunk of a huge old slick-barked oak. It was covered with vines that climbed all the way to the top and twined and twisted among the limbs. Smokey and Red barked a few times, but Rock was our main tree dog. The walls of Mr. Richard's den were covered with trophies that that old dog had won in club hunts against some pretty stiff competition.

The temperature must have been hovering in the twenties by that time, and I tried not to think about the warm spot in my bed next to my little brother, Darrell. Instead I turned my light up into the darkness, trying to shine the coon's eyes.

"There he is, Larry," Mr. Richard said. I looked where he was pointing his light and saw a pair of bright orange eyes, and then, on another limb, I saw another pair.

"There's two of them up there, Mr. Richard. Wait a minute, there's another pair. There's three coons up there!"

He moved his light around in the other branches. "You think you can climb it, son?"

I looked up at the trunk. It was too big for me to reach all the way around, but I was pretty sure I could "coon it" up to the first limb. The vines would either help or hinder me. I took off my belt and passed it through the handle of my lantern and looped it over my shoulder. I stepped up to the tree and hollered at Smokey. He leaned up on the bark and howled a few times, and I wrapped my legs and arms around the trunk as far as they would go. By pulling up with my arms and legs, I could usually gain about eight inches with each effort, depending on how big the tree was.

I found out quickly that the vines were going to present a problem. They were between me and the tree, keeping my belly pushed away and making it hard for me to get a good grip. Mr. Richard saw I was having a hard time getting started, so he came over and pushed me up as high as he could reach, then stood back and watched. He always had great faith in my ability as a tree climber, and he bragged on me every chance he got.

I made it up past the thickest of the vines, but my arms were aching and tiring quickly. I knew I couldn't rest until I made it to the first limb, so I kept doggedly gripping, higher and higher into the black night. When I finally touched that limb, it was strong and live and as big around as my leg. I hauled myself up on top, and straddling the limb, rested for a few minutes. Both of us shined the

coons again to see how much farther I had to go, and that's when I
got a very big surprise. There were three coons up there all right,
but the one in the middle was snow white. I could hardly believe it.
Mr. Richard's light must have been too dim for him to see it.

"Hey, Mr. Richard," I yelled. "One of these coons is white."

"Aw, Larry," he laughed, "don't be pulling my leg like that. Get
on up there and jump one of 'em out."

I thought I might be seeing things so I stood up on the limb and
climbed higher in the tree, about fifteen more feet. I got directly
under the coons, and they backed up a little and bunched together, huddling fearfully in the glare of the light and from the
racket the dogs were making at the base of the tree. The dogs knew
a coon was about to come sailing into their midst, and they were
ready to fight. I couldn't decide what to do at first. I couldn't figure
why three grown coons would be running together and climbing
the same tree. That was the reason the dogs had been messed up so
bad on the track. Young coons will run together like that in roastin'
ear season, but this was the dead of winter.

"There ain't no doubt about it," I called. "I'm right under 'em
and this middle one's white."

He couldn't get over it, and we talked back and forth, trying to
decide what to do. Season was open, but we didn't want to kill all
three of them at once. I wouldn't have done it, and Mr. Richard
wouldn't have allowed it. We decided that he'd hold all three dogs
away from the tree, and I would start jumping them out, one by
one. He would try to hold the dogs off the brown coons to let them
get away to run another night. When I jumped the white coon out,
he'd turn the dogs loose.

Some people might not think it's fair to jump a fifteen-pound
coon out of a tree into the middle of three or four fifty-pound dogs,
but a mad coon is something you don't want to tangle with. When
he hits the ground, he's all teeth and claws. I've seen dogs come
away from a fight looking like they'd been into it with a buzz saw.

Mr. Richard caught Rock and Red and Smokey, and I could see
his light moving away far below me on the ground. After all the effort of climbing that tree, I wasn't cold anymore. Mr. Richard yelled
he was ready, so I went up and got on the limb with the coons. One
of the brown ones ran out to the end of the limb and stopped, looking back at my light. I gave the limb a little shake and hissed at him.
He leaped, spreading his four legs wide, just like a big flying squir-

rel. I heard the thump his body made when he hit the ground, and the dogs went crazy when they saw him. Mr. Richard had a hard time, but he held them tight.

The coon made his escape into the bushes, and the dogs didn't like it at all. They were howling and lunging as hard as they could, trying to get loose. The other brown coon went off to one side and walked quietly down the tree to the ground. I don't think the dogs even saw him.

I inched up on the limb and actually got to within five feet of that beautiful creature. As I looked at him, I wondered: Did he know he was different from his brothers? Were these other two his litter-mates or were they only rutting on this cold night? This may sound crazy coming from someone who's killed as many of them as I have, but I love coons. I'm guilty of sending a lot of them to their deaths. Any man who has a real love of hunting is always a little sad over the death of his game.

I took one long last look at his elegant white fur. It was milky white and looked as soft as down. His eyes held no fear or anger or accusation that I could see, only a slight bewilderment at this large one-eyed monster that could follow him to his last refuge. I shook the limb hard, almost regretfully, and he made his leap. Mr. Richard turned the dogs loose, and I started back down as quickly as I could go without falling. The white coon's high-pitched chattering cries mingled with the savage voices of the dogs as they caught him, and by the time I reached the ground, it was all over for him.

A Boy's Mistake

I helped Mr. Richard pull the dogs away, and we knelt side by side to look at his snow-white pelt, thick and lustrous a few minutes before, but spotted now with blood and dirt. He wasn't a true albino, we could see now. He had a black mask over his eyes and black rings around his tail like any other coon, and he didn't have pink eyes. We looked at him for a while, but it was already late, and it would be much later when we got back to the truck. I picked him up, and Mr. Richard whistled at the dogs and asked me what I was going to do with him. I thought about it for a minute and said, "I don't know. Dress him when I get home, I guess."

"Boy, it'll be daylight before you get the hide off that thing," he said. I knew he was right. It was close to two o'clock in the morning, and my school bus came by at 7:15. That would give me a little over five hours to dress him, clean up enough to get in bed, get a little sleep, and then get back up to eat breakfast in time to catch the bus.

We started out of the woods with Mr. Richard pulling his two dogs on leashes, and me carrying the white coon in one hand and leading Smokey by his chain with the other. It was cold, bad cold, and we were wet and tired and the truck was a long way off. The coon got heavier and heavier, and I had to keep changing hands as one cramped and got cold, then the other one.

Listen to me making all these excuses for what I did halfway back to the truck. There's nobody to blame but myself. We all do things that we regret, and then look back years later and think, *Why did I do that?* It never does any good because you can't call it back.

I'd like to be able to say that the white coon's hide is mounted on a board and hanging on a wall in my house, or that we had him stuffed and he's sitting in a lifelike pose in my bedroom, but I can't. The truth is that a young boy got so cold and tired of carrying a once-in-a-lifetime trophy that he handed the leash of his dog to the man walking beside him and dropped back until the dogs couldn't see what he was about to do. He walked over to a slough filled with icy black water and dropped the trophy into its murky depths.

I don't suppose I'll ever be lucky enough to see another one like him because I don't figure God makes very many of his kind. But if I did, I wonder what I'd do this time. I like to think I'd turn my light off and carefully back down out of his way in the darkness, hoping he wouldn't jump out before I reached the ground. Maybe then the debt would be paid.

DEREK ZUMSTEG

Bugs Bunny, Greatest
Banned Player Ever

FROM USSMARINER.COM

From a dead raccoon to a hyperactive rabbit. Never before read
anything quite like this. Never before heard of U.S.S. Mariner. First
thought: it could have used an editor. Second thought: an editor
likely would have ruined it.
— D.M.

WITH THE DVD RELEASE of *Looney Tunes Golden Collection* it is at
last possible for us to examine in detail one of the most famous
baseball games ever played, and see what lessons the contest holds
for the analytical community.

"Baseball Bugs" (1946) depicts a game held at the Polo Grounds.
No date is given, but artifacts shown such as public address equip-
ment and advertisements ("Filboid Studge," "Nox, 2 for 25," "Manza
Champagne") definitively place it during the 1946 season. The vis-
iting Gas House Gorillas are playing against the home team, the
Teatotallers. It is a day game and conditions are good.

The first view of the scoreboard shows the Gorillas at 94 runs (10-
28-16-40) after the first four innings. This appears to be footage inserted out of order, as we'll determine later the score then was not
96–0 but rather 54–0. While obviously neither team was a major
league affiliate and it is almost certain that the game played is an
exhibition, the score is already notable. The total of 54 runs was far
more than the previous all-time run scoring record for a team in a
game (held by the Chicago Colts, who scored 36 against Louisville
in a game on June 29, 1897), and the score of 40 runs in an inning

would be significantly above the most runs scored in any inning by one team (18, by the Chicago Colts in the seventh inning on April 14, 1883).

The stadium is entirely filled, and as we know that the Polo Grounds could hold 55,000 fans in that year's configuration, it is fair to assume that this was a game of some note, and that the players participating were extremely popular.

We open to see "a screaming liner" hit by the home team. The outcome of the hit is not defined, and the hit itself seems an indicator that the game was not official: the ball appears to be a shade of gray, and makes an almost-human screaming noise as it travels, neither of which was normal behavior for a regulation baseball in play. Since the balls used in the remainder of the game are white, and since we also see that the Teatotallers are a horrible offensive team, it is reasonable to conclude that this footage is from some kind of pre-game hitting contest, or perhaps an entirely different game.

The initial comparison of the teams' players offers a startling contrast, as well as a further confirmation that this is not an official game. In 1946, baseball was in transition. During the first half of the decade, as the equipment and personnel needs of the war took precedence, baseball had become a slap-and-dash game, characterized by little hitting and little power, but with many stolen bases. After the war's end, with returning players came plate discipline and power hitting, and almost all of the wartime players were quickly forced out.

This is obvious even in the first shot of the Gorillas pitcher as compared to the Teatotaller. Both wear uniforms without a team name, number, or other identifying characteristics, but they otherwise could not be more different:

I have summarized major differences in Table 1.

The Teatotaller identifies himself as being "ninety-three and a half years old." It is unclear whether this is a humorous exaggeration by the player, but he is extremely slow to swing and awkward, as if once he has put the bat in motion he is unable to control it effectively. Clues offered from his appearance and analysis of other Teatotallers' biomechanics, in particular their posture and stylistic hitches in their method of play, suggest that no one on the team is under fifty. While today this seems only a little odd, we should remember that modern nutrition, training, and medical support allow players much longer and more productive careers. In 1946,

Table 1 A Comparison of Characteristics of Players

Characteristic	Gorilla Pitcher	Teatotaller Batter
Height	Over 6'	Apx 5'5"
Weight	Over 220 lbs	Under 125 lbs
Uniform colors	Dark gray and blue	Light gray and red
Eyeglasses	No	Yes
Gray hair	No	Yes
Illegally ragged uniform	Yes	No
Visible facial hair	Stubble	Sideburns
Slouching	Yes	No
Smoking cigar while playing	Yes	No

there were few players forty or older: three in the National League, and the oldest player in either league was Ted Lyons at forty-five, pitching in only five games.

You can also see that the Gorillas' catcher wears no facial protection of any kind, even turning his hat around. This brash display of fearlessness must certainly have been intimidating to the other team, given their age-related susceptibility to broken bones if hit by a ball.

This raises a series of troubling questions I admit that I cannot answer, either in viewing the game or in subsequent attempts to research it using primary sources:

1. Why would a team of extremely strong, young men play a game against a team of extremely old, weak men?
2. Why would over fifty thousand people attend such a game?

The second pitch of the game is quite high, and the Teatotaller does not swing. It's initially called a ball, but the Gorilla catcher (who, like his teammate, is extremely large) hits the umpire on the head, driving him fully into the ground. The umpire apologizes profusely and changes his call to a strike.

While it is tempting to look at this as part of the long history of player-umpire violence, instead consider this as a demonstration of the raw power of the Gorillas' catcher. Given the coloration and quantity of the dirt displaced in the act, it is clear that the area behind home plate is extremely loosely packed matter, such as sawdust, possibly mixed with sand.

A further limitation to the force of the blow is the survival of the umpire. At first the umpire is able to respond in an apologetic manner on realizing his error. The umpire then passes out, presumably with a concussion. However, the history of head trauma injuries is filled with strange tales of lucidity after horrible injury, and this is no less believable than what many trauma rooms see on a daily basis. A presence of an umpire at home later is inconclusive in establishing the struck umpire's survival or replacement.

And yet, even given those caveats and boundaries on how great the force must have been, the amount of acceleration applied to the umpire so suddenly, and without noticeably harming the catcher at all, testifies to the physical condition and hardiness of the Gorilla players.

When the Gorillas are up to bat again, we see for the first time the ineffectiveness of the Teatotallers' pitching. A frail elderly gentleman with long sideburns that swing during his delivery throws a slow, overhand pitch, which is hit directly at him. Gorilla players are shown walking to the plate, getting a hit on the first pitch, and immediately starting toward first as the next player steps up without even waiting for the previous batter to reach first. The traumatized pitcher continues to throw, and each pitch is hit smartly at him, causing him to duck. This occurs three times.

At one point, we are able to see over thirty Gorillas circling the bases, so close that they actually put their hands on the person in front of them and form a conga line as they walk around the bases, careful not to pass the person in front of them, for fear they will be called out for advancing in front of the previous runner. That there are over thirty tells us several things:

1. The teams playing were allowed to carry a full major league roster.
2. In the carnage, even the Gorilla coaches, bat boys, and other uniformed staff were able to bat and hit against the weak pitching, and neither the Teatotallers nor the umpires noticed this and called the illegal batters out.

It's a further testament to the addled mental condition of the Teatotallers during this drubbing that they were unable to take advantage of the congested base running by fielding any ball and throwing it to any base, where it would have immediately forced out three runners and ended the inning.

A shot displays a rapidly changing score of 42 runs in that inning so far. This shot establishes a scoreboard discrepancy that is not noted anywhere else or in contemporary accounts. Early on, before the Teatotallers bat, we are shown a scoreboard:

Table 2 Scoreboard as Initially Displayed

Gas House Gorillas	10	28	16	40
Teatotallers	0	0	0	

After which the Teatotallers bat and do not score. Then, in this, the conga-line inning, the scoreboard is shown as

Table 3 Scoreboard as Displayed the Second Time

Gas House Gorillas	10	28	16	40*
Teatotallers	0	0	0	

*increasing to 41 and 42

During the short footage of the Gorillas circling the bases, we see several hitters cross the plate. There are several possible explanations:

- The home team scoreboard operator decided to restart the fifth inning as the fourth, given that the fifth had gone so badly for his team, and we happen to see the Gorillas pass the 40-run mark a second time. This is ruled out, however, by the presence of the crowd and the fact that it is still day. Even though we can see that the Gorillas are aggressive batters and swing early at pitches, and that the Teatotallers are inept hitters, the sheer amount of time it would take to play a 134-run game (to that point) makes this unlikely. This is supported by analysis of game lighting: given the lack of discernible shadows but with a well-illuminated park, we can tell that the game was played either at midday under light cloud cover or at dusk. Later events (specifically the extended Bunny comeback) rule out the latter.
- The earlier shot is an accident, an insert of footage taken later. While we can determine that everything else is in chronological order, it is the most likely of the explanations and the one we'll accept here.

There is an important lesson from this inning: run scoring is not dependent on taking walks or even on seeing a lot of pitches. The Gorillas score 42 runs in this inning alone by drilling single after single right at the pitcher. By keeping the pace of the game extremely fast, they kept the pitcher in the game, presumably because he had a low pitch count and was not tired, but also there was no pitcher warmed up to relieve him, and the Gorillas scored so quickly that they drove the score up before one could even be told to begin stretching. There is an additional psychological effect to be considered, as well: faced with a team that can score 42 runs in an inning, the opposing manager must have been so stunned by the offensive onslaught that he was unable to make a move, and further that his coaches and other staff were similarly disabled. It would be difficult to apply this advantage in a game situation, but is a situation worth watching for because once gained, it can clearly be exploited to great gain.

We are then introduced to the shabby state of both the groundskeeping and of stadium security at the Polo Grounds, as we see an angry rabbit (Bugs Bunny, RHP/UT) is able to heckle the visiting team from left field, where he has dug a fairly substantial hole, and is enjoying a carrot-dog and (it appears) has consumed a large bottle of wine through a straw.

The Gorillas, presumably bored at the level of competition offered at the game, force Teatotallers equipment upon the rabbit and he enters the game. The new lineup is announced:

C: Bugs Bunny
LF: Bugs Bunny
RF: Bugs Bunny
P: Bugs Bunny
3B: Bugs Bunny
CF: Bugs Bunny
1B: Bugs Bunny
SS: Bugs Bunny
2B: Bugs Bunny

Using an orthodox delivery, Bugs delivers a pitch which appears quite fast but is then able to take the catcher's position and (as the catcher) encourage himself (as the pitcher). When he catches the ball, the force of the impact throws him back and shatters the backstop.

This provokes a most interesting investigation. Clearly, the ball cannot have been thrown with much force, or he would not have been able to have run and caught it. We can be especially sure of this given that catching the ball imparted far more force than he could have expended throwing it. However, from what we can see from the ball's path as it is caught is that it is nearly flat and extremely fast. Relativity prevents us from believing that he is able to travel at nearly luminal speeds, as it rules out traveling extremely fast and arriving three seconds before the ball without (as one barrier) himself experiencing massive and noticeable aging.

What can we make of this then? Two theories appear initially viable:

1. There is a wormhole as theorized by Feynman and others that allows Bugs to step off the mound and be transported back just slightly in time and over about sixty feet in distance without affecting anything else.
2. Bugs's delivery of the pitch is deceptive, and it is actually extremely slowly thrown with respect to the plate, and it is his encouragement of the pitch that accelerates the ball toward the plate, "flattening" its trajectory.

When thrown, the pitch must be traveling at least as slow as 15 ft/s (to give him time to run to the plate and then talk). At the same time, it can't touch the ground before crossing the plate, or be ruled an automatic ball, so it must actually be thrown upwards at least as fast as to resist the force of gravity (as $g = 32$ ft/s^2). Since the pitch crosses the plate at approximately the same height it was thrown, we know when it left Bunny's hand it was traveling at about 64 ft/s. Neglecting air friction and the effects of spin on the ball:

> 0s: 64 ft/s up
> 1s: 32 ft/s up
> 2s: 0 ft/s up
> 3s: 32 ft/s down
> 4s: 64 ft/s down
> 64 ft/s = 3,840 ft/m = 230,400 ft/h = ~44 mph

Therefore, he throws the pitch in the air at about 44 mph and possibly quite slightly toward home. In the time the toss gives him behind the plate, he begins to chatter. In his three seconds of yelling, he's able to cause the ball to accelerate extremely fast. We can estimate the speed of the ball given the force applied to Bugs while catching it. If, as seems reasonable, we figure he weighs 80 lbs, the force to throw him directly into the backstop and do significant structural damage to that backstop can be estimated ("Estimation of pitch speed through re-creation of secondary observations using weighted mannequin and riot suppression weapons," Zumsteg, 2004). We are able to figure that the pitch was traveling at least 150 mph and possibly much faster.

That means that Bunny was able to cause the ball to accelerate by at least 50 mph/s^2. Based on these calculations, it would seem possible for Bunny to actually fly and even to achieve escape velocity and orbit the planet using only his heckling. However, it's important to note that as demonstrated in this game, we can only definitely establish from the footage that he is able to perform the acceleration when drawing an object to him, and only on the baseball. Even if we consider that this demonstration is the only time this happens, it still raises other questions:

1. How is this possible?
2. Why doesn't Bunny throw a ball and then from the mound encourage it back as the batter swings?
3. Why doesn't Bunny use this ability on batted balls as a fielder, drawing balls to him for easy outs?

The possibility that it can only be done while crouching does not rule out either of those uses. It may be that this acceleration through encouragement can only be done while catching, a theory that is supported by circumstantial evidence, but particularly by the fact that if such an effect were available to him, there is no reason he would not use it then. As to the last question, as we'll see later, circumstantial evidence seems to indicate that he does do this, even if the effect is not shown. The issue warrants further investigation.

Almost as baffling is Bunny's "slow ball." Traveling a straight line and barely rotating, it moves so little that three batters take three swings at it and never make contact. Given the ball's extremely minimal rotation, it seems likely that this is not a "slow ball" as we conventionally think of it but instead a knuckleball, which Bunny is using to best take advantage of the known unusual air currents at the Polo Grounds. If we acknowledge that it was a knuckleball, the hitters' inability to make contact becomes much easier to explain.

Bunny's innovation extends to more than possible new discoveries about physics and the nature of perception. In his first hit, Bunny attempts to score an inside-the-park home run but finds a Gorilla covering home plate has received the ball. Bunny then shows him a pin-up of (we must believe) surpassing attractiveness, causing the player to go into fits of pleasure. This allows Bunny to score easily. If such beauty is indeed usable (and use of it does not violate the rules) and can be reliably applied, this is a clear innovation with applications in fields as diverse as anesthesia and crowd control.

Bunny scores, and we are given our first shot of the new scoreboard. Interestingly, the Gas House Gorillas are now the home team. Bunny inherits the first four (see above) innings of scoreless Teatotaller play, while the Gorillas now lead by 96–1. This seems to indicate that the Gorillas, after impressing Bugs to play against them, gave up on that inning. It is not clear why the sides switched, though earlier cheering for the Gorillas seems to indicate wide local support, or why Bunny was forced to substitute in and inherit the score if he replaced the entire opposing team and switched from home to visitor.

In a tense confrontation at home, we see the Gorillas replace the umpire by force with one of their own so that they can call Bunny out at home in the next play. Bunny, to his credit, then manages to argue the fake umpire into reversing his own call. It is a rare application of mental acuity and misdirection in debate that persuaded the umpire to change the call — against the interests of his own team — and allowed Bunny to score again. For those that say that arguing with umpires is guaranteed not to help and is frequently harmful, this will stand as a powerful counter-example. If a player impersonating an ump can be turned to reverse a call in those circumstances, what chance does a neutral arbitrator have against a similarly golden-tongued player? We can only hope that a real umpire, faced with the same kind of oratory jujitsu, would have the presence of mind to focus on the events and continue to make the right call.

We are then shown a disturbing fielding play. A Gorilla, chasing down a line drive hit by Bunny, catches it and is knocked backwards and down into the turf, where he burrows into the ground and disturbs a headstone to appear, bearing the words "He Got It."

While this Gorillas player is much slighter than previous players shown, that a ball could impart that much force seems implausible. For one, a ball traveling so fast would have reached him much quicker, and appeared to be traveling much "straighter" than the one we see. Further, such a ball would not have been caught, but instead would have shattered the player's arm and broken through the glove and proceeded to bore through the player's body. That it does not offers us a possible solution: that players, by shouting at the ball or otherwise, are able to dramatically accelerate it. The outfielder, either not observing or not understanding this apparently temporary phenomenon, was responsible for drawing a ball toward himself, each shout adding to its velocity, until, fatally, he caught it and, unlike Bunny, was unprepared for an impact of such force.

But then how is he able to catch the ball safely and still be driven into the ground? The only plausible explanation is that on catch, the ball continues to accelerate even though the player is no longer shouting. Further evidence that ball behavior is divorced from fielder vocalization comes quickly. On the next hit, Bunny's line drive is able to drive a different Gorilla approximately ten yards into a tobacco advertisement on the outfield wall. This player says nothing in fielding, and so disproves that fielder shouting is the cause.

This would further support the contention that it is Bunny who has a singular ability to accelerate the ball, and that this ability is not limited to catching or to only drawing objects to him.

Catching: while waiting for a pitch, is able to yell and cause the ball to accelerate toward him.

Batting: yells before receiving the pitch, able to hit the ball and then cause it to accelerate equally after contact.

Alternately, we can consider that the mass of the ball is not constant, and Bunny is somehow able to alter or control both the speed and mass of a ball in play to provide beneficial results.

As to the matter of the tombstone, there is no other contemporary or historical account of that incarnation of the Polo Grounds being built on a graveyard. This should be attributed to an unlikely grim coincidence.

Bunny's ability to control energy is further demonstrated on a play when, faced with an unconventional defensive alignment in which all nine Gorillas form up off the third base line, he is able to hit all nine of them with a batted ball, maintaining the ball's speed. Each struck fielder lights up, showing a yellow luminescence characteristic of electrical discharges. This electrical discharge causes the scoreboard to display random colored numbers and text ("TILTED").

We are shown only one other play, in which Bunny tags a Gorillas player out so forcefully that the runner hallucinates.

We next learn that Bunny has taken the lead, 96–95. This means that at some point during the game, the official scorer ruled at least one of the Gorillas' runs invalid, as we had previously established that they had scored 96 runs when Bunny took over for the Teatotallers. The cause and resolution of the disputed run is not documented in available footage.

The game situation as announced is two outs, bottom of the ninth (as the Gorillas are now the home team, they are at bat), with one base runner. The batter chops a tree down to use as a bat measuring approximately twenty feet long and three feet in diameter, affording the hitter plate coverage unequaled in the history of baseball.

Assuming that the tree is of a normal variety and not, say, balsa (what little observation we can do from the footage does rule out exotic and lightweight trees), we can calculate the weight of this bat as

$$Volume * (weight/cubic\ foot)$$

Using a generic weight for the wood of 35 pounds per cubic foot, I estimate the weight of the bat at just shy of 5,000 pounds, including handle. Even if the bat was corked (how this would be accomplished in the time available is unclear), it would still weigh thousands of pounds. That the Gorillas hitter is able to swing this massive tree indicates that Bunny is not the only player on the field with extraordinary powers.

Bunny attempts a "called shot" of pitching, asking the fans to "watch me paste this pathetic palooka with a powerful, paralyzing, perfect, pachydermous percussion pitch."

It is notable that, while appearing to be fast, this pitch is hit extremely well by the Gorillas hitter. It is unlikely that any pitch could avoid contact with a bat of that size if the batter was able to time his swing remotely well. Consider that even an extremely early or late swing would still put wood to the ball, due to the length of the bat. If the ball's trajectory is straight and it does not hit the ground, even a 6-degree swing (rather than a 90-degree one, bringing the bat perpendicular to the batter's foot position) would still allow the bat to make contact (approximately twenty feet behind the plate). Note that such contact would result in a foul ball unless it hit a knot or other irregularity in the bat.

The batter takes a full swing and the ball is hit out of the Polo Grounds. Bunny attempts to pursue the ball in a taxi, but is foiled when his driver turns out to be a member of the Gorillas — that he has a taxi license with his picture on it further supports the earlier contention that the Gorillas are not a professional team, though it makes the question of why fans turned out in such numbers even more baffling if the players were not professionals.

Bunny leaves the taxi and is lucky enough to catch a bus, which delivers him to the Umpire State Building. After taking an elevator to the top, Bunny hoists himself up a flagpole and throws his glove up. The glove then moves to catch the passing ball and returns to Bunny's hand. Fortunately, an umpire was scaling the building exterior, possibly with the intent of suicide arisen from shame over being removed from the game by a contestant. The umpire is able to make the out call, thus ending the game. Note that in major league games, throwing equipment at a ball is not legal, but at this point we have firmly established that the game is not played under the rules of major league baseball and we should not regard this ruling as aberrant. The call so disturbs a Gorillas player that he begins to hallucinate that he's being taunted by both the Statue of Liberty and Bunny.

What can modern baseball analysis tell us about the talent of Bugs Bunny? Unfortunately, we are faced with several problems:

- This game provides us with an extremely limited sample. Bunny plays for only five innings.
- The level of competition is never established.

As the first can't be overcome, let's deal with the second. From the level of fan interest, it is fair to assume that the players involved are good enough to be a major draw: a semipro game of local celebrities would not (and still does not) draw a sufficient crowd to pack in fifty thousand fans who cheer wildly at events (for one example, see the attendance at MLB All-Star celebrity softball games). The best-fit explanation is that the Teatotallers are a collection of former greats of baseball, playing against a team of current pro and semipro players drawn from the New York region. This seems to fit available player data as well. For instance, New York Giants player Johnny Mize was 6'2" and 215 pounds, and a good match for several of the leaner Gorillas players seen, though he batted left-handed, and we do not witness "The Big Cat" or any left-hander take a swing either against the Teatotallers or Bunny. Given the age of the Teatotallers, we can safely assume that they are greats of prewar baseball.

Using modern projection estimation engines, it is possible to guess at the current talent level of the Teatotallers at the time of the game, given their level of performance when forced out of baseball and then again, fifteen to twenty years later, playing an exhibition game at fifty and over. While we must of course look at any results with a great deal of skepticism, as there is little data on the effects of aging deep into later life, even the extrapolation of existing known trends (reduction in bat speed, fielding ability, and so on) provided startling results. Even a team of the greatest players who had retired in the late 1930s would have been poor competition for a regional unaffiliated professional team, or for a modern equivalent, a short-season rookie team (such as the Pioneer League).

At the same time, given what we know about the physical characteristics of the Gas House Gorillas, we can match them up with similar players from the time, favoring players on local teams. Assuming a mix of at least 50 percent local players not affiliated with a major league team, we find that the Gorillas were quite close to major league quality, with a difficulty adjustment of about .900 compared to the major leagues. As a point of comparison, the highest minor league level has a difficulty rating of about .850 in any season. It is worth noting that given the projected roster, they were an extremely poor defensive team. Still, the Gas House Gorillas, even as composed, were nearly major league quality, and facing a team that may have once been good, but was of nearly no present quality.

Why such a game would be scheduled remains unclear. Efforts to find contemporary promotional material for insight into fan motivation or how the game was marketed have proved fruitless.

If we accept that definition of the Gorillas' level, then the performance of Bunny becomes even more astounding but measurable.

While complete stats are not available, we know that he shut out the Gorillas for five innings, when we would expect them to score over two runs against another team. Bunny did this, however, without any defense behind him. Every play had to be made by one player, which interestingly offers us a way out of recent arguments about how much a pitcher contributes to the outcome of balls put into play. With the exception of luck, all factors thought to have a significant effect are here the responsibility of Bunny. While we see him strike out three batters, the actual events matter little. If he struck out the remaining ten batters we do not see, he makes what must be spectacular plays defensively. Either his pitching or his defense are exceptional, and quite likely both.

Bunny's line for outcomes we see:

$$1.6 \text{ IP}, 0 \text{ R}, 0 \text{ H}, 3 \text{ K}, 0 \text{ BB}, 0 \text{ HR}$$

It's clear that as a pitcher and fielder, Bunny excelled in those five innings, holding scoreless a team that would have been good compared to other major league teams. Even assuming that the knuckleball can rarely strike out three batters at once, this demands further inquiry. The limitations of reasonable (or even possible) fielding ability imply that Bunny must have been extremely good at getting strikeouts or that he was able to use his previously established ability to accelerate balls toward him to turn balls in play into easy outs.

While there is no evidence Bunny played in other exhibition games or unsanctioned leagues for which there are records, it is possible that he played under an assumed name. Further investigation may allow us to better delineate how much of his success was in fielding and how much in pitching.

As a hitter, the feat is even more astonishing. We see no evidence that he was allowed courtesy runners, and yet he scored 96 runs. This implies 96 home runs, either inside the park or by hitting the ball over the outfield fence. Given his displayed speed and the Gorillas' almost certain poor defense, along with his ability to improvise when the situation turned against him, Bunny took advantage of circumstances that allowed him to use his talents to take advantage of the other team in an unprecedented display of offensive prowess.

Consider that given 15 outs, Bunny scored 96 times. His RC/27 would be 173. Now of course Bunny could not always face a team so ill equipped to deal with his high-percentage take-all-four-bases running style and bean-all-nine-fielders hitting ability, but even dramatic penalties placed on him would still make him the greatest offensive player of all time.

But this is all speculation based on incomplete footage of an exhibition game. It is a shame that we will never know how good Bunny might truly have been, and that there is but *one record* of his exploits on the field.

The exclusion of nonhuman players like Bunny is another shameful example of the long history of injustices done by baseball's racist policies. That black and rabbit players could only play against white players in nonsanctioned exhibition matches deprived the game of some of the best talent to ever play, and from what we've seen, robbed scientists of a chance to better study phenomena with wide applicability to questions of physics that could have greatly benefited all residents of the earth, be they human or Leporidae.

OSCAR CASARES

Ready for Some Fútbol?

FROM TEXAS MONTHLY

Who knew cartoon characters could play such key roles in sports?
This time, in Texas, and it isn't funny.
— D.M.

SPEEDY GONZALES, the famous cartoon star of the fifties and sixties, has been in the news again lately. It seems the image of the
"fastest mouse in all Mexico" was evoked recently at the boys' 5A
state soccer championship, pitting the nationally ranked Coppell
Cowboys, from North Texas, against the Porter Cowboys, from
Brownsville, the southernmost city on the U.S.-Mexico border. In
an effort to belittle their opponents, the Coppell fans held up a
poster showing Speedy Gonzales about to be squashed by a large
shoe. The sign read STOMP ON BROWNVILLE! (and no, that's not a
typo). When officials forced Coppell to remove the sign, the Porter
fans continued cheering for their underdog team with the chant
"¡Sí se puede!" ("Yes, we can!"), a call to action recovered from the
era of Cesar Chavez's marches with the United Farm Workers of
America. The Coppell fans answered this with their own chant of
"USA! USA!" implying that the Porter players and their fans were
not citizens of the United States. And when that didn't work, one of
the fans called out, "You suck, you beaner!" In the end, though,
their taunts were as effective as Sylvester the Cat's were on Speedy
Gonzales. Porter won 2–1 in overtime.

Interestingly enough, this was all happening while Congress de-
bated an immigration reform bill, including the possibility of a
seven-hundred-mile wall along our southern border (one end of
which would pass about a mile from Gladys Porter High School,

my alma mater), and while hundreds of thousands of undocumented immigrants and their supporters marched in cities across the United States, also chanting *"¡Sí se puede!"* Soon several thousand National Guard troops would be deployed to assist the Border Patrol in certain areas, including South Texas.

What the Coppell fans and the players on the charged soccer field probably didn't realize was that their reaction toward a group they assumed was not American could hardly be counted as new. One of the most concentrated efforts to rid the country of illegal immigrants occurred in 1954, when the U.S. government officially passed Operation Wetback, a mandate to expel all illegal workers, particularly those from Mexico (as the name may have clued you in to). Led by the Immigration and Naturalization Service and aided by the municipal, county, state, and federal authorities, as well as the military, the operation resulted in a massive sweep of Mexican-American neighborhoods and random stops of "Mexican-looking" people.

A year earlier, when these bitter feelings were already escalating, Warner Bros. introduced a new cartoon character named Speedy Gonzales. The original Speedy debuted in a cartoon titled "Cat-Tails for Two," where his character looked more like a rat, mean and sleazy and with a gold tooth the animator must have thought would add a touch of realism. Speedy Gonzales then disappeared for a time, only to make a comeback in 1955 in what could be described as a more user-friendly version of the original drawing. Warner Bros. had fixed his teeth, worked on his English, expanded his wardrobe — from an old T-shirt, barely covering his privates, to white campesino pants and shirt, both finely pressed, and a red bandanna he kept neatly wound into what looked like a bow tie — and then added a bit of panache with the sombrero, worn slightly askew, that would soon become his trademark. Later that same year, Warner Bros. won the Academy Award for Best Short Subject with the cartoon *Speedy Gonzales.*

How strange then that the Coppell fans would choose to taunt their opponents with a poster of a mouse known for running circles around his enemies. What started out as mockery quickly turned into a self-fulfilling prophecy, as the little guy used his speed to even things out against a bigger, more physical competitor. Along the way, the Porter team would prove that the game amounted to more than just some name-calling. Because for all questions of na-

tionality, this actually turns out to be the classic American story: underdog sports team from a small, remote town defies the odds and
earns a bid to play in the championship game, where these players
must now face a formidable opponent in a match that forces them
to look inward if they hope to win.

Gladys Porter High School is located on International Boulevard, about two miles from the Gateway International Bridge,
which crosses into Matamoros. The school is also a block from
Southmost, historically one of the poorest areas of town, where at
one time it was said that even the cops wouldn't go after dark.
Locally, Porter was known as the school that couldn't win, in the
classroom or on the playing field; it seemed the only people who
believed in Porter were from Porter. The school has changed dramatically since I left some twenty years ago — it is now the district's
magnet school for engineering and technology, and in 2003 the
football team came close to capturing the district title — and it has
gathered an almost cultlike following of fans, collectively known as
the Porter Nation.

A few days before the big game, the Porter soccer players loaded
their equipment onto the school bus that would take them the 370
miles from the border to Round Rock, just north of Austin, the site
of the state championship. Now they just had to wait for the drug-
detection dog to inspect the vehicle. The Brownsville Independent
School District has a policy of bringing dogs to check any bus that is
scheduled to leave the region; according to James Kizer, Porter's
athletic coordinator, the searches are done to prevent any "sur-
prises" later. The argument could be made that the inspections are
in the best interest of the team and the school, as a preventive measure, should there be a player who decides to smuggle illegal drugs
and run the risk of serious charges. But in a way, the searches are
not so different from the ones the players would be subjected to if
they were down the street at the bridge, trying to enter the United
States from Mexico.

Once the team passed the inspection, it was clear to leave the
area. That is, until the next inspection some ninety miles later, near
the King Ranch. By law the bus driver was required to stop at the
Border Patrol's Sarita checkpoint so federal agents and their drug-
detection dogs could search the vehicle. To facilitate the process,
the players wore special tags that identified them as student athletes en route to a competition. (These tags prevent the sort of inci-

dent that occurred earlier this year when another team made it through the checkpoint only for it to be discovered later that some of the passengers were not actually with the team and had slipped away from the bus during a stop, supposedly to make their way into Texas illegally.) The Porter players were used to stopping at the checkpoint on their way to tournaments, including the semifinal match that had led to the championship game. Still, there is something disconcerting about being in your own country and having to identify yourself to a federal agent.

This time around, the Border Patrol agent happened to be female. As she boarded the bus, another agent led a dog around the perimeter of the vehicle. The players knew the drill: sit up in your seat and give the agent your full attention.

"Everybody U.S. citizens?" she asked, stepping into the aisle.

The coaches and players all nodded and said yes.

"Where are you coming from?" she asked.

"Brownsville," one of the nearby players answered.

"Which high school in Brownsville?"

"Porter."

"Hey," she said, "I went to Porter!"

After so many such inspections during the season, the players were more than happy to meet another member of the Porter Nation and hear her wish them luck. These warm feelings lasted only until the following afternoon, when they walked onto the field and fully realized the level of competition they were up against. The Coppell team was ranked second in the nation, with three of its players having already been recruited to play at the collegiate level. This was also Coppell's third straight year to compete in the state championship, including 2004, when it won the title. As if this weren't enough to contend with, there was also that Speedy Gonzales poster waving in the stands.

If Coppell fans noticed anything less than American about the Porter team, it might have been its style of play. Spectators in this country are used to watching the type of soccer showcased during the recent World Cup, which tends to be more physical (even when the players aren't giving each other head butts in the sternum). But Porter plays a faster-paced soccer that focuses on shorter passes, in what some people might describe as more of a Mexican style. It certainly isn't the kind of soccer most kids across suburbia grow up with. The quicker technique makes sense because of the smaller size of the players in the Rio Grande Valley. Porter's approach to the game is actually quite common in this region of Texas, as well as on the other side of the river, because until recently, crossing over to Matamoros was the only way for boys to play on leagues year-round.

These contrasting styles just added to what was already happening in the stands. As the game wore on and the tension grew, Porter coach Luis Zarate, who himself had grown up playing on both sides of the river before becoming a place kicker for the University of Houston, called a time-out to center his team and deal with the slurs. "Focus on your game. At the end of the day, people are going to be talking about who won the game, not about these other things," he said, probably in Spanish, since his players are bilingual and this is the common language of soccer along the border.

What Coach Zarate wanted more than anything was to impress upon his players that they had fought hard all season to make it to this final game and had earned every right to be on the field. "You're here. You belong here!"

He repeated this until it began to sink in. "You're here. You belong here!" Here at the state championship, here in Texas, here in the United States. They had traveled all the way from Gladys Porter High School, in the shadows of a proposed anti-immigration wall, to the 5A state championship, and they were exactly where they should be. "You're here. You belong here!" His words held an immediacy, but they also managed to convey a message his players could carry with them off the soccer field.

Jorge Briones, described as "a scoring machine" by his coach, went on to make the two goals that won the game, and the Porter Cowboys became the first Rio Grande Valley team to win a 5A division title in any sport. The team returned to Brownsville to a hero's welcome. Everyone, from alumni dating back thirty years to local politicians, lined up to publicly offer his congratulations. What no one could offer the players, though, was a way to afford the $300 championship rings. The University Interscholastic League, the governing body for most high school athletics programs in the state, sets limits on what gifts a team can receive from its school or school district. Eventually, businesses came together to offer the players jobs at various car dealerships in town. Briones spent a couple weeks washing cars at Marroquin Auto Sales, a used-car dealership along the freeway, so he could earn the money for his state MVP ring.

When I called Coach Zarate on his cell phone, he and his team happened to be the guests of honor, along with a few Dallas Cowboys Cheerleaders, at the grand opening of the new Wal-Mart Supercenter in Brownsville. The store manager had just donated $1,000 to go toward the team's funds for next season. I spoke to Coach Zarate a few minutes before he asked if I wanted to talk to Briones. Then he turned to his star player and in Spanish told him there was a guy from a magazine who wanted to ask him some questions.

"Can I talk to him in Spanish?" I heard Briones ask.

"Sure," the coach said. "He's from down here."

Then Briones came on the line and I congratulated him, until it got so loud at the grand opening that he could hardly hear me. It sounded as if there were a pep rally going on.

"Can you wait a minute, sir?" he asked.

And then we both stayed on the line, listening to "The Star-Spangled Banner" playing in the background.

CHRIS BALLARD

The Game of the Year

FROM SPORTS ILLUSTRATED

A delightful variation on the old Grantland Rice cliché: it's not whether
you win or lose, but how you play one unforgettable game.
— D.M.

JOSEPH PERIDORE couldn't believe it. The senior looked at his
coach, at the one finger he was holding in the air, and stared long
and hard, hoping that the finger might grow a friend, hoping that
his coach would call for a two-point conversion. After all, East
Poinsett County High *always* went for two; seven games into the season the Warriors had yet to try an extra-point kick. Likewise, they
hadn't attempted a field goal because, as coach Dusty Meek put it,
"You can't kick a field goal if you don't have a field goal kicker." In
northeast Arkansas, among the cotton-farming towns of the Mississippi Delta, there weren't many kids who grew up trying thirty-yard
kicks. Open-field tackles? Sure. Throwing a ball through a tire? You
bet. But booting a football? Never.

Until now. Until this moment, four hours into the longest, strang-
est football game anyone around these parts had ever seen — the
one that had seemed *least* likely to yield footage for *SportsCenter*. If
anything, the meeting of EPC and Hughes High on October 13 in
Lepanto, Arkansas, held less importance than any game in the state
that Friday: it was the All-Defeated Bowl. Neither team had a victory in eleven tries, and between them they suited up only twenty-
nine players — including a five-foot-three, 120-pound EPC senior
known as Goose, who in four years had never touched the ball during a game. But the magic of sports is that there is always the potential for great drama, no matter the stage it is played on.

Already the running back for Hughes had scored a state-record nine touchdowns; EPC's quarterback had answered with five touchdown passes of his own as well as 835 yards of total offense. There had been onside kicks and trick plays and now a 72–72 tie in overtime, with the conversion still to come. The concession stand had closed up, the cheerleaders had long since gone hoarse, but 150 or so EPC fans dotted the stands on this brisk Friday night, and now they stood and stomped on the metal bleachers and turned to one another to ask the same question: is Coach Meek *really* going to kick it?

He was. This game had gone on too long, his boys had fought too hard. Now was EPC's best chance to win this thing, to salvage something from a lost season. And as Meek would say later, "I knew Peridore would be fine. He's the type of kid, nothing fazes him. I don't think he gets nervous."

As he jogged toward the huddle, the stadium lights glinting off his helmet and the throb of the crowd rattling inside it, Joseph Peridore — linebacker by choice, place kicker by necessity — steeled himself for what would be his first kick of his high school career, with one thought in his mind: *I think I'm going to throw up.*

First Quarter, 2:54 to Play

Hughes leads 6–0. Kendric Smith, the Blue Devils' senior running back and free safety, has just returned an interception forty-five yards, and now, at the EPC 20, he takes the handoff and bolts to his right. It is a play called "93 Wrong Way," designed to fool the defense into following the blockers to the left. It doesn't fool anyone, but Smith does. He jukes, breaks two tackles in the backfield, then roars around right end and outruns three EPC defenders for a twenty-yard touchdown, his first of the game. He then skips in for the two-point conversion, and it's 14–0 Hughes.

Kendric Smith was always the fastest kid in the football games down at the park in Blackfish, Arkansas. When his family moved to Hughes, a small farming town thirty-six miles southeast of Memphis, all that changed was the playground — the other kids still chased Ken. By the time he got to high school, he was excelling at basketball and football. Only five-foot-eight but built like a blast furnace at 175 pounds, he can dunk with two hands and run the forty-yard dash in 4.4 seconds. He scored eight touchdowns as a sophomore and seventeen his junior year. His senior year he ran for two scores one week and two the next; as coach James Wright puts it, "Ken is our offense." Kendric says Reggie Bush is his idol, but in style and size he more closely resembles Barry Sanders. He runs as if chased by a swarm of bees, jerking and cutting and often reversing field, going five yards back to gain ten.

Smith is soft-spoken and tacks "Sir" or "Ma'am" onto the end of each sentence when talking to adults. "He's a good kid, and I can't say that about all of them," says Charles Patrick, the school's athletic director. It's easy to imagine him a local hero, idolized by little boys, back-slapped by old men, and swooned over by young girls, as small-town sports stars so often are. But there's not much fanfare in town these days. Like many farming communities in the area, Hughes enjoyed a boom during the '60s and '70s. The dark, rich Delta soil was perfect for growing cotton, soybeans, and rice. Jobs were plentiful; on Saturday nights Main Street was jumping.

Then interest rates rose. All those tractors, bought on the promise of a greener tomorrow, became steel albatrosses. A severe drought and new technology — better machines meant fewer jobs — forced the town to change, slowly at first. The population dipped, as people left for work in West Memphis or Forrest City.

To drive through Hughes now is to see a husk of a town. Main Street is littered with boarded-up buildings and stray dogs. The busiest place is Poor Boy's Liquor, down by where the railcars used to run from West Memphis to Helena. The median household income is $18,333, and nearly four in ten people live below the poverty line. Smith lives with his mother, grandmother, sister, and a cousin, Kevin Brown, in a four-room house in a run-down part of town known as Cowan Street, where front yards are pocked with furniture, windows are covered with tinfoil, and every third house is falling down or looks as if it might.

Smith spends much of his time at school. During football season he practices from 2:30 P.M. to 4:30 P.M., then works out with the basketball team until 7:30. He and Brown, a six-foot-five forward and Hughes's best basketball player, walk home together. Both dream of going to college; while a number of Division I schools are looking at Brown, Smith has had a harder time attracting recruiters because of his height. "I'd like to leave," Smith says. "I want to see how things are outside Arkansas, go out into the world."

He's not alone. There's not much left to be proud of in Hughes, though for years the town could count on its sports teams. The boys' basketball team won the state championship in 2001. The football team has been to the playoffs the last five years. This season, though, you could feel the life seeping out of the program. Fewer kids in school, fewer kids coming out for football. Enrollment in grades K through 12, as high as 1,600 in the 1970s, slipped to 1,000 by 2001, then 800, 700, and, this year, only 550. "Town's dying," says Wright, the coach. "Won't be that long until we ain't got a football team."

It's a stretch to say they had one this year. Only twenty-two kids came out for football, and by the time the Blue Devils faced EPC, they were down to sixteen. Six of those were sophomores, and only one, sophomore tackle Lucas London, weighed more than 220 pounds. "We have more cheerleaders than we have football players," says Smith. Coming into the game against EPC, Hughes was 0–5; if the Blue Devils didn't win this game, they weren't going to win any.

Second Quarter, 5:27 to Play

Things aren't looking good for EPC. The Warriors are down 34–14 on their home field, and Smith has run for four touchdowns. But now, an opportunity: on second-and-goal from the 9, EPC's junior quarterback, Brett Hardin, drops back and floats a ball into the left corner of the end zone, where sophomore Carson Tyler — whose dad, Steve, was known as "the fastest white guy in Arkansas" back when he played receiver at Lepanto High, and once had a tryout with the USFL Memphis Showboats — snags it. As always, the Warriors go for two, and Hardin hits Tyler in the end zone.

Ben Gordon, a six-foot-two, 260-pound lineman, sends an onside kick squirreling to the left side. It's the fourth time tonight Meek has tried the strategy. His logic: "I figure if I kick it to their running back, he's probably going to bring it back to the fifty. This at least gives us a chance to get the ball."

On this occasion it works, and EPC takes over at midfield. A few plays later Hardin heaves a deep ball down the left sideline into single coverage for a TD, and, just like that, it's 34–28.

Brett Hardin looks as if he's straight out of the '50s. The handsome, five-foot-ten quarterback has a blond flattop, a powerful right arm, and more than a few female admirers. He plays baseball (he's the team's star center fielder) and has been starting for the football team since he was a sophomore. He can bench three hundred pounds and is an honor roll student.

This season has been hard for Hardin, as it has been for the whole team. For years EPC was a football power, ever since Lepanto and Tyronza, the school down the road, were consolidated in 1986. Under the previous coach, Mark Courtney, EPC ran a spread offense, which helped Marcus Monk, now a receiver at the University of Arkansas, set school records before graduating in 2003. Two years ago the Warriors won the 3AA Conference title; last season they repeated.

Then Courtney left, and EPC hired Meek, who had been the offensive line coach at Stuttgart High, a 4A football school 140 miles to the southwest. He brought with him a modern approach — binders, scouting reports, game plans — as well as a devotion to discipline. Gone were Courtney's lax two-hour practices. Meek expected kids to practice hard for four hours on Tuesdays, to wear ties on game days, and to stay at school during the five-hour break between the last bell and the start of games. Many of the kids walked. Last season the team had thirty-three players. This year the Warriors started with twenty-five, then twenty, and by the Hughes game fifteen, most of whom had never played a down for the varsity. "After the first player quit, they just kept going," says Hardin. "I guess they had better things to do. I guess they didn't like the discipline."

Lepanto hasn't changed much in the last fifty years. It's still the kind of place where young boys grow a mustache as soon as puberty allows, where it's not the law that every man of driving age own a pickup truck but it seems that way, where whole families show up at EPC games dressed in matching camouflage hunting gear. Unlike Hughes, Lepanto is not reeling, though it's by no means flush. The median income is $22,590, and school enrollment and town population are holding steady — "and for a Delta community, that means you're ahead of the game," says school superinten-dent Mickey Pierce. There's still a big crowd on the first weekend of October for the Terrapin Derby, when Greenwood Street is shut down so a thousand people — and a few dozen confused tur-tles — can traverse it. There's also the weekly Lepanto Auction and the catfish fry at the Harvest Grill Diner. Tradition runs deep in Lepanto, and for years no tradition was bigger than Friday-night football.

That's changing, though. In Lepanto, as in many small towns in the South and through middle America, football's hold on the younger generation has loosened. "They all want to get a vehicle, or play video games," says Gary Williams, EPC's principal. "No one's got time for football." The outside world calls; thanks to im-proved roads, kids in Lepanto can quickly drive thirty miles up to the relatively brighter lights of Jonesboro on weekends. Sure, there are still cars parked in the school lot grease-penciled with GO WAR-RIORS #1, still pep rallies before big games, but football is no longer sacred.

Meek knew bringing in a new system meant he might struggle his first year — but he didn't expect this. Twenty years ago no one could have imagined an EPC team fielding only fifteen players. With a roster thick with underclassmen and thin on bulk, Meek had to rely on Hardin all season. Coming into the Hughes game, he was the team's leading rusher, passer, and kick returner, and EPC was losing by an average of thirty-three points. Hardin might have suffered the most — with his athleticism and skills, he's hop-ing for a shot at playing in college. "Coach always said that if I were a little bit taller, he could write me a ticket to any school," Hardin says, "but it's hard to get noticed when you're 0–6."

Second Quarter, 2:53 to Play

Up 40–28, the Hughes players are experiencing a rare feeling: confidence. Smith has run for a fifty-four-yard touchdown, a fifty-two-yarder, and now a twenty-eight-yarder, his fifth TD of the game.

What makes Smith's success tonight even more impressive is that EPC knows the run is coming. The Blue Devils have yet to pass; in fact, they have put the ball in the air no more than a dozen times all

season. "People ask me, 'Coach, why don't you throw the ball,'"
Wright says later. "I say, 'Two reasons: we ain't got no one who can
throw it, and we ain't got no one who can catch it.'"

Instead, Wright runs a single-wing offense, a relic from the
smashmouth days of high school football in the 1940s and '50s.
Imagine eleven kids lining up in a clump and then running around
as if they've been put in a blender. On every play the quarterback
makes a 360-degree spin as he makes (or fakes) a handoff, while
tackles run one way and a decoy runs the other. By Meek's estimation, Wright's the only coach in the state of Arkansas who still runs
a true single wing.

The Blue Devils' offense has its limitations against bigger teams
because their line gets pushed around, but against EPC's undersized defense it's working almost flawlessly. "There were times
where we're thinking, 'Oh, we got [Smith] stopped,'" says Meek.
"And then, all of a sudden, this white jersey pops out, and it's like,
'*Where's he coming from?*'"

Hughes's offense may be clicking, but its defense is another matter. Hardin runs for another score, closing the gap to 40–34 at
halftime. The halftime whistle blows, and the Blue Devils jog off
the field, their coach bringing up the rear. As usual, he is limping
and cussing.

James Wright has been around football the better part of his life. At
sixty-six, he's been coaching for thirty-eight years, the last nine at
Hughes. He won a state championship with Rison, was a runner-up
with Lakeside and Gould, and also coached at Marked Tree and
Fouke. Short and stubby, he has a blocky head that's covered by a
faint swirl of white hair and eyes that look as if they've been squint-
ing for the last forty years. He's easygoing and has a host of self-dep-
recating sayings. For example: "My wife's smart — 'bout the only
dumb thing she ever did was marry me."

Wright doesn't understand why the kids don't want to come out.
"When I was growing up, if you didn't play football, you weren't
anything," he says, echoing the lament of Gary Williams at EPC.
"You couldn't get a date. You *had* to play football."

You can tell he's lost some of his passion. Part of it is his right
knee. Five years ago he tore something while trying to get out of
the way of a halfback sweep.

Each summer he meant to have surgery, but he never got it

done, so he carried crutches in his car and dragged that leg when he walked. (He is scheduled for surgery this week.) He has thought about making this his last season, just teach next year, but there's not enough money in the school budget for both a history teacher and a football coach.

Wright, who lives in a big brick house on the eastern edge of town, is often asked if, like many longtime residents, he plans to leave Hughes. "Why?" he says. "I go to the pharmacy, and he knows what I take and everything my wife takes. I go to the grocery store, and if I forget a check, they charge it to me. Go to the bank, and they give you anything. I know all the cops; all the kids know me. Why would we want to leave when everybody knows us?"

Third Quarter, 4:12 to Play

Smith does it again. EPC had stopped him on three consecutive plays, then he broke off a fifty-three-yarder on fourth-and-seven to make it 54–40. Again Coach Meek feels the game slipping away. And again Hardin answers. He runs for a touchdown (EPC gets stuffed on a two-point try) and, after the Warriors grab the onside kick (their third recovery in eight tries), drives the team again. All night Hardin has been reading the corners, running a play called "94" in which the inside receiver runs a flag and the outside receiver runs a hitch. If the corner comes up, Hardin throws the flag; if he doesn't, he throws the hitch. This time he zips a screen pass to Bucky Chamberlin, a tall sophomore receiver, and now it's 54–52.

Hardin jogs to the sideline for a short breather — as safety, QB, and return man, EPC kickoffs are the only time he comes off the field — and is greeted enthusiastically by a short, slight player in oversized shoulder pads who has tucked pads into his socks to give the appearance of calves. Hardin gives him a high-five, and in return senior Gus Johnson whops Hardin on his helmet, then lets out a celebratory whoop.

Dusty Meek grew up watching games in Lepanto, then went on to play linebacker for the team after it became EPC. His senior year, 1995, he was class salutatorian, and the Warriors won their first conference championship. Now, a decade later, he's back. Although the losing has worn on him, Meek looks young for twenty-eight, with kind eyes, short dark brown hair, and a wide face. He prides himself on being professional, on building a program the right way. Before the season he bought a host of signs for the locker room, among them: THOSE WHO EXPECT TO WIN HAVE ALREADY BEGUN TO CONQUER and TRADITION NEVER GRADUATES.

Williams, the school principal, backs Meek, but neither Williams nor anyone else disputes that it's been a rough year. "Everybody at school makes fun of us for not winning," says Chamberlin, the sophomore receiver, "but I don't think they understand how hard it is to win with fifteen players."

It's tough on the parents too. Cody Brown is a senior, a big kid with a goatee, and this wasn't how he expected his final year to play out. His grandfather owns Fat Daddy's BBQ, the red roadside truck where $6.50 gets you a BBQ plate and a Coke. His mom, Karen, runs it on Fridays but makes sure to close by 6:00 P.M. to get to the game. She says all the losing hasn't changed how the boys play. "They're going balls to the wall out there," she says.

Whatever levity there has been for EPC usually traces back to Gus Johnson. Gus, or Goose as he calls himself, is five-foot-three and weighs 120 pounds with a full stomach. He dresses but never plays. He does, however, engage in elaborate stretching routines during games — that is, when he's not excitedly yelling and pointing at the crowd. Johnson is developmentally delayed; everyone in town just calls him "special." "He's one of those kids, always happy, always got a smile," says Meek. "Football's probably one of the only times he gets into a regular environment with the other kids, because he has the special-ed classes."

In four years Johnson has missed one day of school, and that was for a funeral. He has been to every junior high game as a fan and seen every varsity game from the sidelines. In practice he goes through all the blocking and tackling drills. On the scout team Meek lets him play safety, where he's least likely to get hurt.

Against Hughes, Goose was as animated as ever. He pointed to Mark Hardin, Brett's father, who usually returns the salute from the stands, but for once his eyes were on the field. "It was different," says Mark. "We knew this was our only chance." On the sideline Meek knew it too. It's one thing to rebuild a program and take some lumps, another to preside over the first winless season in school history. He paced, frowning.

Fourth Quarter, 3:36 to Play

After 118 combined points the Warriors take their first lead of the game, at 66–60, on a Hardin touchdown toss. Though the game is three and a half hours old, fans are not leaving . . . and more are arriving. Some locals got word of what was happening, and they drove over, cheering as they climbed into the bleachers.

The celebration is short-lived: soon after, Smith sweeps left to tie the score at 66–66. Over the loudspeaker an announcement is made: "Kendric Smith has just scored his eighth touchdown of the game. That ties the Arkansas state record."

The score stays tied, and the two teams head into overtime — in which each team gets four downs to score from the 10-yard line. Hughes gets the ball first. Smith runs once, twice, three times, and finally, on fourth down, wriggles through the right side of the line for his ninth touchdown, breaking the record. Hughes goes for two, running "93 Wrong Way" again, but this time Smith is stopped short, gang-tackled out of bounds. It's 72–66.

On EPC's third play in overtime, Hardin scores on a two-yard run — he's now accounted for ten touchdowns running, returning, or passing — and the Warriors players prepare to go for two. Except there's Meek, on the sideline, calling for one. Suddenly, it's Joe Peridore's moment.

Four hours of play and it comes down to this. Lucas London, the big tackle on Hughes — a kid who volunteered to be team manager in the fourth grade, who has yet to win a varsity game — takes his place on the line. "I figured if I could just get to the middle, I might get a hand on it," London says. If anybody could block the kick, it would be the Blue Devils' biggest player.

The ball is snapped, Peridore takes two steps and boots the ball hard, toeing it gracelessly, and for a moment London thinks he has it blocked. But the kick soars over his hand, over the helmets of his teammates, and through the uprights. EPC wins it 73–72.

Talk about jubilation. "You'd have thought we won the state championship," says Mark Hardin. Parents run onto the field, EPC's cheerleaders hug the players, and Gus Johnson looks as if he's trying to walk on air, leaping and bicycling his legs. On the other sideline the Hughes players file off, consoled by the ten or so fans who made the one-hour drive. It is a long bus ride back for Smith and his teammates, near the end of a long season that will only get longer. "Heartbreaking," says Smith, who not only set the state records for touchdowns but also finished with 425 yards, the third-highest total in Arkansas history. "It was heartbreaking."

Meek doesn't get home until 1:00 A.M. because the papers kept calling him at the school's football office, and they couldn't quite believe what they were hearing. He spent forty-five minutes on the phone with the Jonesboro paper, and Nick Walker from the *Arkansas Democrat-Gazette* had to call back — "Just to double-check," he said. "All of this happened in *one* overtime?"

For a brief period Hughes football matters again; *Hughes* matters again. For a brief period these kids are heroes. It doesn't matter that Kendric Smith lives on Cowan Street, that Brett Hardin is undersized, that there will be no playoffs for either team. For one moment what happened on a football field in Lepanto is the most important thing in this little corner of the world.

Smith begins getting calls from friends and family that night. Over the weekend he starts to realize the magnitude of the record, but it doesn't fully set in until Monday morning when Brown, his cousin, nudges him. "Wake up, Ken," Brown says. "Look at this."

And there on the TV is footage of Smith from the EPC game, taken by a Jonesboro TV station. Not on local TV, on ESPN. "Hey, congrats to Kendric Smith," the anchor is saying. "You hear about this one? He's a running back out of Hughes High School in Hughes, Arkansas. Friday night he scored nine touchdowns, including one in overtime." Smith can't believe it.

The next week he gets calls from Arkansas State and Central Arkansas. Their coaches want to talk to the kid who scored nine touchdowns. Then a reporter from *Newsday* in New York City calls, wanting to impose a *Friday Night Lights* narrative on Smith's feat. Kids come up to him in the hallways at school, want to shake his hand, all for a game that Hughes *lost*. And that's the part no one can comprehend. "Everybody wanted to know the same thing," says London. "How does your running back score nine touchdowns and you *lose*?"

Wright can't quite believe it either. "I've been coaching for thirty-eight years, and I've never gone 0-fer," he says. "Of course, the year that I do, now we have to get the attention." Still, he appreciates what Smith's record means to Hughes. The program might be dying, but it won't go quietly. "That might have been the last hurrah," Wright says, "but it was one hell of a hurrah."

Over in Lepanto, Brett Hardin sees the ESPN footage too. He first gets calls, then letters and cards from his distant relatives. People are in awe. "My friends down in Marked Tree were mad," says Hardin. "They're like 8–1, the best team around, and *we're* getting all the attention."

The publicity doesn't change much at EPC. Kids don't suddenly come out for the team. The Warriors don't go on a winning streak, as they would in a Disney movie. There *is* talk of the talented junior high kids coming up next season, of how the program will regenerate. Still, going into the final game of the year, senior night against division powerhouse Barton High, EPC is 1–8. Some people at school joke that this promises to be such a blowout that they shouldn't even play the game.

It is a frigid October night, and the fans who arrive with blankets and hot chocolate are there out of dogged loyalty; by halftime it is a rout, Barton up 41–14. At the end of the third quarter the game is over for all practical purposes. The EPC band plays just to keep warm, boys in the stands practice their duck calls, students slip off into the night.

Those who do leave early will wish they hadn't. Down on the EPC sideline, word of something unusual begins to circulate: Goose is going into the game. With 5:55 remaining in the fourth, and EPC down 58–14, Meek grabs Johnson by the shoulder pads. "All right, Goose, you're going to get the ball, and when you do, I want you to take it straight to the house, you understand me?" Johnson nods, then jumps up and down, waving his arms to get loose.

It takes a second for the crowd to realize what's happening, but when they do, a murmur goes through the stands. *Goose is in!*

The ball is snapped, Johnson takes the handoff at his own 25, and starts running . . . straight to the sideline, right at the EPC coaches, who worry he might sprint straight out of bounds. Instead, slowly but surely, he begins making a wide arc, turning up field. Of course, he's running a sweep! And then he's off, chugging down the sideline, a convoy of EPC blockers in front, a host of Barton defenders running alongside, somehow knowing how fast they have to run to make it look as if they might tackle Goose. (The Barton coach had heard about Gus Johnson, that this was his final home game.)

Goose hits the 50, the 40, then the 30, and now the crowd is up and yelling, the EPC subs sprinting after him down the sideline. As Johnson charges into the end zone the PA announcer roars as if he's Telestrating the apocalypse: "TOUCHDOOOOWWWWN, WARRRIORRRS! GUS JOHHHHHHNSON ON THE CARRY!"

In the stands some are crying, others are laughing. Mark Hardin is pointing at Goose, who for once doesn't see him because he's getting mobbed by cheerleaders. The EPC players are jumping and high-fiving. Sophomore wide receiver Bryant Woodson says to no one in particular, "Man, I'll remember that for the rest of my life."

He's not the only one. EPC loses 58–22, but nobody cares. Johnson is carried off the field, people slapping him on the back. Assistant coach Josh Hill can't stop smiling. "That made the whole season bearable," he says. In the locker room Gus struts around, jersey off, in just his pants and those giant shoulder pads, and what he keeps saying, over and over, is "Can't *nobody* stop the Goose!"

Since it's the Warriors' final game, they pile their jerseys in the middle of the floor, as if building a mesh funeral pyre. Johnson doesn't comprehend the magnitude of the moment for his fellow seniors, doesn't understand that there is something profound and melancholy about the end to any boy's high school career, an unspoken understanding that, for most of them, sports will now change in a fundamental way — from being the watched to doing the watching. Big Cody Brown, the senior tackle, understands this, and he breaks down in tears.

One by one, they file out, saying their good-byes to one another. Goose is escorted out by his older brother, Jeff, who announces, "We're going to go home and watch *SportsCenter* because Gus is going to be on it all night." After thanking Coach Meek for a good season, Brett Hardin leaves with his dad.

Fifty miles away, in Hughes, Kendric Smith and his teammates are doing the same thing, turning in their jerseys, heading home, moving on from football.

The paths of the boys from EPC and Hughes will continue to diverge, but the thirty-odd kids and their two small towns will remain linked, at least in the Arkansas record book, by one night and by one game that wasn't supposed to matter. "It's funny about kids that way," Wright, the Hughes coach, would say later. "They can be getting their ass handed to them on the field, week after week, and it don't matter. To them, it's all about that next Friday. Who knows what can happen on that next Friday?"

DAVE HYDE

Filling in the Pieces
of Jake Scott

FROM THE SOUTH FLORIDA SUN-SENTINEL

In the whatever-happened-to genre, Jake Scott again breaks the mold, from urinating in the Arctic to holing up in the Pacific.
— D.M.

IN THE LAST STATE. On the last island. Down the last road. At the last speck of a no-stoplight town before the United States drops into the Pacific Ocean.

This is where sports' reigning hermit possibly lives, protected by friends, geography, and a six-foot hedge. Public records say he owns this unassuming, two-story home. But no family member or former teammate will confirm it. No telephone number is available. And there's only a decades-old football photo to measure the man in the front yard against.

"Hi, Jake Scott?" I ask.

"Jake's up in the house," the man says, pointing up a half-dozen stairs to a wooden porch with a screen door. "Who're you?"

"A writer from Florida," I say, walking toward the stairs, leaving the man chuckling a this-could-be-good chuckle.

He knows what everyone does: Jake Scott doesn't do interviews, rarely surfaces in public, divorced himself from the Dolphins, declined a College Football Hall of Fame bid, didn't join most other Super Bowl MVPs again last year in Detroit, and has pulled such a Howard Hughes that a sports memorabilia dealer, showing the kind of focus that sends others in search of

Sasquatch, once hired a private investigator to contact him. It took two years.

"*Hey, Jake!*" the man in the driveway yells up at the house. "*A writer's here to see you!*"

Scott's final Dolphins moment in 1976 was spent yelling with Don Shula. Defensive lineman Manny Fernandez says Scott wasn't asked to sing his college fight song like other rookies his first training camp because "he's the one guy no one messed with." A Colorado mountain man once heard Scott was a football player and picked a bar fight, saying, "I'm the toughest guy in here." Scott dropped him like a shirt off a hanger, and then asked, "No one's tougher in here than him?"

These are some dots. Connect them and you understand the possibilities as the screen door opens and the ghost walks out in a purple golf shirt tucked into faded blue jeans. It must be him. It's that football photo time-aged forward.

At sixty-one, he's still trim. He's completely bald. Oversized glasses cover his face like two storm windows. And he's smiling, thank God. I double-check to be sure.

"Hi, how you doing?" he says.

He shakes hands. He talks in a soft, friendly voice still rooted in Georgia. He says, "I'm not hard to find." He says, "I don't want a story written." He says, "If you'd ask questions, then I'd have to tell the truth." He says, "I live the simplest life you can imagine — wake up every day and decide whether to golf, fish, or have a drink."

From this front porch, the Pacific peeks through palm trees across the quiet road. Warm air rides in on a noonday breeze. Scott puts one foot up on the railing and allows the conversation to drift. He tells how his home sat alone on this road when he arrived in 1982. Now the world has joined him. A small place beside him just sold for $1.9 million. A big lot across the road, against the ocean, went for $29 million.

He says, "That's how it goes." He says, "Beautiful here, isn't it?" He says, "Too bad my boat just had its propeller damaged or I'd take you out fishing — just you and me, not for a story."

After ten minutes, it seems I've scaled the mountain, found the wise man, but won't get to ask the three questions carried across time: What the heck has he been doing with his life? Are the testosterone-rich stories teammates tell about him true? And what's up between him and Shula?

Then Scott says something I find out later makes his friends listening inside look at each other in surprise:

"I'll be at the Tahiti Nui at five if you want a drink."

Regulars at the Bar

5:00 P.M. The bar's first stool, the corner view, the spot nearest the open double doors, belongs to Richard Pasakai, a Hawaiian everyone calls "The Mayor." He is fifty-four, nearsighted, autistic, grew up on this westernmost Hawaiian island of Kauai, and is such a known commodity that Scott has him chaperone visiting *haole,* or white people, around the island to ensure they have a local's stamp of approval.

The second stool belongs to Art Wills. Art is cool. Art is funny. Art is a seventy-year-old construction worker and Hawaiian. At age six, he remembers standing on a Honolulu rooftop watching the Japanese bomb Pearl Harbor — "I thought it was a fireworks show at first," he says. Four years ago, he moved into the bottom apartment in Scott's home for two weeks and never left.

The third stool is Scott's. As I enter, he is taking a peanuts can to the other side of the small bar and sprinkling some before four tourists from San Francisco. He waves me over to where he's sitting. One rule of the Tahiti Nui, known only to locals, is this side of the bar is for them and that side is for tourists.

Another rule is these three men sit on these three stools. They're as much of the daily scenery as the thatched roof, Polynesian masks, dozens of ribbons from local canoe-paddling competitions, and the framed photos on the walls of fishermen with their catch.

"We meet here at five," Scott says from stool number three.

Every day?

"It's a simple life," he says, drinking a Salty Dog (vodka and grapefruit juice). I get a Hawaiian beer and sit down on the fourth stool.

6:00 P.M. The idea was not to be a slave to fame or money. Create a life. Take a machete and make a path. Hanalei fit with that when Scott discovered it on a visit to see Terry Hermeling, a former

Washington Redskins teammate who owned rights to Burger King stores on the outer Hawaiian islands.

Scott had a Colorado place then. He and fellow Dolphins safety Dick Anderson had taken their 1971 Super Bowl winnings and bought a Colorado ranch together. When they sold it a few years later, Scott built an A-frame log home 9,400 feet up a mountain north of Vail. It was so isolated he laid the electrical lines himself. In winter, he'd snowmobile up the final two miles on the otherwise impassable road.

Hanalei became Colorado's geographical alter ego for Scott. Kauai is 550 square miles with 60,000 people. But Hanalei is the farthest stop on the island, cradled between the Pacific and the world's wettest spot of Mt. Waialeale, which gets 480 feet of rain annually.

Main Street consists of five blocks where you can eat taro burgers, drink papaya smoothies, sign up for surf lessons, or give a hitchhiker a ride for six ocean-hugging miles to where the United States ends on a beach.

"The beauty of this place got me," Scott says. "And the people. They're just like the South in some ways. The food's the same, pork and chicken. And they'll sit just around with the children playing in the ocean, the men drinking beer and the women talking.

"Nothing fancy to it. People just living. That's what I was like."

7:00 P.M. Scott points to a framed photo on the wall of him holding a 130-pound ahi tuna. He learned to fish in the rugged seas of the island's North Shore from David Kahoone, a neighbor, friend, and Hawaiian. He has fish tales. Just last week such a big marlin hit that it took all his line and had to be cut loose.

But he also has too many tales like this: Kahoone, dying of cancer two years ago. He helped care for him, right to the end. The three men on the bar stools then took Scott's boat to a remote, oceanside cave where, as a boy, Kahoone rode out a storm in a boat with his grandfather while a hammerhead shark sat in the water. There, they scattered their friend's ashes.

"It's what he wanted," Scott said.

8:00 P.M. Scott introduces me to a Hawaiian taro farmer in jeans and T-shirt. We small-talk for a few minutes. About taro, the potato-like crop grown in Hawaii. About fishing. When he leaves, Scott says he's worth millions.

By evening's end, it seems he's introduced most of Hanalei's 800 residents, many Hawaiians, some *haole*. There's J.D., who has a stuffed 550-pound lion in a room of his house; Scrappy, nicknamed because he liked to fight as a kid; a golf buddy, a neighbor, a player in the Wednesday night poker game at Scott's home for which he makes his special chili.

Somewhere amid the dozens of greetings, a Hawaiian and friend of a friend introduces himself to Scott, saying, "I've never met a Super Bowl player before."

Scott clinks his Salty Dog glass against the man's beer, says in the pidgin Hawaiian he sometimes breaks into, "How you doing, brud-dah."

9:00 P.M. Scott made more Pro Bowls (five) in the Dolphins' glory years of 1970–75 than four Hall of Fame teammates. He remains the Dolphins' all-time leader in interceptions (35) and punt returns (10.5-yard average). But the Pro Bowl plaques, two Super Bowl rings, college All-America awards from his days at Georgia, and his 1968 Southeastern Conference Player of the Year trophy that he didn't even bother attending the banquet to pick up all sit in his mother's Atlanta home.

He holds up the only football souvenir he carries around: five screws in his left hand from breaking it against Kansas City fullback Jim Otis in the 1971 AFC Championship game. He shows the right wrist he then broke in that ensuing Super Bowl. That put both hands in casts and led to him saying at the time: "Now I find out who my real friends are when I go to the bathroom."

10:00 P.M. Art asks Scott, "You really talking to a writer?" Scott shrugs. I grab a pen and a cocktail napkin off the bar and ask question number one: what the heck has he been doing with his life?

"You're looking at it," he says. "You can make life real simple if you want."

The broader answer sounds like a nonstop adventure. He's single, hasn't worked a day of his nonfootball life, and lives half the year in Hawaii. The other half, he returns to his native Georgia or is off like a dart at the map. He's off to New Zealand this winter for a month with his Atlanta girlfriend. British Columbia is a common stop.

He once had the idea to urinate in the Arctic Ocean, he says, and so spent four months in a motor home in Alaska, "driving down every dead-end road they had." Another year he rode his Harley motorcycle from Georgia to Mexico City.

"We were getting run off the road in Mexico, hard, when the guy I was with pulled out a .45 and started firing," Scott said. "I didn't even know he had it."

Was anyone hit? "I don't know, but they stopped trying to kill us."

Last Super Bowl, when most other MVPs were gathering in Detroit, Scott was scheduled for another preferred destination: Australia. One previous trip there, he ended up in Perth and befriended some blokes. They took a helicopter to the remote town of Exmouth, where they spent some good time fishing.

He had planned to fish for barramundi this time. "Huge perch," he says. "Great to catch."

But his buddy got sick, the trip was canceled, and Scott ended up watching the Super Bowl at Jake's Compound, which is what friends call his home that includes four apartments. (Art lives in one. Two are for visitors. The fourth is kept locked for whenever his sister and her husband visit from Key West.)

Scott didn't mind missing the MVP gathering considering what the NFL was offering. Fly to Detroit? Sign several hundred memorabilia items? Put up with "all the a—— kissing"? he says. For $8,000?

"I don't need the money," he says. "I don't need it for my ego. And I'd rather sit here and have a drink with Art."

He looks over at Art, who's listening to the bar's band, the Road Warriors, play "Lay Down Sally."

"Tells you what an idiot I am," Scott says.

11:00 P.M. Hall of Fame quarterback Bobby Layne once told Scott the goal in life was to run out of money and breath at the same moment. Scott likes that efficiency, though he has been broke and nearly broken.

He invested his football money into car dealerships. For years, everything hummed along nicely, meaning Scott had several million in the bank and lived in Hawaii and Colorado. In 1991, the owner of the dealerships filed for bankruptcy. Scott lost every cent.

"Good thing I was here," he says. "If I'd been around him, I might've killed him."

A Georgia alum and investor would help Scott to his financial feet again. But, to do so, Scott needed to find money to invest. He had to decide what to sell from his life: Colorado or Hawaii? "I hated to sell the place in Colorado," he says. "Had to, but hated it."

Midnight. Question number two: Are the wild stories his teammates tell about him true? Of his University of Georgia report card being all As and Fs, depending if he cared about the subject? "That's true," he says.

Of his legendary drinking stamina to the point he once drank forty-three beers in a setting? True. Of so many women flocking to him that on one visit Joe Namath said, "And I thought I had women in New York"? True.

Of his ability to unlock an opposing quarterback's secret — noticing, for instance, Namath always studied the break of Scott's free-safety position to read coverage, so Scott would take a false first step to fool him?

"Yeah," Scott says, adding that Namath would curse at him across the line of scrimmage.

Of him telling a nervous Shula, on the bus to Super Bowl VII, "What's the matter, you thinking about going down as the losingest coach in Super Bowl history?"

"That's true," Scott says. "I'm never late to anything. I'm always early. That day I was outside the bus giving tickets to some people. Shula yells out, 'You're going to be late to the biggest game of your career.' So I said that to him."

Of him taking a $5,000 pay cut to leave the Canadian Football League and join the Dolphins?

"It was $10,000," he said. "I remember reading [general manager] Joe Thomas say in the papers, 'We got a first-round talent for seventh-round money.' But I got them back."

When the World Football League bought Larry Csonka, Paul Warfield, and Jim Kiick in 1974, Scott says he bluffed the Dolphins that he had a big-money WFL offer too. That's why the Dolphins offered him a five-year, $600,000 deal. He became the NFL's first $100,000-a-year defensive back.

Of him riding his Harley up the concrete columns and over Georgia's basketball arena?

He smiles. "That's the rumor, isn't it?"

1:00 A.M. Scott turns to me. "I knew you were coming. I got a call at four o'clock this morning saying you were on the island."

I look. He's serious. Every teammate and friend from Anderson to Csonka to Jim Mandich has repeated the same thought: Scott never lies. Ever. So I think back. I had called his mother in Atlanta the day before leaving, fishing to assure he was in Hawaii so as not to waste a five-thousand-mile trip. She hinted he was there, but like everyone refused to pinpoint where there was. Scott won't say that was the tip-off.

"It's a small island," he says. "But think about it. I wasn't surprised when you showed up. If I'd been surprised, you might have been thrown off the porch." He laughs. He's joking. Maybe.

1:17 A.M. "Don't tell anyone this is a beautiful place," Scott says, as I get up to leave. "We don't need more people here." As I look back, he's moved closer to the band, playing "Against the Wind."

Good Friends

The Kauai Taro Festival is held the next afternoon in an open field. Several hundred festival-goers stand amid the occasional spitting from Mt. Waialeale and take in music, art, and every food of the potato-like taro. Smoothies. Poi. Pork- and chicken-wrapped Hawaiian lau-laus.

After an hour, I wander a few blocks into the Hanalei Gourmet Restaurant.

"Hey!" Scott calls over. "Sit down. Have a beer."

He introduces me to Paul the Bartender, who once rented one of Scott's apartments; Hag, who owns a transportation business in town and plays in Scott's Wednesday poker game; and the Road Warriors' bass player and his girlfriend, who is suggesting she could join the poker game.

"Okay, do you *know* how to play poker?" Scott asks her. "Do you know hi-lo?"

She hesitates. "Yeah, I think."

Scott laughs. "Just have your boyfriend give us $200 and save yourself the time."

He wears jeans, sandals, and a white golf shirt with the insignia of Fuzzy's Place, an Atlanta bar whose owner played football at Georgia with Scott. Fuzzy Cawthon, fifty-six, had died the previous week. Scott, who gave Cawthon his nickname, might not surface much, but he holds friendships fiercely. A few years ago another Georgia teammate, Dick Young, was dying and Scott rushed from Australia hoping to see him but arrived too late.

Cawthon was the second close friend Scott lost in October. The first was more traumatic. It came aboard the custom-made, forty-one-foot catamaran Scott bought earlier this year. He named it the *Mele Kai*, Hawaiian for either "Mary of the Seas" (Mary is Scott's mother's name) or "Song of the Seas."

Beyond personal fishing trips, the idea was to have tourists rent the boat for trips. Bill Lawrence, a longtime friend and Hawaiian boat captain, became Scott's business partner and would go out with tourists.

On October 8, Scott and Lawrence were carrying officials of a major Hawaiian canoe-paddling competition from Kauai to the island of Molokai. Scott was in another part of the boat when he noticed it drifting. Lawrence, he found, had suffered a heart attack.

"We tried CPR, mouth-to-mouth, everything," Scott says. "There wasn't anything to do to help him. We could only cover him up."

He takes off his glasses, wipes his eyes.

"It makes you look at things, reminds you what's important, what's not. It also means I'm getting old."

Falling-Out with Shula

Question number three: what's up between him and Shula?

"Don Shula is a good man," Scott says. "He was a great coach. And he made a mistake."

There, in three definitive sentences, stories are unlocked that rumble across the years. If his friends' deaths tell how deeply Scott can love, these stories tell how long he can remember.

Let's start here: Legendary Georgia coach Vince Dooley says Scott is the best athlete he ever coached. Yes, better than Herschel Walker. But in 1968, after winning its final regular-season game, the team sent Scott into Dooley's office carrying oranges as the players' vote for an Orange Bowl bid and national title matchup. But Dooley, in a move he regrets, privately had signed already to play in a lesser Sugar Bowl.

Scott cut Dooley from his life right there. This wasn't just a football issue to him. It went deeper. It was about loyalty and trust. College juniors weren't eligible for the NFL draft then, so Scott left for the Canadian Football League and stayed away from Georgia until Dooley left.

In 2001, Dooley offered to lobby Scott for the College Football Hall of Fame. Having no way to reach him, Dooley sent word through a friend that Scott only had to promise he would attend the induction ceremony. Scott sent word back not to bother.

Scott and Shula once were close. Shula took a snowmobile with his family up to Scott's Colorado home. They had lunch together in Vail. His oldest son, David, wore number 13 in football because Scott "was his idol," Shula says.

But at some point that changed. Scott loved the mind and tactics of Shula's defensive coordinator of the Super Bowl years, Bill Arnsparger. But like many teammates, he didn't respect Arnsparger's successor, Vince Costello.

During one practice in 1974, Scott yelled at Costello, telling the coach he didn't know what he was talking about. When Shula hustled across the field to ask what happened, Scott said, "I wasn't f—— talking to you."

Then, after the 1975 season, Shula announced in a team meeting that players' attendance was mandatory at a banquet. "I won't be there," Scott said.

"Everyone will be there or they'll be fined $5,000," Shula said.

Scott didn't go. He was fined. That offseason he asked for a trade. "Shula said I'd never have to wear a Dolphins uniform again," Scott says today. Scott was on the team in preseason but didn't practice because of a bum shoulder.

Shula says doctors told him Scott was healthy. When he told Scott this, Shula remembers, "He told me he'd say when he was ready to practice and play. I said, 'We can't operate like that. I can't have one set of rules for you.'"

Scott, to be sure, was respected for playing through pain: he played the final eleven games as a rookie with a separated shoulder; he played Super Bowl VI with that broken hand and wrist, even receiving punts in the game; he was MVP of the "Perfect Season" Super Bowl despite such a battered shoulder that Jimmy "the Greek" Snyder moved Washington from a two- to a three-point favorite with the idea Scott couldn't play.

Still, when he wouldn't shoot up the shoulder with painkillers for an exhibition game, Shula and Scott got in a yelling match in the locker room. The next day, Scott was traded to Washington for the forgettable Bryan Salter.

But that's not the mistake Scott harbors today. Several teammates asked don't know this one. They think he never has attended a Perfect Season reunion. But he says he was there in 1982, at the ten-year celebration, ready to join in. As Scott tells it, he and Shula were in an Orange Bowl elevator together.

"I said to him, 'We've got to meet next week and iron out this thing between us,'" Scott says. "Shula said to me, 'F—— you.'"

Shula says today: "I don't remember that. Why would I say that?"

When the elevator door opened Scott walked out of the Orange Bowl, rolling away like a dropped coin, never to be seen again. Shula wishes he would return, saying, "I loved Jake on that team and I know the kind of player he was. I don't think there has been a better safety combination than him and Anderson."

When the Dolphins announced this summer that Anderson would be inducted in the Ring of Honor, Scott called his former safety partner to congratulate him. There was some thought Anderson and Scott would enter together, like Mark Duper and Mark Clayton. Scott says it was never offered, and he hasn't talked to any Dolphins official in more than a decade.

"I'm not bitter or angry," Scott says. "I'm living a great life. I do whatever I want. And I love the Dolphins. I just didn't want to come around and be an issue with [Shula]."

Asked whether he'll come back someday, he answers: "*Na kuli ana.*" He lets it sit a moment. "That's Hawaiian for, 'It's not in my future.'"

And so he lives in the world he's created, not the larger one asking to see him, touch him, and remember him as someone thirty years ago. There's a sense of nobleness to this, the ex-jock not defined by his glory. There's also an equal and opposite sense of loss at not joining his team in the occasional whiff of public nostalgia.

He surfaces occasionally. He attended one Super Bowl MVP gathering in 1986 (he was the only one without a tie). He signed autographs at a card show in Broward County in 1993 and another in Virginia in 2001 only after that promoter's private investigator tracked him down. ("I see a ghost," teammate Jim Langer said in greeting him.)

He has agreed to be an honorary Georgia captain for the coin flip before the Georgia Tech game on Saturday. Dooley, if it matters, and no doubt it does, is no longer officially with the school.

But across one weekend, in hours of conversation, his eyes narrowed just once in the manner his reputation still holds. I asked about taking a photo for this story.

"I don't want one taken," he said. "Hawaiians think it's bad luck to have their picture taken."

"Do you think it's bad luck?" I asked.

"Hawaiians do," he said.

"But you have your picture on the wall at the bar."

His eyes flattened. "There'll be no picture."

A few seconds later, he was laughing about his friend, Paul Hornung, losing so much weight that his pants fell down while speaking at Notre Dame. And telling how he took Csonka elk hunting in Colorado. Then how he'll boat friends to a small island off Kauai, open only to Hawaiians, and let them off there while he'll fish for a few hours before picking them up.

Scott drains the last gulp of Budweiser, puts the bottle down, and opens his hands, palms up: "That's it. There's no big mystery. I'm just living the simple life I saw." He stands up, shakes hands, and walks out the door.

An Invitation

As my airplane taxis to the gate after the fifteen-hour trip home, a message pops on my cell phone: "Hi, this is Jake. Just wanted to make sure you got back okay. Come on back here sometime and we'll go fishing. Bring your wife."

There's a chuckle. "Call ahead next time, though, or I really will throw your a—— off the porch."

WRIGHT THOMPSON

Fading Away

FROM ESPN.COM

Was it us, or that substance of which he will not speak, or just him?
— D.M.

IN THE LAST house on the left, behind two gates in a heavily se-
cured Orange County community, Mark McGwire is reinventing
himself.

One part of his life, the public part, is over. A second act, in a
new place with new friends, is just beginning. Bunkered within the
walls of his exclusive enclave, across the street from a U.S. congress-
man of all things, he can look out the windows and see the mountains rising in the distance.

He likes it here on lots 82 and 83 in the Shady Canyon neighborhood, billed as a place for folks with "quiet wealth." Far from the
glitz of Beverly Hills and from the O.C.'s oceanfront palaces, it's for
people who don't want to be found. A computer system scans license plates for undesirables; security guards stop strangers and, if
a homeowner doesn't say "yes," send them on their way. From the
outside, the houses look like battleships.

This is where the forty-three-year-old McGwire spends his days.
Five years ago, he retired as one of baseball's most beloved players.
His legacy is different now. The Hall of Fame ballots went out last
month, and no one knows if he's in or not, or if he even cares or
not. That's how he likes it, of course. He's not here to talk about
the past.

He sidestepped questions from Congress. He doesn't do interviews, including one for this story. He didn't go back to St. Louis
during the World Series. But it's more than just avoiding the media

and fans. McGwire never seems to talk about the past. To anyone. In fact, he seems intent on leaving his past behind.

"I haven't even spoken to him since he retired," says Randy Robertson, a buddy from childhood and one of his college roommates at Southern Cal. "I don't know who his best friend is now."

"I haven't spoken to him in a while," says Mark Altieri, the slugger's former spokesman.

"I haven't seen him in ages," says Tom Carroll, his high school baseball coach.

"He just wants to slink away," says Ken Brison, son of a former McGwire foundation board member.

"We never talk about politics or baseball," says U.S. Representative John Campbell (R-Calif. 48th), his neighbor.

His Mediterranean-looking mansion at the end of a cul-de-sac is such an unlikely end for a star of one of the most magical summers baseball has ever known. McGwire's future will be inside Shady Canyon, with his new wife, Stephanie, and young kids, Max and Mason, and at the breathtakingly expensive golf course nearby.

"That's where he is all the time," says friend Justin Dedeaux, son of the late Rod Dedeaux, McGwire's coach at USC. "He stays behind those walls and that's it. No one ever sees him. He just completely dropped out. I don't know if he talks to anybody."

But what of the past he wants everyone to forget about? Even if he cuts ties, it's still there. The places where he grew up, the friends he once knew, the life he once lived, that's McGwire's legacy. Even if he doesn't speak, it speaks for him.

Only ghosts remain at McGwire's boyhood home in Claremont, California. Bits and pieces of a former life, things left behind. The pink and white chairs in the living room. The white wraparound couch. The blue wallpaper upstairs.

There are a few clues that he once lived here. The tub is extra large and the closet is a walk-in and the couch is a room-filler and the dining table is more suited for a battalion than a family.

"Everything is big," current owner Paul Martin says, laughing.

It should be. This is where John McGwire raised his five boys, including a baseball slugger, an NFL quarterback, and a bodybuilder. He designed the place himself. When the McGwires moved about a decade ago, Martin bought it from them.

He points behind the sparkling blue pool, toward another relic from the days when McGwire on television meant home runs, not testimony.

"The satellite dish was John's so he could watch all his kids," Martin says. "We just never took it out."

Nearby is a small putting green with three holes. Now, the flags are strewn about in disarray, but back in the day, the ultra-competitive McGwires had many a showdown out there. Often neighborhood kids, like Patrick Kirk, would join in.

"It was just brutal, the competition," says Kirk, now a lieutenant colonel in the army. "We would hang out at his house. His mom was a phenomenal cook. She fed us like there was no tomorrow."

McGwire was around five when his folks moved here. On this quiet cul-de-sac, he read about his sporting heroes and dreamed. Kirk still laughs, remembering Mark running down the street one Christmas, yelling, "Pat! Pat! I just got a prescription to *Sports Illustrated*!"

They were all the same then. No stars or fans, no winners or losers, no heroes or cheats. Relationships were real. Life was simple, something out of a black-and-white sitcom. The neighborhood was full of kids, and they were the support group for a shy McGwire.

"He was a very private person," Kirk says. "He had a core group of friends that he hung out with that he felt comfortable with, that he spent time with."

Eventually, McGwire distanced himself from his old buddies. It started, friends say, when one of that core group tried to capitalize off Mark's name. An already private man was realizing that trust and fame didn't often go hand in hand. The journey that ultimately led to the walls of Shady Canyon had begun.

"When that trust was betrayed," Kirk says, "he looked at that inner circle and said, 'How can I trust those guys?'"

The last time Kirk and McGwire spoke, when Mark was with the A's and both were home visiting their families, Patrick knew the bond they once shared was no more. His old friend was gone, a wary superstar in his place.

"I could even tell when Mark and I talked in the cul-de-sac, there was this feeling of keeping an arm's distance," Kirk says. " 'Good to see you. Glad to see you're doing well.' But you know, it was strained. I feel bad. You hang out with these guys and you form a bond with them, and you think you'll never be separated."

With bonds broken and his family gone, there isn't much left of

McGwire in the neighborhood anymore. The fan mail to his old address is down to a trickle. He hasn't visited his boyhood home since it was sold a decade ago. He probably doesn't know Kirk was in the Pentagon on September 11. He doesn't know that his old putting green has seen better days. His junior high school, just a few blocks away, is closed.

Then there's the biggest loss: the pride the cul-de-sac felt at their native son's success has been tempered. Martin was watching when McGwire hit seventy, and he was watching when McGwire went in front of Congress. The alpha and omega.

"That was so sad," Martin says. "And so unnecessary. I was sitting here, thinking, 'Just tell them what you did and everyone will think better of you.'"

The seasons are changing on Siena Court. One day, no one in this neighborhood will know anything about McGwire. Maybe they won't even know this is where he grew up.

That might not be too far away. Martin's wife, Pan, has Alzheimer's, and earlier this year, he was diagnosed with leukemia. "Not much time," he says softly.

The Martins stand inside the garage, just outside the door to the house. There's still a piece of freezer tape that the McGwires put up, letting people know that the button that looks like a buzzer actually raises and lowers the garage door. The next owners might never know who put it up.

He smiles. She does too, but her eyes are vacant. Paul Martin understands the past is gone for his wife, and he understands that all we are, in the end, is a collection of the things that happened to us.

A few feet inside the front door of Damien High School, on the door of the old coach's office, there's a poster. It's from 1998, and it's got a big photo of McGwire and a star with the number 70 on it.

"Nobody does it better than our hometown hero," it reads.

Everybody had them eight years ago. Now they're difficult to find.

The one on Tom Carroll's door is worn, the edges starting to roll back. If you're looking for signs that Mark McGwire went to high school here, this is about it. Some schools turn into shrines for famous alums, with retired jerseys and big plaques. The only other hints that a great man got his start here are a few entries in the basketball record book and a trophy or two.

Come take a ride with Carroll, now the school's athletic director. He drives around the campus in a golf cart. A lot has changed around here since the class of 1981 threw their caps in the air and moved on. The little dairy down on Bonita Drive where everyone hung after school is gone. The old gymnasium is locked, used only for special occasions. A new athletic facility just opened.

Standing at the old gym, Carroll fishes out a key. He swings open the door, walks over to the trophy case, and starts looking. One of the taller trophies is for baseball team MVPs. Not many people see it behind these locked doors.

"His name should be on there," Carroll says, scanning through the years.

Sure enough: 1981. McGwire shared the honor with a guy named Mike Alexander. That was a good team. They were even better the season before, McGwire's junior year. The Spartans won their conference for the first time ever. That trophy is around here too. It's the only other piece of McGwire left.

"The plaque has fallen off the trophy," Carroll says. "They better not have taken that."

It's not here. He knows one more place to try: the trophy case in the new gym. Driving around in his golf cart, Carroll talks about the conundrum the people who love McGwire face. They were once so proud to have even a small part in baseball history — Carroll, for instance, turned USC scouts on to Mark — and now all of that is so muddy.

Anyone who sat in the stands in 1998, or checked their papers every day, knows how they feel here at Damien High. That summer meant so much to so many people, and its unraveling is a hard thing to contemplate. Was what I watched real? Were my emotions fake too?

"I saw the bit with the Congress," says Jack Helber, McGwire's American Legion coach. "And that was somewhat, ahhhh, that was disappointing. If you try to hide it, you really aren't hiding it. You're pretty much admitting things."

Some just don't talk about it; Carroll, for instance, doesn't remember anyone coming up to him in the halls to talk about the congressional hearings. He's chosen his own stance: it isn't true, and if it is, baseball is more at fault than the shy kid he once knew.

"I wouldn't believe that SOB who wrote that book," he says of Jose Canseco's *Juiced*. "But I could be wrong. I don't know if they even tested McGwire for steroids. They are the ones at fault. They encouraged those guys. A lot of McGwire's hard work was swept under the carpet. I know he was very self-motivated, and he loved the game of baseball."

Carroll is in the new shiny facility now. A stained glass window, gift of the class of 2006, carries a few words from the school song. The lyrics are about faded glory.

> A certain word, a thought remembered
> Will stir within someday
> We'll recall the nights of victory
> Time has swept away.

Standing in front of the glass case, Carroll still can't find that trophy.

"Now where in the hell is this?" he says. "I hope they didn't steal it."

Finally, he spots it, next to the 2003 water polo trophy. No plaque to tell what year or what it was for. Just a team photo attached. That's been almost forgotten. Only the old-timers know that if you look closely, the kid down at the end, with the red hair pouring out the sides of his cap, is Mark McGwire. Or he used to be, at least.

"Margaritaville" is rocking on the stereo at Dedeaux Field on the USC campus. The frosty cans of MGD are flying out of the clubhouse. Ah, the annual alumni game.

Time for former USC baseball players to show up, kill some beers, see old friends, tell a few stories. Lots of people come. Recent World Series champion Randy Flores — certainly not the most famous USC alum to play for the Cardinals — sits on the dugout bench.

He wasn't about to miss this, even bringing a disposable camera to take photos with his buddies. He sits next to Craig Jones, a former Trojan and minor league pitcher. Jones, now a cop and real estate agent, has a little guy with him.

"Is this yours?" Randy asks.

"This is Luke," Jones says proudly.

"What's up, Luke?" Randy says, leaning in.

They're all laughing, trying to figure out where the years have gone. Craig has a son and Randy won a World Series title?

This is why they all return. For moments like these. A lot of guys show up who played with McGwire in 1982–84, but not the man himself.

Just a year ago, they were all sitting around, trying to figure out how to get his butt down to the stadium. Only, no one had his phone number.

His old friends miss him. His old program misses him.

"We pride ourselves on 'Trojan family,'" says Don Winston, USC senior associate athletic director. "I don't think he's mad at us. . . . He doesn't want to be involved in anything, and it's a shame."

Everyone has a theory. Some believe he doesn't trust people. Some believe he's embarrassed. Justin Dedeaux, son of the legendary coach, has his own idea.

"I don't think he's embarrassed as much as I think he's crestfallen by the whole thing," he says. "Hurt. He's a highly sensitive person. He really is that way. Some guys it just rolls off their back. But Mark takes things to heart. This has hurt him terribly, and I don't think he knows how to approach this."

Not even Randy Robertson has spoken to him. They grew up a few streets apart. They went to junior high school together, played Legion ball together. They were roommates as sophomores at USC. McGwire was in Robertson's first wedding, for God's sake. Now Robertson doesn't know how to contact his old friend. He wasn't at McGwire's wedding four years ago in Las Vegas.

"I haven't seen him since his last year," Robertson says. "I've never even met his [second] wife or his two kids."

The last time they were together was at Dodgers Stadium in 2001, the year McGwire retired. They talked for about fifteen minutes, just catching up, and Robertson had no idea that it would be the last time he would see his old college roommate.

Now it has been five years, and he sits in his airy home just off an L.A. freeway and wonders if McGwire is going to Cooperstown.

"I don't think the Hall of Fame is something he needs," Robertson says. "Me, personally, I'd love him to be in the Hall of Fame, and I think he's deserving. I don't think he feels that way. I don't think he needs it. It would be another award that doesn't validate his life."

No matter what happens when the ballots are returned before the December 31 deadline, USC has decided that McGwire will remain a prominent former player — at least from its end. The museum down the right-field line is packed with memorabilia. Jerseys from St. Louis and Oakland. A cutout of him swinging. Framed paintings. They didn't stop loving McGwire at USC after the congressional hearings.

"I think he got some bad advice," says Dedeaux, whose father, Rod, died in January. "I can't for the life of me figure out why he didn't say, 'Hey, this is what I did. I took this, I took that, and at the time it was okay.' At least he didn't lie like [Rafael] Palmeiro. He didn't lie. You can say that about him."

Maybe someday he'll be back in the fold. The entrance to Dedeaux Field is named Mark McGwire Way. It's the first thing fans see when they come to a game. Only, USC still hasn't had the dedication. It has been years.

"We didn't have a ceremony because he wasn't here," Winston says. "We haven't done it because we haven't been able to communicate with him."

So, for now, another part of McGwire's past waits for him to return. There are teammates to drink beers with, new children to meet, stories to tell. There's a life left behind.

"A lot of people," Dedeaux says, "would like to say, 'Mark, we love you.'"

If he's not with any of his old friends, then where is Mark McGwire? If the weather's even close to nice, which it usually is, he's out on the links at Shady Canyon Golf Club. One look at the parking lot lets you know what kind of place this is. Ferrari. Jaguar. BMW. Mercedes. Ford GT.

McGwire has his handicap down to zero. He tried to qualify for the U.S. Open two years ago. He won a golf skills competition a few years back, beating the likes of Greg Norman, Rich Beem, Colin Montgomerie, and Paul Azinger.

"He's a good player," says Shady Canyon head pro Kirk Manley. "He's got a good golf game. He works at it very hard."

Most of his neighbors see him regularly, usually coming or going from a round. The guy they see doesn't seem like someone who is hiding or avoiding old friends. McGwire feels safe behind these walls.

"He always stops and waves and talks," says John McMonigle, a real estate mogul who lives a few houses down. "I see him in his golf cart on his way back from the club. I see him at Starbucks. I see him at the grocery store. I see him at the drugstore. I see him all the time. He's very friendly and outgoing, and we just think the world of him."

Inside Shady Canyon, McGwire is simply another person, albeit a two-dimensional one. No deep digging here. Just casual talk about his two young children, born post-retirement, or about his golf game. The best place to hide isn't in a cave or on an island. It's in the monotony of a daily routine.

"We usually talk about his kids or we talk about my cars," Campbell says. "He wants to be a father, a friend, a neighbor, and a husband. And the fame thing? He doesn't seem to be caught up in that at all."

No one asks about steroids or the Hall of Fame, two subjects awkwardly parked between the old and new phases of McGwire's life. Those questions are kept outside the gate. And who knows? Robertson might be right. Maybe McGwire doesn't care about Cooperstown. At least not right now.

"As you get older," says Jim Dietz, who coached McGwire in the Alaska League, "things like that become a lot more important to you. I'm sure that will happen to Mark."

Things like the Hall of Fame are for a man's children, and his grandchildren. By rejecting his past and creating a new future, McGwire is altering the arc of his family. He is changing all of their futures, and the way they will all view their past. Instead of the Hall of Fame defining them, his disappearance will. These are the decisions that shape a family.

Says Nancy Boxill, granddaughter of 2006 inductee Cumberland Posey: "I am delighted beyond words that from now until the end of time people will go to the Hall of Fame and they will be confronted and engaged by the contributions that my grandfather made. Knowing that I come from a very strong and capable and excellent grandfather means that I have to do my best to be strong and capable and excellent."

Maybe that has occurred to McGwire. But if you want to ask, you've got to get past the security guard and the gates — one large one out front and a smaller one past the golf club. Unless he gives his blessing, the gates remain closed, keeping his past locked safely outside, his future neatly barricaded behind these walls.

JOHN KLIMA

Deal of the Century

FROM THE (TORRANCE, CALIFORNIA) DAILY BREEZE

"Bonus baby" — one of the most evocative phrases in sports. Nothing like fading away so quickly that strangers feel free to tell you what you once were.
— D.M.

THE LETTERS INEVITABLY arrive in April. They come from different points across America, but all ask the same thing.

"Dear Paul: You were the first $100,000 bonus baby," one started, as if Paul Pettit had forgotten. It is a classic fan letter to a baseball player, a sugarcoated attempt at knowledge, disguised as a friendly ruse for a signature. "I am sorry that you didn't play in the majors longer, but it still means something to have been there. If you have a photo to autograph for me, I would like it. Thank you."

They all end with the same question, and sometimes the letter writers even say please. The letters always find their way into Pettit's garage at his home in Hemet, the place where the walls have been covered with photographs from his career, but this is no shrine. You can find his photos by his workbench, where his tools are neatly organized, next to the dusty set of golf clubs. Time and bad knees have caught up to him, he said, and he stopped playing a few years ago. He is seventy-six now, and on the kitchen table is a pill-box with his daily medications.

He takes the time to accommodate each letter, but sometimes it strikes him as funny that someone wants the signature of a pitcher who won one lousy game in the major leagues fifty-three years ago. It is as if they are waiting on a young man's promise as a pitcher long since lost.

"The only thing I can think of," he said with a laugh as he walked past images of former teammates, some now gone, the happy faces of ballplayers confined to black-and-white images, "is that someone thinks it's worth something."

There is tremendous irony in his statement. Once, his signature was worth more than any other high school player in the history of the game. In 1950, he made a deal that shook the baseball industry and served as a precursor to the way modern athletes are bought and sold.

For years, he autographed copies of the photo of him wearing his Narbonne High uniform in 1948. In that photo, he stands tall and proud. The photo is taken from an upward angle, so the young man looks poised and polished. He looks strong and powerful, unaware what $100,000 in 1949 would mean for the rest of his life.

"That's my favorite picture," he said. "I was just a young kid who happened to be able to throw a baseball."

He happened to be able to throw a baseball so well that he was the first $100,000 bonus player. His legacy is not as a pitcher with one major league win, but as a cautionary tale.

Here, days after Major League Baseball's annual amateur draft, when many promising baseball players expect the future to unfold as planned, Pettit is a living reminder that no matter how certain one's career looks, there are no guarantees.

His wife, Shirley, walked in. Pettit stopped to look at a framed mural of Forbes Field, a montage made up of all the names of the Pittsburgh Pirates who played there. Pettit can never remember where to find his name, but Shirley, his wife since 1950, knows exactly where to look.

She pointed at the front column, and there is Pettit's name. He smiled. She always knows where to find him.

If you listen closely, the stories are all here. There is a photo of George Pettit, a native Englishman who arrived in Los Angeles in 1909 with a love of soccer and not much else. He quit school and never became a rich man, but he always found a paycheck and a soccer game. He spent twenty years working as a milkman, and when he was thirty-five, he married a nurse from Philadelphia named Valerie.

The couple had a daughter, Valerie, followed by a son, George William Paul, who was born at the height of the Depression, on November 29, 1931. "I got Paul," he said, "because my mother thought it was a lucky name."

His father worked in the alphabet soup programs, gaining employment in the Works Progress Administration as a landscaper at Fort McArthur in San Pedro. In 1941, the family moved to the low-rent Harbor Hills housing project in Lomita where, by 1950, no family was allowed to have an annual income of more than $3,000.

Growing up in Lomita made Pettit cherish what little his family had. George's only son understood the value of modesty, a trait that would serve him well in a career he did not predict.

"We weren't dirt poor," Pettit remembered, standing in front of his Mercedes, "but we didn't have much extra to spend either."

Occasionally, Pettit recalled, there was just enough to walk to the movie theater. Sometimes, if they were lucky, they would get to watch "Flash Gordon" serials, directed by Frederick Stephani, a wonder kid with a flair for the future.

Pettit has only one photo of Stephani because the man is a mystery. Ambitious and clever, Stephani arrived in Hollywood in the early 1930s from the University of Bonn and Heidelberg Film School, one of a generation of European filmmakers who recognized Germany was changing.

Neither Pettit nor Stephani could have foreseen that, in 1950, they would make a deal that would begin to change the way baseball does business. Pettit, in unassuming fashion, signed an agreement that made professional baseball players question their own value and the right to determine their own careers. Stephani, the *Breeze* believes, became the first amateur player agent in baseball history.

It led leading baseball executives, such as Branch Rickey, to urge owners to accept an amateur draft, which was instated in 1965, partially in an effort to curb bonus payments, a decision that had the opposite effect on signing bonuses.

The deal angered baseball owners, who feared losing control of players and resented negotiating with agents.

Baseball is a business of unspoken truths, and in judging the trajectory of Pettit's own career, it is difficult not to speculate that he was blackballed nearly ten years later when, having reinvented himself as a power-hitting first baseman, he nearly hit his way back to the big leagues. But instead of a stirring end to a struggle, Pettit was left to languish in the minor leagues.

The decision he made as an eighteen-year-old high school pitcher was one of the first signs that a new era was coming. He did this as a teenager, not to challenge authority, but because he recognized the rare opportunity to help his family escape from life in a housing project.

Instead, Pettit would only be remembered as the pitcher who turned in one major league victory for $100,000, but his story is about more than a signature. Like finding his name hidden within a mural of a long-gone ballpark, Pettit's truth lies somewhere in a black-and-white past.

The Lefty from Lomita

His fastball came out of a folktale.

"There hasn't been a schoolboy pitcher around like him for a long time," Branch Rickey told the *Los Angeles Times*. "He's the Bob Feller type, definitely, and maybe by this time next year a lot of people will know it."

High school hitters rarely stood a chance. Pettit threw a no-hitter against San Pedro as a Narbonne sophomore in 1947, his first of six no-hitters in three years. He went 16–0 for a semipro team in Hermosa Beach. In the summer of 1949, he threw three consecutive no-hitters: one in high school and two in American Legion, racking up at least eighteen strikeouts in each game.

Pettit's reputation was sealed when, as a senior in 1949, he took the mound against Banning High and pitched a game he never forgot. "I had that little extra fastball," he says. "Confidence was abounding."

Pettit gave up four hits and struck out twenty-seven batters and won the game, 2–1, in twelve innings. It was the most strikeouts in a California high school game since Walter Johnson in 1905.

The late Howie Haak, then a young Brooklyn Dodger scout, was stunned.

"I saw him at his best and never saw his equal," Haak told Pittsburgh writer Les Biederman in 1954. "He had a major league curve in high school and just blazed his fastball by all the batters. If the other team hit a ball in the air, it was a big event."

Pettit was the best pitcher from Lomita since the Dodgers signed Erv Palica out of Narbonne as a sixteen-year-old sophomore in 1945. He had been sent to Ebbets Field courtesy of scout Tom Downey.

You couldn't miss Downey, who barreled into town driving his two-door, baby blue Cadillac. Former players claim he kept a liquor cabinet in the trunk. When the Dodgers played in the 1947 World Series, Downey had originally signed four of their starters. In 1944, Downey had signed a promising multi-sport athlete from Compton, Duke Snider.

Downey was a former Mexican League pitcher with a reputation for making deals under the table, according to players who knew him. Downey centered his attention on finding a way to bring a wad of Pirate owner Frank McKinney's Indianapolis bankroll to Pettit's pocket.

"Downey was real good," Pettit says. "Real supportive. He just thought I had all the potential in the world."

For a scout, discovering a hard-throwing, six-foot-two, 205-pound left-hander is like finding an oasis in the desert and having to pay for a drink.

"I knew my value," Pettit said. "I was going to sign for at least $90,000."

Yet in the back of Pettit's mind there were terrible reservations. He had thrown so many innings that he feared the worst. George Pettit had learned how to compile his son's pitching statistics and tallied 945 strikeouts in 545 innings over three years, an average of 181 innings per season as a teenager.

Pettit also kept a secret. He had injured his elbow when he landed awkwardly in a basketball game. He had the opportunity to make more money in one moment than his parents had made in their entire lives. It meant no more menial jobs for George, who was then working as a night watchman. Some days, his mind felt as tired as his arm. He didn't feel young anymore. He was only eighteen.

"I think he was under pressure in those days," former player and manager George Genovese said. "All eyes were always on him. In a way, it was like the kiss of death, getting all that money."

Deal of the Century

Tinseltown hadn't been kind to Stephani of late. His run as an MGM contract producer ended when, after a string of box office failures, studio chief Louis B. Mayer flicked his cigar ashes at Stephani and never hired him again.

Down on his luck, the best Stephani could find was a freelancing job to write and produce a forgettable movie named *Johnny Holiday*. Shot on location in Indianapolis during the summer of 1949, it brought Stephani to the city where McKinney kept his headquarters.

Enter singer-actor Bing Crosby, a 25 percent owner of the Pirates. Though no sources can directly place McKinney meeting with Stephani, and though Stephani and Crosby never collaborated on a film, studio records show that Stephani and Crosby were both under contract at Paramount in the early 1930s.

Unlike Crosby, an avid golfer, Stephani never had any interest in sports. A complete review of his career with film synopsis obtained from the American Film Institute in Hollywood reveals no stories tied to sports.

Rumors swirled that Crosby had helped orchestrate an arrangement between McKinney and Stephani in the summer of 1949 that would allow the Pirates to evade the "high school rule," prohibiting teams from signing players before graduation. Most observers believed a handshake deal in which the Pirates agreed to purchase Pettit's contract from Stephani was arranged prior to his graduation in January 1950, a move which further added to the firestorm Pettit was about to walk into.

"I felt all along," said Haak, who became a legendary Latin American scout for the Pirates before his death in 1999, "[that] the Pirates had the inside track."

There was precedence. That winter, Crosby had helped the Pirates sign future major league left-handed pitcher Vernon Law to a minor league contract.

Some published reports claimed Crosby visited the family home in Lomita, but Pettit denies that. When Pettit finally arrived in the minor leagues in the spring of 1950, many players believed Crosby had been the instigator, pairing Stephani with McKinney and delivering Pettit to Pirates general manager Roy Hamey.

"Through Bing Crosby, you mean?" said Len Yochim, a former teammate of Pettit's, by phone from his home in New Orleans, Louisiana. "That's the big thing that came along with it. He assisted in the signing. That's what we players thought."

Stephani maintained he was in the movie business.

"I long had in mind doing a sports picture," he told the *Los Angeles Times* in 1950, "but the cost to an independent producer of signing established stars like Pancho Gonzales, Ben Hogan, Ralph Kiner, and the like is prohibitive. So I decided to take a chance and sign some promising youngster to a long-term contract."

Even today, Pettit has difficultly describing the eccentric Stephani.

"He was a hard personality to pin down," Pettit said. "He just seemed to be kind of . . . well, I don't know. He didn't really know baseball that well, I knew that."

Yet in the fall of 1949, Pettit received a curious letter from Stephani. It would lead to the decision that shaped Pettit's career.

Stephani made a handsome offer to sign Pettit to a motion picture deal, with the sole purpose of reselling the contract to the highest-bidding major league team, while retaining the movie rights to Pettit's life. Stephani, in effect, would be acting as Pettit's agent, a revolutionary idea that outraged the baseball community.

"I have no quarrel with Pittsburgh," Cardinals owner Fred Saigh told the Associated Press. "I just don't like the idea of dealing with agents."

Even with the potential consequences to his career, the offer was too good for Pettit to pass up.

"It was all through Stephani," Pettit said. "He's the one who came to me and said, 'Hey, I'd like to make this movie.' He wanted me to sign a contract for less money and resell it. I knew my value at the time. When he finally upped the ante to $85,000, plus $5,000 per picture, up to three pictures, and if we made a life story I got 10 percent, it started to add up. That's why I signed with him. As long as I had the say as to what team I signed with."

That was the question. In an era when owners had the right to control players, what right did a high school player have to choose his own fate?

Stephani made it appear that he was sifting through offers from various teams. Because Pettit's price had soared so high, many teams dropped out. Pettit says he was never sure what teams were really in the running, nor would he admit that a deal was in place before he graduated.

"I liked the Red Sox, I liked the Yankees," he said. "They were all interested, but I can't remember too much."

Added Genovese, who became a successful scout: "I think perhaps they had already verbally agreed to terms, if not [had] an already written agreement somewhere, so it would still not be illegal."

The Pirates had been there all along. Downey had won over Pettit with hints of what was to come.

"I was really interested in that Cadillac," Pettit said. "He said, 'When you sign, you'll be able to buy one.'"

When Pettit graduated from Narbonne in January 1950, he and his father drove to Stephani's office on Sunset Boulevard. Paul Pettit sat at the table, surrounded by two lawyers, as well as Stephani, Downey, and Hamey, Pittsburgh's barrel-chested general manager. The deal was to be for $85,000 until the former milkman had the final say.

"My dad spoke up and said, 'We'd like $100,000,'" Pettit said.

There was silence in the room.

"They went outside of the office for five minutes," Pettit recalled. "They came back and said, 'You got it.'"

The photo of the signing is on Pettit's wall. In it, the young pitcher stares up at a grinning Hamey. It is suggested to Pettit that he has the look of a man who has just sold his soul to the devil. Pettit only laughed and moved on to the next picture.

Size, Speed, and Cash

There was little patience. Because he was a bonus player who received more than $6,000 to sign, Pettit was required to be on the Pirates' major league roster within a year. Mindful of the scrutiny and perhaps leery that Pettit was not at full strength, Pirates manager Billy Meyer expressed concern. "I only hope they don't spoil him before he joins us," he said in 1950.

Pettit said he anticipated some of the attention, but was not ready for the scrutiny. "They could have put me anywhere," he said. "That was [Pittsburgh's] mistake. Part of the problem, when I went to Double-A, [was] they put a lot of pressure on me. There was a lot of publicity. There were three newspapers in town and I was in one of them every single day."

There was also the $100,000 question. Though Pettit's contract was spread over ten years, and though he spent most of his first year's salary to buy a new home for his parents, Pettit learned to live with a label.

"What is to stop any player from putting himself in the hands of an agent?" Yankees general manager George Weiss asked in a 1950 statement. "Someone must determine where baseball law ends and civil rights begin."

The battle lines were drawn.

"As for dealing with an agent, what was Roy Hamey to do?" Rickey, then the Dodgers general manager, told the *New York Times*. "The agent had the boy tied up. On the boy's part, he had a perfect right to have an agent and it was no evasion of the high school rule if the club did not negotiate ahead of time."

Arthur Daley, the *New York Times* columnist, reserved a special contempt for Pettit. A yes man with a typewriter, Joe DiMaggio's ghostwriter, Daley was essentially a publicist for the Yankees. He took several shots, writing as if he was praying for Pettit to fail.

"Lean and hungry fellows make better ball players than rich and fat ones," he wrote in 1951. "It takes a pretty strong character to be able to punish himself and drive himself when he has all that folding money hidden under the mattress."

Some players were encouraged that the system could be compromised. Others were enraged about how much Pettit made beating it.

"I venture to say that when the Pirates paid that boy $100,000, each member of the Pittsburgh club lost about $4,000 in salary," Cardinals shortstop Marty Marion told the *Washington Post*. "I'm for the up-and-coming young fellow getting all he can out of baseball, but when he deprives those who have already made their mark in the game of making money, it's high time to take steps to stop it."

The most insightful comment may have come from catcher Clyde McCullough.

"He has everything," McCullough told the *Post*. "Size, speed — and cash."

While players mulled over Pettit's money, *Post* columnist Shirley Povich wrote a passage that was prophetic.

"What Pettit's agent did was to expose a loophole in the rules and open up what could amount to a new promotional profession — signing up promising schoolboy athletes while major league clubs are restrained, and then peddling their contracts to the highest bidder."

The sum and the duration of the contract were considered outrageous. A week after Pettit signed, Ted Williams re-signed for the

1950 season for $125,000, baseball's top salary. When Rickey re-signed his double-play combination of Jackie Robinson and Pee Wee Reese for the 1950 season, he paid Robinson $35,000 and Reese $30,000. In 1953, the Yankees trimmed veteran left-handed pitcher Ed Lopat's contract from $30,000 to $21,000 when he went from twenty-one victories to eleven in an injury-shortened season. All of it added up to a burden Pettit would carry for the rest of his career.

"To get $100,000 as a high school kid in 1950," Genovese said, "would be like giving a high school kid $30 million today."

"It does seem a trifle ridiculous, doesn't it?" Daley asked. "An untried and unproven schoolboy reaps a fortune without having played one game of major league ball — or minor league ball?"

Even the supportive Rickey, who became Pittsburgh's general manager in 1951, had worries.

"That is the great fault of the bonus in my business," he wrote in his personal papers. "There should be joy in the chase, zest in the pursuit."

In other words, a player should feel compensated by his opportunity alone.

"That's more than I got in my whole life," sixty-three-year-old Grover Cleveland Alexander grumbled to the *Los Angeles Times* in 1950. Alexander said he signed his first major league contract for $1,500 in 1911. Broke, hard of hearing, and nursing the bottle, the aging right-hander couldn't fathom that baseball would give a high school player so much money.

"I was just working," he said.

Still other players believed Pettit's contract represented the start of a new era. Observed forty-two-year-old knuckleballer Dutch Leonard in the *Los Angeles Times* in 1951: "More power to them. When I was a kid, I was tickled to death just to get a chance to play. I didn't ever receive a bonus, but baseball has given me enough reward — a lovely family, a home, some security . . . and it took me out of the coal mines."

There was enough attention on Pettit to make him wish he could hide. It didn't help when he labored in a pair of spring training games. He was pitching over his head, a high school boy against experienced professionals, shelled when he should have been learning at a lower level. Some observers began to question if Pettit was ready. The Pirates maintained he was.

"We think that he is capable of playing Double-A baseball and we are perfectly content in sending him to the [New Orleans] Pelicans," Hamey told the Associated Press.

Pettit felt the pressure. There was a naysayer for every step, a whisper for every walk, or a breath of optimism for every strikeout.

"They expected me to do well off the bat," he said. "Maybe they thought I was better than I was. I don't know what it was."

True, Pettit had to be in the big leagues by 1951. But why start him at a level where most observers believed no high school pitcher could succeed?

Noted Genovese: "The bonus rule was really unfair to a young player. Many a ballplayer ruined his career, not willfully or intentionally, but for the fact that they weren't ready to play at a high level so soon. Sometimes, you had to carry a kid because that's what you had to do. You put him in, he'd try too hard, and a lot of them got hurt that way."

While looking at the photo from the day he signed, Pettit paused. Perhaps he really had sold his soul.

A Star Is Torn

"A lot of guys who go into professional baseball say, 'I need to get a chance,'" Pettit said. "As a bonus player, you get a first shot more than some other guys because the money is invested. I had a shot at New Orleans, but I wasn't handled properly. I started too high. They thought I was ready to pitch at that level but I wasn't. I was nineteen. Those guys were twenty-five or twenty-six. They can hit any fastball hard."

"That wasn't a league for a young player," recalled Yochim, a left-handed pitcher who was one year older than Pettit and his teammate in New Orleans. "I should know. I got raked over the coals."

Pettit's first professional start was slated for a Sunday afternoon against Chattanooga. The fans were roped off in the outfield. Cameras were everywhere. Pettit remembered the isolation. For all the money the Pirates spent, there was no pitching coach in New Orleans to monitor his progress. Pettit was not trained. He was not protected. He was simply handed the ball. It was baseball in the dark ages.

"It was a big pressure cooker," Pettit said. "It probably pumped too much adrenaline in me and I tried too hard. I was just out there firing as hard as I could."

Said Yochim: "He was always singled out. I tend to believe that may make you try harder, press too much."

Pettit pitched seven innings and struck out nine, but after the game, he joked that half his pitches wound up in Mississippi. He threw the ghastly total of 154 pitches, walked eleven batters, and gave up six runs and seven hits and lost.

"I had never walked eleven in my life," he said, still sounding embarrassed fifty-six years later.

His arm began to bother him. Again, he said nothing.

"I'm not convinced he wasn't already hurt when he signed," Yochim said. "You would seem to think he was supposed to have a blazing fastball to have the all-time highest bonus."

In only his third professional outing, Pettit felt a pop in his elbow. The Pirates sent him to Dr. George Bennett at Johns Hopkins Hospital in Baltimore, the same physician who treated DiMaggio. But sports medicine in 1950 was primitive. Arm surgery didn't exist. Pettit told the eager press that nothing was wrong.

"I think I started throwing too soon," he said. "There's another example of pressure, of wanting to push it. I didn't have the right medical advice. If I had a cortisone shot or a deep heat, maybe, but they didn't even have that. I thought, in two weeks, I should be fine, but it didn't work out that way."

The Pirates had made an investment, and the Pirates' front office ordered New Orleans manager Hugh Luby to pitch Pettit. It was nearly 100 degrees one night in Memphis, but Pettit couldn't get his arm loose. He didn't say a word, yet grunted each time he threw.

"That was the lowest day of my life," he said. "My arm was hurting so badly."

Luby had been in baseball since 1931. He recognized that Pettit was in over his head. In rushing Pettit, Luby believed they were ruining him. On July 4, the Pirates dismissed Luby.

"I am not telling a tale out of school when I say the Pirates realize now [that] they brought young Paul Pettit up too fast," Luby told the *Los Angeles Times* weeks after he was fired. "He should be pitching in a Class D league. And by the bonus rule, he must go up next year to Pittsburgh."

Pettit was never the same.

"Even today, I still feel the remnants of that injury," he said. "Right in here," he says, tapping his elbow and forearm.

He finished his first professional season 2–7 with a 5.17 ERA. He would come to the big leagues as a wounded animal.

In his final start of the season, he was pitching in New Orleans against Atlanta. Eddie Mathews, a young third baseman from Santa Barbara, wouldn't let Pettit forget his identity. Facing him in the first inning, Pettit struck him out with a high-and-tight fastball. Moments later, Mathews stood at the top step of the dugout, shouting at Pettit, "You bonus baby son of a b——!"

Pettit labored into the tenth inning. "I was just walking around the mound in a daze," he said. "Picture a guy walking around the desert without a drink of water. That was me. I was so exhausted, I think I lost ten pounds that night. And in the tenth inning, here comes Mathews again, and I tried to get him in that same spot. Now, it was 420 feet to center field and it was a high fence out there. Mathews hit it, and the ball kept carrying right over the Coca-Cola sign."

Pettit laughed heartily when he relived the home run, and it doesn't seem to matter that the ball never lands in the story. The rest of his career would be marked by a mission to become not Paul Pettit, the first $100,000 bonus baby, but Paul Pettit the husband, the father, the ballplayer, the professional. There would always be a nice payment awaiting him before the start of each of the next ten seasons, but the money wasn't there to make him as rich as the critics would believe. He would always have to work hard to be seen as more than a dollar sign.

"I suppose that because I had such a tremendous amateur record, I think they felt I was a shoo-in. They thought I was the next coming of Walter Johnson or something," Pettit said. "It just didn't come out that way."

The $80,000 Joke

Pettit made his major league debut on May 5, 1951, against the Giants at the Polo Grounds. Meyer put him in the game as an afterthought, an eighth-inning mop-up assignment in an 8–1 loss. Later, he summoned Pettit to meet with Rickey at Forbes Field.

Rickey informed Pettit that the club had placed him on waivers.

No one claimed him. At twenty years old, every team in the major leagues thought Pettit's career was over. With no recourse, he began to laugh at the severity of his situation. The laughter grew stronger, and soon, Meyer was laughing.

"I didn't want to be disrespectful," Pettit recalled. "But I laughed because $80,000 was still owed on my contract, and who was going to pick me up? It was quite obvious that no one wanted me."

Pettit began an injury-plagued odyssey that took him from the majors to Single-A. While he was in the minor leagues, a transformation of his reputation occurred. Players who had never met him, who thought that because he was the $100,000 kid he might be arrogant, realized that Pettit was as modest as his Lomita upbringing. He may have lost some arm strength, but he'd lost none of his father's sensibilities. Pettit became a working man, and if one hadn't known he was a ballplayer, one could have assumed he was a milkman, a watchman, or a landscaper.

"He was the hardest worker you would see," Yochim said. "He did everything he could to get the job done. He was a fine person on a club. Not a guy who would say, 'I got a hundred thousand.' He wasn't chesty and all that. He was none of that. He was just a down-to-earth, hardworking young man."

Pettit went to spring training with the Pirates in 1952, but Rickey decided that Pettit wasn't ready to return to the major leagues. Rickey assigned him to Triple-A, the Hollywood Stars, but no matter how Pettit played, some still considered him the bonus baby bust. One *L.A. Times* headline shouted at him with four simple words: "Poor Little Rich Boy."

Hooray for Hollywood

Long before Jack Nicholson grinned courtside at Lakers games, showtime was Milton Berle and Groucho Marx along with an ever-present and never-ending line of aspiring starlets in high heels and short shorts. It was ballplayer heaven.

Pettit pitched for the Hollywood Stars when Gilmore Field was the favorite show in town. "In many ways," he said, "this was one of my most satisfying years."

Satisfying, in part, because he didn't have to be a celebrity. Pettit finished 15–8, but admits that he was getting by with savvy instead of stuff.

There were also days when his hitting ability made his teammates wonder if Pettit was in the wrong line of work. He ended the season with a .320 average. At the very least, he would be able to help his own cause as a major league pitcher. He would get another crack with the Pirates in 1953, and this time, Pettit was determined to become more than the $100,000 kid.

Pettit pitched well enough to make a believer out of an unexpected guest. Pettit had not seen Stephani since the day he signed.

"He came by and saw me at Gilmore Field," Pettit said. "Things were going good at the time, and he seemed to be personally interested in my career. I think he was in Spain making pictures at the time, but I don't know. I never saw the man again."

Stephani's last Hollywood credit was in 1957. He was married at least twice. His second wife divorced him when he went to Africa and didn't return for months. Stephani surfaced in the early 1990s, trying to front a production to make a sequel to *Casablanca*, a project that never got off the ground. He faded into obscurity. There are no known obituaries.

Even Stephani's most mischievous muse could not have predicted the legacy his deal with Pettit would leave on sports culture and business. Every sports agent should pay a commission to the movie man's memory. True, Stephani had a flair for the future, but he never anticipated the creature he created.

One and Done

Catcher Clyde McCullough was disgusted with Pettit's lack of control at the start of the 1953 season. He stomped to the mound and wouldn't give Pettit the ball.

"He came out and said, 'Where'd you throw that to?'" Pettit said. "I said, 'My arm hurts, Clyde.' He didn't say a word. He just gave me the ball, turned around, and walked back to the plate."

When his arm felt good, Pettit proved he could win. He made his first major league start on May 1 against the Reds at Forbes Field. He worked six and a third innings and gave up four runs (one earned) and got his only major league win. A day later, it hurt again.

"It was the arm," Pettit said. "The arm just didn't respond. I started that game in Pittsburgh, and I had them eating out of my hands."

Pettit lost his confidence. He next pitched against the Giants at the Polo Grounds and couldn't finish the first inning. He got a start against the Chicago Cubs, who knocked him out of the game. With his arm hurting and his effectiveness dwindling, the Pirates sent him to the minor leagues in June. He came back to the big leagues in September and pitched well enough to give himself hope despite finishing the year with a 1–2 record and a 7.71 ERA in ten games. But when he came back to spring training in 1954, his arm still would not respond.

"I didn't know what the hell was wrong," he said. "I just couldn't throw. My arm wasn't hurting, and yet, it was like it was dead. I went to spring training and I didn't even get into a game. They just sent me down."

Pettit wound up in Huntsville, Texas, at minor league camp. It was a prisoner-of-war facility from World War II, where players slept in barracks. It was a depressing place. Pettit no longer knew what to expect.

Rickey wondered if the former bonus baby might still have some unforeseen value. Rickey told Pettit that he would return to Hollywood, where manager Bobby Bragan asked Pettit how he felt about playing first base.

Pettit was at a crossroads. It had been four years since he signed as a pitcher, but his arm had never healed. He made a decision. "As a pitcher," he said, "I couldn't throw the gloss off the ball."

Genovese believes Pettit had a chance to return to the big leagues not as a starting pitcher but as a left-handed-hitting first baseman or outfielder.

Pettit batted .324 with 20 home runs and 103 RBIs at Salinas, and while again playing for Genovese in Mexico City during the 1955 season, Pettit hit .382 with 9 home runs and 80 RBIs. He also had a twenty-three-game hitting streak.

In 1957, Pettit's confidence returned. He had reinvented his career as a legitimate power-hitting threat. He had his best season as a hitter, batting .284 with 20 home runs and 102 RBIs for Hollywood. He batted cleanup and played right field. He was twenty-seven years old, seemingly young enough to return to the major leagues and help the last-place Pirates. The Pirates had twenty-two-year-old

Roberto Clemente in right field, but Stars manager Clyde King believed Pettit could hit at the major league level.

Genovese agreed.

"He would have been on my twenty-five-man roster," Genovese said. "Two outs, man on first, here's a man who might tie it up with one swing. You look down the bench and you're not going to put a singles hitter in there if you have someone you think can tie the score. If I send George Genovese, five-foot-six, 150 pounds, up to hit, you think I'm scaring anyone? Paul was put together. Paul was not a shrimp."

As Pettit is prone to say, it never worked out.

When he did not receive an invitation to major league camp, he was devastated. Did he never get a second chance because of how he got his first?

"I don't know the answer to that," Pettit said. "I thought I really had the chance to go back to the major leagues as an everyday player. You're twenty-six and you had a good year and you don't even get a chance to go to spring training? What do you think that does to your ego? I just lost my mental edge. I never did well from that point on."

His confidence drained, Pettit retired at age thirty in 1962. He returned home to raise his family and began a teaching career in the South Bay that lasted nearly thirty years.

Like Father, Like Son

For a few dollars on eBay, you can buy his autograph on an index card, but the seller is mistaken. Paul Pettit, the first $100,000 bonus baby, is not a "deceased ballplayer."

Now he knows where some of those autograph requests end up.

The letters always arrive in April, and the price tag follows him into his old age. There is nothing he can do about that, but like his playing days, he lets it go. He's just a former ballplayer now, he said, and the grandkids don't know too much about his career, and that's fine by him.

Pettit gazed at a photograph of himself steaming down the first-base line. His leg is outstretched as he makes a final lunge for first base, but the ball is already in the first baseman's mitt.

"This is me, playing at Richmond, Virginia, being thrown out by half a step," Pettit said. He chuckles and says without a trace of bitterness, "Story of my life."

Shirley came to remind him that it was getting late. "She was the best part of the whole thing," he said. When Pettit signed, someone had the idea to throw in $750 for a honeymoon. Shirley laughed. She said she's still waiting.

There is the value of Pettit. No matter what didn't happen, the people who know him the best say he has remained the same kind of person. This is the fine line of being a professional athlete. Pettit never lost what his father gave him. He worked hard, had a hell of a laugh, and enjoyed the memories. Who knew? The greatest gift wasn't the salary. It was in the satisfaction.

WILLIAM C. RHODEN

An Unknown Filly Dies, and the Crowd Just Shrugs

FROM THE NEW YORK TIMES

A simple, powerful reminder that nothing is how our modern celebrity culture makes it appear, not even horses.
— D.M.

THERE WAS NO ARRAY of photographers at Belmont Park yesterday, no sobbing in the crowd as a badly injured superstar horse tried to stay erect on three legs. There was no national spotlight.

Instead, there was death. In the seventh race at Belmont, a four-year-old filly named Lauren's Charm headed into the homestretch. As she began to fade in the mile-and-an-eighth race on the grass, her jockey, Fernando Jara, felt her struggling, pulled up, and jumped off.

As the race concluded, Lauren's Charm collapsed. No one, except those associated with the horse and two track veterinarians, seemed to notice.

The scene was in stark contrast to what unfolded at Pimlico last Saturday when the Kentucky Derby winner, Barbaro, severely fractured his ankle in the opening burst of the Preakness. A national audience gasped; an armada of rescuers rushed to the scene. In the days that followed, as the struggle to keep Barbaro alive took full shape, there was an outpouring of emotion across the country and heartfelt essays about why we care so much about these animals.

But I'm not so sure we do, and I'm not so sure the general public fully understands this sport. When people attempt to rationalize the uneasy elements of racing, they often say: "That's part of the business. That's the game."

But there was nothing beautiful or gracious or redeeming about the seventh race at Belmont. This was the underside of the business. The nuts-and-bolts part, where animals are expendable parts of a billion-dollar industry.

The two vets raced to the stricken horse, followed by the assistant trainer Anthony Rodriguez; his mother, Doreen, who served as the hot-walker; and the groom. By the time they reached her, Lauren's Charm was dead.

Dr. Jennifer Durenberger, the second vet to reach the horse, said the filly had apparently died of a heart attack. "This was very uncommon," she said afterward in a telephone interview from her office. "It happens to one in twenty thousand horses."

I'm not sure how many fans in the meager crowd of 3,741 paid attention to the white equine ambulance that pulled onto the track, or saw the filly being loaded in it.

The filly's owner, Joseph Dirico, was watching a simulcast of the race at a track in Massachusetts with his father and uncle. "She started dropping back," he said last night of the horse he had named after his wife. "That's what I saw. I didn't expect to get a phone call saying she'd had a heart attack. I'm glad I wasn't there. I would have run down to the track, I would have had tears in my eyes. She was a nice horse, a really correct filly."

Last Saturday evening, Barbaro's devastated owners said that these things happened in racing, that it is part of the sport. Yesterday, Dirico said, "I guess that's part of the game."

What is the nature of this game?

Horses go down much more frequently than the general public realizes, and many in the business have noted that had Barbaro not been the winner of the Kentucky Derby, he might have been destroyed after being injured.

Jara, an eighteen-year-old Panamanian, seemed to take Lauren's Charm's death in stride. He had finished fourth aboard Jazil in the Kentucky Derby, his first Triple Crown race. He said that in his four years of racing, this was the first time he was in the saddle when a horse died.

Asked if he was going to think about the horse during the rest of the day, he said no. "There is another race to come," he said. "You have to think about the next race."

"Everything is equal," he added as he compared Barbaro to Lauren's Charm, who won one race in her career and earned all of $77,363. "But Barbaro could have won the Triple Crown."

The dead animal was loaded in the ambulance and carted to the track's stable area, where it was put on its side, legs bent as if it were still running. The horseshoes had not been removed. The carcass was then half carried and half pushed into an area designated for autopsies. An earthmover helped push the horse against a concrete wall.

I asked one of the track supervisors what would happen now. He said if the horse was insured, there would be an autopsy. If not, then he would wait to hear from the owner to determine if there would be an autopsy at the owner's expense.

Dirico said he indeed might order an autopsy. "I had no insurance on her," he said. "If reasonable, I'd like to have it done for my own peace of mind."

I wondered why he didn't have the horse insured. "Insurance is so expensive," he said. "I never thought it would come to this. I've had good luck with horses."

The gate to the fenced-in area was closed. I glanced back at Lauren's Charm, lying on the ground. Just days ago, the cameras were trained on Pimlico, and a nation cried for Barbaro. I wonder what the nation would have thought about this.

One animal breaks an ankle on national television in a Triple Crown race and sets off a national outpouring of emotion. A four-year-old collapses and dies in full view on a sunny afternoon and not many seem to notice. Or care.

As they say, it's the business.

But what kind of business is this?

Let Us Now Raze Famous Men

FROM SPORTS ILLUSTRATED

From the obscure to the . . . my man! . . . obnoxious. Worth it just for the doppelgänger formulation of the two Dons, King and Trump.
— D.M.

I

THIS IS AMERICA?" The German is perplexed. That the world-renowned Friars Club celebrates the world-class achievements of a world-famous American — in this case Don King — by repeatedly telling him that the world would be better off without him is a tricky idea to master in any language. What a world.

The German is tall and slender, in his late twenties, lank blond hair capping the milk bottle of a long, pale face. The expression on that face is one of earnest curiosity. Across the white hotel table-cloth and the white hotel plates and the florets of white hotel butter and the white-noise clatter of dull hotel cutlery he emphasizes neither "This" for sarcastic effect nor "America" to indicate scorn.

He is a sportswriter from *Bild* — arguably the best-selling news-paper in the Western world, thanks, inarguably, to full-page nude-photo essays with headlines like "Ich Bin Die Miss Playboy!" — and having flown 3,800 miles from Hamburg to New York City to write about Don King, *der grosse Boxveranstalter* (super fight promoter), and finding himself among 1,200 howling *Amerikaner*, and sitting below the immense cut-glass daggers of the icicle chandeliers and the 10,000 yards of blood-red velvet draped above them all in the ti-tanic ballroom of the New York Hilton, on the occasion of the

Friars Club Roast of Herr King, and having asked, "This is America?" he bends a pen to his notebook, raises his eyebrows high in a gesture of abject innocence, stares at his American colleagues, and waits for an answer.

His American tablemates squint briefly at him across that arctic expanse of starch-stiff linen. At last one shrugs. "Sure, Georg," he says with a tired smile of uncertain sincerity, slowly twirling his index finger to indicate the room and everyone and everything in it. "This is *America.*"

The German nods and, as the drawbridge brows swing down, begins to scribble.

In the most basic way, this is correct. We are on the island fortress of Manhattan after all, and are therefore tethered to greater America, even if only tenuously. And we are on the Avenue *of* the Americas, in a huge ugly room, shoehorned wall-to-wall with decidedly American types — stand-up comics and beat-down boxers, nightclub wiseguys and their inflatable molls, politicians and press agents and cabaret singers, sportsmen and showmen, cutmen and cornermen and chorus girls — familiar to everyone everywhere who has ever seen an American movie of the 1930s.

From the dais to the back row the grand hall is a lively diorama of clichéd young movers and palsied old shakers, of the great and the ingrate, of has-beens and might-bes, of nugget cuff links and Prada knockoffs, of dandruff and adultery, of cauliflower ears and mammaplasty scars, of hand-painted leopard-skin neckties and tans from a can, of hair delivered precut from a warehouse in New Jersey and gray-market cologne so potent you could clip it to your key ring and use it to take down a mugger. There's Botox in Spandex and Viagra in vicuña seated shank to bony shank, and everywhere the crippling weight of gangster bling — gangblang — even by the wet and diamond-studded mouthful. Deep cleavage, sure, and deeper cynicism and, even unfired, there are cigars being waved around that could bring down the walls of a city.

Harder to explain, perhaps impossible, is that these nearly fictive citizens of our national imagination have gathered today in the grand American show-business tradition of pretending to honor a man by pretending to love him by pretending to hate him. Are there words enough in any tongue to explain that they've come not to praise Don King, but to bury him — beneath a ceremonial mound of their obscene and ornate scorn?

It's much easier, really, and more correct, just to point at the honoree himself, to point at Don King and say, "*This* is America."

II

Now seventy-four years old, Don King has through four decades been the one boxing promoter anyone anywhere might reasonably be able to name, his fame dating to 1975 and the mythic beginnings of his second life: the promotion of that epic fight, the Ali-Foreman Rumble in the Jungle. That African adventure would have broken a smaller man, a weaker man, a less flexible man; that Conradian paddle back up the river Congo should have finished King before he'd even started — *"Mistah King, he bankrupt"* — but instead made his global bones. He has been the constant, outrageous presence on the ring apron of our collective consciousness ever since.

King's successes and failures are the stuff of rumor and report and folklore, of books, essays, articles, jeremiads, polemics, documentaries, and movies of the week. He's been named in more lawsuits than you've had hot meals. By dint of his junkyard doggedness and our national habit of forbearance, though, and eased by a thousand TV interviews and a hundred magazine covers, he has aged somehow into our most beloved buccaneer, our comic Blackbeard, the laughing captain of our happy damnation.

Having inherited the corkscrew DNA of storied manager-promoters like Doc Kearns and Mike Jacobs, those backstage giants who guzzled the heavy cream off the careers of Dempsey and Louis, King has long been their natural, merry heir. And like them the conflict of his interests runs so deep that his negotiations are a kind of comic schizophrenia — King haggling only with himself.

Chanting his mantra, "Only in America!" and wrapping himself literally and figuratively in the flag, he presents himself as the living embodiment of the American dream: a good man, self-made and self-reliant, up from the gutter by his storied bootstraps to dazzling fame and fortune, his hardworking life a triumph of personal industry in the Land of One More Chance, his success and reputation lofted into the sunshine on the very wings of free enterprise.

But he also seems the very nightmare American, the man of whom we all despair, the Promethean exaggerator and Faustian bamboozler, a man for whom the simplest truth is never less than a three-rail bank shot. He is either the perfection of sweet patriotism or the apotheosis of patriotic hypocrisy — the incorruptible red, white, and blue devoted solely to eternal honor, or to the further purchase of his own magisterial luxuries. Last refuge of a scoundrel and so forth, he carries those little American flags he's always waving even when no one's looking.

Let's say also that King is the ravenous American id, eager consumer of everything in reach, and coveter of all things out of it. And stipulate while we're at it that he's the two faces of America and that he harbors multitudes: black and white, rich and poor, sacred and profane, good and evil. Look long and honest and hard and in Don King we find the worst *and* the best in each and every one of us. And by caricaturing every American trait and impulse, every wanton appetite and violent itch, he is, thus, America itself.

It is too easy to say, as many have, that the real trip into the heart of darkness is the one we've all taken in the years since that jungle rumble, trying to plumb the lightless mystery of Don King's nature. Wouldn't it be quicker and more illuminating to simply acknowledge the love of hucksters and of violent spectacle in our own American nature? At least that would explain why he's more recognizable by far than any fighter anywhere currently plying that ancient trade.

His stature, of course, is largely associative. By seeing him stand with greater men in greater times, it is possible to think him great as well. Leaving the combat to others, he is universally known by his conquests. From Tokyo to Reno, five hundred championship fights and not a mark on him. Flyweight to heavyweight and all sizes in between. Soliloquizer, elegizer, spoonerizer — crackpot supersizer of the King's own English — his deft and grasping reach is planetary, his global puppet shows sold by satellite from dateline to dateline and pole to pole.

We know King too by his tirades and indictments. We know the rap sheet and the mug shots and the injunctions, suit and countersuit, all the hard work and the dirty work. We know the names of the two men he killed in his first life — one in anger, one in self-defense — back on the cracked and hopeless streets of East Cleveland: Sam Garrett and Hillary Brown. We know his crime and punishment. The time served and the debt paid and the pardon won. The reputations made and squandered, the boxers broken on the adamantine fists of their own ambitions. Some say King bought trouble for every fighter he ever touched, but still forgive him everything. Others damn him forever just for letting Ali stay too long in harm's way, and see in King's smiling eyes the withering evil at the root of Ali's diminishment.

And yet, while any case pitting King's storied history against our sporting sense of fair play may never be resolved, that history proves his business acumen uncanny from first to last. For example, 1973, the not-yet-famous but insatiably ambitious Don King rides in the limousine — and on the coattails — of his titleholder-client Joe Frazier to a boxing ring in Jamaica, where King takes his seat in the cham*peen*'s corner for a title fight. George Foreman, challenger and unholy brute, lays waste to Smokin' Joe through each successive round, and as he does so King changes seats and sentiments, one chair at a time, until the moment Foreman hammers Frazier down and takes away his fancy belt. By which climax King, ass and aspiration, has arrived around the ring at a seat in Foreman's corner. Leaping through the ropes and over suddenly smokeless Joe, King swaps coattails, then cars, and rides back home with new chum and champ, Furious George.

Says King at the time, and to this day, "*I came with the champion, and I left with the champion.*" It is his mission statement and business model. He is as God made him, a scorpion in a world full of willing frogs.

He is loud, huge, brash, and funny. By turns brilliant and banal. Indefatigable. Brazen, charitable, shameless, rich. He is by instant turns your welcoming enemy and your terrifying friend. Yes, he's magnificently generous, as befits a king, but the killing's in the vig. His ominous contracts are famously simple; under his hard stare, you make your mark for his whispered promises. He is smarter than you are, avid as a shark, bulletproof. Question him, and he will batter you with nonsense. If you think him witless, he will outwit you. Shiftless, he will outwork you — then break you for the insult.

He is the ruthless clown, the numbers-racket genius, the self-mocking jailhouse cribber of misremembered Shakespeare, the inexhaustible transcendentalist negotiator misquoting Thoreau in search of inner peace and another 7 percent of the gate. And brush up on your Bible because even Satan uses Scripture when it suits him.

He has been the P. T. Barnum of our age, the infinitely striving, endlessly spieling barker at the tent mouth of the Don King Big Top. Once inside, we find that he's the only returning attraction on the bill. Ali, Frazier, Foreman, Tyson come and go, tracking bloodied sawdust after them, but the ringmaster never leaves.

He is modern boxing's ruin and its only real asset. He is the creator-destroyer of today's dying fight game, the man who puts the *shiv* back in Shiva.

He remains insatiable, always famished. I watched him eat a bowl of soup in a New York café a couple of days before the roast, and his eating was mechanical. The big spoon small in his hand and slow in the bowl, his eyes fixed on his meal, he brought each steady spoonful to the great mouth, unhurried, never a drop spilled. Quiet, tidy, and rhythmic, he leaned to the bowl as he emptied it. And as he did so, two television executives, men of stature in their field, certainly, but childlike in the presence of the monster Mac Daddy, sat down and presented him a contract. A couple of fights on a premier cable network. This boxer or that one, on one night or another. Who knows? Who cares? Plug them in later.

King held the contract in one hand and cut furrows in that cooling soup with the other. He ate as he read. For the next five minutes the executives fidgeted in their Hickey Freeman suits, tapped their cap-toe oxfords, and watched King's soup spoon.

The spoon stopped. King, in his offstage voice, the dealmaking voice the public never hears, spoke down into the soup. "The skeleton is there. But we *need the meat.*"

He chuckled low, and the spoon resumed its work.

Hungering, even as he eats, he is hunger itself, voracious, and the feeding makes him hungrier still.

For better and worse Don King embodies in the vastness of his good-natured greed the hungering abundance of America in all its mindless dualities and stubborn oppositions; in its soaring entrepreneurial spirit and its murderous bureaucracy, in its loving charity and its sterile lust for money and power. It's all there in one man. As it is in each of us. Love him or hate him, this wealthy and impoverished man, this pardoned sinner, this earnest huckster, this violent advocate of sweet peace in the world is just like you. He is us.

"My magic lies in my people's ties!"

He is Horatio Alger with a gun!

"I work for the day when all people will be clothed in dignity!"

Or have at least had the wool of dignity pulled over their eyes!

"Only in America!"

He *is* America!

And this is his day.

III

Up and out of the limo and into the Hilton lobby, Don King is greeted by hoots and squeals of recognition and a lightning storm of camera flashes. "Yes, yes, yes!" he trumpets as he strides across the polished marble, that nasal voice cutting the air like a cleaver, that one voice a klaxon above a hundred others. "Only in America!"

He is energized now — larger than life and his blue-ribbon smile dazzling — and he moves with a graceful sense of mighty purpose, Father Bountiful sowing prosperity with his every step. Through the knots of well-wishers and confused traveling salesmen, his overcoat billowing, the crisp tuxedo worn as we've seen it on hundreds of occasions — the fine shirt of Egyptian cotton stretched tight on the belly and the tie one size too big, too *Cleveland* — King, resplendent in his natural plumage, makes his way upstairs. "Let's go get slaughtered!" he keens, sweeping up the escalator in his evening dress.

It is 10:30 in the morning.

Today's affair is a luncheon, the surreality of which requires a dozen comics working blue to bring their filthiest material to bear in broad daylight on an audience neither sufficiently lubricated nor adequately unhurried to fully appreciate it. In fact, the whole megillah has a furtive vibe to it, half shameful, as if we're all crowding into the TomCat Triple-X for the businessman's matinee. This is going to be a tough house.

"Big Pussy! Big Pussy! Big Pussy!" King hollas across the greenroom, those plosive Bs and Ps popping like corks as actor Vincent

Pastore from *The Sopranos* walks in. "Yes, yes, yes! My man, my man! Nobody doesn't like Big Pussy!"

And so the tone is set.

"Michael Spinks!" King bawls. "My man!"

"LeRoy Neiman!" King crows. "My man!"

"Pat O'Brien!" King wails. "My man!"

"Kreskin!" King bellows. "My amazing man!" He pumps the mentalist's hand as if trying to draw deep water from a desert well handle.

To which the nightclub swami replies, glasses dancing on his nose, "I knew you were going to say that."

On and on they arrive, the lounge-act tenor and the weatherman, actors forgettable and forgotten, comics on their way up or on their way out — a telethon's worth of men and women who've made the climb but never reached the summit, citizens in good standing on America's celebrity B-list.

Joe Frazier limps in, the legs that carried him so near immortality now barely able to carry him across the room. His son Marvis steadies him at his elbow as he walks, every bowlegged step a tender reminder of Joe's legendary doggedness, of his fearlessness when within range of another man's fists. "Joe Frayzhuh! Joe Frayzhuh! Yes, yes, yes! Smokin' Joe! Smokin' Joe! My man!" oompahs the human sousaphone.

Frazier, who deserved more affection and respect from America than we ever gave him, wears a wide-brim black Stetson atop a double-breasted suit of electric teal over a thermal-underwear tee. You suspect the suit was chosen from a closet full of such Technicolor dream clothes, Frazier's subconscious fashion palette a vivid one, that he might remain visible to us even beneath Ali's lifelong eclipse. After shaking King's hand — a moment for the cameras in which the two men's eyes never meet — Noble Joe moves to a seat nearby to ease his legs and back. As he passes he trails behind him, fittingly if not exactly magically, the smell of recent, mellow smoke. His breakfast cigar perhaps. A small crowd of true believers follows, to bathe his aches with their belated regard.

Freddie Roman, fifty years a comic, Dalai Lama of the mystic Catskills, and dean of the Friars Club, walks in and is gathered under King's heavy arm for a photo-op, as is actor Abe Vigoda, old as the pharaohs.

Above all these septuagenarians hovers a three-foot microphone

on its eight-foot flexible boom, borne aloft by a young TV techni-
cian dressed all in black and poised there to record the labored
gibes and wisecracks. Seen from across the room, the audio rig
looks dire indeed, remarkably and unfortunately like the Reaper's
own eager scythe held high.

IV

Corralled by publicists and herded out, we are driven down a chute
into another, larger room, where fifty or more shooters stand ar-
rayed in front of a small stage. For the next hour it's "Look to the
left! The LEFT!" and "Over here! Over HERE!" as the paparazzi
raise their photo-op prayers to these low-hanging stars.

King is paired and re-paired with various attendees, that smile
frozen hard on his face as he and his brother Friars are arranged
like puzzle pieces by their various publicists. This is perhaps the
only moment in history when the words "Where's Dick Capri? Get
me Dick Capri!" have been spoken with real urgency.

King is shown the commemorative he will receive as part of the
day's honors: a cut-glass Friar standing in a ring of cut-glass flames.
Depending on the heresies of *your* misspent youth, this will remind
you either of your parents' dusty bottle of hazelnut liqueur or of
the Spanish Inquisition. And while vaguely aware of the historical
horror of the latter, I must confess to an intimate teenage acquaintance with the horrors of the former.

King then holds aloft for the cameras a pair of red boxing gloves
— "To the left! To the LEFT!" — an autographed gift from the
president of the United States on the occasion of Don King's roasting day. King campaigned vigorously and sonorously for George
W. Bush in Florida and Ohio in 2004. Given the slim margins of
the President's victories in these states, it is possible to argue, at
least if you're Don King, that Don King, by mobilizing the African-
American vote in these areas, tipped the election in Bush's favor. In
return for which the President himself might have appeared here
today, but couldn't, according to King, because he was "embroiled
in so much other minutiae." The Global War on Terror being, if
nothing else, a real scheduling headache.

Spinks and Frazier and heavyweight contender Lamon Brewster
and comic Gilbert Gottfried have all been photographed with their

fists cocked beneath King's chin, and the photo pros from the world's tabloids are running out of visual clichés and steam. Just as the energy threatens to drain entirely from the room, Donald Trump arrives. Still wearing his trademark scowl and a faceful of stage pancake — from his day job at *The Apprentice*, one assumes — he is late. Fittingly, Trump will be the roastmaster for this afternoon's ribaldries, having been the roastee a year earlier. "What a great, great event this is," he says to no one as he enters. "Very prestigious."*

Excepting certain tinhorn heads of state with large standing armies, Trump is the only person in the last quarter-century to publicly rival King's matchless ego or to equal his self-loving zeal. Trump is King's tonsorial doppelgänger, and the funhouse mirror in which King's rags-to-riches tale is bent into the shortshort story of rich to richer. Trump's business plan over the years, as simple and efficient as King's, is a two-step philosophy. It works, apparently, like this:

Step 1: Take credit.

Step 2: Assign blame.

Accountable only to themselves, the double Dons have built their empires on bluster; each man floating majestically above the American skyline in a giant bologna skin filled with his own hot air. That they remain aloft against the stubborn gravity of reality speaks to our endless credulity in the face of celebrity.

These few moments of Trump l'oeil having finally produced sufficient imagery to litter every news desk worldwide for the next twenty-four hours, the flacks holster their cattle prods, gather up the dignitaries, and lead them through a backdoor to the ballroom.

V

Seating seventy dusty luminaries from the antique worlds of vaudeville and the fistic arts, the dais is more than two hundred feet long. At its midpoint is a lectern, above which hangs the Friars' motto,

---

* In the interest of full disclosure, I must alert the reader that Mr. Trump once took public exception to a book review I'd written, in which I jokingly theorized that many New Yorkers would be willing, even eager, to drop a nonlethal flowerpot on his incredible head.

Prae Omnia Fraternitas — translated loosely from the Latin as, How many of you folks are from out of town?

Stand-up comedy and boxing have a great deal more in common than one might think. Both look easy. Both are hard. Both abide outside the inflexible margins of polite suburban propriety. Both are solitary acts of bravery and barely controlled aggression in which one party struggles to provoke a reflex in the central nervous system of its target. In boxing the desired response is the unconsciousness of the concussed opponent; in comedy, Carrot Top notwithstanding, the sought-after reflex is the helpless laughter of the paying customers. In the second case the audience is the adversary. Why, after all, do you think they call it a punch line?

But there's no time for etymology now, as Freddie Roman, having warmed up this chilly daytime crowd, has at last brought to the lectern Roastmaster Donald Trump, who leans into the microphone for his opening remarks as if to bite it.

"HEY, FREDDIE, how come HE has to SIT so NEAR ME? Move OVER, DON. . . . You know he KILLED PEOPLE? This guy KILLED PEOPLE. I'm going to say things about him, and I DON'T WANT TO BE KILLED. . . ." He waits, maybe for comic effect, maybe to let the echo fade. "How come there are so FEW BOXERS HERE? Because DON KING has SCREWED so many BOXERS, nobody WANTS TO COME!"

There is an awkward silence, punctuated by a flurry of nervous laughs. If this *were* a fight, Trump would have hit the canvas before his corner even pulled the stool. King sits a few feet away, casually holding aloft an unlit cigar the size of a fireplug, grinning gamely but inscrutably. Trump, to his thick-skinned credit, breathes deeply, rises up, and loudly, EMPHATICALLY, tries again.

"Let's FACE it. DON KING IS A BIG, FAT, F—— THIEF!"

There is another brief, but undeniable, pause while the audience considers its options. Laugh, and they'll only encourage him. Sit quietly, and it's going to be the longest afternoon this side of the planet Saturn. The crowd, some of whom have paid $1,000 a plate for a chicken breast and a side of those dollhouse carrots and desperately need a laugh, decides to tie its opponent up in a clinch and keep him on his feet the rest of the way. It gives him, likely out of self-interest, his first wall-to-wall laugh.

"HE F—— EVERYBODY HE TOUCHES!" comes The Donald's subtle *thank you.*

"Here's the KIND OF CRAP they WRITE," Trump shouts, reading from his script. "'I have a CATCHPHRASE, You're FIRED! Don has a catchphrase, Not GUILTY!' . . . This is FREDDIE and his GREAT group of GENIUS writers. . . . 'Don is a big FAN of *The Apprentice*. IN FACT he'll SOON have his own show, it's called *THE ACCOMPLICE*.' . . . LISTEN to this piece of CRAP. 'Don King wants to write a BOOK about this EVENT, *Old JEWS and the NEGROES Who Frighten Them*.'"

Having assigned blame, thereby also taking credit for whichever parts of the script he has "punched up," Trump is free to introduce the first professional comic, Stewie Stone, which, blessedly, he eventually does.

Stone, who looks exactly like the picture you have in your head right now of a man in late middle age named Stewie, selects as his opening target the roastmaster himself. "You're a mean c——. I didn't know that about you. You're getting a million and a half dollars to give lectures on how to be a millionaire? Your father *gave* you forty million dollars, that's how! . . . Don King at least did it with a gun — you're just full of s——."

Which generates the first belly laugh since we all walked in. Trump scowls that well-known scowl, all gunfighter squint and powdered jowls, a dour look that must have bought him all kinds of street cred with the other kids at military school. Stone works a solid five-minute set. The barely printable highlights:

"What can I say about Don King that hasn't already been said by a DA, a judge, and a parole officer?"

To Don King: "Trump's got worse f—— hair than you do!" Then to Donald Trump: "Do you realize you're turning prematurely orange?"

And, to cover his exit, directed at either or both of the two Dons, at once apt and poignant, "You deserve what's coming to you."

In an inexplicable theatrical miscue, the next two speakers are civilians. Suffice to say that by comparison they make Trump look like Fanny Brice, and that they squander what little comic steam Stone had managed to stoke. It becomes apparent why the various dignitaries fight so hard to sit on the dais: so they don't have to watch.

A brief moment here while the entire audience frantically reloads its wineglasses.

VI

The Friars Club is a fraternal order of outsiders who made themselves insiders, of comedians, actors, publicists, and other show folk who invented for themselves a century ago just about the only club in that anti-Semitic age they'd ever be invited to join, then perfected these savage roasts as a way to express their fierce loyalty to one another. Still, even after luring some of the bright new lights of comedy to join them in the last few years, the membership has a median age somewhere between "He used to open for Louis Prima at The Sands" and "He's coding!"

The best-kept secret of these roasts is not how hard and yet fragile a thing stand-up comedy is (or how profoundly lonely), but rather how hard it is to find a guest of honor. Whomever you see in the hot seat next year, or in one of those staged Page Six photos the day after, he or she likely wasn't the Friars' first choice. Or even the second. Or seventh.

"That's always our biggest problem," I was told by an elder Friar in good standing a few nights before the event. (In service of that standing, I'll maintain his anonymity.) "People are terrified by the idea of being roasted. Most celebrities have no sense of humor about themselves. We go through a dozen candidates sometimes before we land anybody willing to do it."

Don't be deceived by the soft-core imitations and broadcast spin-offs you've seen over the years, like the PG-rated *Dean Martin Celebrity Roasts* of the '60s and '70s, or the popular (and heavily edited) Comedy Central version of Friars Club roasts. In its unadulterated form a Friars Club roast isn't merely obscene, it's also brutal. "I think we made Chevy Chase cry," said the insider.

"Worst day of his life," added another.

VII

In a fine display of synchronized drinking the audience has refilled, tossed back, and refilled their glasses again. Thanks to those two unfunny *farshtinkener momzers,* and the quick ingestion of two hundred gallons of institutional wine, the crowd is head-rushed, restless, and desperate for real laughs. Lisa Lampanelli, all energy and offense, comes out swinging and delivers.

Sadly, most of her aggressive best cannot be printed in most magazines. Here's a schematic example of a Lisa Lampanelli joke: *Don King is so BLANK BLANK that he has to BLANK his BLANK in his BLANK when he BLANKS to BLANK.*

In deference to the trademark holders at *Mad Libs®*, *Match Game* fans, and the prevailing moral standards of your community, and by subtracting the n-word, the c-word, the t-word, the a-word, the b-word, the d-word, and the p-word, I transcribe these few excerpts:

"There's no denying it's been a great year for Donald Trump. First and foremost, he's happy with his beautiful wife, INSERT NAME HERE. But what do you say to a barber to get that kind of a haircut, anyway? 'I f—— your daughter'?

"The Amazing Kreskin is here. He's a mentalist, that guy — he can read people's thoughts. What a horrible gift. How many times tonight alone did he hear people walk by him thinking, 'Man, what a d—— bag!'?"

Other than Don King, she's the only person on this dais who actually killed.

Al Sharpton's up next, and as he stands at the lectern between Donald Trump and Don King, it's like seeing your favorite characters from the novels of Tom Wolfe gathered for a portrait, a trinity of charismatic rascals. The Reverend, one of the few presidential candidates of the modern age with a demonstrable sense of humor, does not disappoint.

"Thank you, Donald Trump. . . . I was in the bathroom having a meeting of the Black Tenants of Trump Real Estate Properties.

"Racism's still alive. You'll notice we have two slicksters up here — one they call a mogul, one they call a mugger. That's race in America."

The Rev knows better than most that you should always leave your audience wanting more. And he does.

As the day wears on, one senses a grave and growing tear in the very fabric of the time–good taste continuum. Dick Capri, a yeoman comic of forty years' service, opens thus: "A quadruple amputee's lying on the beach. . . ." He works fast, the jokes well tuned to the room — filthy, offensive, unprintable.

Next up is Jackie "the Jokeman" Martling, best known for his work with Howard Stern. His signature is that he giggles at his own jokes. Today he's the only one laughing. "What can you say about a man who combs his hair with electricity?" Nothing evidently. The twilight sound of crickets overwhelms the ballroom. At the mid-point of his infinite five minutes, Martling notes, "Wow, it's quiet up here," and even the crickets are silent. He actually closes with the words, "I'm sorry I didn't do better."

Colin Quinn, greeting the silent audience, gets his biggest laugh the instant he opens his mouth. "I don't know if I can follow Jackie, but I'll try." And his topper, upon seeing Trump, Sharpton, and King posed arm in arm for a photo: "Their hair looks like the three stages of a forest fire."

Norm Crosby, a charming little apple-core doll of a man, a pro's pro and indomitable, throws down a solid-blue set from the old school. The audience pours sugar all over him for having done so. Here's the only joke that's printable: "Don King is a smart man, he knows things. . . . He knows the similarities between Bill Clinton and Abraham Lincoln. One got his brains blown out. The other was assassinated."

VIII

Don King sits mildly by with one long arm draped over the chair next to his, fiddles with his cigar, laughs when the moment requires it, smiles beatifically at all other times. Good comic or bad, he takes his lumps with apparent fine humor and in the spirit, whatever that might actually be, of the occasion.

The comics tee off on the man's mythology, busting him on all the familiar signifiers — the hair, the criminal history, the famous names on the fight cards, the money, and the jewelry — all the things you already knew you knew about him. The man himself re-mains unmoved. In that way he is perhaps the best honoree the Friars have ever had, fireproof, shockproof, shtickproof. What can any of these people say that might somehow wound or touch or even interest him?

The honor and duty of closing the show go to Pat Cooper, an-other stand-up stand-up veteran from the long-gone tail-fin days of Ed Sullivan, supper clubs, and crepe de chine cocktail dresses. Cooper has no act to speak of, and is the first to admit it; rather he relies on the moment, and on his perpetual state of consummate rage, to carry him through. It is comedy as peeved improvisation.

To try to transcribe more than a sentence or two would be a disservice to history, and to Cooper.

"I shouldn't have bothered with that shower. . . . What the f——
is your story, Trump? . . . I saw you six years ago. . . . You sent me a
letter, Don, and you said, 'Pat, anything you need, please call me.'
I've been calling you for six f—— years. When the f—— do you
[pick up] the f—— phone?

"It's been a nice afternoon that I'll certainly forget. I'd like to get
off, ladies and gentlemen, but I've got no ending."

The audience, grateful to Cooper, rewards him with a generous
hand. But it is now almost 3:00 P.M., the show running very late indeed, so the energy beneath the applause feels nearly frantic, as if
the crowd can't wait to go. As the Cooper ovation subsides, people
fold their napkins, fuss with their coat-check tickets and beaded
bags, yawn and stretch. It is into the palpable tension of this impending getaway that the final speaker of the afternoon is introduced. The unspoken covenant with the audience is, of course,
that he will keep things brief. But brevity is not Don King's long
suit. Nor is linearity of thought. Nor are his remarks organized in
written form.

In consideration of space, sense, and trying to reproduce the exact manner in which the address was received by the wine-woozy,
enervated audience in the Hilton ballroom that day, I compress
here as best I can the twelve minutes of King's remarks, drawn from
the torrential stream of consciousness into which sportswriters have
been dipping their little buckets for the last thirty years. Ironically,
the rhetorical adhesive that holds many of King's sentences together is the phrase *Do you know what I mean?*

"Thank you. . . . Well, it's been a great day. Many people have
come up here to abuse and misuse, do wild accusations, unfounded,
unwarranted; nevertheless I've been the recipient of all this pain,
but from pain comes gain. . . ."

*(Various historical discursive asides now follow, including, but not limited to, olden days, a joke about a funeral home, slavery, prejudice, the Civil
War, the Reconstruction, and the indiscriminate, prolific roasting of strangers not named, but. . . .)*

"The Friars bring people together. . . ."

*(Asides now on Donald Trump and his rich father, his turn in military
school, then at Wharton, how he handles himself with "aplomb," and how*

one might even consider Trump, with his "extracurricular peccadilloes," a "macaroni" or a "playa," which leads naturally into the biblical instruction to go forth and bear children. Trump, the prolific paterfamilias, the story of Abraham and Sarah, be fruitful and multiply, etc. . . .)

"I'm standing up here blamed for everything that's ever happened in this country from the Johnstown Flood to World War II to the Lindbergh kidnapping, you know. I accept it graciously. . . ."

(Asides now referring to sticks, clubs, running through the jungle in a loincloth, Al Sharpton crying out in the wilderness, and the general — albeit painfully slow — trend toward the moral progress of mankind. . . .)

"I have to say to all of you who don't like George Walker Bush . . . George Walker Bush is a revolutionary!"

While King's enthusiasm at this point is unquestionable, several people in the audience moan audibly; others simply start leaving. "Many blacks may not realize this, but he did more for blacks image-wise than any president in the history of the United States. . . ."

(Asides now include "chic and steel," Condoleezza Rice, Colin Powell, and the security of "350 million people," "lyin', cheatin', stealin'." "He raised the bar of dignity, he raised the bar of pride, he raised the bar of hope." The Klan, the CIA, and "the slide and glide," camaraderie, conviviality, "God bless America!" and "Danny Aiello! His arms too short to box with God!" Freddie Roman and the "sweat poppin' off his brow!" "Which only a crazy man would do!" "Levity and jobs and programs and the brave sacrifice of the Screamin' Eagles — and the Friars too." "Patriotism is the greatest thing in the world." "More sacrifice," "the Friars exemplify bravery and perfect union." A submarine. . . .)

At which moment a man at the table behind us gets up and leaves, saying, "This is nonsense, just nonsense."

("Performance is what counts . . . I am the godfather of hip-hop. . . . Treat your woman as your equal if not your superior. They don't understand that, but a macaroni does." . . .)

"This has been a wonderful day!"

("Legitimize the articulation. . . . That's the blackology that Don has, . . . that smile, that infectious smile that's so addictive." . . .)

"I love America! George Walker Bush! Only in America!"

Sensing an end, or at least willing one, the audience rises and applauds as it jogs for the exits — a rolling ovation out the door. "We only roast the ones we love," says Freddie Roman to their backs as the room rapidly empties.

"This is America?" the German reporter asks again.

IX

Trump flees the scene like a line handler beneath the *Hindenburg*. In his haste he leaves behind his script. A millionaire perhaps, but not a strong speller, and he has indeed made several edits, including the elimination of any jokes poking fun at himself.

In his wake Lloyd Price, the singer who first brought King and Ali together in 1972, judges the day "magnificent," as he slips into his cashmere coat, laughing. "Just a wonderful, wonderful day."

Evander Holyfield stands a few feet away. Saying nothing, staring into the middle distance, he waits for a word or two with King, a chance to plead for one more money fight. Against the blur and hurry of overworked waiters and stagehands on overtime, he is an impossible stillness, his face as stoic and unknowable as any statue on Easter Island.

King circulates quietly in the afterglow with a handful of friends, tired now, signing autographs for stragglers in the abandoned ballroom. He is told by one of his several attendants that they will be leaving the hotel through a side entrance. There is a process server in the lobby. King is being sued. Again. Even today, or perhaps *especially* today. He says nothing. It is somehow possible in this moment to feel sympathy, even empathy, for Don King. To pine on his behalf for a day's rest, a day's respect, a day's fun, for a truce, however momentary, in the unending battle he himself set in motion so long ago.

Someone asks him how he feels.

"Hungry," comes the reply.

X

Out the side door and around the corner to a steakhouse. New York in October, a careless east wind kicking the city's trash through the streets. That hot yellow Lamborghini Gallardo parked out front belongs to Zab Judah, the soon-to-be-ex-welterweight champ. Elaborate as a Mars lander, sexy as silk stockings, the car costs $200,000. Inside the restaurant King stands in a quiet corner counting out crisp fifty-dollar bills so Zab can put some gas in it. King smiles. Zab murmurs "thanks" through diamond-studded teeth.

King never got to eat his rubber lunch, but this is Zab Judah's

birthday party too. He turned twenty-eight yesterday and was on
the dais for the roast; King had ordered a cake and brought a
dozen and a half folks — friends and employees and entourage —
over here to celebrate both moments with a very late, very large
lunch. King often gathers his intimates for meals like this while
away from home. This is his traveling family, his musical-chairs defense against the loneliness of the road. And Father Bountiful, ever
gracious, ever generous, inviting you in with his hand on your
shoulder and his eyes on your wallet, is a perfectly charming host.

At a fine big table in the private dining room King judges his day a
fair one. "I thought it went very well," he says. "They're supposed to
level pain on you there. It's a good coming together, though. It
makes you feel good."

He speaks clearly but softly as he sits back in his chair, taking his
ease. Only the week before he had undergone angioplasty, a well-
kept secret, the heart at the heart of darkness now threatened
rather than threatening. He passes the mashed potatoes and reminds us all to clean our plates.

Later, still working, *always* working, he will talk with Holyfield.
And that too-old fighter and that ageless promoter, sitting bent in
the lamplight, far from the others, will whisper, heads drawn close,
about a deal you can only pray never gets made.

To sit with Don King is to visit something singular in the American
character, at once admirable and appalling, a man all restless vigor
and every appetite unchecked. That he made a life so large for so
many on the strength of his wits and his will is somehow inspiring.
But at what cost? And to whom?

Only in America.

Near irresistibly, you are drawn to him. Despite your fears, he
carries you willingly to the very brink of something. Once there,
unbidden, you look down. And there you see the two unmistakable
faces of the great American grotesque — the benevolent malevolent, carrying all good and bringing all evil, welcoming you, arms
flung wide, affection and death both beckoning, America itself
gathering you up for a loving hug as it suffocates you.

When Zab Judah's cake arrives, the candles firing shadows up the
walls, the room kindled orange and red, Don King, American,

happy and famous and rich, a man at once soothed and amused and enraged by the dire light of his terrifying fame and comforted by the hard-won luxuries of his terrible prosperity, will smile yet again, unashamed, unchastened, and unafraid, and in full voice, loud with his multitudes, yours and mine, the voice of America itself, will sing out clear and happy and strong.

And you will try very hard, in that flickering moment of joy, to forgive him. But in your despair, you will fail.

SALLY JENKINS

Only Medal for
Bode Is Fool's Gold

FROM THE WASHINGTON POST

Sally Jenkins takes out Bode Miller, "not because of the way he skied the mountain, but the way he acted at the bottom of it."
— D.M.

FOR WEEKS NOW Nike has advised us to "Join Bode." Join him where? At the bar? That's one place you might find Bode Miller after the Turin Games, unless he's in his motor home, finding new ways to duck all that pressure he put on himself.

Miller is the biggest disappointment in the Winter Olympics, not because of the way he skied the mountain, but the way he acted at the bottom of it. The fact that he didn't win a medal at these Games, going 0-for-5 in the Alpine events, is beside the point. It's not the winning, it's the trying. The point is that he acted like he didn't try, and didn't care. Failing is forgivable. Getting fatter on beer while you're here is not.

If there has been a weaker performance by an American athlete on the international stage than that of Miller, I'm hard-pressed to think of one. To hear Miller tell it, he spent more time in Sestriere's nightclubs than he did in actual competition, which amounted to less than eight minutes. Miller's final Olympic event, the slalom, lasted all of sixteen seconds. He bulled out of the start house, did a couple of quick scrimshaw turns, and promptly straddled a gate.

Fair enough — Miller has struggled in the slalom this season, finishing just two of eight races, and it was a tough course. Nine of the top twenty-nine skiers in the competition did not finish. It was Miller's behavior afterward that sealed his reputation as the goat of the Games. He thrust his hands in the air, stuck out his tongue, and waggled in mock celebration. Then he skied off the course, avoiding the cameras and throngs of people at the bottom of the hill. When Associated Press reporter Jim Litke found him later, he declared, "Man, I rocked."

Then he delivered a disquisition on his Olympic experience. "It's been an awesome two weeks," Miller said. "I got to party and socialize at an Olympic level."

Let's review his awesome two weeks. Miller arrived in Turin sullen and defensive, and blew his chance in the downhill when he lost time on the bottom of the course, probably as a result of his lack of fitness. He blew another medal in the combined when he led after the downhill portion, but straddled a gate in the slalom. Next, he blew up a gate in the Super-G, and then insulted his rivals afterward by saying he wasn't one of those guys "who skies 70, 80 percent and gets on the podium."

Miller has worked awfully hard to reach this point; the relationship he has built with the public is the one he himself has constructed over many months. He was impossibly over-hyped coming into the Winter Games between Nike's ad campaign, his autobiography, and those nipple-baring magazine covers, all of which he cooperated with and cashed in on. Miller took the world's biggest ego bath — until he realized it was going to be difficult to satisfy Olympic expectations, especially in a field chock-full of Austrians.

Now he wants to distance himself from all the hype and commerce. "The expectations were other people's," he told the AP. "I'm comfortable with what I've accomplished, including at the Olympics."

The about-face has left Miller so confused that he can't get his stories straight. In one breath, he talks about giving it his all, and in the next, he talks about how hard he drank during the Games. "I just did it my way. I'm not a martyr, and I'm not a do-gooder. I just want to go out and rock. And, man, I rocked here."

Or: "My quality of life is the priority. I wanted to have fun here, to enjoy the Olympic experience, not be holed up in a closet and not ever leave your room."

Miller's act has clearly worn on his coaches, and Bill Marolt, chief executive of the U.S. Ski and Snowboard Association, suggested that officials would have "a heart-to-heart" talk with Miller at the end of this season regarding his behavior. Nor would Marolt speculate if Miller would be back on the team. "I don't believe we should have conversations like this in the media," Marolt said. "But clearly it will be something we will address at the year's end, and I don't know where that will go right now."

What they should tell Miller is this: Everyone can sympathize with his struggle to meet unrealistic expectations. And everyone respects what Miller has done on skis, from his two silvers at the Salt Lake Games to the overall World Cup title last season. But nobody respects the Bode Miller who showed up here — maybe not even Miller himself — and unless he can compete respectably, he shouldn't return to the team. There are few things less worthy of respect than the athlete who pretends not to care about the outcome. It's a bail-out position, a protection, and an excuse. If you pretend not to care, then no one can say you really lost. Miller never committed to these Olympics, never put his ante on the table. He sauntered around the Games as if he was just here to watch.

Which is mostly what he did.

DANIEL COYLE

That Which Does Not Kill Me Makes Me Stranger

FROM THE NEW YORK TIMES PLAY MAGAZINE

Completely uncoachable nutcase. Sound like an NBA player?
No, much better for Daniel Coyle's sensibility, an indefatigable
Slovenian cyclist.
— D.M.

JURE ROBIC, the Slovene soldier who might be the world's best ultra-endurance athlete, lives in a small fifth-floor apartment near
the railroad tracks in the town of Koroska Bela. By nature and voca-
tion, Robic is a sober-minded person, but when he appears at his
doorway, he is smiling. Not a standard-issue smile, but a wild and
fidgety grin, as if he were trying to contain some huge and mysterious secret.

Robic catches himself, strides inside, and proceeds to lead a swift
tour of his spare, well-kept apartment. Here is his kitchen. Here is
his bike. Here are his wife, Petra, and year-old son, Nal. Here,
on the coffee table, are whiskey, Jägermeister, bread, chocolate,
prosciutto, and an inky, vegetable-based soft drink he calls Commu-
nist Coca-Cola, left over from the old days. And here, outside the
window, veiled by the nightly ice fog, stand the Alps and the Aus-
trian border. Robic shows everything, then settles onto the couch.
It's only then that the smile reappears, more nervous this time, as
he pulls out a DVD and prepares to reveal the unique talent that
sets him apart from the rest of the world: his insanity.

Tonight, Robic's insanity exists only in digitally recorded form,
but the rest of the time it swirls moodily around him, his personal

batch of ice fog. Citizens of Slovenia, a tiny, sports-happy country that was part of the former Yugoslavia until 1991, might glow with beatific pride at the success of their ski jumpers and handballers, but they tend to become a touch unsettled when discussing Robic, who for the past two years has dominated ultra-cycling's hardest, longest races. They are proud of their man, certainly, and the way he can ride thousands of miles with barely a rest. But they're also a little, well, *concerned.* Friends and colleagues tend to sidle together out of Robic's earshot and whisper in urgent, hospital-corridor tones.

"He pushes himself into madness," says Tomaz Kovsca, a journalist for Slovene television. "He pushes too far."

Rajko Petek, a thirty-five-year-old fellow soldier and friend who is on Robic's support crew, says: "What Jure does is frightening. Sometimes during races he gets off his bike and walks toward us in the follow car, very angry."

What do you do then?

Petek glances carefully at Robic, standing a few yards off. "We lock the doors," he whispers.

When he overhears, Robic heartily dismisses their unease. "They are joking!" he shouts. "Joking!" But in quieter moments, he acknowledges their concern, even empathizes with it — though he's quick to assert that nothing can be done to fix the problem. Robic seems to regard his racetime bouts with mental instability as one might regard a beloved but unruly pet: awkward and embarrassing at times, but impossible to live without.

"During race, I am going crazy, definitely," he says, smiling in bemused despair. "I cannot explain why is that, but it is true."

The craziness is methodical, however, and Robic and his crew know its pattern by heart. Around Day 2 of a typical weeklong race, his speech goes staccato. By Day 3, he is belligerent and sometimes paranoid. His short-term memory vanishes, and he weeps uncontrollably. The last days are marked by hallucinations: bears, wolves, and aliens prowl the roadside; asphalt cracks rearrange themselves into coded messages. Occasionally, Robic leaps from his bike to square off with shadowy figures that turn out to be mailboxes. In a 2004 race, he turned to see himself pursued by a howling band of black-bearded men on horseback.

"Mujahedeen, shooting at me," he explains. "So I ride faster."

His wife, a nurse, interjects: "The first time I went to a race, I was not prepared to see what happens to his mind. We nearly split up."

The DVD spins, and the room vibrates with Wagner. We see a series of surreal images that combine violence with eerie placidity, like a Kubrick film. Robic's spotlit figure rides through the dark in the driving rain. Robic gasps some unheard plea to a stone-faced man in fatigues who's identified as his crew chief. Robic curls fetuslike on the pavement of a Pyrenean mountain road, having fallen asleep and simply tipped off his bike. Robic stalks the crossroads of a nameless French village at midnight, flailing his arms, screaming at his support crew. A baffled gendarme hurries to the scene, asking, *Quel est le problème?* I glance at Robic, and he's staring at the screen too.

"In race, everything inside me comes out," he says, shrugging. "Good, bad, everything. My mind, it begins to do things on its own. I do not like it, but this is the way I must go to win the race."

Over the past two years, Robic, who is forty years old, has won almost every race he has entered, including the last two editions of ultra-cycling's biggest event, the 3,000-mile Insight Race Across America (RAAM). In 2004, Robic set a world record in the twenty-four-hour time trial by covering 518.7 miles. Last year, he did himself one better, following up his RAAM victory with a victory six weeks later in Le Tour Direct, a 2,500-mile race on a course contrived from classic Tour de France routes. Robic finished in seven days and nineteen hours, and climbed some 140,000 feet, the equivalent of nearly five trips up Mount Everest. "That's just mind-boggling," says Pete Penseyres, a two-time RAAM solo champion. "I can't envision doing two big races back to back. The mental part is just too hard."

Hans Mauritz, the co-organizer of Le Tour Direct, says: "For me, Jure is on another planet. He can die on the bike and keep going."

And going. In addition to races, Robic trains 335 days each year, logging some 28,000 miles, or roughly one trip around the planet.

Yet Robic does not excel on physical talent alone. He is not always the fastest competitor (he often makes up ground by sleeping ninety minutes or less a day), nor does he possess any towering physiological gift. On rare occasions when he permits himself to be tested in a laboratory, his ability to produce power and transport oxygen ranks on a par with those of many other ultra-endurance athletes. He wins for the most fundamental of reasons: he refuses to stop.

In a consideration of Robic, three facts are clear: he is nearly indefatigable, he is occasionally nuts, and the first two facts are somehow connected. The question is, How? Does he lose sanity because he pushes himself too far, or does he push himself too far because he loses sanity? Robic is the latest and perhaps most intriguing embodiment of the old questions: What happens when the human body is pushed to the limits of its endurance? Where does the breaking point lie? And what happens when you cross the line?

The Insight Race Across America was not designed by overcurious physiologists, but it might as well have been. It's the world's longest human-powered race, a coast-to-coast haul from San Diego to Atlantic City. Typically, two dozen or so riders compete in the solo categories.

Compared with the three-week, 2,200-mile Tour de France, which is generally acknowledged to be the world's most demanding event, RAAM requires relatively low power outputs — a contest of diesel engines as opposed to Ferraris. But RAAM's unceasing nature and epic length — 800 miles more than the Tour in roughly a third of the time — makes it in some ways a purer test, if only because it more closely resembles a giant lab experiment. (An experiment that will get more interesting if Lance Armstrong, the seven-time Tour winner, gives RAAM a try, as he has hinted he might.)

Winners average more than 13 miles an hour and finish in nine days, riding about 350 miles a day. The ones to watch, though, are not the victors but the 50 percent who do not finish, and whose breakdowns, like a scattering of so many piston rods and hubcaps, provide a vivid map of the human body's built-in limitations.

The first breakdowns, in the California and Arizona deserts, tend to be related to heat and hydration (riders drink as much as a liter of water per hour during the race). Then, around the Plains states, comes the stomach trouble. Digestive tracts, overloaded by the strain of processing ten thousand calories a day (the equivalent of twenty-nine cheeseburgers), go haywire. This is usually accompanied by a wave of structural problems: muscles and tendons weaken, or simply give out. Body-bike contact points are especially vulnerable. Feet swell two sizes, on average. Thumb nerves, compressed on the handlebars, stop functioning. For several weeks after the race, Robic, like a lot of RAAM riders, must use two hands to turn a key. (Don't even ask about the derrière. When I did, Robic pantomimed placing a gun in his mouth and pulling the trigger.)

The final collapse takes place between the ears. Competitors endure fatigue-induced rounds of hallucinations and mood shifts. Margins for error in the race can be slim, a point underlined by two fatal accidents at RAAM in the past three years, both involving automobiles. Support crews, which ride along in follow cars or campers, do what they can to help. For Robic, his support crew serves as a second brain, consisting of a well-drilled cadre of a half-dozen fellow Slovene soldiers. It resembles other crews in that it feeds, hydrates, guides, and motivates — but with an important distinction. The second brain, not Robic's, is in charge.

"By the third day, we are Jure's software," says Lt. Miran Stanovnik, Robic's crew chief. "He is the hardware, going down the road."

Stanovnik, at forty-one, emanates the cowboy charisma of a special-ops soldier, though he isn't one: his background consists most notably of riding the famously grueling Paris-to-Dakar rally on his motorcycle. But he's impressively alpha nonetheless, referring to a recent crash in which he broke ribs, fractured vertebrae, and ruptured his spleen as "my small tumble."

His system is straightforward. During the race, Robic's brain is allowed control over choice of music (usually a mix of traditional Slovene marches and Lenny Kravitz), food selection, and bathroom breaks. The second brain dictates everything else, including rest times, meal times, food amounts, and even average speed. Unless Robic asks, he is not informed of the remaining mileage or even how many days are left in the race.

"It is best if he has no idea," Stanovnik says. "He rides — that is all."

Robic's season consists of a handful of twenty-four-hour races built around RAAM and, last year, Le Tour Direct. As in most ultra sports, prize money is more derisory than motivational. Even with the Slovene Army picking up much of the travel tab, the $10,000 check from RAAM barely covers Robic's cost of competing. His sponsorships, mostly with Slovene sports-nutrition and bike-equipment companies, aren't enough to put him in the black. (Stanovnik lent Robic's team $8,500 last year.)

Stanovnik is adept at motivating Robic along the way. When the mujahedeen appeared in 2004, Stanovnik pretended to see them too and urged Robic to ride faster. When an addled Robic believes himself to be back in Slovenia, Stanovnik informs him that his hometown is just a few miles ahead. He also employs more time-honored, drill-sergeant techniques.

"They would shout insults at him," says Hans Mauritz. "It woke him up, and he kept going."

(Naturally, these tactics add an element of tension between Robic and team members, and account for his bouts of hostility toward them, including, in 2003, Robic's mistaken but passionately held impression that Stanovnik was having an affair with his wife.)

In all decisions, Stanovnik governs according to a rule of thumb that he has developed over the years: at the dark moment when Robic feels utterly exhausted, when he is so empty and sleep-deprived that he feels as if he might literally die on the bike, he actually has 50 percent more energy to give.

"That is our method," Stanovnik says. "When Jure cannot go any more, he can still go. We must motivate him sometimes, but he goes."

In this dual-brain system, Robic's mental breakdowns are not an unwanted side effect, but rather an integral part of the process: welcome proof that the other limiting factors have been eliminated and that maximum stress has been placed firmly on the final link, Robic's mind. While his long-term memory appears unaffected (he can recall route landmarks from year to year), his short-term memory evaporates. Robic will repeat the same question ten times in five minutes. His mind exists completely in the present.

"When I am tired, Miran can take me to the edge," Robic says appreciatively, "to the last atoms of my power."

How far past the 50 percent limit can Robic be pushed? "Ninety, maybe 95 percent," Stanovnik says thoughtfully. "But that would probably be unhealthy."

Interestingly — or unnervingly, depending on how you look at it — some researchers are uncovering evidence that Stanovnik's rule of thumb might be right. A spate of recent studies has contributed to growing support for the notion that the origins and controls of fatigue lie partly, if not mostly, within the brain and the central nervous system. The new research puts fresh weight to the hoary coaching cliché: you only think you're tired.

From the time of Hippocrates, the limits of human exertion were thought to reside in the muscles themselves, a hypothesis that was established in 1922 with the Nobel Prize–winning work of Dr. A. V. Hill. The theory went like this: Working muscles, pushed to their limit, accumulated lactic acid. When concentrations of lactic acid reached a certain level, so the argument went, the muscles could no longer function. Muscles contained an "automatic brake," Hill wrote, "carefully adjusted by nature."

Researchers, however, have long noted a link between neurological disorders and athletic potential. In the late 1800s, the pioneering French doctor Philippe Tissié observed that phobias and epilepsy could be beneficial for athletic training. A few decades later, the German surgeon August Bier measured the spontaneous long jump of a mentally disturbed patient, noting that it compared favorably to the existing world record. These types of exertions seemed to defy the notion of built-in muscular limits and, Bier noted, were made possible by "powerful mental stimuli and the simultaneous elimination of inhibitions."

Questions about the muscle-centered model came up again in 1989 when Canadian researchers published the results of an experiment called Operation Everest II, in which athletes did heavy exercise in altitude chambers. The athletes reached exhaustion despite the fact that their lactic-acid concentrations remained comfortably low. Fatigue, it seemed, might be caused by something else.

In 1999, three physiologists from the University of Cape Town Medical School in South Africa took the next step. They worked a group of cyclists to exhaustion during a sixty-two-mile laboratory ride and measured, via electrodes, the percentage of leg muscles they were using at the fatigue limit. If standard theories were true, they reasoned, the body should recruit more muscle fibers as it approached exhaustion — a natural compensation for tired, weakening muscles.

Instead, the researchers observed the opposite result. As the riders approached complete fatigue, the percentage of active muscle fibers decreased, until they were using only about 30 percent. Even as the athletes felt they were giving their all, the reality was that more of their muscles were at rest. Was the brain purposely holding back the body?

"It was as if the brain was playing a trick on the body, to save it," says Timothy Noakes, head of the Cape Town group. "Which makes a lot of sense, if you think about it. In fatigue, it only feels like we're going to die. The actual physiological risks that fatigue represents are essentially trivial."

From this, Noakes and his colleagues concluded that A. V. Hill had been right about the automatic brake, but wrong about its location. They postulated the existence of what they called a central governor: a neural system that monitors carbohydrate stores, the levels of glucose and oxygen in the blood, the rates of heat gain and loss, and work rates. The governor's job is to hold our bodies safely back from the brink of collapse by creating painful sensations that we interpret as unendurable muscle fatigue. Fatigue, the researchers argue, is less an objective event than a subjective emotion — the brain's clever, self-interested attempt to scare you into stopping. The way past fatigue, then, is to return the favor: to fool the brain by lying to it, distracting it, or even provoking it. (That said, mental gamesmanship can never overcome a basic lack of fitness. As Noakes says, the body always holds veto power.)

"Athletes and coaches already do a lot of this instinctively," Noakes says. "What is a coach, after all, but a technique for overcoming the governor?"

The governor theory is far from conclusive, but some scientists are focusing on a walnut-size area in the front portion of the brain called the anterior cingulate cortex. This has been linked to a host of core functions, including handling pain, creating emotion, and playing a key role in what's known loosely as willpower. Sir Francis Crick, the co-discoverer of DNA, thought the anterior cingulate cortex to be the seat of the soul. In the sports world, perhaps no soul relies on it more than Jure Robic's.

Some people "have the ability to reprocess the pain signal," says Daniel Galper, a senior researcher in the psychiatry department at the University of Texas Southwestern Medical Center at Dallas. "It's not that they don't feel the pain; they just shift their brain dynamics and alter their perception of reality so the pain matters less. It's basically a purposeful hallucination."

Noakes and his colleagues speculate that the central governor theory holds the potential to explain not just feats of stamina but also their opposite: chronic fatigue syndrome (a malfunctioning, overactive governor, in this view). Moreover, the governor theory makes evolutionary sense. Animals whose brains safeguarded an emergency stash of physical reserves might well have survived at a higher rate than animals that could drain their fuel tanks at will.

The theory would also seem to explain a sports landscape in which ultra-endurance events have gone from being considered medically hazardous to something perilously close to routine. The Ironman triathlon in Hawaii — a 2.4-mile swim, 112-mile bike ride, and marathon-length run — was the ne plus ultra in endurance in the 1980s, but has now been topped by the Ultraman, which is more than twice as long. Once obscure, the genre known as adventure racing, which includes 500-plus-mile wilderness races like Primal Quest, has grown to more than four hundred events each year. Ultra-marathoners, defined as those who participate in running events exceeding the official marathon distance of 26.2 miles, now number some fifteen thousand in the United States alone. The underlying physics have not changed, but rather our sense of possibility. Athletic culture, like Robic, has discovered a way to tweak its collective governor.

When we try understanding Robic's relationship to severe pain, however, our interest tends to be more visceral. Namely, how does it feel?

"I feel like if I go on, I will die," he says, struggling for words. "It is everything at the same moment, piled up over and over. Head, muscles, bones. Nobody can understand. You cannot imagine it until you feel it."

A few moments later, he says: "The pain doesn't exist for me. I know it is there because I feel it, but I don't pay attention to it. I sometimes see myself from the other view, looking down at me riding the bike. It is strange, but it happens like that."

Robic veers like this when he discusses pain. He talks of incomprehensible suffering one moment and of dreamlike anesthesia the next. If pain is in fact both signal and emotion, perhaps that makes sense. Perhaps the closer we get to its dual nature, the more elusive any single truth becomes, and the better we understand what Emily Dickinson meant when she wrote that "pain has an element of blank."

It's a gray morning in December, and Robic is driving his silver Peugeot to one of his favorite training rides in the hills along Slovenia's Adriatic coast. The wind is blowing fifty miles an hour, and the temperature is in the forties. If Robic's anterior cingulate cortex can sometimes block out negative information, this is defi nitely not one of those times.

"This is bad," he says, peering at the wind-shredded clouds. "It makes no sense to train. You cannot train, and I am out there, cold and freezing for hours. I am shivering and wondering, *Why do I do this?*"

Robic often complains like this. Even when the weather is ideal, he points out the clouds blowing in and how horrible and lonely his workout will be. At first it seems like showboat kvetching that will diminish as he gets more familiar with you, but as time wears on it's apparent that his complaints are sincere. He isn't just acting miserable — he is miserable.

The negativity is accentuated, perhaps, by the fact that Robic trains exclusively alone. What's more, he's famously disinclined to seek advice when it comes to training, medical treatment, and nu- trition. "Completely uncoachable," says his friend Uros Velepec, a two-time winner of the Ultraman World Championships. Robic in- vents eclectic workout schedules: six hours of biking one day, seven hours of Nordic skiing the next, with perhaps a mountain climb or two in between, all faithfully tracked and recorded in a series of battered notebooks.

"I find motivation everywhere," Robic says. "If right now you look at me and wonder if I cannot go up the mountain, even if you are joking, I will do it. Then I will do it again, and maybe again." He gestures to Mt. Stol, a snowy Goliath crouched 7,300 feet above him, as remote as the moon. "Three years ago, I got angry at the mountain. I climbed it thirty-eight times in two months."

Robic goes on to detail his motivational fuel sources, including his neglectful father, persistent near poverty (three years ago, he was reduced to asking for food from a farmer friend), and a lack of large-sponsor support because of Slovenia's small size. ("If I lived in Austria, I would be millionaire," he says unconvincingly.) There is also a psychological twist of biblical flavor: a half-brother born out of wedlock named Marko, Jure's age to the month. Robic says his father favored Marko to the extent that the old man made him part owner of his restaurant, leaving Jure, at age twenty-eight, to beg them for a dishwashing job.

"All my life I was pushed away," he says. "I get the feeling that I'm not good enough to be the good one. And so now I am good at something, and I want revenge to prove to all the people who thought I was some kind of loser. These feelings are all the time present in me. They are where my power is coming from."

As a young man, Robic was known as a village racer, decent enough locally but not talented enough to land a professional contract. Throughout his twenties, he rode with small Slovene teams, supporting himself with a sales job for a bike-parts dealer. It was with the death of his mother in 1997 and his subsequent depression that Robic discovered his calling. On the advice of a cyclist friend, he started training for the 1999 Crocodile Trophy, a notoriously painful week-and-a-half-long mountain bike race across Australia. Robic finished third.

In October of 2001, Robic set out to see how far he could cycle in twenty-four hours. The day was unpromising: raw and wet. He nearly didn't ride. But he did — and went an estimated 498 miles, almost a world record.

"That was the day I knew I could do this," he says. "I know that the thing that does not kill me makes me stronger. I can feel it, and when I want to quit I hear this voice say, 'Come on, Jure,' and I keep going."

A year later, he quit his job and volunteered to join the Slovene military, undergoing nine months of intensive combat training (he surprised his unit with his penchant for late-night training runs). He earned a coveted spot in the sports division, which exists solely to support the nation's top athletes. For Robic, the post meant a salary of 700 euros (about $850) a month and the freedom to train full-time.

This day, despite the foul conditions, Robic trains for five and a half hours. He rides through toylike stone villages and fields of olive trees; he climbs mountains from whose peaks he can see the blue Adriatic and the coast of Italy. He rides across the border checkpoint into Croatia, along a deserted beach and past groves of fanlike bamboo. He rides in a powerful crouch, his big legs churning, his face impassive.

While I watch from the car, I'm reminded of a scene the previous night. Robic and his support crew of fellow soldiers met at a small restaurant for a RAAM reunion. For several hours, they ate veal, drank wine out of small glass pitchers, and reminisced in high spirits about the race. They spoke of the time Robic became unshakably convinced his team was making fun of him, and the time he sat on a curb in Athens, Ohio, and refused to budge for an hour, and the time they had to lift his sleeping body back onto his bike.

Stanovnik told of an incident in the Appalachians, when Robic, who seemed about to give up, suddenly found an unexpected burst of energy. "He goes like madman for one hour, two hours," Stanovnik recalled. "I am shouting at him, 'You show Slovenia, you show army, you show world what you are!' I have tears on my face, watching him."

At the end of the table, Rajko Petek wondered whether he could continue to work on the crew. "It is too much," he said to a round of understanding nods. "This kind of racing leaves damage upon Jure's mind. Too much fighting, too much craziness. I cannot take it anymore."

Robic sat quietly in their midst, his eyes darting and quick. Sometimes he'd offer a word or a joke, but mostly he listened. At first it seemed he was being shy, but after a while it became apparent that he was curious to hear the stories. The person of whom they spoke — this sometimes frightening, sometimes inspiring man named Jure Robic — remained a stranger to him.

Robic finishes his ride as the winter sun is going down. As we drive back toward Koroska Bela, a lens of white fog descends on the roadway. We pass ghostlike farms, factories, and church spires while Robic talks about his plans for the coming year. He talks about his wife, whose job has supported them, and he talks about their son, who is starting to walk. He talks about how he will try to win a record third consecutive RAAM in June, and how he hopes race officials won't react to the recent fatalities by adding mandatory rest stops. ("Then it will not be a true race," he says.) In a few months, he'll do his signature forty-eight-hour training, in which he rides for twenty-four hours straight, stays awake all night, and then does a twelve-hour workout.

But this year is going to be different in one respect. Robic is going to start working with a local sports psychologist who has previously helped several Slovene Olympians. It seems that Robic, the uncoachable one, is looking for guidance.

"I want to solve the demon," he says. "I do not want to be so crazy during the races. Every man has black and white inside of him, and the black should stay inside."

He presses the accelerator, weaving through drivers made timid by the fog. "This will be good for me," he adds, his voice growing louder. "I am older now, but I have the feeling that I am stronger than ever before. Now I am reaching where there is nothing that is too hard for my body because my mind is hard. Nothing!"

Robic attempts to convey the intensity of his feeling, but can only gesture dramatically with his hands, which unfortunately are needed to control the steering wheel. The car veers toward a ditch.

Acting quickly, Robic re-grips the wheel. After a shaky second or two, he regains control of the car. We barrel onward through the mist. His sidelong smile is pure confidence.

MIMI SWARTZ

Polite When in Neutral

FROM THE NEW YORK TIMES PLAY MAGAZINE

Brazilian warmth that is like the morning sun. Thanks for that, Mimi
Swartz, and may Bia's rays shine forever.
— D.M.

TO THE UNINITIATED or the uninformed, Bia Figueiredo might
seem like a very bad driver. She zigs and zags through the clogged,
smoggy streets of São Paulo — either in her jet-black Honda Fit or
her mother's Chevy Corsa, depending on which car's license plate
number allows her to beat the air pollution controls and drive le-
gally that day. She downshifts, she upshifts, she tailgates like there's
no tomorrow. She passes on the left, passes on the right, ignores
various white stripes designating this or that lane, and, at particularly tense times, talks about having me open the passenger door to
stop the motorcyclists who zoom past between paralyzed cars. "Why
don't we try?" she asks, her eyes merry but her lightly accented
English tight. The only thing that seems to be keeping Bia's behavior in check, in fact, is that she is just two tickets away from losing
her driver's license. "This is the traffic," she says dolefully. "I hate it.
I hate it so much."

At this moment she looks and sounds like any other pretty, pouty
twenty-one-year-old child of São Paulo prosperity, her long brown
hair flawlessly highlighted, her skin unlined, unfreckled, and a
pale, perfect pink. Her robust figure, today as most days, is clad
courtesy of Puma, one of her sponsors: form-fitting T-shirt, form-
fitting workout pants, shoes and bag, all color-coordinated in black,
white, and apple green. Her CD player flits from Shakira to Shania
Twain, and her cell phone twitters frequently, but she remains

oblivious, focused on the road, looking for an opening, anything that might give her a small advantage in this stultifying daily ritual. This deep concentration I recognize as what she referenced earlier, without a trace of irony, as her "animal instincts."

"I am so sad about it — the traffic," she says, shaking her head. "The drivers just don't go, okay? Drivers in São Paulo get used to the traffic and they just don't go."

Not going isn't Bia's problem. Ana Beatriz Figueiredo (pronounced Fee-gay-REE-do, though in Brazil she's just getting famous enough to be known by her nickname, like Pelé or Ronaldinho) is currently on a mission to become not merely the most successful female Formula One driver but the first female Formula One world champion. In the process, she hopes to bring back the era of great Brazilian drivers that ended with the fiery and martyr-like death of the greatest of all, Ayrton Senna, on an Italian racetrack in 1994. Among its participants and fans, Formula One — or Grand Prix racing, as it is also known — is considered the fastest, most difficult, and most technologically sophisticated of all motor sports. This is not stock-car racing, or drag-racing, or even Indy. The engineering marvels that are Formula One cars are painstakingly built and can cost in the millions. The track is not the conventional oval that many associate with car racing, but a winding, varied course; in Monaco, it runs through city streets.

So far, Bia has done well, advancing through the various levels of car racing with something that looks like ease. She was named Rookie of the Year for the Brazilian Formula Renault series in 2003, and in 2005 became the first woman to win a Formula Renault race in South America. (In Formula Renault, the cars are not custom-made, as they are in Formula One, and reach top speeds of about 150 miles per hour. Formula One cars can hit 200 miles per hour and higher.) In 2006 she moved up to the faster cars of Formula Three, which reach speeds of 170 miles per hour, and she is currently ranked fourth in South America in that category. Bia's fans have set up an adoring website, which is available in both Portuguese and English (www.torcidabiafigueiredo.com.br). She has major sponsors — not just Puma, but guy-guy companies, like Bardhal, which makes auto products — and has been compared favorably with Danica Patrick, who finished fourth at Indy last year and is the first woman ever to have led that race. Currently, Bia's manager is negotiating her next step, a spot on a European Formula Three team, bringing her ever closer to what she calls, with equal parts modesty and ferocity, "my objective."

Back in traffic, Bia shifts into neutral and stews. She reacts to this poky, exhaust-laden morass the way a great author might respond to the first pages of a hack novel, or a fine painter to a landscape on black velvet: it's a deeply personal affront. She falls uncharacteristically silent and then takes a sharp, fed-up breath. Glimpsing an opening, Bia stomps on the accelerator, flying onto the shoulder just long enough to get a G-force jolt before pulling into traffic again. No one, it seems, is in a bigger hurry than she is.

For those of you who have not brushed up on your Brazilian history recently, São Paulo is one of the biggest cities in the world and, not coincidentally, is the center of Brazil's auto industry as well as its auto racing. That São Paulo is a city of strivers is obvious not just from its tony restaurant culture but from its aggressive skyline and carefree pollution. From Bia's descriptions of the rich in Brazil and from stories that described her as middle-class, I somehow imagined that she had come from a family of high school teachers or salesclerks, a notion I am quickly disabused of when she takes me to her home.

On the way there, the road begins to open up, and she does too. Bia has a laugh that is deliriously gay, and she has that Brazilian warmth that is like the morning sun — sweet and soft. She has a way of saying "Yes" in response to queries that is simultaneously definitive and encouraging. She is pretty, but in a Katie Holmes way, not a Nicole Kidman way, which means she is approachable. And she is not at all — or not yet — jaded. Listening to Nelly Furtado's latest hit, she asks what the word "promiscuous" means, and looks a little squeamish at the answer, and when I tell her why "condoms" is not the best shortened form of "condominiums," she looks abashed.

We speed past clumps of luxury high-rises adjacent to the infamous Brazilian slums known as *favelas*. As the city falls away, more *favelas* squat between gated communities, one of which is Bia's. The neighborhood looks like a jungle version of Bel Air, with large, well-landscaped homes twining up a hill paved with brick streets. The Figueiredo house is a whitewashed, two-story contemporary with a balcony overlooking an expansive swimming pool. A uniformed servant is in attendance. Bia's father is a noted psychiatrist with a specialty in drug and alcohol rehabilitation, and her mother is an oral surgeon. In other words, if soccer is the game of the masses in Brazil, auto racing remains, as always, the province of the wealthy and sophisticated. Since Henry Ford built a plant in Brazil in the 1920s, the car has been synonymous with the country's global ambitions. Brazilian Grand Prix champions showed the world that their country could compete on an international scale, not just by winning races but also by handling cars that were so technologically advanced.

The most renowned Brazilian driver was the handsome, charismatic Senna, who, twelve years after his death, still holds the third-highest number of victories in Formula One history. Senna possessed not only great courage but also tremendous grace and style, qualities that are revered by his countrymen and that he displayed both on and off the track. The loss of Senna still haunts Brazil, most particularly São Paulo, and the hopeful, nostalgic search for a replacement continues to this day. It is therefore not surprising that Bia keeps a photo of Senna tucked under the glass of her bedside table, and that her fervent fan club sees in her the stirrings of opportunity. As the site's founders, Larissa and Cinthia Leite, wrote me giddily in an e-mail: "We met Bia 2004, May, 10 years after that sad May of 1994 and Bia was in #10 car. We felt something unique coming from that car, a wish to do the best, to go beyond of limits. . . . Like something wished tell us . . . that feeling . . . is back!"

That feeling certainly dominates the Figueiredo household. "Our life now is racing," Bia's mother, Marcia, says with a shrug, though she doesn't frequent the races. ("She'd make everyone too nervous," cracks Bia's older sister, Ana Luiza, who also lives at home.) Marcia is warm, with a crinkly, eager smile. Bia's father, Jorge, is the somber one, his sense of humor best described as parched. When I ask what school of psychiatry he favors, he fixes me with a level gaze and answers, "Jorge Figueiredo." But when he has the chance to talk about Bia's accomplishments he becomes more animated.

The Figueiredos raised their girls the modern way: both went to exclusive schools, both studied English in the United States as exchange students, both were raised, in the great democratic tradition, to believe they could be anything and anyone they wanted to be. Today, there are plenty of pictures around the house of Ana Luiza — "the intellectual," according to Bia — and her parents are clearly happy with her ebullient beauty, her success in her chosen career (tourism), and the boyfriend who, baseball cap reversed on his head, seems to have become part of the family. On the other hand, Jorge has at least twelve photo albums devoted to his younger daughter. Showing me shots of Bia's victories, Jorge points out that she refused to accept her trophies from bikini-clad babes, like the boys, but instead asked a family friend to do the honors.

The Figueiredos also have the video equivalent of a highlight reel, which we watch from a plush, burnt-orange couch in which all the seats recline. We see Bia as a child, racing around in her hot-pink go-cart at upwards of sixty miles per hour. As she grows, she progresses to bigger, faster rockets on wheels. Older Bia watches appraisingly as younger Bia speeds around the tracks, blocking off drivers, overtaking them, and even crashing. (We all observe calmly as, onscreen, her demolished car is lifted by crane onto the back of an eighteen-wheeler after Bia hit a wall and spun out. When I ask whether she had been frightened, she shakes her head dismissively.)

The most instructive clips, however, are Bia's post-race interviews from when she was eight or so. She told me that she was shy when she spoke to the inevitably bemused local TV reporters, but in fact she seems remarkably self-possessed. Her fingernails are already black with grease, and she seldom displays a child's eager smile or willingness to please. Instead, she thinks about her answers carefully before giving them up:

Was she scared of crashing? "No."

Did she play with dolls? "Yes."

Did she have a boyfriend? Of course not.

Asked about Senna's death, Bia bows her head and seems, just for a moment, to leave the premises. She finally responds somberly, which causes her sister, translating from the couch, to erupt with laughter. "She says, 'Life goes on,'" Ana Luiza explains, and it is sort of a crackup, watching this child wax wise, though her father has told me that the only time he has seen Bia cry was, in fact, when Senna died.

What does Bia think about when racing? the reporter onscreen persists. The little girl looks at him steadily. "You can't step on the brake," she says. "You have to go on."

"Bia grew up at Interlagos," her mother tells me, and this is not an understatement. The fabled racetrack, located between two reservoirs on what was once the outskirts of town, now sits surrounded by a large *favela*. Bia takes me in through a back entrance, near a newsstand crammed with racing magazines that carry news of the announced retirement of seven-time Formula One world champion Michael Schumacher. We stand in a sun-bleached parking lot between what are actually two courses. To our right is the sprawling track officially known, since 1985, as the José Carlos Pace Autodrome, named for the Brazilian Formula One driver who died in a plane crash. Aficionados still call the place by its old name, however, which dates back to when the track opened in the 1940s. Next door is the far smaller go-cart track named after Ayrton Senna, where Bia demanded to be taken at age six. (Her father made her wait until she was seven before she could get behind the wheel.) "This is where I started," she says. It is worth noting that the go-cart track here — or "go-go cart," as Bia calls it, with typical acceleration — is nothing like the homey, litigation-proof sites rented for kiddie parties in the United States. Instead, it is a fast, grueling training ground for racecar drivers, or pilots, as they are more aptly called. All the Brazilian champions got their start in carting, which partly explains Bia's early attraction to the place. She loved the speed, the noise, and the crashes, but she also knew, from a young age, that to accomplish her goal of becoming a Formula One driver she would first have to master this miniature version of the sport.

Bia strides to a nondescript building between the track and the street and raps on a heavy metal door. It is opened by an inordinately fit older man with a haunting, gleaming smile. Naylor Borigis de Campos, who goes by the name Nô, is one of the most famous cart trainers in Brazil, known for his uncanny ability to spot and nurture talent. He has worked with many of the country's best drivers, even loosely with Senna, whose picture appears among those of Bia and many others lining his office walls. A collection of brightly colored helmets — gifts from grateful drivers — graces another wall. Sitting down on a weary black leather couch, Nô grins and takes a faded Brazilian identification card out of his wallet and shows it to me: it is Bia at eight, her tiny thumbprint and name in perfect script beneath her picture. Nô has carried this card with him for the last eleven years.

It is entirely likely that much of Bia's career would not have happened without Nô, and that his, too, would have ended long ago without her. Their intertwined stories make for one that the Life-time network might reject as too implausible: when Nô was the age of Bia in her ID photo, he came to São Paulo from Bahia with his desperately impoverished family, which included nine siblings. Opportunity in São Paulo proved to be scarce, however, and the family left. But Nô chose to stay on, cleaning public bathrooms by day and sleeping in them at night. School was out of the question — he hasn't had any formal education — but he had a gift for mechanical things, and eventually taught himself to work on cars. Like many from the *favelas*, he was drawn to Interlagos.

Then, in 1995, one of Nô's protégés, a gifted driver named Marco Campos, died in a racing accident in France. Nô had also recently lost his wife and, deeply depressed, was thinking of giving up his career entirely. But one day — cue the music — he saw a dark-haired, determined little girl racing around the go-cart track. (Nô had already tried to train a few other girls, with no success.) "When he saw me," Bia says, translating from Nô's heart-tapping, hand–clasping, heaven-peering Portuguese monologue, "he thought, 'It's her.' He had energy again. He thought he could start again."

Nô guided Bia toward a fifth-place finish in the Brazilian carting championship when she was ten, and over the next few years, she almost always ranked in the top five in that event. At sixteen Bia graduated to Formula A (a faster cart on a faster track for older kids) and for two years running won the Gold Helmet Award for the Best Brazilian Cart Driver. (She was also, incidentally, the first female to win Formula A races in Brazil.) In 2003 she came in second in the Petrobras Cart Selective, a prestigious South American competition.

What Nô has done for Bia is both tangible and intangible. Yes, he is her mentor. Yes, he found the right man to repair the engines on her cars, and, yes, he drew upon his myriad contacts to find her the right manager (the well-known and well-regarded former racer André Ribeiro) and the right racing team (Cesário Fórmula, owned by Augusto Cesário, also a former racer). But Nô also makes sure, on a daily basis, that Bia faces the world — their chosen, shared world — with resolve and focus. Over time, he has grafted his natural asceticism onto Bia's instinctive determination: "You have to focus 95 percent on racing, 3 percent on school, and 2 percent on family," he has told her.

It's obvious that this collaboration makes a statement that transcends racing. It is nothing new in Brazil that the drivers are white and privileged, while those who work in the pit have darker skin and started with little, if anything. It's one of the few ways for people of limited means to escape Brazil's pervasive poverty. But in this case, an older man (Nô is fifty-seven) and a younger woman work together as equals, something that has not always been easy for Brazilians to accept. That Nô loves Bia like a daughter is clear — he keeps her generous gifts and old uniforms locked away in his luxury high-rise — and it is hard not to wonder what might happen to him when and if the time comes for them to part. That time may not be so far away, given that Bia's manager thinks she should move next year to a European Formula Three team, possibly Cesário's British squad, the next step on her path to Formula One. "All these manufacturers have a specific plan for young drivers," Ribeiro tells me, and those plans don't necessarily include a go-cart guru, no matter how gifted he is.

The next day, Bia and Nô take me to the place she calls "the Team," a gigantic auto mart on the outskirts of town where, in a sprawling garage, the car she races for Cesário Fórmula is housed. The place smells thickly of oil and is as spotless as a surgical ward. About half a dozen cars are parked inside, each worth hundreds of thousands of dollars, painted bright primary colors and stickered with sponsors' logos. They look malevolent — long and narrow, needle-nosed with just a sliver of a windshield — and settling into the driver's seat is not unlike nestling into a coffin. The steering wheel is about the size of a salad plate, and there are two tiny sideview mirrors with which to scan for gaining cars. On what would be the left door of Bia's car (if there were a door) is pasted a small map of the first track she will race in the upcoming fall season. It's color-coded to show her the best places to accelerate, slow down, and take a curve. Bia has already begun to study her strategy, even though this race, in Buenos Aires, is still about two months away. She will also eventually walk the track, committing trouble spots to memory so that her moves during competition will be almost automatic. Just before the race, she, like all competitors, will be allowed two runs that will establish her starting position.

Even when she isn't staring down a race date, Bia works out almost daily with her longtime trainer, Fernando Conceição. Racing is one of the few sports where the strength difference between men and women is not really a factor in determining victory. Still, Bia needs endurance to withstand the G-forces of driving forty minutes straight in a Formula Three race, and she needs to keep her arms, neck, and shoulders strong to avoid the tendinitis that can develop from steering and shifting. Otherwise, it's pretty much reflexes, strategic ability, and mind-set that will determine the difference between victory and defeat — assuming, of course, that the pit crew and car do their part too.

There are currently two drivers each on Cesário's South American Formula Renault and Formula Three teams, and a staff of about sixteen engineers and mechanics. (The men's room at the garage is, understandably, much bigger than the ladies' since the only other female I see working here is a secretary.) They all wear spotless Cesário Fórmula T-shirts and jeans, and some of them are handsome enough to be featured in a "Boys of Interlagos" calendar. Bia doesn't socialize with the other drivers — "There's a lot of jealousy, so it's hard," she says. Instead, the crew serves as her office colleagues. One of them, clowning around, snaps the black steering wheel cover from Bia's car and wears it on his head like a shower cap.

When Bia steps into her yellow-and-black racing uniform, with its fireproof quilting and sponsor patches (Bardhal, Puma, Samsung, and others), nobody is tempted to whistle. "No one knows what sex you are when you are in uniform," she has said, and she's right. She looks like a slightly more feminine version of the Michelin Man, her buoyant walk subdued by all the padding into a slew-footed waddle. At her waist Bia wears a belt with "A+" embroidered next to her name. I think it's a ranking and then realize it's her blood type. In case of fire, she tells me, she has exactly five seconds to get out of her car.

Nô watches Bia's transformation from a distance, arms folded, a slight look of anxiety clouding his face. "Should I stick with her?" he asks me, out of the blue, resuming another round of heartfelt pantomime. "What do you think? Would that be the right thing to do?"

I shake my head and ask him to repeat the question.

"'Yes.' You should say, 'Yes,'" one of the mechanics interjects.

Nô, it seems, is already preparing himself and Bia for the next stage of her career, whichever way it goes.

*

In both the Brazilian and European press, most of the stories focus on Bia's difficulties as a woman in a man's game. She is constantly asked whether she thinks men are stronger, smarter, and faster, and even at this early stage in her career, she has her stock answers. (They would be "No," "No," and "No," sometimes with the added comment that she wants to "thump the next guy" as much as anyone.) It's also true that every man racing against Bia wants to thump her. "They cannot accept losing to a girl," her manager, André Ribeiro, says. There is another school of thought, however, that suggests being a woman is a major advantage these days, owing to the current state of Formula One racing. The fact that Michael Schumacher was such a consistent victor actually eroded enthusiasm for the sport over time. Many hope that a new face, particularly a female face, might reignite interest in Formula One, just as Danica Patrick has brought new life to Indy car racing. (Indy's sagging television ratings soared in 2005, thanks largely to her participation.) Lots of people follow racing only casually, Ribeiro says, so they need someone who stands out.

"You have twenty guys and her [to root for]. Everyone picks her."

Which explains, on many levels, Bia's visit to the salon of Wanderley Nunes, close personal friend of the Brazilian supermodel Gisele Bundchen and the country's answer to Frédéric Fekkai. There are attendants in sparkling white uniforms, and clients with more than a passing knowledge of cosmetic surgery. Nunes himself wears a black button-down and black slacks, his hair in a tangle of blond highlights. He has an air of irrepressibility faintly evocative of Santa Claus. Bia greets him lavishly, which is fitting because Nunes not only does her hair but is also one of her sponsors. She wears the "W" logo for his salon on her uniform, just above her heart. The public couldn't care less about Michael Schumacher's coiffure; not so when it comes to Bia Figueiredo, who is here for a cut and blow-dry. Brazil may be ready for a woman racecar driver, but she has to be a particular kind of woman. "In today's world, motor sports is a business," Ribeiro says. "You need people who represent the sponsors in a nice way. Bia is feminine in a masculine environment."

This obligation is true not only with fans but, more importantly, with sponsors, who help defray the costs of putting Bia on the track. Car maintenance and race fees can amount to almost $400,000 a year, and Bia earns nothing: no salary from the team, nothing from endorsements. She won't make money unless she gets to Formula One. Bia's sponsors currently cover about 40 percent of her racing costs; Cesário makes up the rest. Her parents are paying all her living expenses. "This is a thing that really worries me," she says, "because if I weren't a driver I would have been working since I was twenty and making money on some other thing. I try to forget this and think that this is my career, and one day I will make money from it. I really trust in it, and my parents support me."

There are other pressures. Specifically, the passing of time: Ribeiro believes Bia has only three more years to make her mark — "Maximum," he says. "It's very difficult. You don't have time to do something parallel. It's a very short period of time." Therefore, instead of a good college, to which she would have surely gained admission, Bia goes to the local community college. She doesn't go to parties or even hang out much with friends. "I don't have time," she says. Her behavior in public must be above reproach: no one wants her to become a tabloid heroine, and no one wants her appearing, like Danica Patrick, in stiletto boots and a bustier in the magazine *FHM*. In fact, Cesário has warned her never to appear at the racetrack like the guys do, with the tops of their uniforms unzipped and their T-shirts exposed. When Bia and her boyfriend of three years broke up, there was great relief among her management. "We drove together," she says, with more than a small trace of nostalgia. "He was a great guy." Subsequently, Ribeiro asked her to stop dating altogether. "The guys can have one night with a girl. They think a woman can't do that," Bia says, shaking her head in disgust. She says she wants to get married and have children, but figures that can wait until her thirties.

Has it been worth it? I ask as we drive home from the salon. We are on an empty stretch of highway, damp from a recent rain, and she has moved her speed from forty to sixty to eighty kilometers per hour. Does she miss having a normal life?

Bia shakes her head and wrinkles her nose, and doesn't even flinch when a motorcyclist in front of us falters slightly before recovering on the uneven pavement. "No," she says. "No way. I have won a lot of maturity. For twenty-one, I am very old in a lot of ways, and a lot of people respect that. I have my life, and I have my objectives."

The road curls sharply, and she accelerates into it. "I love this curve," she says.

IAN FRAZIER

Snook

FROM THE NEW YORKER

Wasn't sure from the opening sentence (warning sign: the word "tangent") where this one was going, but Ian Frazier could write about anything . . . snook? . . . and make it fascinating.
— D.M.

WHEN I WAS IN high school in Hudson, Ohio, I had a neighbor named Pete Snook. The Snooks lived one street over from us, and our backyards met on a tangent, in a brushy, unlandscaped area of the kind you don't see much today. I made a path through it in the mornings walking to Pete's house so he could drive me to school. He drove a Volkswagen that had no trash on the floor and never broke down. I believe it was his own. Pete was a serious, straightforward, imperturbable guy with a wiry figure and short dark hair and dark eyes. He acted older than the rest of us, like a grownup consigned for a certain number of years to the body of a teenager. He was a grade ahead of me, and, aside from the trips to and from school, we didn't hang out together, but I admired his style.

One morning we got to school and were standing near our lockers by a hallway intersection in the main building during the bustle of kids coming and going before class. A younger kid stopped and ragged Pete. The kid was a wiseacre, funny and smart with a big mouth, though not a bad guy. As he was running on, he made a remark about a girl in town. Pete said something back to him, and the kid followed up his first remark with another. All at once, Pete turned and took the kid by the lapels — ours was a boys' school, we had to wear jackets and ties — and lifted him with a quick thrust of his forearms against the wall. With an expression of intense seriousness, he told the kid never to say anything like that again. I remember the poor kid's mouth open so wide he had several double chins, and the wideness of his eyes. He said he was just joking, sorry, don't get carried away — what a person in that situation usually says. Snook then set him back on the floor, and we went on with our day.

The incident passed by in a second and had no consequences that I know of. I never heard it referred to afterward. But it has stayed with me, I'm not sure why. For a blink, I glimpsed through an everyday surface to the machinery working inside. Also, I would have given a lot to be able to make such a move. At sixteen and seventeen, I wanted desperately to be tough. I used to practice my toughness in front of a mirror: "I'm gonna hit you so hard it'll put your entire *family* in the hospital!" Even given the latitude of fantasy, the effect was laughable. I could not figure out how Snook had pulled it off. Now I think the secret was, first, that he had right on his side, and, second, that his purpose was as much instructional as it was threatening: cheesy comments, especially about girls, have an unpredictable aspect that can call down a thunderbolt. Mostly what I'm remembering, I guess, was a moment of real and instant justice, a rarity in the world.

I think I also admired Snook simply for his name. My grandmother lived in Florida, and when I visited her I fished, dreamily and unskillfully, and, among the many kinds of fish I never caught but wanted to, number one was the snook. I read about snook in sporting magazines, saw them mounted on the walls of tackle shops and restaurants, and thought they were cool. The snook is an elegantly constructed fish. It's narrow, but not too — not snaky like a pike or a barracuda — nor does it grow to be chunky like its distant relative the bass. The snook's shape is close to the platonic ideal for a fish, in my opinion. The slight concavity of its upper jaw gives it a racy, rakish profile. A narrow, ruler-straight line the color of tattoo ink runs along its side, which is an understated silvery-white. The snook does not have the pointy teeth that make similar predatory fish look forbidding and comical, the implication being that it hunts so well it doesn't need them.

Snook live in tropical and near-tropical places. They're an oceanic fish, but they also like brackish water inland — coastal rivers and mangrove swamps subject to big fluctuations of tide. A snook finds a good place in a dark pool beneath some mangrove roots and waits, and when prey comes within range he strikes swiftly and with authority. He moves seaward, occupying new ambuscades, as the tide recedes.

For years I never got a good look at a snook in the flesh, or in the fish. At a New Year's Eve party in Key West, I recall people drinking on a pier, dock lights overhead, baitfish gathering underneath in the light, and suddenly a big fish scything through the bait, strewing them around in splashes as they tried to escape. We looked over the edge and watched. Someone said it was a snook. I was still deciding whether to run to my grandmother's and get my fishing rod when the predator vanished and the commotion died down. Another time, I was on a bottom-fishing boat when the mate yelled for everybody to come to the bow and cast to a school of snook chasing mullet. Again, in half a minute they were gone.

But if you love fish, and keep watching for them, every so often fate grants you a vision. One spring, I hitchhiked north from Key West along the Overseas Highway, headed eventually for New York City. (I have written about this trip before, but not this part.) On one of the middle Keys, I got a ride from a young guy from Kentucky with a bushy beard and dark-rimmed glasses. The Kentuckian said he had come down to the Keys to take a look at a sailboat he wanted to buy. He said that if I didn't mind riding around with him while he searched for the sailboat, and didn't mind waiting while he examined it and talked to the owner, he would then give me a ride some hundreds of miles north to the Florida town where he lived. I said okay.

This Kentuckian was a troubled soul. He had quit the Kentucky National Guard because he had been upset by the shootings of students at Kent State University by the Ohio National Guard a few years before. The Kentuckian had friends in the Ohio National Guard, and could not understand how any Guardsmen could have acted as the ones at Kent State did. He thought perhaps they had been framed, or hadn't known their ammo was live, or something. He kept turning this painful puzzle over in his mind. Now he had decided he wanted to live on a sailboat for a while. As he talked, he followed some handwritten directions he had. They led to a turnoff from U.S. Highway 1 onto a white marl road that went among encroaching mangroves and ended at a neat little development by a canal. Each pastel-colored one-story house sat back among palmettos and poinciana trees, and next to each house was a slip big enough for a good-sized boat. We found the house, got out, and walked down to the single-masted sailboat tied up alongside.

A bright sun shone from almost straight overhead. The sailboat floated in the clear water; extending below it to the sandy bottom was its precise, hull-shaped shadow. I looked more closely. In the middle of the shadow, between the boat and the bottom, finning almost imperceptibly, was a snook. My idling, time-killing mood stopped as if I'd just tromped on the brakes. A snook! Twenty-five feet away! With a snookish sense of aesthetics, the fish made a symmetrical third among the images of sailboat and shadow. He had even positioned himself facing the same direction as the boat's bow. The way he was holding there, you could have easily missed him, so boldly did he mimic boat and shadow, hiding motionless in plain sight.

In the other shadows — of the pilings, of the dock — baitfish flickered. Soon one would forget the snook was there and wander into the boat's inviting shade, and — *pow!* I could have watched all day. But the word had just got out, apparently. In a minute along the dock came a skinny, darkly tanned man with kinky blond hair. In one hand he carried a plastic bucket of water with half a dozen live shrimp, in the other a spinning rod. He plucked a highly unwilling shrimp from the bucket, hooked it just once through the shell behind the head, gauged the distance, and flipped the shrimp under the boat. The shrimp, knowing what he was in for, shot backward and downward for the sand at maximum speed. The snook hit him before he'd gone two feet.

With a jerk the hook was set, and there followed the wildest close-quarters angling battle I'd ever seen. The snook dove this way and that around the boat's keel, veered for the pilings, jumped, thwapped his tail against the boat, splashed, cartwheeled, all as if right before us in a bathtub. The angler had foreseen the street fight. His line was extra-stout, his hook strong. Soon he had the fish up on the dock and was pushing a stringer through his gills. Before he carted him off for supper, he let me marvel at the trophy lying there gasping on the planking. The older guy I am now wishes the snook had been left alone in his ingenious lie. But the young guy I was then had really wanted to see what would happen, and stare close up, and touch the wonder with his hand.

As the Kentuckian and I drove off, I kept talking about the snook. I said that I loved fish and fishing, and I also mentioned that

I had always wanted an aquarium but had never taken the trouble to provide myself with one. At this, the Kentuckian looked at me sternly through his glasses' dark rims. "You've always wanted an aquarium? And yet you never went out and bought yourself one?" He paused to let the weight of my negligence sink in. "You should be horsewhipped!" he pronounced.

I did go to New York City on that trip. There I got a job, found an apartment, and for a while didn't travel to much of anywhere. In the city, I missed the rest of the country, especially the Midwest; I wanted to go fishing again in unfabulous places far from anybody. My friend Don was working in Chicago and also eager to escape. He told me he had heard about a northern Michigan river called the Pigeon that was supposed to have good fly-fishing for brown trout. Late one May, I flew out to Chicago and met him, and we drove seven hours north to give the Pigeon a try.

Midwestern trout streams tend to get less press than the free-stone rivers of the East and the Rockies. Midwestern rivers are slower, swampier, muddier, grassier; they often have tunnel-effect overhanging trees and fewer opportunities for long, photogenic back casts. The riverbeds are more likely to be clay or sand, ideal for burrowing mayfly nymphs that hatch into big winged insects like the brown drake or the *Hexagenia limbata,* perfect food for big trout. There's a humming, humid lushness to nighttime trout fishing in the Midwest (the big insects often stay on the water until late at night) that fills the senses and staggers you back on your heels.

Don and I knew nothing about the Pigeon. When to fish it, with what kind of flies, imitating what kind of bugs — those key details remained a mystery. We pitched Don's tent at a state-forest campsite on the riverbank, and immediately action started popping everywhere. The big mayflies were hatching, the trout were jumping and feeding and stuffing themselves, so that it made even us hungry. We tried every fly in our tackle boxes. We changed leader size, found different stretches of river to fish, cast endlessly, endlessly. Not one fish, not one strike. This happened day after day while our bafflement assumed gigantic proportions.

About two miles from camp, the river curved against a clay cliff maybe twenty feet high. Just downstream from it, the current ran close to the bank in a deep and slow stretch lined by tag-alder bushes. Fish took up feeding positions here one beside the next, so that a cast to the first fish would also float the fly over four or five more after him. One evening, I was fishing this stream while Don, upstream, cast to the opposite bank. I kept dropping the fly right in the middle of the bull's-eye left by the lead fish's rise form. Not only didn't he strike; he nimbly picked real insects from the surface an inch or two to the right or left of my artificial, and then his companions downstream did the same. I began to cast frantically in the craven hope that I might snag one of the fish by accident. In mid-cast I looked up and saw a man watching from atop the cliff.

In certain moods, I hate running into other anglers on the stream, so I quickly looked away, following with fake concentration the progress of my despised fly. Had I examined the man more closely, I would have seen a master fly-fisherman, in scuffed waders and flop hat, smoking a stubby cigar to discourage mosquitoes. He asked how I was doing, and I said something surly, not looking up. He stood a bit longer, then wished us a cheerful good-bye and good luck, and disappeared.

We returned to camp in the dark — wet, fishless, and bummed. The next morning, we decided that we had to find a tackle shop at all costs and ask somebody, anybody, what was going on. Fly-fishing had not become so popular then. In the hardware stores and sporting goods stores we searched out in little towns, nobody knew about trout flies. Finally, at a phone booth in Vanderbilt, Michigan, we found a yellow pages that showed a more promising tackle store in Gaylord, nine miles away. We drove over, parked in front, went in. Standing behind the counter was the man I'd seen on the cliff the night before. "You should've been using an Adams, size twelve," he said, even before "Hello." "I had some I could've given you. After I saw you I caught a couple twenty-two-inch browns, and a brookie seventeen inches long."

The reason I mention this man is that his name was (and is) Fred Snook. In later years, Don and I fished with him, met his wife and kids, had dinner at his house. With Fred, the affinity between last name and fish had become explicit: Fred owned the Alphorn Shop, a sporting goods store stocked with all kinds of fishing equipment, especially fly-fishing gear and highly effective local trout flies tied by Fred. (As you go through life, by the way, you will find surprisingly often that people take up professions suggested by their last names. When I began to write that sentence, I thought many examples would come to mind, but now the only one I can think of is my former optician in New York City, Dr. Morton Blinder.)

Fred Snook was the first truly gifted angler I ever fished with. He took us out on local waters — the Sturgeon River, as well as the Pigeon — and showed us how he fished in heavy brush. Fred could put a dry fly in a saucer-size hole among a confusion of branches and twigs where even visualizing the cast seemed to call for trigonometry and string theory. When the only open airspace around him was directly overhead, Fred could make his back cast go straight up. You wondered how Fred himself ventured through some of the places he fished, like you wonder when a buck with big antlers comes out of a dense thicket. He had an otherworldly facility for not getting person or gear tangled, and he always found a quick out when, rarely, he did.

From Fred I learned that if your fly snags on something, under water or above, you mustn't bow the rod and yank and cuss, but (if possible) pull the line through the line guides and reach the rod tip to the fly until it's right on it. Some jiggling around then often pops the hook free. Once when we'd been fishing the Sturgeon and Fred was almost late to attend one of his kids' school plays, he humped double time through swamp brush and pine trees as thick as dog hair while Don and I, twenty years younger than he, straggled far behind. I absorbed a lesson there too — about always fishing to the limit, but not making your family mad.

Fishing, of course, is faith. You have to focus on each cast as if it were the very one that is going to produce the fish of your dreams. In fact, on almost every cast nothing happens. Maintaining faith through blankness repeated hundreds of times is the sport's essential discipline. In my case, I tried to put the fly in the exact spot I thought a fish would be and, when I received the usual nothing in return, often I lost interest and sulked. "You gave up on it! Stay with it!" Fred said whenever he saw me do that. He always fished out each cast and gave each little piece of water his hopeful attention. I saw him get huge strikes when his fly was on slack current a few feet from the tip of his fly rod. Because he often hooked fish close in, where the shock was heavy and sudden, he checked the end of his leader after every few casts to make sure nothing had frayed it. Meticulous care was his liturgy. He waded dextrously, watched an expanse of good water for a few minutes before he fished it, stayed calm when he saw a big fish. One of the sharpest underwater vis-

tas I recall is of Fred's weighted pink-salmon-egg fly — a pattern
called the Thor — about three feet below the surface of the pew-
ter-tinted, perfectly clear Sturgeon, skirting shaggy tree roots and
the tangled branches of drowned logs on a controlled path as neat
as if cut with an Exacto knife.

But this is a story about snook as well as Snook, so it now returns,
circuitously, to Florida.

Years later, I was married and living in Brooklyn with my wife and
our two young children. She was planning our spring vacation. For
sentimental reasons involving the city of Sarasota and a pay telephone (in earlier times she and I had split up; I had moved from
New York to Montana, she had gone to Florida; her apartment in
Sarasota had no phone; one day out of the blue she called me from
a pay phone on the street; I was sitting in my cabin in the woods
forty miles from Kalispell; we talked; when her coins ran out I wrote
the pay phone's number on the wall and called her back; before
hanging up we agreed in principle to get back together; the next
evening I was feeling happy about that and wanted to give her a
call; the only number I had was of the pay phone; as it happened,
she and her sister at that moment were walking back to the apartment from a bar; their route happened to go by the pay phone; as
they passed they heard it ringing; when she picked up on the
fourth ring, I was not particularly surprised; and so on), we chose
Florida for our first long vacation with the children.

We flew to Orlando, spent a few days at Disney World, and then
went to Sarasota, where we showed the children the pay phone.
They were perhaps more impressed with it than they let on, or not.
From there we drove down the Gulf Coast to the small town of
Everglades City. My wife had included it for my benefit because a
guidebook said that it had good fishing. Not since I was a kid had I
seen anyplace in Florida I liked so much. The town reminded me
of the pre-modern, unfancy Florida I used to visit with my grandmother. As soon as we arrived, I set about to hire a fishing guide
and catch some snook.

Later, it turned out that the guide I'd found was a semi-famous
tarpon angler. He assured me he could put me on to lots of snook,
but somehow every place we went, every time we turned around,
we met another pod of tarpon. I ended up catching two tarpon, including one of about five feet, the biggest fish I'd ever caught of

any kind. Tarpon have big scales and a lower jaw that's overshot, like a bulldog's. In that flat coastal landscape — tidal river, mangrove islands, horizon — the giant I hooked was a sudden stroke of verticality, leaping and splashing and spinning like a waterspout touched down. Tarpon are noble and bilingual fish that make long migratory journeys between the American coast and Mexico and back again. I liked watching them cruise by two or three abreast in the shallow bays and then continue into the far distance, the long front spines of their dorsal fins tracking above the surface like whip antennas. After such a successful day, to mention that I'd really been hoping for a snook would have seemed small.

Then, last spring, I got another chance to go to Everglades City. I was writing a short article for *Architectural Digest* about the Rod & Gun Club, a venerable motel where we'd stayed. This time when seeking a guide, I asked around for one with credentials for snook (which people there pronounce to rhyme with "fluke"). The name several people gave me was Don McKinney. At seven on a Saturday morning, I was driving down gravel roads in the neighboring town of Chokoloskee looking for the place where I was supposed to meet him. A guy came riding by on a wide-tire bicycle holding an unwieldy bouquet of fishing rods in one hand. Barely glancing over, he guessed who I was and waved with the rods for me to follow him.

"This boat ain't as fancy as some," Don McKinney said as we climbed down into it from the dock where he keeps it, behind a friend's trailer home. Indeed, the craft suggested a piece of fiberglass stamped into boat shape from a blank with a single blow. A Pollockish decorating scheme of random paint spatters had worn off all its surfaces but the vertical ones. Don McKinney stowed the gear and then unfastened a long fiberglass pole from the gunwale and began to pole us out of the canal, grounding now and then in muck because of the low tide. On the bank, a neighbor stood and jawed with him awhile as we inched around embedded hurricane debris. "I caught a twelve-pound jewfish right under that piece of roof last week," he told the neighbor, pointing to a rusted rectangle of corrugated metal we had just passed. The neighbor asked if he had kept the jewfish, and Don McKinney said, "No-o-o-o, I did not. I don't know who this guy sitting here might be" (pointing at me).

"You ain't allowed to keep jewfish anymore, anywhere in the state of Florida," he explained once we'd left the neighbor behind.

"They're an endangered fish, so you gotta let 'em go, big and little. You're not supposed to call 'em jewfish no more neither. Their new name is the Goliath grouper. I don't want to offend nobody, so I try to remember. But I'm sixty years old and I been callin' 'em jewfish all my life, and I imagine I'll continue to."

Poling steadily, Don McKinney took us past the waterfront of Chokoloskee. The whole place still seemed to be wincing from the last hurricane. The sky-high Washington palms leaned away from the water as if the huge fist out there were still raised. At their frazzled tops, a few thin fronds dangled. Many houses in Chokoloskee had bright-blue tarpaulins on all or part of their roofs where the shingles had blown off. A houseboat sat awkwardly on the shore, tilted sideways on its port pontoon. Most of the dock pilings towered thirty feet or more in the air, mud marks up three-quarters of their length; the hurricane waves had hammered on the dock boards from below, driving the pilings up out of the mud and eventually knocking most of the boards away. Now the pilings were of a height from which you could step onto a midsized naval vessel. Don McKinney said that insurance won't pay for fixing docks, so people aren't sure what they'll do.

Once we had enough draft, he let down the engine and we roared across one reach and then another, heading inland, until we turned into the mouth of a tidal river and swooped up it like *Apocalypse Now.* As the river narrowed we slowed, the boat rocking on its own wake, and then coasted into a quiet intersection where this river met a smaller one. We eased next to the mangroves on our left, and Don McKinney shoved the pole among them into the muck and tied us to it. Mangroves enclosed us, their thicket of flying-buttress roots chuckling softly in the falling tide. He took out a cigar and lit it using a Zippo lighter emblazoned with a leaping fish in gold — a present from a high-ranking executive at Zippo for whom he sometimes guides. With that he seemed to complete himself, finally. Don McKinney has pale-blue eyes and a long, shrewd face that a cigar seamlessly becomes part of.

He began telling me just where in this particular intersection a snook might lie. Beneath that crotch of old tree trunk, veined like bridge cable; next to that stump; or right over there, against that far bank, where the water looks deep and dark and likely. When the perturbation of our arrival quieted down, the surface became glass-still again. The spot he indicated, pointing to it now with the tip of his bait-casting rod, reflected the mangroves above it, their shiny green oval leaves with here and there a yellow one, and a few white, dead branches corkscrewing out, and on the branches several air plants, a lovely parasite that grows on dead wood and resembles the top of a pineapple. Don McKinney cast his topwater plug into the heart of the likely spot, inches from the bank. He let the plug sit a moment, then gave it a twitch. At that, a snook struck with a violent swirl that twisted the surface reflection around itself like a bedsheet.

The sight caused me to become overwrought, shouting quietly and fumbling with my spinning rod. I was exaggerating my reaction, but only a little; earlier, I had heard Don McKinney say to his neighbor by the canal that he hated guiding highly experienced fishermen who make a point of how hard to impress they are. I wanted to demonstrate that I was more the overly excitable sort, as well as serious about catching a snook. After I calmed down and got a grip, I laid about three hundred casts in that intersection, back in all the mangrove-root culs-de-sac I could reach — but no go. Looking up the river, I saw a strange surface bulge coming at us. As it came even and passed, I saw below it three immense manatees. They swam by in a second about two feet down, as graceful as fat people who can really dance.

After that first excitement we fished for hour upon hour without another strike from a snook. Don McKinney said the first one hadn't been too interested either, or he would have taken the lure. Sometimes the rivers we went up became tunnels in whose ceilings the mangrove branches met, and we snapped through cross-river spiderwebs in the gloom. The heat came down and sat on us and on everything like a slab of sheet iron. Still no strikes. Nothing was going on at all. Extreme boringness in fishing has its fun side sometimes. Don McKinney sat in the boat and ate generic fig newtons and told me how much cheaper they were at Kmart than at the A&P. Then we talked about the horrible cost of health care, and the immigration problem, and how lousy country music is today.

I kept casting with a pleasant sense of pointlessness. Don McKinney changed our venue every once in a while, and smoked cigars. He buys them through the mail from a company called Thompson, in Tampa. They send the cigars and an invoice, and he mails them a check — they're a trusting company, in other words, and their cigars are number one. The only irritant in the day, kind

of welcome in its variety, arose whenever the lure I was casting became stuck in the mangroves. I had thought that Fred Snook was
the best I ever saw at getting stuck lures out, but Don McKinney can
claim even higher levels of skill. When my own pulling and wig-
gling of the line and myself did not avail, I handed the rod to Don
McKinney. His first address to the problem involved a no-hands re-
positioning of his cigar, shifting it by lip motion from one side of
his mouth to the other and reclenching hard with his teeth. Then,
after he did some jerking, flipping, wand-waving, and a bit of pizzi-
cato plucking on the line, the lure usually dropped free.

In my experience, fishing guides who've had no luck all day are
usually ready to quit by midafternoon. They know a bad day when
they see one, and at about two o'clock they write it off and move on
to the next in their minds. Thinking Don McKinney might be of
this stamp, at two-thirty I told him I was ready to accept reality here
and give up. From under the long bill of his light-blue fishing cap
he looked back at me with such reproach and disappointment that
I quickly added, "But of course I'm up for more if you are." He
started the engine, and we sidled through more mangrove passage-
ways and then into a broad river, the Lopez River. We ran down that
for five or six miles to where it widened into a bay, just before the
Gulf. Tall trees on one side of the bay partly enclosed a cove. Because they blocked the wind, the yellow-green, slightly murky water
in the cove lay flat calm. We came within casting distance of the
shore, and Don McKinney pushed his pole into the bottom and
tied us to it.

Like Fred Snook, I scoped out the water before I cast. In the middle of the cove, motionless after our wake died down, was a floating
door. We had seen hurricane debris off and on all day, but no other
doors. In fact, I couldn't recall in all my previous years of fishing
ever encountering a floating door. In this bay no other object besides us floated anywhere nearby. Somehow I enjoyed seeing a
door there, framed by the calm surface of the cove. Don McKinney
said he thought it was a door from a shed, but certain design
touches — the recessed panels in the top, middle, and bottom —
made me think it might be an interior door from a house, perhaps
a bedroom door. The late-afternoon sun hit the cove at an angle
and caused the prism of the door's shadow to descend into the water on a slant.

Of course I remembered the snook in the shadow of the sailboat thirty-odd years before. I cast my lure to the door three times, five times, twelve times. I put it just shy of the door, near the top, near the bottom, and beyond the door. I landed the plug with a rap right on the door itself, and then, carefully so as not to get hooked, pulled the plug off and swam it away. I really peppered that door. Nothing doing . . . oh, well.

I made a less careful cast past the door and to the left of it. I turned to say something to Don McKinney. Maybe pausing for that extra moment or two I let the plug sink longer than I'd been doing before. Still looking at him, I began to retrieve, and felt a jolt. He was looking at my plug. On his face I saw the joyful ignition of angling triumph. I turned back. A large and handsome snook with my plug in its mouth leaped head over tail in the air.

WILLIAM FINNEGAN

Blank Monday

FROM THE NEW YORKER

Inside the world of surfboards, and the black, dying art of blowing foam. Good-bye, Jan and Dean — and Grubby.
— D.M.

GORDON (GRUBBY) CLARK did not invent the modern surfboard. It just began to seem that way, as the decades passed and his company, Clark Foam, of Laguna Niguel, California, founded in 1961, came to dominate the production of the polyurethane-foam "blank" — the lightweight alabaster core without which there would be no modern surfboard. For many people, Clark Foam and surfboards became conceptually inseparable. Clark's monopoly was estimated, as of last year, to cover 90 percent of the American market and 60 percent of the world market. The surfing press routinely described him as its industry's Bill Gates — or, because he was eccentric, reclusive, and rich, as surfing's Howard Hughes. In 2002, *Surfer,* the leading American surf magazine, published a list of the "Twenty-five Most Powerful People in Surfing." It put Clark at number two, behind Bob McKnight, the head of Quik-silver, a surfwear company. Clark hasn't granted an interview in more than thirty years, but the piece was accompanied by his photograph. It showed an older man in a Hawaiian-print shirt, with his face hidden by sunglasses, and two burly forearms, two big fists, and, directly in front of his eyes, two thick middle fingers raised at the camera.

When Clark, who is now seventy-three, started surfing, in the early 1950s, there were perhaps two hundred surfers in California. "We slept on the beach, drank wine, chased girls, ate abalone and lobster that we caught ourselves, worked some odd jobs, but mostly, if there were waves, we surfed," recalled Dick Metz, one of Clark's oldest friends and the first employee of Clark Foam. Today, the world's surf population is said to exceed twenty million. Although most surfers have never had much money, Clark single-mindedly built a company that's estimated to be worth as much as $40 million.

Then, on December 5, 2005, Clark, with no warning, faxed a seven-page letter to his customers announcing, "Effective immediately Clark Foam is ceasing production and sales of surfboard blanks." He alluded to run-ins with government regulators, primarily over the chemicals and equipment he used, and to claims filed against him by ex-employees or their survivors: "I may be looking at very large fines, civil lawsuits, and even time in prison." His equipment, most of which he had invented, could never, by definition, meet the government's standards, he wrote. Indeed, "for the majority of my equipment and process I am the 'standard.'" To Clark, this implied a limitless liability. In any case, he was done trying to satisfy the government. "When Clark Foam was started, it was a far different California," he wrote, and went on:

> The only apology I will make to customers and employees is that I should have seen this coming many years sooner and closed years ago in a slower, more predictable manner. . . . My full-time efforts will be to extract myself from the mess that I have created for myself.

It was not entirely clear what he was talking about, even to industry experts. None of the relevant regulatory agencies were taking any known action against him. But Clark began dismantling his plant immediately and, soon afterward, destroying much of his irreplaceable equipment. He ordered his workers to smash his eighty-odd concrete master blank molds — all of them based on designs provided by the world's best shapers. (Shapers are the craftsmen who turn blanks into surfboards, ready for glassing.) Luis Barajas, who worked for Clark for thirty-two years and was his wood-mill foreman, told me, "Mr. Clark told us to cut up the glue presses, with torches." Clark seemed unable to watch, Barajas said, and he walked away. "It was hard for us too." Surfers made pilgrimages to the concrete recycling plant where the broken molds were dumped — piled askew, like huge robbed caskets. A local shaper could still identify, for his companions, which molds had produced the blanks for boards that were ridden to world championships.

Rage and disbelief roiled the American surfboard business. Many shapers didn't know where their next blanks would come from. Glassers, sanders, and salespeople would all be unemployed; the price of boards would double. The age of the handmade board was over. Clark alone had been keeping the Chinese, and multinational corporations, out of surfing. Many surfers were convinced that they would now be riding clunky, mass-produced plastic boards, waiting for somebody to rediscover how to blow foam as well as Clark had. How could an entire industry have relied on a single supplier? The cover of *Surfer* carried, instead of the usual colorful surf shot, a stark image of two white blanks, one unshaped and one shaped, against a black background, with the caption "This Changes Everything." December 5 became known as Blank Monday.

Clark got his start working as a laminator for Hobie Alter, who had been making balsa-wood-and-fiberglass boards in his parents' garage in Laguna Beach since he was a teenager. In 1954, Alter opened Hobie Surfboards, one of the first surf shops, along a quiet stretch of the Pacific Coast Highway a few miles south of Laguna. He hired Clark about three years later. Clark and Alter were devoted surfers, but they also shared a certain intensity on land. "Most of us seemed to take a long time to grow up," Metz said. "But they were already there." Clark had a real job, in the oil fields of Huntington Beach, a gritty town twenty miles north, but drove back after work to Alter's shop, where he slept in an old pickup truck. Both men knew well the drawbacks of balsa wood, the standard core at the time. It soaked up water like a sponge through any crack in a board's fiberglass skin, and the supply was unreliable: balsa came from Ecuador, and southern California's airplane builders were buying up most of the better wood for use in their planes' skins. Board builders had experimented with Styrofoam and other plastics, but none had proved practical. Then Alter began working with a rigid form of polyurethane, a lightweight foam. "And I thought, *By God, this is really it*," he told me recently.

Clark, who had a strong background in engineering — he had studied math, physics, and chemistry at Pomona College — saw polyurethane's potential immediately. "Grubby had a really deep mechanical brain," Reynolds Yater, another early Laguna surfer and shaper, told me. Alter rented a shed in Laguna Canyon and installed Clark there. They painted the windows black to keep the project secret. It was frustrating work, with far more setbacks than successes, but after six months or so they began to produce blanks that Alter could plane and fine-sand into surfboards that were better than balsa. In June 1958, they put their first foam-core board on the market.

They were just in time for a national surf craze, inspired by the movie *Gidget*. In 1961, Alter and Clark realized that to increase production Clark would need bigger equipment, and to pay for the machines he would need to start selling to other board-makers. Clark bought a few tools from Alter, built a new plant, deep in the ranchlands of the Laguna Hills, and formed his own company, Clark Foam.

There was still a lot to learn. Foam blanks, for example, need stringers — strips of wood down their centers, for strength — but sawing them in half wasn't working, Metz told me. "So Grubby came up with the idea of a hot wire. He put electricity through this very taut wire, got it red-hot. Then we tried to run a blank through it, and the wire snapped. We were in shorts, barefoot, diving for cover — that wire would take your head off if it caught you in the neck. We kept trying to make a better wire, but it kept breaking. We had wires whipping around every other day. Finally, we got it right."

The basic design quest was (and is) for greater lightness without loss of strength — for a faster, more maneuverable, more responsive surfboard. In the midst of the sixties craze, some companies from outside the surfing world began to make molded boards. These were crude knockoffs, and although they were inexpensive, surf shops refused to carry them. They were sold, instead, at Sears and Montgomery Ward, and bought only by the clueless. Serious surfers wanted to ride the same boards that the top riders — featured in magazines and surf movies — rode. A real surfboard was hand-shaped and hand-glassed, and could be made only by a surfer.

I started surfing in the mid-sixties, and though fairly clueless myself, I knew enough not to go near a "pop-out" — a mass-produced, molded board. I first got a good look at pop-outs on the beach at Waikiki, where they were rented to tourists. They were huge, indestructible pink-and-white beasts. They seemed more related to barges or scows than to surfboards. The first board I bought, when I was eleven years old, was secondhand, but it came from Dave

Sweet, a reputable builder. My next board, financed by weed-pull-
ing, was made for me, and cost a hundred and twenty dollars. I ordered it, carefully specifying the length, the tail width, the color,
and anything else I could think to specify, from Larry Felker, a
shaper in my southern California hometown, and then prayed that
it would arrive in less than six months.

Felker was a celebrity in my adolescent world, though his company was, in truth, just a half-step above a garage operation. Even
the big board-makers, with shops on the Coast Highway, were only
a couple of steps above the garages. But the difference in price between a factory-made knockoff and a top-of-the-line custom board
was surprisingly small. That was in part because the shapers and
other surfer-workers were so poorly paid — an exploitation relieved,
in theory, by the unquantifiable benefit of working in the coolest
possible industry. (Also, when the surf was good nobody was really
expected to show up at work.) Board-makers believed, moreover,
that if they raised their prices surfers would just go down the street.
Despite the sport's popularity, nobody was getting rich selling surfboards. Gordon Clark, however, was doing very well making blanks.

"Blowing foam is a black art," Bill Bahne told me. Bahne, a sun-
browned, cheerful man who seems to have carefully divided his
time, over a long career, between the surf and running various factories, is chairman of the board builders' group at the Surf Industry Manufacturers Association. He went on, "If the sun is out, your
foam will come out different. Humidity is crucial. Gordon tried to
control all the variables, at huge expense. Even the big chemical
companies that make the raw materials — Bayer, BASF — couldn't
make foam as good as Clark's."

To make a blank, the main components of polyurethane are
mixed together and poured into a two-and-a-half-ton concrete mold,
roughly surfboard-shaped, where they froth and rapidly expand.
Innumerable things can go wrong — air bubbles, soft spots, hard
spots, pour streaks. Clark's tinkering was meticulous and tireless.
Much was made of his "formula," which he refined constantly. He
also wrote long, fantastically detailed manuals for his workforce,
which grew to more than a hundred. In an interview with an obscure surf magazine in 1972 — the last formal interview I've been
able to find — Clark said, "It takes a long time to develop your
particular process and it's just a lot of little two-bit tricks." He

added, "There's no romanticism in foam. . . . It's dirty, messy, and it's hard work."

It's also hazardous. Clark made his own resins, in a polyol reactor, from isocyanates that he bought by the ton. Bill Bahne told me, "That polyol reactor was like an A-bomb. You really wouldn't want to have a reactor without the safeguards and knowledge that Gordon had." Bahne, contemplating starting a foam-blank company himself, once showed part of Clark's polyurethane formula to polymer chemists at a major company. "And they said, 'This is dangerous. This is for a guy who can drive an eight-thousand-horsepower dragster.' Gordon could do it. But these polychemists said, 'No way. Do *not*.'"

Of the blanks produced by the various early manufacturers, Clark's were not the easiest to work with. Chuck Foss made big, soft, powdery blanks that shaped like butter but lacked strength. Harold Walker's were creamy, spongy, and a pleasure to have in the shaping bay. "Grubby's blanks were brittle, and mean to work," one early shaper told me. "But they had the best cell structure: small and tight. And he listened to shapers."

Clark could be morbidly competitive. Don Hansen, an early boardmaker in Encinitas, once hired two Clark ex-employees to help him make his own blanks. Clark sued Hansen. In the small community of board-makers, people were appalled. Hansen won the case, and Clark did not lose gracefully. Until then, he had sold his blanks exclusively to the established board-makers. Now, in his view, they had betrayed him by moving into his niche. His revenge was to start selling blanks to anyone — amateurs, garage shapers, kids — at the same low price he charged big customers.

Clark also started punishing disloyal customers. If his deliverymen spotted someone else's blanks in the racks outside a shaper's bay, the board-maker would hear about it. "His drivers would say, 'Hey, you got some oddball blanks in here. What's going on?'" a second-generation California board-maker told me. "And maybe you'd get a call from Grubby, or somebody else at Clark Foam. But your deliveries would definitely start slowing down." A few board-makers stopped using Clark Foam. But nobody could make blanks as efficiently, as cheaply, or with such consistently high quality as Clark. Walker Foam — Clark's last real domestic competitor, though only a fraction of his size — closed in 1973.

Clark's was an unusual monopoly, though. For all his forward-thinking industrial practice (and competitive ruthlessness), he had done more to keep board building a cottage industry than anyone. Thanks to his inexpensive blanks, garage shapers were flourishing in every beach town on both coasts, in Hawaii, even in Europe, South Africa, and South America. And they were crucial to a board-design revolution that started in Australia, in 1967, and that soon reduced the average size of a surfboard from nine and a half feet long and more than twenty pounds to seven feet and less than ten pounds. (Later, it would fall toward six feet and six pounds.) Many big-name board-makers, saddled with large inventories of long boards, got hit hard. Some of the new backyard shapers found favor with the top riders and became the next big-name board-makers. Clark Foam was the only established company that slid through the short-board revolution unscathed.

Clark had always tried to give shapers blanks of whatever shape, size, density, and stringer arrangement they wanted. As board de-sign got dramatically more subtle and varied, he began to build special concrete molds based on "plugs" that the top shapers pro-vided him. Eventually, he was publishing a catalog offering blanks in more than seventy shapes, at eight densities, with stringers in four different woods, along with a library of five *thousand* tem-plates for the "rocker" — the lengthwise curve in the bottom of the board. The variations were effectively endless.

Rocker is a critical element in short-board design. Once, in the days of redwood and balsa, boards were basically flat from nose to tail. Today, serious surfers believe that every sixteenth of an inch of rocker in a blank template matters. Clark developed what be-came known as the "close-tolerance blank." His foam cores were no longer big, rough approximations of a surfboard for a shaper to transform with saw, planer, and sandpaper, but something very close to a board's finished shape. A skilled shaper could turn one into a wafer-thin, high-performance wave-riding instrument, ready for the glasser, in less than an hour. And, while the price of a fin-ished short board ranges from $400 to $800, until last year blanks still sold for less than $100.

Clark's plant, which by 2005 had been in the same spot in the Laguna Hills for more than forty years, worked three shifts a day, often seven days a week, and was said to ship a thousand blanks a day. That number has never been confirmed, since Clark didn't release any figures. Still, Bill Bahne told me, "as a business model, it ranks with what anyone's done in the U.S."

Peter St. Pierre and his partners have run Moonlight Glassing since 1979. Many thousands of surfboards have been shaped and glassed in the bright warehouse space they lease in an industrial zone a few miles from the coast in northern San Diego County. St. Pierre is an affable, bearded craftsman in his early sixties. In his opinion, Clark's close-tolerance blanks weren't good for the latest generation of shapers. "Grubby took a lot of the guesswork out of it for them — they could poach other people's rockers," he told me, one morning in June. "We get young guys who call themselves shapers who will bring us a board without fin markings. They just say, 'Put 'em where you want.' They don't even understand fin theory!" Fins are inserted after a board is glassed — and glassing is the basic service Moonlight provides, along with custom paint jobs — but their placement, number, shape, and size are supposed to interact dynamically with a board's design. However, St. Pierre also sees some of the best artistry around. Wandering through his shop, I noticed racks of magnificently shaped blanks, awaiting color and glassing. In a rack of boards to be patched, I saw the scribbled names of some of the world's top surfers.

Moonlight is a word-of-mouth establishment. It doesn't sponsor any surf stars, or feel the need to advertise. In that sense, although St. Pierre is well known, his business is pure garage. "I don't want to just mindlessly send out boards," he said. "I like to have interactions with the customer. I see our boards in the water, I want to know how they're riding. How's it flexing? Everything, good and bad. It's the only way to archive what really works — at the beach." He took a sip of tea. "Boards can be like a tennis ball. They can go flat after a few weeks. And they can come alive again too." He laughed. "You know how it is."

After forty years of surfing, I suppose I do. But I still have no idea what part of a board's performance to attribute to the glass job, to foam density, to fin placement. I generally figure the main variable is my state of mind.

At that moment, a trim, dark-haired man appeared, accompanied by a boy. They were carrying newly finished boards, looking shy and pleased, and they thanked St. Pierre. "He shaped those himself," St. Pierre said. The man's board was a rudimentary shape, but his son's was a tiny, finely wrought three-fin shape known as a thruster. It looked to be of professional quality. On the bottom of the board was a graceful painting of a compass rose. I assumed that was Moonlight's work. But St. Pierre said, "He did that too. All we did was the glass and fins."

Not many surfers shape their own boards these days — or ride boards shaped by their dads. "But the backyard guys are the heart and soul of design innovation," St. Pierre told me. He rattled off a list of shapes and shapers, all famous in the world of surfing. "The Campbells made the Bonzer in their backyard. Stevie Lis made the Fish in his backyard. Even the short board came out of a backyard — it was a grassroots revolution. Surfboards have always been a homemade thing. All the businesses are just offshoots of some guy's garage."

In the early nineties, top shapers began to experiment with computerized shaping machines. They would supply a master blank of a shape that rode especially well, elaborate measurements would be taken, and these would be programmed into a foam-cutting machine, producing a virtually identical board that required very little hand finishing. This represented a large savings in labor, and as the price of shaping machines dropped, some of the major board-makers bought their own. Clark opposed this development, on the ground that it jeopardized the health of the handmade-surfboard industry. But machine-shaped boards were an attractive option not just for overworked shapers but for professional surfers as well. Their boards are, as a rule, the lightest, thinnest, most highly refined instruments in use — meaning, also, the most delicate. Pros ride their boards unusually hard. They take big chances, in powerful waves, and may break any number of boards in the course of a season of competition. They do not want to have to adjust to a handmade board's quirks every time they jump on a new one.

There was also a new line of pop-outs being developed by experienced surfers and shapers who believed that polyurethane foam had reached the limit of its potential. It was time, some board-makers believed, for the development of a stronger, lighter board from new materials, perhaps some form of molded plastic. Prototypes were built in California, but when these were ready to go into mass production the work was done in Thailand. For Clark, this was a double blow — post-polyurethane pop-outs that were not barges, and that were made overseas with cheap labor.

Although Clark gave no interviews, he had, for many years, sent roughly annual state-of-the-industry letters to his customers. In 2004, he devoted much of his letter to the threat of overseas, particularly Asian, manufacturers. "Their approach to production and distribution will not follow our traditions but will be based more on conventional business school theory," he wrote. The "backyard" quality of American board building would be highlighted, humiliatingly, by the innovations of low-salaried engineers. "Looking at other manufacturing industries within the United States," Clark warned, "you will note that they have disappeared 100 percent. That could happen to surfboard manufacturing!"

The main hope of the American industry lay with what Clark called the "sophisticated buyer." This was a surfer who, in the hardcore case, insisted on working directly with a shaper, but anyone who could pick a board to ride from a well-stocked shop rack and give a "sound technical reason for the choice" qualified. Sophisticated buyers, presumably, would continue to reject the whole notion of generic surfboards produced anonymously by nonsurfers, in faraway places, like pool toys.

The downside to increasing the number of such buyers was that the surf was too crowded already. This is the bane of most surfers' lives, and the main reason so many of us travel to the ends of the earth, camping on the sides of volcanoes and in equatorial rain forests. Clark largely stopped surfing in California long ago. After he bought a place in a rural area of the Big Island, in Hawaii, in the 1970s, and was introduced to some uncrowded local breaks, he is said to have resumed.

The crowds weren't only in the water. Orange County, a sprawling place that contains Laguna Beach, has grown in population fivefold since the days when Clark and Alter began their experiments. The Clark Foam factory, when it was built, was surrounded by cow pastures, orange groves, and bean fields in the Laguna Hills. Today, it is in the middle of an upscale suburb, Laguna Niguel, population sixty-five thousand. The hills around it are laced with tile-roofed subdivisions and shopping malls. A minatory pale-glass office building dominates the nearest bluff.

This encroachment brought Clark unwanted attention, mainly from the Environmental Protection Agency, several state environ-

mental agencies, the county fire marshals, and something called
the South Coast Air Quality Management District. There were concerns about toxic fumes, fire hazards, and worker safety: the polyurethane used in surfboards contains a possible carcinogen called
toluene diisocyanate, or TDI. Clark revamped his ventilation system. But he grew frustrated with the inspectors. "They don't know
chemistry," he complained to Reynolds Yater, and in one of his industry letters he wrote about having "to prove to some government
idiots that my system worked."

In a non-union, cottage industry where glassers and shapers often work shirtless and in shorts, amid clouds of poisonous dust and
fumes, Clark eventually had his employees who worked with foam
wearing elaborate air-supply apparatuses, and regularly tested for
chemical exposure. Still, he got hit with at least four workers' compensation claims. (One of these cases, turning on exposure to TDI,
was also filed as a wrongful death suit in late July.) Clark's insurance went up, and so did his sense that he was being persecuted.

In 1993, Clark bought a large working ranch in central Oregon,
and he began to spend more time there than he did in California.
But he talked almost daily to his managers at the plant, and continued to micromanage his company's strategic planning. And his
business touch wasn't getting any lighter. His old partner, Hobie Alter, had begun designing sailboats in the sixties — his Hobie Cat
eventually became one of the world's most popular catamarans. Alter's board business was now a long-board specialty house. (Long
boards, which are easier to ride, both for beginners and for aging
surfers, had made a comeback, of sorts, beginning in the eighties.)
His sons ran the surf business, using Clark blanks. Then Clark
heard that they were trying to get some soft-top boards made in
China. (Soft-tops are a new niche item, for beginners; they don't
use polyurethane.) Clark apparently started giving them a hard
time. Hobie heard about it, and they spoke. There were angry
words, and they have had little contact since. "Gordon's always
been very opinionated," Alter told me tightly. "And his opinions always work to his advantage."

As Clark passed seventy, the question of succession was raised occasionally. He had two children from his first marriage, but neither
had shown an interest in the business. He had a stepdaughter from
his second marriage, and she worked at Clark Foam for a while,
then left. Clark seemed in no hurry to retire anyway. His 2004 in-

dustry letter was widely considered one of his sharpest. It contained a lecture on tariffs and a disquisition on brand value that used, as an example, a prostitute who claims she's from Paris, and the prices she can charge, compared with a prostitute who says she's from Calcutta — vintage Grubby.

Then, in the summer of 2005, Clark took a trip to China. When he returned, he spoke to Luis Barajas, his wood-mill foreman. "He said, 'Luis, they got us. They build an Orange County every couple of days,'" Barajas told me.

Not long afterward, according to friends, Clark was in Hawaii, dirt-biking with Jimmy Pflueger, who is something of a local magnate, on Kauai. During a break, Pflueger told Clark a story. He had got into trouble with the state and the EPA over some grading he'd done without a permit. There had been a rainstorm and a mudslide, and a lot of dirt had ended up on a coral reef. The state fined him $4 million. The worst part, though, Pflueger said, was the way the government calculated some fines, compounding sums daily by a formula that, given time, could break the Federal Reserve.

Clark flew back to California. He brooded all weekend, according to a friend. On Monday morning, December 5, he went into Clark Foam and approached the first worker he saw pouring foam into a mold. "That's it," he said. "That's the last foam we pour."

In the immediate aftermath of Blank Monday, the price of a blank doubled — if you could find one at all — and the prices of boards went up as much as $200. Foreign blank manufacturers diverted shipping containers to California, Hawaii, and Florida, where shortages were most acute. Harold Walker, of Walker Foam, who had reopened, in a modest way, during the nineties to service the long-board revival, began ramping up production. There was a general scramble to hire Clark's ex-employees. And, within six months, there were two dozen new companies making, or preparing to make, polyurethane blanks for the American market, including four new factories in Mexico.

"There's good foam out there, but you've got to shuck and jive to get it. Nobody's up and running with a real program now," Tim Bessell, a veteran shaper, told me. I visited Bessell at his shop in La Jolla in June. He had a grab bag of blanks stacked outside his shaping bay. "These are from Brazil, England, Australia, South Africa,

California," he said, pulling out blanks from the rack, grimacing. Bessell, who has been shaping for thirty years, had his worst quarterly loss in fifteen years during the first three months of 2006, and his second quarter was just as bad. "My gripe isn't Grubby quitting, but how he did it," he said. "This was a rash old man who decided, 'I'm taking my toys out of the sandbox, and fuck all you guys.' All he needed to do to be a hero was give three months' notice."

Alongside his traditional polyurethane-foam-core boards, Bessell had a number of alternative designs for sale. There were boards with cores of expanded polystyrene (EPS, the stuff of coffee cups), which has recently been refined to make it more shaper-friendly, and which does not have the TDI problem. There was a board with a core of extruded polystyrene, a material that Bessell praised. There were no examples of the most commercially successful popouts — the California-designed, Asian-made molded boards from a company called Surftech — but there was a remarkable-looking hollow board. It was black, and astonishingly light, with a carbon-fiber weave under an epoxy-resin skin. It even had a plug for draining any water that managed to get inside. At $1,150, it was roughly twice what a regular short board costs. Some shapers believe that, in the long run, the forced innovation Clark brought about will be good. Even Bessell is excited about the possibilities. The big question, though, is whether the independent hand-shaper will be able to survive, economically, without the extraordinary support that Clark Foam provided. Everyone, including Bessell, says, "There will never be another Clark Foam."

Clark did end up selling most of his wood mill, where the stringers were made, along with his library of rocker templates. Green Valley Mill, in Oceanside, bought both, and hired Luis Barajas and his crew.

When I visited Green Valley, I got to see the great rocker library — thousands of long, curved, color-coded strips of wood, covered with runic markings — as well as the special basswood from Wisconsin that Clark found after a lengthy search. The basswood's unusual grain makes it extra strong when cut into a banana shape for a stringer, and it became known as Clark Select. But the glue presses at the mill, compared with the ones Clark destroyed, were primitive — a bunch of hand clamps on blanks that were anchored with rusty, concrete-filled car-wheel rims. No one has figured out how to rebuild the lost machines.

At Green Valley, I met Bill Bahne, the surf industry veteran. He is a principal in one of the new blank-production companies, which owns Green Valley Mill. Some of his blanks were there, waiting to be glued up with stringers. They were made of a new, TDI-free poly-urethane, but they had consistency problems. Bahne studied them dubiously. "It's a lot of trial and error," he said. I had seen his cata-log; it offered three plugs, and like every new blank catalog I'd seen, it described its meager offerings in terms of the Clark plug that each model was meant to replace. When Clark said he was the standard, he wasn't wrong. In some ways, despite the futuristic talk now filling surf magazines — about greener, stronger new materi-als and technologies — board building has taken an evolutionary step backward.

I got a glimpse of the post–Clark Foam world in May, when I went to Indonesia in search of uncrowded waves. Half a dozen of us had booked a boat, with a home port in West Java, to sail to an uninhab-ited island farther west. Much of the discussion before we left con-cerned what boards to bring.

Peter was bringing a Surftech, which shocked me. He's a serious, skilled surfer, with plenty of boards, and here he was relying on a weird molded-plastic contraption that he hadn't even test-ridden. The thing was indestructible, he said, and he liked the challenge of learning to ride it. Kevin brought a couple of boards, including a brand-new thruster with an EPS foam core. That was going to be his experimental ride.

I settled on an odd pair: the first board Owl Chapman shaped for me, ten years ago, and a nearly identical one that he had made more recently. Chapman, who was a top big-wave rider in his youth, was working, last time I saw him, in a ramshackle shed in the jungle on the north shore of Oahu, living pretty much board to board. (I tried to reach him to get his views on the Clark Foam shutdown, but he has no phone.) I had been trying to get someone to repro-duce the first board, which I adored, since shortly after I got it; Chapman himself had failed when I asked him to try. I heard about a kid on Long Island with a reputation for being able to replicate any board, and he made a valiant effort. The board he shaped rode well, but it was more conventional than my great Owl board, and it didn't drive through waves with the same authority. And it snapped within weeks, in Fiji.

That first Owl had been retired for years — it had so many dents and patched dings that it looked like a piece of tropical flotsam. But I happened to get it down and ride it earlier this year, on a whim, and was stunned to find that it had as much life in it as ever. St. Pierre was right: resurrection sometimes occurs.

Once we reached the island, Kevin's new board broke almost immediately — snapped in two by a relatively small wave. We couldn't decide if the EPS core was at fault; maybe the glasser had been unfamiliar with epoxy resin, and had just made the shell too light.

Peter seemed mystified by his Surftech's performance. His surfing is usually flowing and powerful; now he was throwing his board around in small, weak arcs. He fiddled with his stance, his fin arrangement. Finally, he borrowed a saw from the boat's skipper and cut a big piece off his middle fin. That seemed to improve matters, but he still wasn't himself. I blamed the Surftech.

I want to see independent shapers survive, but I don't see how anyone can stop Costco from selling Chinese-made knockoff boards at half the price of American originals. Parents buying first boards for their kids will shop there. Experienced surfers — the "sophisticated buyers" — are looking for something else, and somebody will figure out how to make it. In the meantime, if surfboards generally get more expensive and less satisfying to ride, the crowd problem may even ease. Not that I've seen anything to suggest that yet. In the bay off the uninhabited island west of Java where we went in May, three other boats full of surfers — from Europe, Australia, and New Zealand — also showed up and anchored, looking for waves.

MICHAEL LEWIS

What Keeps Bill Parcells
Awake at Night

FROM THE NEW YORK TIMES PLAY MAGAZINE

Why do you do what you do? Few sportswriters get inside that question better than Michael Lewis. Parcells answered, then, once again, stopped doing it.
— D.M.

Monday

IT'S MORE THAN sixteen hours since the Dallas Cowboys finished their first game of this season, and twenty-five journalists are still waiting to hear what happened. Of course, they know that the Cowboys lost to the Jacksonville Jaguars, 24–17. After racing out to a 10–0 lead, the Cowboys collapsed. They threw interceptions, dropped passes, allowed sacks, committed penalties. The journalists know this, but they also know that they saw only the same tiny slice of the game that the fans saw on TV. They don't really know why the team fell apart, and the only way to find out is from the inside — from some coach with a knowledge of the plays, who has studied the game film. But since the head coach, Bill Parcells, forbids his fourteen assistant coaches from talking to the news media, the pool of possible informants is one. It's as if a sensational crime has occurred in broad daylight and there's only one witness. And he is an extraordinarily reluctant witness.

The journalists and cameramen loiter for a good hour in the hallways of the Dallas Cowboys' practice facility until Parcells finally arrives. He walks to what is in real life a small lunch table in an atrium but that on television will appear, thanks to a cloth backdrop behind him embellished with logos of the Dallas Cowboys and the Ford Motor Company, as dignified as an official briefing room.

"Fire away," he says, and glares at them.

Bill Parcells is the only coach in NFL history to take four different teams to the playoffs, but that only begins to set him apart. In 1983, in his first NFL head coaching job, he took over a New York Giants team that had one winning season over the previous decade, turned it around on a dime, and led it to Super Bowl titles in the 1986 and 1990 seasons. In 1993, he became head coach of the New England Patriots a year after they finished 2–14. Two seasons later they were 10–6 and in the playoffs for the first time in eight years; another two seasons later, they were in the Super Bowl. From there Parcells went to the Jets, who were coming off a 1–15 season, and coached them to a 9–7 record in his first year and a 12–4 record in his second. The Cowboys had finished 5–11 three seasons in a row before Parcells arrived in 2003. His first year they were 10–6 and reached the playoffs. No NFL coach has ever proven himself so clearly to be a device for turning a losing team into a winning one. And yet, even now, as he begins his sixteenth season as a head coach in the NFL, he lives the psychological equivalent of a hand-to-mouth existence.

After the late-night flight home from Jacksonville, he went to his condo to catch a few hours' sleep. He woke up not long after he nodded off, choking on his own bile. "It only happens to me during the football season," he says. "It happens no other time of the year. And it wasn't something I ate." After that, he couldn't sleep at all. He found that his ex-wife, Judy — they divorced in 2002, after forty years of marriage — had left a message on his answering machine. She saw the game on TV. "Please don't let it affect your health," she said.

He still returns in his mind to a question his wife often asked him: why do you do what you do? Coaching football doesn't make him obviously happy. Even in the beginning, in the late 1960s, when he was an assistant coach at West Point, he would come home after games so evidently displeased that his eldest daughter would sit on the sofa next to him, silently, and put on a long face. She was five years old and had no idea what had happened; she just picked it up from his expression that postgame wasn't happy time. "When my wife asked me that question," he says, "I never had a good answer. There was no answer. There is no answer."

"Fire away," he says to the twenty-five people who are here to ask him why he lost. And they do. They ask the same question ten different ways: who messed up? And he gives them the same answer ten different ways: none of your damn business.

Thus begins what Parcells calls assignment-of-blame day. He knows exactly who is to blame, of course, because he has spent hours watching the video. At 5:00 A.M. he gave up trying to sleep and came into his office to study it. It wasn't until then that he really saw the game. When watching video, Parcells doesn't usually waste a lot of time studying his quarterback. That's one player he can see pretty well during the game. But this morning has been different. Against the Jaguars, Drew Bledsoe missed throws he once made in his sleep. He was indecisive and slow to see open receivers. As a result, he held the ball far too long. Last season Bledsoe was sacked forty-nine times and smacked in the act of throwing eighty-two times, a league high. He has been showing the symptoms of a quarterback who is looking at the rush instead of his receivers — which is to say a quarterback who should no longer be playing in the NFL. Parcells studied the video to determine if Bledsoe had indeed lost his nerve. The video didn't say. But the video did reveal that the Cowboys' cornerbacks were soft and that his left tackle's inability to handle the pass rush had the potential to ruin the Cowboys' season.

It galls him that the media's curiosity so closely echoes his inner concerns (by far the most common question is, are you thinking about benching Bledsoe?), and makes him even less inclined than usual to satisfy it. "We're in the business of collecting information," Parcells likes to say. "We're not in the business of exchanging information." His practices are closed to reporters after the first fifteen minutes, and he's comically slow to divulge the most basic facts about the state of his team — like, for instance, which players are injured. At this very moment the Dallas Cowboys have several key players hobbling around the trainers' room, looking distinctly unwell. Left tackle Flozell Adams walks as if he should be on crutches, and cornerback Aaron Glenn is supposed to have arthroscopic surgery in eight days. And yet Parcells's postgame injury report consists of a single player, a third-string wide receiver named Jamaica

Rector. When I ask him why Flozell Adams runs with a distinct gimp, Parcells laughs and says, "That's just how he runs."

He isn't exchanging information. He isn't saying who's hurt. And he isn't voicing his doubts about his quarterback. The fifth time a reporter asks Parcells what, exactly, might lead him to replace Bledsoe with the backup, Tony Romo, he glares for a beat or two, and then says, "Bledsoe's starting on Sunday, okay?"

Tuesday

You can tell which day of the week it is by the video Parcells selects at six that morning. On Mondays it's the Cowboys' most recent game. On Tuesdays it's the next week's opponent — in this case, the Washington Redskins. For several hours each morning, he sits behind his desk staring at a screen, making notes on a white legal pad. This Tuesday he motions for me to pull up a chair beside him.

His office is vast and impersonal and without a trace of self-importance. Parcells has had his picture taken with presidents and movie stars, but the only photograph in the office lies face down on a bookshelf. He turns it over to reveal a snapshot of him with three tough-looking young men — tattoos, sleeveless shirts — from a boxing gym in North Jersey he likes to visit.

His few possessions are confined to the tiny space behind his desk. At his feet rests a single, thick binder in which he has organized every last bit of his personal and financial life: divorce settlement, coaching contracts, book contracts, endorsements, agent agreements. On the desk is his other thick binder, containing practice schedules and other coaching materials. Parcells carts the baggage of his youth wherever he goes, but its contents are mainly the attitudes and emotions of a tough kid raised on the streets of North Jersey. If he decided to quit his job, he wouldn't need a trip back to collect his stuff; he could walk out the door with all of it. The only physical evidence of his past is three small elephant figurines. Parcells's mother passed on to her son an odd superstition: elephants with their trunks pointed toward a doorway bring good luck. In his condo, Parcells keeps a collection of elephant statues. Here he has just three little ones, pointed the wrong direction.

There's just one other thing that connects this office to its occupant: a thick whiteboard beside the desk, on which the Cowboys' depth chart is scribbled. Balanced on top of the board is a baseball bat. "I got that because I got a couple of St. Bernards on this team," Parcells says. "You know why they're called St. Bernards?" I don't. "Because I got to hit them with a stick to get 'em to do anything."

Then he resumes his study of the Washington Redskins, looking for player weaknesses and strategic tendencies. His greatest fear is the threat posed by Redskins wide receiver Santana Moss. One way to deal with Moss — the conservative solution — is to assign two defensive backs to cover him at all times. But that leaves one fewer defender to cover other receivers, tackle running backs, or rush the quarterback. Parcells decides he would rather risk having cornerback Terence Newman cover Moss man to man. When the Cowboys are in man-to-man coverage, Newman will go where Moss goes. Parcells points out Redskins right tackle Jon Jansen. "This is Jansen getting pushed back," he says. "He doesn't look like the player he was a couple of years ago." The right side of the Redskins' line seems to have trouble with twists. If Newman can cover Moss long enough, Jansen won't be able to hold off Greg Ellis or Marcus Spears, the Cowboys' pass rushers he has to block.

When Parcells turns his attention to the Redskins' defense, he tries to see the game as the Redskins' coaches see it, with a view to the weaknesses and strengths of their opposition, so that he can guess what the Redskins are trying to do. Parcells spots an opportunity, and his fear momentarily disappears: no matter who the Redskins play, their cornerbacks have been giving opposing receivers far too much space — leaving the short routes uncontested — while still managing, on occasion, to get burned on deep routes. The Redskins' coaches obviously do not trust their corners to play tight. "I think they might be vulnerable at the corner position," Parcells says. "But we go out to exploit that, we may be vulnerable." The Redskins' cornerbacks may be relatively weak, but their pass rushers are relatively strong. Now Parcells begins to worry all over again about his left tackle, Flozell Adams, the critical barrier between the other team's pass rush and Drew Bledsoe. Against the Jaguars, during the game, Adams looked exposed; on video, he looks worse. He gave up a sack, was penalized for a false start, and was routinely beaten by quick defenders.

Again, there are ways to compensate. The Cowboys might play with extra tight ends, to help Adams block. But if they do that, the Redskins will respond by inserting extra linebackers — by going into what they call their "Diamond Point" defense — and Parcells believes the Redskins' defense is more effective in this mode. So he decides the Cowboys will tempt the Redskins with a vulnerable Flozell Adams all on his own and hope that he proves invulnerable.

Having zipped through all of Washington's preseason games, Parcells then studies the Redskins' first regular-season game, against Minnesota, when their offense looked like it belonged to a different team. As the video reaches the end of the first quarter, Parcells points to the screen and says, "They've shifted more than they did the entire preseason." The Redskins' offense suddenly looks less like the handiwork of their head coach, Joe Gibbs — whom Parcells has faced twenty times over the years — than of Al Saunders, the associate head coach for offense the Redskins poached from the Kansas City Chiefs in the offseason. Parcells moves on to examine the 2005 Chiefs. "If you can just understand what they're about, a lot of other things follow," he says. "It's like finding a common denominator in mathematics." What the Chiefs have long been about — and what the Redskins are newly about — is exploiting the width of the field. Their running game tends to avoid the inside, or the middle of the field; it's built instead on sweeps and reverses. Their passing game has a lot of quick screens to the outside. And before every snap there's a lot of running around. "One of the worst things you can do on defense is be a reactive defense," Parcells says. "You can't worry about what they're doing. All that shifting, all that movement before the snap, is designed to get you worried about what they're doing. They don't want you to get a good fix. They don't want you to stare down for ten seconds. They want to create indecision."

Over the next couple of days, Parcells and his coaching staff can drill his team to be ready for pretty much everything that the Redskins can do. He can design a game plan to exploit slow tackles and weak cornerbacks; he even sees an advantage for the Cowboys in the Redskins' new fast-strike style. Referring to Al Saunders, Parcells says: "This other guy, I think, he's a lot more indiscriminate. I think he's not going to be as concerned about the effect on his defense." In other words, the Redskins' defense will pay the price — in time spent on the field, in fatigue — for Saunders's disinterest in controlling the ball and the clock.

The game plan doesn't take long to create. Parcells has a dozen assistant coaches studying the same video. There will be no secrets.

Information about the surface of the game is not the problem; if anything, there's too much of it. I ask Parcells if there is anything he would like to know that he doesn't know: that is, if he had a spy inside the Redskins who could provide him with answers to any of his questions, what would he ask? He thinks a bit before he finally answers. "I'd like to know their mechanism on audible," he says. "I'd like to know how they were changing the plays."

What has him troubled — what has him waking up choking on his bile — isn't what you might expect. It's not concern that the Redskins' coaching staff could spring something on the Cowboys for which they are entirely unprepared. And it's not his team's raw ability. It's a thing that's harder to put into words, and impervious to strategy. Even as he is trying to study his next opponent, he can't shake what happened on Sunday. How his team, the moment the Jaguars pushed back, collapsed. How, the moment the players felt the pressure, they began to commit penalties and the sort of small but critical mental errors that only a coach watching video can perceive. In their performance he smells the sort of failure he defines himself against.

At the back of Parcells's personal binder there are a few loose, well-thumbed sheets that defy categorization: a copy of a speech by Douglas MacArthur; a passage from a book about coaches, which argues that a coach excels by purifying his particular vision rather than emulating a type. Among the papers is an anecdote Parcells brings up often in conversation, about a boxing match that took place nearly thirty years ago between the middleweights Vito Antuofermo and Cyclone Hart. Parcells loves boxing; his idea of a perfect day in the offseason is to spend it inside some ratty boxing gym in North Jersey. "It's a laboratory," he says. "You get a real feel for human behavior under the strongest duress — under the threat of physical harm." In this laboratory he has identified a phenomenon he calls the game quitter. Game quitters, he says, seem "as if they are trying to win, but really they've given up. They've just chosen a way out that's not apparent to the naked eye. They are more concerned with public opinion than the end result."

Parcells didn't see the Hart-Antuofermo fight in person but was told about it, years ago, by a friend and boxing trainer, Teddy Atlas. It stuck in his mind and now strikes him as relevant. Seated, at first, he begins to read aloud from the pages: how in this fight twenty-nine years ago Hart was a well-known big puncher heavily favored against the unknown Vito Antuofermo, how Hart knocked Antuofermo all over the ring, how Antuofermo had no apparent physical gifts except "he bled well." "But," Parcells reads, "he had other attributes you couldn't see." Antuofermo absorbed the punishment dealt out by his natural superior, and he did it so well that Hart became discouraged. In the fifth round, Hart began to tire, not physically but mentally. Seizing on the moment, Antuofermo attacked and delivered a series of quick blows that knocked Hart down, ending the fight.

The Redskins video is still frozen on the screen behind Parcells. He is no longer sitting but is now on his feet. "This is the interesting part," he says, then reads:

> When the fighters went back to their makeshift locker rooms, only a thin curtain was between them. Hart's room was quiet, but on the other side he could hear Antuofermo's cornermen talking about who would take the fighter to the hospital. Finally he heard Antuofermo say, "Every time he hit me with that left hook to the body, I was sure I was going to quit. After the second round, I thought if he hit me there again, I'd quit. I thought the same thing after the fourth round. Then he didn't hit me no more."
>
> At that moment, Hart began to weep. It was really soft at first. Then harder. He was crying because for the first time he understood that Antuofermo had felt the same way he had and worse. The only thing that separated the guy talking from the guy crying was what they had done. The coward and the hero feel the same emotions. They're both human.

When Parcells finishes, he says: "This is the story of our last game. We were Cyclone Hart."

Then, with the greatest care, as if they're an old and cherished possession instead of a couple of grubby sheets of paper, he returns the pages to the binder that holds his private business. He returns to watching video of the Washington Redskins. "Their receivers are upgraded from last year," he says. "If we aren't able to cover Moss man to man, we'll lose."

Wednesday

Terence Newman has no idea that he is so high on Bill Parcells's list of concerns. "What else did he say?" asks the fourth-year cornerback when I tell him that Parcells seems to think that his ability to handle Santana Moss in man-to-man coverage is the key to shutting down the Redskins' offense. "Coach doesn't say too much," Newman says, "unless you do something bad. If he's not saying anything to you, you must be doing something good."

At different times, Parcells tells me that the Cowboys will lose if (a) his left tackle, Flozell Adams, cannot protect his quarterback, or (b) Newman fails to shut down Santana Moss in man-to-man coverage, or (c) his quarterback, Drew Bledsoe, makes poor throws. He refers to no other player or position as a necessary condition for victory. He can survive poor play by his linebackers, or interior linemen, or receivers, or backs. His concerns about his quarterback are predictable. His concerns about his left tackle and the cornerback are telling: they mirror almost exactly the shift that has occurred in football finances since Parcells became a head coach. When free agency arrived in 1993, defensive backs were the lowest-paid players on an NFL defense. Offensive linemen were just about the lowest-paid players on offense, and the left tackle was paid no more than any other lineman. The cornerback is now the best-paid defensive position and the left tackle the second-best-paid offensive position; indeed, after the quarterback, the left tackle is the highest-paid position on the field.

Adams is listed at six-foot-seven, 340 pounds, and he is, if anything, heavier. Terence Newman is listed at five-foot-eleven, 195, and he is, almost certainly, smaller. That they are even allowed to engage in a contact sport together is a cause for wonder; that Terence Newman has survived as long as he has is something of a miracle. But they have several things in common. Both do much of their job while running backward. Both operate on the edge of the play and find themselves in hand-to-hand battle with recognized superstars. The left tackle typically blocks the best pass rusher, who attacks from the quarterback's blind side; the cornerback frequently covers the most threatening offensive player. And both needed free agency for the NFL to reward and publicize their importance.

I tell Terence Newman that in addition to worrying that Newman may single-handedly blow the game, Parcells is also worried Flozell Adams may single-handedly blow the game. This doesn't make Newman feel better. He confesses that he spends at least some small amount of his time wondering what Parcells thinks of him.

What's odd about this is that he doesn't appear to spend a great deal of time wondering if he's any good — nor should he. Newman was the first player Parcells drafted after arriving in Dallas, and he has proven to be a shrewd choice. In his rookie season with the Cowboys, he was a Pro Bowl alternate, as he was again in his third season, when he didn't give up a single touchdown.

"But isn't Moss faster than you?" I ask.

"He's fast, but I don't know if he's faster than me," he says.

"How fast are you?"

"Come on in here," he says, and I follow him into the film room used by the defensive backs. He hits a few buttons on a computer terminal and up on the screen pops a play from last year's game between the Cowboys and the Oakland Raiders. The ball is on the Oakland 14-yard line. Oakland's star receiver, Randy Moss — no relation to Santana — lines up across the field from Newman, and is covered by the other cornerback. Moss finds a seam in the middle of the field, snags a pass, and appears bound for the end zone. There isn't anyone within ten yards of him, and no one between him and the goal line. But what should be an uninterrupted eighty-six-yard dash ends after seventy-nine yards, when Newman pulls Moss down from behind. "I'm that fast," he says.

And then Terence Newman smiles almost shyly. He looks about fifteen years old, and now fesses up: when he was at Kansas State, he was the Big 12 100-meter and indoor 60-meter sprint champion. Speed isn't a problem. "I'll just try to buy as much time on the line of scrimmage as possible," he says. Then he wanders off to another endless meeting.

Because it's Wednesday, Parcells is watching video of his own team. For the next three days he will study not game videos but videos of the Cowboys' practices. When he does this, he tends to focus on what he couldn't see clearly from the sidelines. And what he can't see from the sidelines is usually pretty much everything that happens along the line of scrimmage. His obsession is with space — creating it on offense and filling it on defense. Parcells is interested especially in the first step or two that players take, because that is when almost all of their critical mistakes are made. He's looking for bad angles, missed assignments, confused play. He'll watch the first one-third of a second of a play, stop the video in a fury, and holler for an assistant coach. He does this now.

"Freddie!" he screams, loud enough that the Cowboys' tight-ends coach, Freddie Kitchens, can hear him two offices down the hall. On his television screen, the players are all frozen two steps into a play. "*Freddie!*"

But there is no need to shout twice; Kitchens is already hustling into Parcells's office. Parcells rewinds the video and replays the first millisecond. It appears to be a passing play, though Drew Bledsoe has only just begun to turn and drop back. But in those first two steps, says Parcells, the rookie tight end, Anthony Fasano, has managed to doom the entire play. Fasano's job is to block Redskins linebacker Marcus Washington. But the angle Fasano takes as he leaves the line of scrimmage means he'll push Washington inside instead of taking him outside, as he's supposed to.

"I know," Kitchens says. "We already talked to him about it!"

"You go over it with him again," says Parcells. "You tell him Coach is a little *disturbed*." And with that Kitchens leaves.

"All we need is about four or five of those in the game," Parcells grumbles, "and we're done." Then he fast-forwards the video in search of the next seemingly trivial error, which he knows he will find and yet is unsure he will be able to correct. "Just because you can identify a problem," he says, "doesn't mean you are any closer to fixing it." He's an odd combination of fatalism and can-do spirit. He seems both to believe and yet not to believe that he can get through to his players. On the one hand, he says, "the players now have so many people telling them what they want to hear that it's harder to get through to them with words." On the other hand, the Cowboys' locker room is decorated with words to live by:

"Blame nobody, expect nothing, do something." "Losers assemble in little groups and bitch about the coaches and the system and other players in other little groups. Winners assemble as a team." "Losing may take a little from your credibility, but quitting will destroy it." "There are many exit doors in pro football. Don't take them." "Don't confuse routine with commitment."

Each of Parcells's little inspirational sayings comes with a provenance. The one about routine and commitment, for instance: Parcells directed that at a young Aaron Glenn in the Jets' weight room nearly a decade ago. A few months later, Glenn, a defensive back, confessed that it had stuck with him. And so now it's stuck on the Cowboys' white cinder-block wall. The players can't go to practice without being hectored, silently, by their head coach. Parcells says he has no idea if his words have any effect.

Thursday

The second and final day of full-scale practice. Never have so many millionaires been so regimented and subdued as when an NFL team gathers to practice. If they didn't wear numbers on their jerseys, the stars would be indistinguishable from the scrubs. The only exception today is wide receiver Terrell Owens, who reminds everybody of his own importance. In huddles he stands apart. In wind sprints he races out into the lead — look at me! — and then, midway through, gives up altogether and falls to the rear (look at me, again!). There's no such thing as too much attention, and no event too trivial to disrupt, albeit mildly. The team's owner, Jerry Jones, strolls onto the field, and the first thing he does is seek out T.O. to make overeager chitchat, like an airplane passenger trying to distract the guy with the shoe bomb. Even Parcells, when T.O. joshes with him, seems uncharacteristically willing to be distracted.

One of the strange things about professional football players is how little time they spend playing football. Their schedules begin at dawn, and their coaches don't have time to sleep. But the players spend more time sitting in meetings, lifting weights, and taking showers than they do playing football. If you added it all up, they probably spend more time wrapping various body parts in surgical tape than they do playing the game. Wednesday and Thursday are the two days the Cowboys practice longest and hardest, but even these practices last just a few hours and only faintly resemble an actual football game. Football is the sport in which practice is least like the game. Because the risk of injury outweighs the reward of repetition, they don't hit each other and they seldom run all out. And it's never truly competitive; the players who aren't good enough to start are assigned to imitate the opposition for the benefit of the first-string offense or defense. The scrubs play the role of the Redskins so that the Cowboys' starting defense can pretend to stymie the Redskins' offense, and the Cowboys' starting offense can run up the score on the Redskins' defense. If the coaches didn't scream and yell so much, you'd never guess that any of it actually mattered.

During practice Parcells says little, but what he says tends to make an impression. (To defensive end Kenyon Coleman, after a mistake: "You just happy to be here again, Kenyon? Ain't gonna last long this year!" To the rookie wide receiver Sam Hurd, after he runs the wrong route: "Not good, Sam! I'm trying to get comfortable with even the idea of putting you in a game.") But for the most part he stands on the sidelines with his arms crossed high over his chest, hands tucked under his armpits, collecting information.

Today, without seeming to, he's making a study of his troubled place kicker, Mike Vanderjagt. Last season the Cowboys finished 9–7, but essentially missed the playoffs by a field goal. Against Seattle in the fourth quarter, "we miss a *field goal* from the ten-yard line," Parcells says. "On Thanksgiving Day we miss a thirty-four-yarder versus Denver, and the game goes into overtime. Last season we had eight games decided by three or less, and eleven games by seven or less." This isn't too far off the league average: half of all NFL games are decided by seven points or fewer, and a quarter are decided by three points or fewer. "I knew I was in trouble last year," Parcells says, "when my long snapper, my punter, and my field goal kicker were all from out of the country."

To fix their kicking problem, the Cowboys signed — and gave a $2.5 million bonus to — a Canadian, Mike Vanderjagt, formerly of the Indianapolis Colts. At that moment, Vanderjagt was the most accurate place kicker in NFL history. His final act before the Cowboys signed him, however, was to miss a forty-six-yard field goal in the last minute that would have tied the AFC Championship game and given the Colts a shot at getting to the Super Bowl.

He turned up at the Cowboys' camp with a pulled muscle that the Cowboys' trainers couldn't locate, and sat out most of the first three preseason games. In overtime of the Cowboys' fourth and final preseason game, against the Minnesota Vikings, he missed a potential game-winning thirty-three-yard field goal. The Cowboys got the ball back and drove to the Vikings' 14-yard line, and Parcells, thinking it might help his new kicker get over the humiliation of the miss, sent him back out. He missed again. ("*I* could have made that kick," Parcells says.) Against the Jaguars, Parcells didn't even have his expensive kicker dress for the game, but instead used the guy on the taxi squad, Shaun Suisham. "You miss the kick that puts your team in the Super Bowl. . . ," Parcells says, without finishing the thought.

It's an elemental thing — that mysterious something in a player under pressure that either snaps or holds — and elemental things are what interest this old coach. Golfers with the yips, big-league catchers whose careers end when they find themselves suddenly unable to throw the ball back to the pitcher — these he understands. He was in the stands during a spring-training baseball game when the St. Louis Cardinals tried to bring back their mentally broken young pitcher, Rick Ankiel — and watched Ankiel throw the ball over the catcher's head, several times. "Ian Baker Finch!" Parcells exclaims, once he has warmed to the subject. "Ian Baker Finch *won* the British Open. Two years later he couldn't hit a golf ball with a golf club." Fear of failure can infect the mind and turn sport into a kind of walking death. "If you can find a solution to *that* problem," he tells me, "quit writing. You'd make a fortune. You got all these sports psychologists. *None* of them can help these guys."

Now, as he conspicuously pretends not to notice his $2.5 million kicker shanking thirty-yard field goal attempts in practice, Parcells wonders if he's witnessing another one of those inexplicable and total collapses of nerves. ("And don't tell me that it can't happen with kickers," he says.) He doesn't talk to Vanderjagt, and Vanderjagt doesn't talk to him: all this drama and anxiety occur without a word of direct, verbal communication. "But," Parcells says, "even when he doesn't think I'm watching him, I'm watching him." Standing on the sideline, staring at his first-team offense as it scores yet another touchdown against the scrubs, the coach who is in the business of collecting information listens to a report from Tony Romo, the backup quarterback and the one who holds the ball for the place kicker. Romo tells him that Vanderjagt is finally hitting the ball squarely. "Yeah," Parcells says. "In practice."

Toward the end of practice, right after the defense stuffs a cheap imitation of the Redskins' offense, and just before the offense triumphs over a cheap imitation of the Redskins' defense, Parcells strolls out onto the field from his usual place on the sidelines and chats with Terence Newman. He has noticed that just before the ball is snapped Newman, instead of being set and square to the line of scrimmage, is slightly turned (the better to call back and forth to other players). Parcells is worried that Newman is falling into a habit of never being exactly ready. He can get away with this on some Sundays, but starting sideways to the line will cost him half a step, and that half-step could be all Santana Moss needs to run right by him.

Every Thursday afternoon after practice and after watching that practice on video, the coaches meet around an oblong table to make their final personnel decisions. They have already pretty much decided how many players at each position they will dress for the game — seven offensive linemen, three running backs, four wide receivers, and so on — but there is one last unanswered question: one kicker or two? It's highly unusual to dress more than one kicker, but this is a highly unusual situation: a kicker on the verge of a nervous breakdown.

"Anyone got anything to say?" Parcells asks.

No one has anything to say. Parcells relates the news, reported by Romo, that Vanderjagt is hitting the ball more squarely.

One of the coaches pipes up: "At least he looks like he's kicking the ball instead of just flailing away at it."

"I don't know if there's a right decision," Parcells says. "It's a coin flip."

He declines to flip the coin. He wants to preserve the mystery of who will kick on Sunday, right up to game time. So the coaches spend the entire meeting figuring out which of the other forty-four players on the game-day roster might be dropped, with the smallest ripple effect, to make way for an extra kicker. There's no longer such a thing as a bench warmer in the NFL — every one of the forty-five players allowed to suit up for a game must be able to play, to justify his spot on the sidelines. Back and forth the coaches go, between a rookie linebacker named Oliver Hoyte and a third-string tight end named Ryan Hannam, before deciding Hannam will sit out, because he's less useful on special teams.

Once that's settled, they toss around a few plays that might work and a few that might not. Parcells is one of those people who find out what he's thinking by what he does. He trusts his gut, and so spends a lot of time rationalizing actions that did not arise from logic or argument. "I do a lot of things on the fly," he admits. Now he blurts out to his offensive coaches that there's no point practicing a certain pass play with Bledsoe as quarterback because he thinks that, for that play, he holds on to the ball too long. But, he says, "you can run that with Romo."

Friday

Friday is the best day of the week, Parcells says. On Friday the game plan is set in stone, all preparations are finished, and there isn't

anything to do. "What about tomorrow?" I ask. If Friday is a picnic, Saturday should be a cakewalk. "Tomorrow you start worrying
about the game," he says.

And with that he goes to have the chiropractor break down scar
tissue in his upper thigh. He hurt himself playing golf. He doesn't
actually play much, but he'll go out on the range and hit hundreds
of balls. "I like practicing," he says. "It's therapy for me."

Rich Dalrymple, the Cowboys' director of public relations, walks
in and says, "Gibbs is saying Portis isn't playing."

"Get out of here!" His defense just spent the week focusing on
Clinton Portis, a Redskins running back.

"It was on the wire," Dalrymple says.

"That means Duckett's playing," says Parcells. That would be T. J.
Duckett, acquired just three weeks earlier by Washington from
Denver.

"I don't know," Dalrymple says.

"Find out!"

"How am I supposed to find out?" Dalrymple asks.

Parcells shakes his head: not my problem.

"Give a guy a morsel and he wants a fillet," says Dalrymple, and
Parcells laughs.

Saturday

It's heresy in the NFL to suggest there should be free time, or that
there is such a thing as diminishing returns to work. But the truth
is that there are some days when there is more to do than others,
and on Saturday there is next to nothing to do. All strategic decisions have been made, all plays practiced, everyone who needs to
be yelled at has been yelled at, at least twice. When I ask Parcells
how he spends Saturday, he says, "Worrying about the game." One
sign of how little actual work needs to be done is that he sets aside
the morning for the photographers to take this season's official
team photograph.

By the time the players — sixty-three of them — have arranged
themselves on the scaffolding, there are, in addition, thirty-two
coaches, trainers, and other support staff. The number of jobs on
the playing field has remained steady for decades, but the number
of ancillary jobs has boomed. (This is one of the two notable differ-

ences when you compare current team photos with those from the early 1960s that decorate the Cowboys' hallways. The other is the increasing numbers of black players.) In 1961, the Dallas team photo had just six men out of uniform; as late as 1980 it had a mere thirteen. The turning point came in 1990, when the team photographer could no longer cram all the nonplayers into a single row and began to stick two at both ends of the rows. As the price of the asset — the NFL player — has skyrocketed, so has the value of those, however peripheral, who can extract a bit more value from it. As the game becomes more complex, it requires more people to understand it, and as more people are brought in to parse it, it becomes more complex. By about 2030, the Cowboys' team photo will be a handful of players nestled among hundreds of trainers and coaches and God knows what else. Competitive forces break people's nerves. They also reshape football teams.

The photographer shoots twelve pictures. In between, the players laugh and joke. But the moment the photographer says, "One, two, three," the laughter evaporates and their faces freeze in expressions of grim manliness. Even T.O., fixing his mouth the exact same way each time, is as serious as a debutante posing for the society pages.

Sunday

More than any other sport, football is meant to be viewed from a God-like angle. Pacing up and down the sidelines, the head coach has the worst view in the house — except for everyone else on the sidelines. The sidelines are an obstacle course of thick cables, Cowboys cheerleaders, flatbed trucks with TV cameras, pushy cameramen, and wide people with even wider sound dishes. So the only way to tell if a play is good or bad for the Cowboys is by the crowd's reaction and the replay on the Jumbotron, which the players themselves watch when they're curious about what has happened. The closer you are to the action, the more desperately your eyes search for the televised image. All in all, the sidelines illustrate that physical proximity to a complicated event doesn't necessarily help you understand it.

Removing myself to the press box, I see that for almost an entire half all goes well for the Cowboys. More than well: none of

Parcells's fears and all of his hopes are realized. Flozell Adams is as impenetrable as a symbolist poem, and Drew Bledsoe resembles a quarterback in his prime. The Redskins' cornerbacks are indeed vulnerable, exactly as Parcells had imagined. Double-teaming Terrell Owens, they leave the receiver Terry Glenn in man-to-man coverage, and Glenn makes them pay. The Redskins' cornerbacks, increasingly insecure, commit dumb holding penalties. The Cowboys' offense moves at will, despite dropping nine passes and committing nine penalties. The defense establishes the virtuous circle that has been the signature of Bill Parcells's defenses since he rejoined the Giants in 1981 and unleashed Lawrence Taylor: Terence Newman covers Santana Moss well, which in turn forces the quarterback, Mark Brunell, to hold on to the ball a fraction of a second longer than he should, giving the Cowboys' fastest pass rushers just enough time to hit him. In response, the Redskins' tackles assigned to block the pass rushers grow twitchy and jump offside. Midway through the second quarter, a Redskins cornerback beaten on a deep route by Terry Glenn is called for interference. The Cowboys punch it into the end zone, and go up, 17–3. The game is on the brink of turning into a rout. Midway through the second quarter, the Redskins have more yards in penalties than from gains.

But if all you saw of the game was Bill Parcells's face, you'd never know life was good. Over and over again, NBC cuts to a close-up of Parcells on the sidelines. When he took over the Giants in 1983, the television cameras seldom found the coach. Now the coach is the go-to guy for the emotions of the game. Parcells's face appears four times for each shot of Joe Gibbs, and it's not hard to see why. Gibbs gives the cameras nothing. He keeps his head down and fails to convey much at all. Parcells, on the other hand, is a study in dissatisfaction, and the TV people have figured that out: they focus on him only after some Cowboy has screwed up. Disapproval to Parcells is like snow to an Eskimo: he has spent so much time living with it that he has developed an elaborate range of signals, many of them nonverbal, to express the subtle shades of dissatisfaction. One time he looks as if he has eaten a bad oyster, another as if he has just been told his car has a flat tire. In any case, NBC relies on him to convey what is wrong with his team, but not what is right.

The material rapidly improves. The Cowboys kick off, and the Redskins' Rock Cartwright — to whom no attention was paid by the Cowboys' coaches during the past week — returns the ball one hundred yards for a touchdown. This is the first time the Cowboys have allowed a kickoff return for a touchdown since 1993. Now the score is 17–10, and in a mere thirteen seconds, the mood of the game has changed. The Cowboys have become Cyclone Hart. They make so many mistakes; they drop passes ever more egregiously and commit ever more foolish penalties. Just like that, the Cowboys are back in another tight game.

At halftime there's no chance for a speech — several of the Cowboys reappear on the field four minutes after they left — but Parcells has taken precautions. This morning, before the game, he called a meeting of the players without the assistant coaches. "I don't want to talk with the coaches around," he told me beforehand. "I want the players to know that I am trying to make a point." This morning, he broke into his personal binder, took out the story of Vito Antuofermo and read it to his players. All week long it wasn't strategy that occupied him; it was character. There's a tendency to believe that, to be successful, a pro football coach must have a gift for the chessboard aspect of the game. But strategy isn't what chiefly interests Parcells. His success depends on his ability to demand, and to receive, higher levels of performance from his players. He doesn't say so explicitly, but his actions speak for him: he spends much more time thinking about getting inside his players' heads, and their skins, than about anything else. He tries to make them uncomfortable. On a baseball team or a golf team, this sort of pressurized approach might lead to a team-wide nervous breakdown. In football — at least for him — it works magic.

But midway through the third quarter there is no sign that Parcells has had any effect. Once again, his Cowboys reel the moment they are jolted. Their mistakes become more and more outrageous and self-defeating until, finally, they fumble away the ball in their own half of the field. The Redskins begin to drive. On a crucial third-and-nine, on the Cowboys' 21-yard line, Brunell drops back. He spots and throws to an open wide receiver, Chris Cooley, streaking down the sideline. Out of nowhere comes Cowboys safety Roy Williams. He intercepts the pass, on the 1-yard line. And then — just like that — the rout is on again. Terry Glenn catches a bomb for a touchdown. Mike Vanderjagt hits a fifty-yard field goal. The Cowboys win, 27–10, but it could have easily been two touchdowns worse for the Redskins. Still, Parcells allows himself no obvious pleasure and exhibits only the most fleeting hint of relief. He passes Terence Newman and tells him he has done a good job. (And he has: on Newman's watch, Moss caught just one pass for seven yards.) He walks over to left tackle Flozell Adams and pats his cheek, and Adams, whose idea of an emotional outburst is a wince, actually smiles.

But mainly the old coach looks sick to his stomach. As the clock winds down, and the camera lingers on Parcells, lips pursed as if he has just finished sucking the world's largest lemon, NBC's play-by-play commentator Al Michaels laughs and says, "You'll never see an expression indicating pleasure on Bill's face."

Monday

Before the game I asked Parcells what time to expect him in his office the following morning. "If I can't sleep it could be as early as five," he said. "If we win it could be as late as seven. Probably win or lose, I'm not going to be in the best of moods. *Something's* gonna happen."

I turn up at seven and find him well settled in. He got out of bed at four, was in the shower at four-twenty and at his desk at five, consumed with loathing for self and team. "We had seventy yards in gains negated by sixty yards in penalties," he says. "That's nine points." I ask him if there was any pattern to the penalties. "Yeah," he says, "they were all stupid." It's the same problem: the Cowboys just happened to win in spite of it. "When your players do dumb things, either they are dumb players or you are not doing a good job of getting across to them what causes you to lose games." The moment the Cowboys hit the locker room after their victory, Parcells told them, "You know, guys, I just want my team to play better."

Now he begins to review the video. It's seven hours before he will meet with the news media for what he calls distribution-of-credit day, when the only positive thing he'll go out of his way to stress is Mike Vanderjagt's clutch kick, which wasn't clutch. (There's no shame in missing a fifty-yarder. It is, from a kicker's point of view, all upside.) He was right: there is always something. One tight end, Anthony Fasano, missed blocks; the other, Jason Whitten, dropped balls. Parcells arrives at the play just before Roy Williams intercepted the pass that, had the Redskins caught it, might have tied the game. "Right now," he says, "I think we're going to lose." They didn't lose, of course, but you wouldn't know it from Parcells. He's seeing what's wrong. Four times, for instance, his rookie safety, Patrick Watkins, goes low to make a tackle and leads with his neck and shoulders. "He's block tackling," says Parcells. "I've seen more guys get hurt doing that than any single thing in football."

He calls one of his trainers for an injury report. "I apologize to you for being a little rough on you last night," Parcells says. (He barked at the trainer for taking Terrell Owens into the locker room before the end of the game to have his finger X-rayed. In the first place, it made it harder for Parcells to claim Owens wasn't injured. In the second place, it was a *finger.*)

"I appreciate you saying that," says the trainer, who then explains that it was Owens, not him, who insisted on the X-ray. "I asked him, 'You want to go in?' and he said yes," the trainer says.

Parcells sighs and says, "Now, Terry's not hurt that bad, is he?" Terry Glenn has something wrong with his shoulder.

The trainer — no doubt sensing that his injury report is about to be edited — says he's unsure.

"Well," Parcells says, ending the conversation before any other players have a chance to get hurt, "you better order a coffin for Watkins. The way he's tackling, he'll need it soon."

He was right: there's always something. It's in the nature of the job. "Guys can't take it," he says. "That's why they get out." Some of the best coaches the game ever saw — Bill Walsh, John Madden — quit simply because the strain was too great. Parcells won't quit. He now knows that about himself: he needs it more than it needs him. He just turned sixty-five. His marriage is over, and his daughters are grown. "My whole life I've always had some guys," he says. "You gotta have some guys. That's probably one of the fears I have when I get older: that I won't have any guys." His younger brother Don died last year. Most of his close friends who haven't died are back in New Jersey. His legacy is secure: he will one day have a bust in the football Hall of Fame. But then his legacy was secure in 2003, before he took the Cowboys' head-coaching job. Before he did so, he had a surprising number of plaintive phone calls from former players. "My old players didn't want me to take the job," he says. "They were afraid I'd embarrass myself. They didn't get it. It's not about your legacy."

Right now he is living alone in what amounts to a hotel room in

Irving, Texas, whose sole virtue is that it is a ten-minute drive to both the Cowboys' practice facility and Texas Stadium. It's just him and whatever it is that keeps him in the game. For the longest time he pretended that he didn't need it. He walked out of two jobs without having another in hand, and he has played hard-to-get with NFL owners more times than any coach in NFL history. After he quit the Jets, in 1999, he said at a press conference: "I've coached my last football game. You can write that on your little chalkboard. This is it. It's over." Now, even as his job appears to be making him sick, he has abandoned the pose. "As you get older," he says, pointing to a screen, where the play is frozen, "your needs diminish. They don't increase. They diminish. I need less money. I need less sex. But this — this doesn't change."

What *this* is, he can't — or won't — specify. But when your life has been defined by the pressure of competition and your response to it, there's a feeling you get, and it's hard to shake. You wake up each morning knowing the next game is all that matters. If you fail in it, nothing you've done with your life counts. By your very nature you always have to start all over again, fresh. It's an uncomfortable feeling, but it's nonetheless addictive. Even if you have millions in the bank and everyone around you tells you that you're a success, you seek out that uncomfortable place. And if you don't, you're on the wrong side of the thin curtain that separates Cyclone Hart from Vito Antuofermo. "It's a cloistered, narrow existence that I'm not proud of," says Parcells. "I don't know what's going on in the world. And I don't have time to find out. All I think about is football and winning. But hey —" He sweeps his hand over his desk and points to the office that scarcely registers his presence. "Who's got it better than me?"

ROBERT HUBER

The Madness of John Chaney

FROM PHILADELPHIA MAGAZINE

Another obsessed coach, captured by Huber with one perfect expression: "Yesterday was a long, long day. And the collective unconscious of black men of a certain age holds it forever."
— D.M.

HOW YOU START is how you finish.

The old man loves little sayings that capture the whole deal, and he sprinkles them through practice on an early December morning. Sipping a twelve-ounce Dunkin' Donuts coffee, in sweats and a Temple baseball cap, John Chaney, born almost three-quarters of a century ago, edges around the Liacouras Center court stiffly, pigeon-toed, calmly watching his players scrimmage before the sun is up on North Broad. Then the ball is passed carelessly out of bounds.

"I'm looking at your head, Dustin!" Chaney yells in his pebbles-in-a-pipe voice. "What you can't see will hurt you. But what you can't see but know, will help you." Coach is full of stuff like this. What's he mean? It's not always obvious. He wants his kids to think, to figure it out.

A few minutes later, Coach is holding forth near midcourt, his team in a loose semicircle, dripping with sweat, all eyes on him. He is talking foundation, he is talking how you start, as a player: "With one step. Catch it, pass it, ex-e-cu-ting your plays. Your job, when you come out on the floor, is, one, no turnovers. Two — what's the second one?"

Someone calls out, softly: *Establish the floor.*

"Establish the floor!" Chaney yells. It means, and they know this because he's been drumming it home for a month of practices,

Take control. Make it yours. Chaney is quickly heating up to something larger, and his eyes seem to go opaque with intensity: "You do that in marriage, you do that in a home, you do that in a business, everything you do involves what you do the first day. The first day!"

A momentary silence, everyone still watching him. Then, louder still:

"Even today, this country right now, this country that you live in, they're going back to how this country was BORN! The Constitution. And they're STILL all fucked up in the head about it. The Constitution says, CLEARLY, separation of church and state. . . . The motherfuckers are still fucking around right now, trying to appropriate church, religion, into the Constitution. They haven't found it yet. And you're going to find that that's how you're going to look at life! Keep coming back to it! All the time!"

His players, they're still staring at him.

To Coach, though, there's nothing strange at all in his leap to the Constitution, *their* Constitution, because it is, after all, the basis of things, and it is an injustice, what is going on. And injustice, all injustice, is personal. It's about all of them, and he's still fighting it.

Chaney has been the head coach at Temple for twenty-four years now, saving kids like these and making the Hall of Fame to boot. And he knows the end is coming, just like it does for everybody. But *how* it's coming, how they're trying to take it from him, it's not right — and he's not going to let it happen. He has come so far, a black boy from the hellhole of Black Bottom, Florida, born during the height of the Depression. He knows injustice. Just as he knows how they're fucking up the world now. The war. The lies.

"How can you keep making the same mistakes?" he wants to know. Back to his team, back to b-ball. Back to a foundation. More on life as John Chaney sees it. "You start with a constitution, as a player — always go back to that. You have to find your way in this basketball world. How you start is how you finish!"

And so there was, last year, the strange odyssey of the Goon and the War, the mating of injustice on a personal and an apocalyptic scale, and it seemed that at seventy-three, John Chaney was, just maybe, finished. Or that he'd lost his marbles. Chaney has a history of violent outbursts, which have tended to focus on opposing coaches:

his third game at Temple, in 1982, he got Stanford's Tom Davis in a chokehold; ditto Gerry Gimelstob of George Washington in 1984; and in '94 he screamed "I'm going to kill you!" at John Calipari of Massachusetts during a postgame press conference. All three times, some alleged manipulation of the games' referees pushed Chaney's hot button, which is a hellfire mix of competitive fairness — justice! — and straight-out competitiveness. Chaney can reach the brink of a fistfight over weekend tennis — he'll get, a friend says, a little "Calipari-ish" — never mind the big-time games he coaches.

But last year's blowup was different. In February, the day before the season's second meeting with city rival St. Joe's, Chaney announced in a media conference call that he was fed up with how St. Joe's was setting picks (where a stationary player gets in the path of a defender to free up a teammate for a shot). Chaney claimed that St. Joe's pick-setters were moving — That's wrong! Illegal! — and if the refs continued to let it happen, he would dispatch "one of my goons and have him run through one of those guys and chop him in the neck or something." Nobody paid much attention, given Chaney's penchant for saying all kinds of things. However, early in the second half of the game, with Temple behind by six points, Chaney got a technical foul for arguing a call against his team, and then, obviously agitated, sent in Nehemiah Ingram, 250 pounds of football player who almost never saw basketball action. Ingram proceeded to throw elbows, bump, and shove his way to five fouls in four minutes — astonishingly quick work. The last one was a push that sent St. Joe's forward John Bryant, who'd leaped for a dunk, down to the floor, where he writhed in pain for several minutes. After the game — Temple lost by seven points — a still-aggravated Chaney said, "I'm sending a message. And I'm going to send in what we used to do years ago — send in the goons. That's what I'm going to do."

It came to light, two days later, that Bryant's arm was broken. Chaney — who had issued a threat, followed through on it, and then told us exactly what he'd done, as if all of this flowed as naturally as A-B-C — was in a lot of trouble. His suspension, first self-imposed at one game, was stretched by Temple to five. The media began calling for his head, and racially charged calls and e-mails flooded Temple. Though Coach still had some backers: Bill Clinton phoned to say that he and Hillary loved him, and he should stick with it. So did Ed Rendell, to tell Chaney how much the state needs him.

All this came on the heels of inflamed comments Chaney had made on President Bush and Iraq. When Temple played Xavier in Cincinnati last January, Chaney told a reporter how much it bothered him that Ohio's electoral votes had put the president back in the White House: "I hate everything out here. It's not the people I hate, it's what they did that I hate." Noting that Ohio unemployment was high, Chaney added, "Sometimes you get what you deserve."

A few days later, at a Philadelphia Sportswriters dinner at the Cherry Hill Hilton, ex-Eagle Gary Cobb, in opening remarks, ribbed Chaney about his politics, suggesting that the values to live by that Coach instills in his players are really *Republican* tried-and-trues. The red flag had been waved: when Chaney spoke, he went off on Cobb, Bush, the war. *Where are the weapons of mass destruction? All these young people dying before they have a chance to live. The lies! . . .* This at an event where he was being honored for winning seven hundred college basketball games. There were catcalls from the audience to shut up and sit down; Chaney challenged one heckler to meet him outside. His friends there — and Chaney has a lot of friends everywhere — were embarrassed for him.

But Chaney has never started a fire that didn't deserve a little more gas. The next day, he was a call-in guest on Michael Barkann's *Daily News Live* TV show and got into it with columnist Bill Conlin, hammering Bush and the media in one fell swoop: *Our boys are dying because somebody lied to us, because the president of the United States lied to us, and you all know it and nobody says anything.*

Later in the show, he bellowed, "You guys all belly up. You're all Republicans!"

"Don't lecture me," an annoyed Barkann responded. "This is a sports program, John, not foreign policy. But I still love you."

"I don't care if you love me!" screamed Chaney, sounding unhinged. "This is America!"

It's not that his theater-of-the-absurd opinions were so outrageous — as opinions. Neither was sending in a player to commit hard fouls — intimidation has always been part of the game. What was disturbing was the *intensity* of it all. Chaney had always been cranky and loud, but now the volume had been turned even higher, over wrongs as disparate as uncalled fouls and an unjust war. Why was he so *angry?*

This season, it appears little has changed: after the first game against St. Joe's, another loss, Chaney was whining to reporters once again, that the refs were anticipating trouble where there wasn't any and had made *six straight calls* against his team at the end. The injustice! And: "Philadelphia don't let nothing go. You guys don't let nothing go," he said of the goon controversy.

The thing was, none of the reporters had even asked him about it.

Get with John Chaney away from basketball (and sportswriter dinners), though, and you meet a different guy, one who, over a few hours in his Temple office, will take you on a tour through poetry, Sinatra, philosophy, politics, religion (no use for it), sex, and food (an abiding obsession). "I can remember when I was a kid," he goes off in his gravelly whisper. "Oh my, my mother would take me to the Italian Market, and I carried the bags, and if I did a good job, she'd take me to George's, and get one of those pork sandwiches where juices run out the side of your mouth. I still go there and eat them!"

Happy as a hog in slop, leaning forward at his desk, his hands on either side of his face in an "Oh my" punctuation — Chaney's small head peers, turtle-like, from hunched shoulders as he pages through a little black book and shares his favorite jottings: *The game has to break your heart, before you know you love it.* And: *Tell me where to stand, I can move the world.*

"That's Archimedes!" he says. "I got shit all over this book. Here's something! Thurgood said, 'A black snake or a white snake, it's still a snake.'"

He turns to his favorite Sinatra song, "One for My Baby," and for no apparent reason does a complete, and surprisingly soft and slow and sweet, rendition of it. He tosses aside Jonathan Kozol's *Savage Inequalities* to hand over Derek Bok's *The Shape of the River* — "It talks about affirmative action, how necessary it is." On sex: Chaney just had one of his players in to warn him he was getting carried away in that department. "You can't do that! You fucking all the time and you get out of bed and your legs are all wobbly, you can't do that! *My* coach told me that. You can't train and fuck. When I first came here, I told guys they weren't allowed to fool around with girls. Well, I've grown old, so now I want to know what girl they're fooling around *with*."

It's true — not the sexual nosiness, but knowing what his players are up to. Chaney is famous for taking kids from broken homes and nurturing them, *willing* them, into manhood. What we don't know is how much fun he has doing it. One day in early December, freshman Anthony Ivory is summoned to explain where he was yesterday, a Sunday. Chaney was trying to get hold of him — not for any particular reason, just to check in. "What if your momma calls me and wants to know where you are, and I don't know?" he chastises. "What am I supposed to tell her?"

Ivory, a three-hundred-pound seven-footer from Washington, D.C., is rendered nearly mute, then manages to claim that he was studying all evening, and deep into the night, with a friend.

"Then have him call me," Chaney commands.

A couple hours later, Ivory phones — it turns out his "friend" is female. "What!" Chaney barks. "I'm going to interrogate her ass!" It also turns out that, along with a credible Sinatra, Chaney does a very good Bob-Newhart-on-the-phone impression, when he gives studymate Renee a call:

"I want to know why he's in your room at two A.M. when practice is at six."

- - - -

"You say helping each other."

- - - -

"I want you to come in here. I want to see what kind of person —"

- - - -

"Oh. How did you sprain your ankle?"

- - - -

"Then I want a picture of you on crutches."

- - - -

"I know I'm funny! Shut up!"

- - - -

"No, I'm not giving you money for a camera."

They go on to discuss how she got hurt. Chaney worries over her lack of health insurance. All this for the girlfriend of a player, Chaney confides later, who has only an outside chance of becoming any good. He suggests, finally, that Renee continue helping Anthony, but that she consider doing it *during the daytime*.

So it is easy to see why when those who know Chaney well — his assistants, writers who have covered the team forever, janitors at Temple — talk about the two sides of Coach, they say that this one, the one that cares so deeply and takes us all on a funhouse ride, is the real one. Because it's so clearly, well, *good.*

But what to make, then, of the Chaney who raged before the St. Joe's game last year and kept raging afterward and as a matter of fact, when you ask him about it now is only too happy to start raging all over again, since he only did *what all coaches do, sending a player in to play hard?*

Even as Chaney insists that the St. Joe's episode was a natural part of the game, his buddies who go back a long way — Sonny and Claude and Jay, black men who've been friends with Chaney fifty years — all know better. "It doesn't take long to remember yesterday," his old friend Andy Hinson says, talking about Coach's long-ago past. Hinson attended college with Chaney in the early '50s at Bethune-Cookman, a black school in Florida. Yesterday was a long, long day. And the collective unconscious of black men of a certain age holds it forever.

Chaney started from nothing down in Florida, where when it rained the water came right up, flooding the porch ankle-deep where the kitchen was, leaving frogs and mud and bugs and shit for his poor mama who made three dollars and fifty cents a week cleaning houses for rich white folk. His dad brought the family — his mother, his younger brother and sister, his auntie — north during World War II. First day, heat of August, fourteen-year-old John walked around South Philly in the one wool outfit he had, a stick-figured yahoo. Every day at school that fall, a kid named Dante would take his lunch money. John would eat nothing, go home crying with a headache. Had to go get the belt so Momma could teach him a lesson. *You stand up for yourself!* One night, sleepless, John hatched a plan. Next morning when he got to school, he went to the metal shop, got inside the cage where they kept the tools, and found a wooden mallet. He was going to crack Dante right on the back of his fuckin' skull. Except he got caught first, with the mallet, and got a week's suspension for the idea. More whippings at home — but Dante never bothered him again. A foothold. . . .

And then he found ball.

He'd sneak off, Saturdays — he was supposed to wash cars in the garage below their place at Seventeenth and Ellsworth with his father, all day, for seventy-five cents. He'd play ball instead. Another whipping when he eventually showed back home. Didn't matter. Ball was his escape — better than escape, it hatched an idea. That he was good. That *he* would do better than the rat-hole they were living in. He went all over the city, looking for games. They called him the Cherokee, he was so skinny and his cheekbones so high he looked like an Indian, but nobody could take the ball away from him. Along about here his mother told him — she had to before he found out somehow — that his daddy was really his stepfather, and she begged him never to tell his . . . well, *half*-brother and *half*-sister. John never told, and never found out who his real father was. He kept playing ball. His father — *step*father — said it was a waste of time, didn't represent nothing. For John, it didn't need to represent nothing. Because becoming Philadelphia public-school player of the year — that was a pretty tall thing in itself. Nobody could take the ball from him.

But his hometown did. Philly colleges — including, *especially*, the Big Five — took a pass. He had to pack a cardboard suitcase and head south to Bethune. And then the Eastern League instead of the NBA — shit, everybody knew he had the *talent* — and then a slow climb in coaching, junior high, Simon Gratz, leap to Cheyney University, where he won a Division II national championship in '78, until, finally — Christ, at this point he was past fifty — Temple president Peter Liacouras took a brave flier, bringing a black coach into the Big Five. All the way to the Hall of Fame! Twenty-four years now. . . .

And counting down. One thing Chaney, a stickler for the truth, can't dispute: his teams have dropped a notch. He took Temple to the NCAA tournament seventeen out of nineteen years, reaching the Elite 8 five times (only three more wins, any of those years, and he would have had a national championship). But the last four years, the Owls haven't been good enough to get to the NCAAs. And then there's Martelli at St. Joe's, getting him seven straight times now and counting. Chaney once owned St. Joe's; when Martelli started in '95, Chaney beat him ten straight.

By all accounts, especially his, Chaney's passion and coaching haven't gone slack. But the players he can still get aren't quite as good. Chaney complains — with this, he's undoubtedly got a point — that other coaches now talk him down in the high-stakes dog-and-pony show of recruiting big-time prospects: *You really want to play in that god-awful slow-down offense, and get up at 5:00 A.M. to practice? And what if the old man decides to quit your sophomore year?*

So it's really pretty easy to understand why Chaney is grasping for any edge he can find — St. Joe's is cheating! — and raging on about refs who refuse to call it.

Oh, it was so painful, getting suspended for those five games, end of last season. Chaney teams almost always start slow, he likes to build to the end, when he can see the fruits of all his work, his boys *finally getting it.* . . . Assistant coach Dan Leibovitz, who'd taken over, called during the suspension to say, "No matter what happens, I want you to know that I'm behind you. And that I love you." They cried. It seemed Chaney was on the brink of getting fired, and one Temple board of trustees member says president David Adamany would have canned him if the board hadn't intervened on Chaney's behalf (though Adamany denies that he considered firing him). When the season was done, Chaney was forced to hunker down and shut up most of the summer, and staying in and silent is not exactly a style that fits John Chaney.

He was too ashamed to see even his tennis buddies, for a couple of months. It was as low as his friends have ever seen him, as bad, Andy Hinson says, as getting snubbed by the city the first time, half a century ago.

Chaney regrouped and came back this season fired up. Which means when his close friend Speedy Morris called to wish him a Merry Christmas, Coach said, "Speedy, how the fuck can I have a Merry Christmas when they're dying over there?"

You always got to keep moving forward. The things he went through, that's yesterday. This is today. You need that to have a tomorrow. He'll take the players he can get and work with them. But sometimes. . . .

A few years ago, Chaney was sure he had Rasheed Wallace coming from Gratz to Temple; now an NBA star with Detroit, he would've been Chaney's best player ever. Assistant coach Bill Ellerbee had helped develop the kid in the summertime, plus he and Chaney were friends with the family; they all but had him signed — suddenly, off Wallace goes to North Carolina, a blue-chip school whose coach, Dean Smith, was white. Andy Hinson, then a coach at Cheyney University, remembers that Chaney came, the very day he got the bad news on Wallace, to guest-lecture his "Scientific Principles of Coaching" class. That day, says Hinson, "the subject became 'You Are Going to Be Black Forever.' John was wide open. It was usually forty-five minutes. He went on for two hours." On white people sweeping in and taking what's yours, what you nurtured. The injustice!

Can he stop it now? Chaney always tells the truth — he *is* old. He's got diabetes and had one cornea transplant and needs another and can tell Danny next to him on the bench during games exactly where everybody should be, but not always — the light is tricky now — whether that was Mark or Dustin who made that move, and are they listening, are they listening anymore when he tells them, again and again and again and again, that speed kills, to take their goddamn time, to PROTECT THE BALL?

Of course, it's bigger than that, it's much more than b-ball. Even Chaney admits this: "My frustration and my anger about things that can be done right, things that don't have a strong foundation, like lies. . . ." Like war.

But come on, he's a coach: Chaney wasn't thinking war and kids dying when he sent in the goon, it was that fucker Martelli getting him *again*. But the spark that set his fire was the injustice. Chaney wants to will the world into a righteous place as he kicks your ass. Or at least still have the goddamn chance to! It's wrong! They're trying to screw him! Even if nobody else could see much of an injustice in a referee's calls, *he* could. He has to. Absolutely, his idea of injustice has broadened — These boys! The war! — but he still operates in the hair-trigger world of a challenge, a fight, the desperate need to win. It's a Chaney aphorism: "There's always another wall to climb. Even when there ain't no wall."

He won't change, all the way to the end. *How you start is how you finish.*

He's still pushing his boys. Sergio Olmos, another seven-foot freshman project of a player, brings his parents, who have come all the way from their home in Spain, into the office to meet Coach one January afternoon. Chaney hugs and kisses them, and *Oh my God, were you at practice? Was my language too bad? But you don't under-*

stand what I was saying, now that's *a good thing!* Coach is a one-man roaring cackling band. He wants to show them — the mom especially — that he's making sweet Sergio tougher, and he paws the air like a dog digging in dirt, and the mom imitates, pawing too, and everyone laughs, as an international language for John Chaney willing another boy toward manhood has been discovered.

MICHAEL WILBON

The Real Deal
in So Many Ways

FROM THE WASHINGTON POST

Wilbon writes the way he talks, with passion and clarity — and fast.
He is the "Blink" of the sports writing world, and his first impressions
in pro basketball are right on.
— D.M.

IN 1956, THE BOSTON CELTICS traded Cliff Hagan and Ed
Macauley to the St. Louis Hawks for the rights to the number-two
pick in the college draft, where they selected a kid who had led his
team to fifty-five straight victories and two NCAA championships,
who averaged twenty-eight points and twenty-nine rebounds his senior year, a kid who turned out to be Bill Russell.

In 1978, while Larry Bird was a junior at Indiana State, the
Celtics drafted him even though he was returning to school for his
senior season.

In 1980, the Celtics traded the number-one pick in the draft to
the Golden State Warriors for a package that would turn out to be
Robert Parish and Kevin McHale, who would join Bird to form
probably the greatest front line in NBA history.

Completing any one of those deals puts you at the top of your
sport.

Making all three of those deals, as Red Auerbach did as boss of
the Celtics, makes you a legend, someone to be loved, hated, en-
vied, studied, and ultimately treasured. There will never, ever be
anyone like Auerbach again.

Never again will a man coach and build sixteen championships in a major sport in one lifetime. No one man will impact the game of basketball, on the court, the way Auerbach did as coach and boss of the Celtics.

He was John Wooden and Branch Rickey, with a touch of Vince Lombardi for good measure.

If all Auerbach had done was make the aforementioned deals and win those nine championships as head coach, it would have been enough to make him the greatest coach in the history of professional basketball. His teams won those nine championships without a league scoring champ, with players such as K. C. Jones and Satch Sanders who were paid primarily to play defense, with great players such as John Havlicek coming off the bench. That's enough of a contribution right there, actually more than should be expected of any one coach.

But Auerbach had to go and have a spine too. He drafted the first 'African-American player (Chuck Cooper). Auerbach was the first to start five black players. Auerbach, when he retired, essentially picked Russell to coach the Celtics, making him the first black head coach in modern American professional sports. Auerbach was doing this, mind you, in a city very often openly hostile to blacks, a city heading into racial upheaval. "Red, to me, was colorblind," former Celtic Kermit Washington said last night in a telephone conversation. "He just didn't care. If you were purple and from Mars and gave an effort, Red was fine. There were a lot of things going on in Boston then. But Red was such a strong personality. He didn't answer to anybody. I think he always knew that if he won, he wouldn't have to answer to anybody. He was a tough, tough man."

Washington, like Auerbach, was a Washingtonian. "I went to American University with his daughter Randy," Washington said. "He was always so kind to me. Some other guys I grew up with in D.C., Adrian Dantley and James Brown, we'd go up and work as camp counselors for Red [in suburban Boston]."

Everybody who hung around basketball circles, particularly in Washington and Boston, has an Auerbach story. The man lived eighty-nine years. You could find him pretty easily, perhaps at a George Washington game at Smith Center, maybe having lunch in Chinatown on Tuesdays. Washington's story is fascinating because he was at the center of the most unfortunate incident in NBA history, the punch that shattered Rudy Tomjanovich's face.

"When they were going to throw me out of the league," Washington said, "Red really stuck up for me. I was really, really ostracized. And Red told Bob Ryan of the *Boston Globe* that people should give me a chance, that he'd known me since I was a teenager and that he knew me to be a good kid. Red's word was gospel in Boston, and that story was in the *Globe*. People gave me a chance in Boston, and it was because of Red. You give him an effort and he loved you. He didn't care about points. He didn't care about the exact number of rebounds. He cared about effort. And he didn't want false effort. He hated that . . . diving on a ball out of bounds you had no chance to save. Red and Pete Newell really stood up for me at a difficult time.

"I'd go by and see him. He had an office right near AU. I hadn't talked to him in a couple of months, but we all knew he wasn't very well. He was good to all of us, all the kids in D.C. You know, Red would sound surly, but there were so many acts of kindness."

It was sometime in the early 1980s when my boss, George Solomon, who was then the sports editor of the *Post*, told me to call Red Auerbach about some issue or another. And he might as well have ordered me to call God. Red's number was listed in the phone book in those days, and while it took me half a week, I ultimately called and asked whatever questions I needed to have answered. I apologized for interrupting his evening at home and I'll never forget him saying, "Kid, if it's a choice between interrupting me or writing something stupid, call."

So, I did, often enough to learn stuff over the years but never so much he'd consider me a nuisance. Sometimes, you could ask one question and if it was the right one, maybe about Bird or Jordan or Barkley or Stockton, Red might talk for six minutes. Recently, the name Phil Jackson might elicit an answer twice that long, some of it funny and much of it less than flattering. If you wanted niceties, Red was the wrong guy to call. And for those of us who love basketball, it was as if we were talking to Moses. My friend Sam Smith, in Sunday's *Chicago Tribune*, called Auerbach "the greatest nonplaying figure in professional basketball history."

The stories coming out of Los Angeles and Philly and all the cities where the Celtics were despised cannot be written without mentioning that Auerbach's cigar smoke could be very annoying, that he did devious things like cut off the hot water to the visiting locker room in Boston Garden, or remove some of the light bulbs or turn up the heat to the point of unbearable. The very mention of Len Bias's name turned his voice into a whisper. It was one of the very, very few moves that didn't turn out the way Auerbach thought it would.

Even so, it is impossible to imagine the NBA without Red Auerbach, the man who built the NBA's greatest dynasty, who on the Mount Rushmore of Coaches sits right there beside Wooden and Lombardi. Fortunately, the greatest contributor in the history of professional basketball has left his signature in enough places that it's not possible he'll ever be forgotten.

BOB HOHLER

$neaker War

FROM THE BOSTON GLOBE

A good old-fashioned newspaper series on a snarky operator in the
world of sneakers and basketball, a world getting ever younger and
sicker.

— D.M.

SPRINGFIELD, MASS. — A brazen foot soldier in a multibillion-dollar war between sneaker makers for the soles of America's youth,
Thomas J. "TJ" Gassnola has peddled basketball dreams to inner-city adolescents across New England despite a lengthy criminal history and prodigious legacy of financial delinquency.

The face of youth basketball in the region for Adidas, Gassnola
is a freewheeling recruiter whose tactics often have clashed with
rules set by the National Collegiate Athletic Association to protect amateur athletes who aspire to careers in college sports. Some
of his practices underscore the inability of the NCAA and other
watchdog agencies to adequately police abuses in summer youth
basketball.

A *Globe* investigation of the sneaker industry's influence on youth
basketball in New England found that Gassnola has handed cash to
members of his Adidas-sponsored summer travel teams for expenses
unrelated to basketball. Several parents of elite players said the
Springfield-based recruiter offered them free airfare or Adidas
merchandise while pursuing their sons, and another parent said he
interpreted Gassnola's sales pitch to mean the recruiter would provide his son improper financial aid. NCAA rules bar amateur players
from receiving anything but "actual and necessary travel, room and
board, and apparel and equipment for competition and practice."

The *Globe* also witnessed Gassnola drive his teenage players in several states, even though his Massachusetts driver's license has been revoked or suspended twenty-four times and was not valid from 1993 until last month.

"You're talking about putting kids at risk in so many different areas," said John Kottori, chairman of boys' basketball in southern New England for the Amateur Athletic Union. "It makes my stomach turn to think about it."

Gassnola, whose supporters include Adidas, and numerous parents and players, has done it all in the company's name. As the sneaker giant's top New England recruiter in its quest to wrest supremacy of the market from archrival Nike, Gassnola operates in a loosely regulated subculture in which Nike, Adidas, and Reebok, a Canton-based Adidas subsidiary, spend millions of dollars on "grassroots" campaigns to curry favor with children as young as twelve in their hunt for the next Michael Jordan or LeBron James, superstars whose endorsements shape the marketplace.

The system has created a cottage industry in which corporate agents such as Gassnola lavish free travel, shoes, gear, and other benefits on predominantly needy youths with basketball skills. For the players, it is a heady environment with a sometimes shady underside: for all the future college and pro stars who have prospered in the system, some have seen their reputations tarnished by their company-backed coaches or recruiters.

One of the most egregious cases involved a Nike-funded coach, Myron Piggie, of Kansas City, Missouri, who was sentenced to thirty-seven months in prison in 2001 for fraud and tax convictions after paying more than $35,000 to five teenagers, including future NBA players Corey Maggette, Kareem Rush, and Korleone Young, to play in his summer program. Three of the players, after enrolling in college, were suspended from basketball competition by the NCAA for periods ranging from five to nine games. (The NCAA has no jurisdiction over amateur athletes until they are enrolled in member schools.)

Subsequent efforts by the NCAA to crack down on abuses in summer youth basketball have produced few results, largely because of its limited jurisdiction.

"Every time we try to make rules, somebody tries to circumvent them," said Tom Izzo, who guided Michigan State to the national championship in 2000 and serves on a select NCAA committee of college coaches.

Gassnola, thirty-four, aspires to make his New England Playaz the top power in summer youth basketball in New England, a distinction long held by the Nike-sponsored Boston Amateur Basketball Club. He declared himself "hell-bent on destroying" the BABC and engaged in a verbal confrontation with BABC coach Leo Papile last winter that nearly became physical during a tournament in Chelsea.

"It's a personal war, a turf war, and a sneaker war," said Gassnola, who has stocked his team with some of the region's best talent, including stars he has poached from clubs in Greater Boston, including the BABC.

"When I die, I want it to say on my tombstone: 'TJ Gassnola, the Guy Who Put Leo Papile Out of Business,'" Gassnola said.

Fierce Competition

Nike invests an estimated $15 million a year on amateur youth basketball, while Adidas spends about $10 million annually and Reebok $6 million a year, according to an industry executive.

Papile, fifty-two, who founded the BABC in 1977, also serves as assistant executive director of basketball operations for the Boston Celtics. His program receives $50,000 a year from Nike plus sneakers, gear, and apparel, while Gassnola said he receives no cash from Adidas but an unlimited supply of merchandise.

Gassnola recently enhanced his program by gaining an endorsement from NBA Hall of Famer Bob Lanier, whose name now appears on the team's uniforms. But Papile, whose program has won eleven national championships and sent more than two hundred players to Division 1 colleges, including NBA Hall of Famer Patrick Ewing and former Celtic Dana Barros, shrugged off Gassnola's challenge.

"I don't know how old he is, but all I can say is, 'Good luck to him, if he lives long enough,'" Papile said. "I've seen guys like him come and go, and when they go, good riddance. They're not good for basketball."

The scramble among the sneaker giants for the nation's elite young athletes has escalated since the early 1990s, spawning dozens of company-sponsored teams that barnstorm the nation from April to July competing in showcases that often attract college recruiters, NBA scouts, and national scouting services.

Nearly every American-bred college and NBA star in recent years has played for a company-sponsored team, and organizers such as Gassnola and Papile have come to wield enormous influence with young players, helping them land lucrative scholarships to private secondary schools, fielding inquiries from college coaches, and advising them on their college choices.

In turn, players who make it big both by turning pro and reaping lucrative sneaker endorsement deals sometimes reward their summer coaches, though Papile said none of his alumni have given back to his program. Gassnola said he receives a combined $20,000 a year from three NBA players whom he declined to identify. (None of his alumni has reached the NBA.)

Indeed, a number of NBA stars, including Tracy McGrady, Tim Thomas, and Tyson Chandler, have designated portions of their multimillion-dollar sneaker contracts to their company-sponsored coaches or handlers.

"This is a big-time business," said Gassnola, a fast-talking recruiter with a self-portrayed "degree in bull" and close ties to former University of Massachusetts coach John Calipari's program at the University of Memphis.

Papile raised eyebrows in the 1980s when he became a Boston-based assistant coach for Cleveland State University after five members of his BABC teams went to play for the school. Responding to rumors that he may have sold players to colleges, Papile issued an emphatic denial in a 1997 interview with the *Globe*.

"Anybody who has the courage to confront me with that, I would go into a steel cage with them and pound them to smithereens, because that's how untrue it is," he said. One summer coach who recently clashed with Papile over a player questioned the propriety of Papile serving as both a high-level scouting adviser for the Celtics and an amateur coach whose former players the Celtics could draft. Two former BABC players, Iowa State's Will Blalock and Notre Dame's Torin Francis, recently participated in predraft workouts for the Celtics.

"It's absolutely absurd that he's getting paid by an NBA team and running an AAU team," said Rick Isaacs, who coaches the H Squad, an elite independent travel team based in California. "Is that not a conflict of interest?"

Papile said he has long reported his BABC role to the NBA, which has approved the activity as a community service. Papile, who said he is not paid by the BABC, also noted that Blalock and Francis worked out for many NBA teams other than the Celtics.

Though Papile has long served as the face of the BABC, his name has not appeared on corporate documents the organization has filed with the secretary of state. Instead, Papile's wife, Kimberly Johnson, is listed as the BABC's president, treasurer, and clerk, while Frank Burke, a basketball operations assistant for the Celtics, and Stuart August, a lawyer, are listed as directors. Papile explained his absence from the documents as a consequence of his work for the Celtics, which requires him to travel about two hundred days a year. He also owns and manages a number of real estate properties.

"All I can do is coach," he said. "I don't have time to do all the other stuff."

Before going nonprofit in 2003, the BABC functioned for many years as a for-profit corporation, though Papile said no one in the organization received a salary and "we never came close to making a profit."

As a nonprofit, the BABC reported raising nearly $99,000 in 2004, the most recent year for which its federal tax return was available. The club reported spending more than $94,000, including more than $6,700 in charitable donations to scholarship funds at Chelsea High School and Charlestown High School.

Numerous coaches, however, have complained through the years about losing players to Papile's higher-profile program — Kalon Jenkins of the Stoughton-based Bay State Magic said the core of his fifteen-and-under team jumped this year to the BABC — yet Papile generally has maintained a favorable reputation while reigning as New England's dominant force in summer youth basketball.

He was inducted in 2004 into the New England Basketball Hall of Fame.

"If I feel my kids need to be at the next level, I deal with Leo only," said Pete Washington, who heads the Young Achievers Basketball Club in Mattapan and previously coached at Roxbury Community College and East Boston High School.

Criminal History

Gassnola, however, has become a pariah among many youth coaches for his history of breaking laws, rules, and promises. The AAU, a major force in youth basketball, has suspended him since 2000 for bouncing an estimated $2,500 in checks for tournament fees.

Gassnola said he has "made a ton of mistakes in my life." He attributed many of the lapses to a "dysfunctional" upbringing and said, "I absolutely robbed Peter to pay Paul to make this [basketball] program work." But he said he has turned his life around.

Gassnola has been convicted three times of larceny over $250 or receiving stolen property, among other charges, and has been ordered by judges in at least eleven civil cases to make good on more than $45,000 in bad debt.

"This is what I do and I love it," he said of his basketball program. "I've stepped on some people's toes I shouldn't have, but I didn't do it intentionally and I'll never do it again."

Court records show Gassnola's criminal record dates to 1988, when he was convicted of delinquent larceny at age sixteen and ordered committed to the Department of Youth Services for a year, with the sentence suspended.

Gassnola said he has applied the lessons of his troubled youth to help a new generation of at-risk teenagers.

"Imagine a guy who sits in juvenile court with a chip on his shoulder the size of you and me," he said, referring to himself. "He went from one juvenile home to another. His father left him at a young age and his mother never understood him. There were a lot of bumps in the road, but he tried to do the right thing. This guy understands kids better than anybody because he used to be one of them, and he doesn't want those kids to go down the same bumpy road."

The road remained bumpy for Gassnola in adulthood. At twenty-two, he was convicted of assaulting a man outside a Springfield bar, for which he received a ninety-day suspended jail sentence.

Less than a year later, Gassnola was indicted on charges of felony assault and unarmed burglary stemming from a confrontation in which one of the alleged victims told police he aimed a licensed handgun at Gassnola to ward him off. The alleged victim also reported a subsequent encounter with Gassnola.

"He told me he could have me killed and that he belonged to one of the highest organized crime families in Springfield," the man told police, according to court records.

A jury in Hampden Superior Court found Gassnola not guilty of the charges. (In an interview, Gassnola denied having any connection to organized crime, though he said he once was involved in bookmaking.)

Gassnola's criminal record also includes convictions for receiving stolen property and uttering a false check in 1998, larceny over $250 in 2000, and larceny over $250 in 2001. (The larceny convictions involved nearly $2,200 he stole from two women.) He received probation or suspended jail sentences in each case and was ordered to pay a total of $3,091 in restitution.

Meanwhile, the list of plaintiffs who have received civil judgments against Gassnola for bad debts include a former basketball associate, a college in Springfield that rented him a gym, and a Hadley company that installed audio equipment in his SUV.

"It's tough to get started in this business," he said, estimating his program costs $100,000 a year. (He said he already has invested nearly $32,000 of his own money this year.)

"You kind of live beyond your means and sometimes you ruffle some feathers," he said.

Gassnola, whom the *Globe* witnessed driving teenage players in Massachusetts, Rhode Island, and Arkansas while his license was revoked, also has amassed a voluminous record of traffic violations such as speeding, operating with a suspended license, and operating an unregistered vehicle. (None of the violations involves alcohol or drugs.) He has been classified five times as a habitual traffic offender, with his latest four-year revocation ending May 3.

"He has continued to drive in blatant violation of the law," Amie O'Hearn, a spokeswoman for the Registry of Motor Vehicles, said before Gassnola regained his license last month.

Registry officials said they did all they could to sanction Gassnola while he continued driving. The rest, they said, was up to police and the courts.

Gassnola has heard critics voice the most derogatory assertions about him, he said, none more incendiary than that he has paid athletes to play for him and has directed players to colleges in return for cash. He said he has done neither.

"I'm not proud of a lot of stuff, but the proudest thing in my life is that I've been able to build this program with a level of success," he said. "I'm trying to do the right thing."

Supporting Cause

Gassnola has helped steer a number of players to major Division 1 basketball programs, including six-foot-six-inch Antonio Anderson to Memphis from Lynn Tech and Maine Central Institute; six-foot-eight Kendric Price of Dorchester to Michigan from Buckingham Browne and Nichols; and six-foot-eight Demetris Nichols of Dorchester to Syracuse from St. Andrew's School in Rhode Island.

An Adidas spokesman, Terrell Clark, said the company has received "no complaints or criticism" about Gassnola.

"We have, however, taken note of a great deal of praise by the parents of players directed to both the club and its officials," Clark said.

Carol Price said Gassnola played a key role in helping her son, Kendric, secure his basketball scholarship at Michigan.

"I can't say anything negative about the experience," Price said. "It was one of the best things that could have happened for Kendric in terms of exposure."

Veronica Brantley credited Gassnola with transforming her son, Jamual Warren, a six-foot-two guard from Springfield, from "a hardheaded little boy to a responsible young man." Warren, whom Gassnola has mentored for more than eight years, attends Globe Institute of Technology in New York and will play next season for the University of Cincinnati.

"From the outside looking in, people will see what they want to see about TJ," said Brantley, a single mother of five. "But TJ has been a blessing for me and my family, and he's done it all out of the kindness of his heart."

Coaches Marvin Avery at Lynn Tech and Mike Hart at St. Andrew's said they have encountered no problems with Gassnola. In 2001, Gassnola also received a recommendation in a sentencing hearing in Springfield District Court from John Robic, who then coached Youngstown State between stints as Calipari's assistant at UMass and Memphis.

"He's a good man," Avery said of Gassnola. "I'm a big supporter."

Yet Gassnola has no shortage of detractors, many of who portrayed him as a hustler more concerned about enhancing his image with Adidas than protecting the interests of young athletes.

"He could end up hurting a lot of kids," said Darryl Bishop, of Roxbury, whose sixteen-year-old son, Darryl, is one of several players Gassnola tried to poach from Papile. "I don't think he's very good for youth basketball and what it stands for."

Bishop, a former football star at Western Kentucky who serves as athletic director of the Shelburne Community Center in Roxbury, said Gassnola arrived there uninvited to try to lure away three of Papile's players: the younger Bishop and six-foot-seven Jamal Coombs-McDaniel of Dorchester, both of whom Papile helped steer to Lawrence Academy, and six-foot-eight Alex Oriakhi of Lowell, a sixteen-year-old phenom whom Papile helped enroll at the Brooks School.

"He didn't offer me anything directly, but he did talk money, about how he had helped out some kids in the past," Bishop said. "I've been there before, so I knew what he was talking about. I told him, 'Anything you do now could hurt my son down the road.' I explained to him that we're not about that."

Bishop, who rejected Gassnola's invitation, said he took Gassnola to suggest he would provide his son improper financial support. Gassnola denied offering anything inappropriate.

"I would never say anything like that," he said. "I don't operate like that."

Still, Gassnola said he is bound by few, if any, regulations, largely because the NCAA is hampered by its limited jurisdiction and no other agency carefully monitors the summer basketball universe.

"You can do whatever you want [because] there are no rules," he said. But while he insisted he would never entice a player or his parents with money, Gassnola acknowledged delivering small amounts of cash to a number of players who have joined his program. He made clear the money was for things unrelated to basketball competition — such as food and leisure travel — and thus a possible violation of NCAA rules on amateurism. He said his only motive is compassion for his players.

"Do I wire a kid forty dollars so he can get something to eat? You're damn right I do," he said. "I'm not leaving a kid on the side of the road who's got nothing at home."

In one recruiting ploy, Gassnola told Coombs-McDaniel's father,

Pernell McDaniel, he would provide the elder McDaniel with Adidas footwear if his sixteen-year-old son joined the Playaz.

"He said, 'What size sneaker do you wear? I'm going to take care of you,'" said McDaniel, who declined the offer.

Gassnola, who acknowledged making the offer to McDaniel, described the goods he receives from Adidas as a valuable resource.

"When a guy like me has product behind him, that makes a difference," Gassnola said. "Kids say, 'That's what T-Mac [Tracy McGrady] wears.' If I had no product behind me, this wouldn't be as easy."

In another recruiting episode, Gassnola failed to impress Doug Millard, of Goffstown, New Hampshire, whose six-foot-eight son, Chad, played as a freshman last season for Rick Pitino at Louisville after starring at Trinity High School in Manchester, New Hampshire, and Brewster Academy. Doug Millard said Gassnola invited his family to dinner at a Manchester Applebee's while he was recruiting Chad, but when the bill came Gassnola produced three credit cards, all of which were rejected. Millard then picked up the check.

"At that point, I said to Chad, 'You're not playing for this guy. How can his team afford to travel if he can't buy a fifty-dollar dinner?'" Millard recalled.

Gassnola then encouraged Doug Millard to let Chad play in a tournament in Memphis. By Doug Millard's account, which Gassnola confirmed, Gassnola said, "If you let Chad go, we have an extra plane ticket. You can go too."

The offers to McDaniel and Millard could have posed a potential problem with the NCAA under a provision that bans prospects and their families from receiving preferential treatment, benefits, or services based on an athlete's reputation.

"We met hundreds and hundreds of people in the basketball world over the last few years, and 99 percent of them were great people," Millard said. "They're not all TJ Gassnolas."

Tactics Questioned

At six-foot-five and about 260 pounds, Gassnola strikes an imposing figure. He wears a diamond earring, gold chain, and Adidas apparel, often from head to toe. A graduate of Springfield's Cathe-

dral High School, where he played basketball, Gassnola has described his occupations through the years as bar owner, car dealer-
ship manager, and real estate entrepreneur.

But his prime pursuit has been youth basketball. He got his
break in 1998 when he steered Warren to the powerful Playaz
Basketball Club of Paterson, New Jersey, an Adidas-funded organization whose alumni include the NBA's Kobe Bryant and Vince
Carter, and became one of coach Jim Salmon's assistants.

With the Playaz's blessing, Gassnola spun off his own team in
their image two years ago. Both Gassnola and Salmon said they
have no financial relationship, and Gassnola said he raises most of
the money for his team from Springfield-area businessmen and the
unnamed NBA players.

At the core of Gassnola's mission is delivering some of the
region's premier talent to major national tournaments and camps,
particularly those sponsored by Adidas. Under NCAA rules, the
events represent the last major showcases for prospective college players before the November period for players to sign with
NCAA schools, further boosting the influence of operatives like
Gassnola.

"It's a world most people don't know very much about," said former Celtics coach John Carroll, whose sixteen-year-old son, Austin,
plays for Papile's BABC. "There are guys like Leo who have been
doing it a long time and have built a good reputation, and there
are bottom-feeders like [Gassnola] who try to make a name for
themselves by going into inner cities and doing whatever they can
to entice kids. It's sad."

Gassnola, who last year incorporated the New England Playaz
as a nonprofit and listed himself as the president, treasurer, clerk,
and sole director, insisted he cares more about helping his players
secure college scholarships than scoring points with Adidas.

"I'm going to make sure they go to college and aren't walking
the streets doing nothing," he said of his players. "That means
more to me than Adidas going, 'Holy [expletive], you got Antonio
[Anderson]. He's a [potential] pro.'"

At times, however, Gassnola has put basketball before education. In 2004, he helped six-foot-nine Travis George of Roxbury enroll at Notre Dame Prep in Fitchburg, only to quickly remove him
over philosophical differences with the school administration. Bill
Barton, Notre Dame's principal and basketball coach, said the dif-

ferences included Gassnola expecting George to leave campus and compete with the Playaz when Barton insisted George remain there during summer school to study.

"We will not take TJ's kids anymore," Barton said. "There are some coaches who should not be guiding young men."

George has attended five prep schools since Notre Dame and has yet to meet the NCAA's academic eligibility standards. For his part, Gassnola acknowledged personally assailing Barton for requiring George to study rather than play basketball.

"[Barton] was killing the kid," Gassnola said. "Travis won't be going to Yale to be an engineer."

Gassnola also acknowledged owing money to Notre Dame after reneging on a pledge to pay Warren's tuition. To date, Notre Dame has taken no legal action, though word of Gassnola's debt has spread through the youth basketball community, further tainting his reputation.

Several AAU coaches told the *Globe* Gassnola has snatched away players from them by making promises the coaches could not or would not match. Most youth teams charge athletes to play, while high-powered programs such as Gassnola's and Papile's cover all the expenses, including travel to tournaments across the country.

No one in Greater Boston has lost more players to Gassnola than Mauricio Vasquez, who runs the Reebok-affiliated Metro Boston program in Dorchester. The players include Anderson, Price, George, and Alvin Lewis, a freshman at Kentucky Wesleyan.

Vasquez said he no longer cares to speak to Gassnola.

"However he got the kids, so be it, I'm not going to sink to those levels," Vasquez said. "If someone sells you a dream and you feel that's going to get it done for you, so be it."

Gassnola said he respected Papile's turf in greater Boston until he learned that Papile advised a relative of Dominique Price, a star guard at Holy Name in Worcester, to steer clear of Gassnola because of his troubled past. (Papile denied the assertion.)

"If [Papile] had shut his mouth, I would have left him alone out of respect," Gassnola said. "But now, it's like I told him in a voice message, 'You know what, bro? Boston is open game.'"

Gassnola has little chance of unseating Papile, according to Sonny Vaccaro, who revolutionized the relationship between sneaker companies and youth basketball players as a Nike executive in the 1980s before he moved to Adidas in 1992 and joined Reebok in 2004.

"That's like taking on the Red Sox or the Yankees if you're the Pirates," Vaccaro said. "It's silly to even say that."

But Gassnola, who hit the road this year with a team he stocked with Division 1 college prospects, said he has no plans to go away.

"Mark my words," he said. "In ten years, the number-one program will be the New England Playaz."

Wading in Cesspool

Fayetteville, Ark. — It's a sleepy Saturday afternoon in the foothills of the Ozark Mountains, and Rakim Sanders, a sixteen-year-old hotshot from a Rhode Island housing project, has created a buzz at a Boys and Girls Club on the edge of town.

Recruiters from major colleges across the country have trekked in April to the gym on a dead-end street in northwest Arkansas to pay respect to Sanders, a sleek, six-foot-five-inch shooting guard. Assistant coaches from Boston College and the University of Connecticut anchor a group watching Sanders from one end of the basketball court while rivals from Providence, Syracuse, and other Division 1 powers stand vigil at the opposite end.

As New England's top college basketball prospect in the high school class of 2007, Sanders — a high-scoring junior at St. Andrew's School in Rhode Island — has received scholarship offers from BC and Providence and has been projected by a basketball trade publication as a 2010 selection in the NBA draft. (Two weeks later, on May 1, he verbally commits to BC.)

Sanders also is the jewel of the Adidas-backed New England Playaz, an elite travel team based in Springfield. And he will receive a special benefit from the Playaz after he performs at the Real Deal on the Hill Tournament in Fayetteville, a major weekend showcase that attracts the nation's top college recruiters and scouting services.

Playaz president Thomas J. "TJ" Gassnola has paid for Sanders to travel not only from New England to Fayetteville, as Gassnola has done for the entire team, but also to fly after the tournament from Arkansas to Orlando to vacation with his brothers and sisters at Disney World. Gassnola then will pay for Sanders to fly home from Disney World.

Never mind that NCAA rules bar amateur teams such as the Playaz from paying for anything but "actual and necessary travel, room and board, and apparel and equipment for competition and practice."

Gassnola, who has a lengthy criminal record and rich history of financial delinquency, says he also will slip his star player $100 to spend during his Disney vacation.

"The kid has no money, so I'm helping him out," Gassnola says. "You want to throw me in jail for that? Go ahead."

Since Sanders will not be subject to NCAA rules until he enrolls in college — and since no other agency closely regulates such activity — the chances of anyone facing sanctions for Gassnola's special gift to Sanders are remote.

"It's all loosely regulated, at best," says Robert Kanaby, executive director of the National Federation of State High School Associations. "We may just have to hope for some sense of voluntary compliance by the individuals who are making [the system] so lucrative and rewarding."

"Michael" Motivation

So it goes in the shadowy corners of the high-stakes scramble by multibillion-dollar sneaker conglomerates to adorn America's basketball stars of tomorrow in their brands. Each of the three major companies — Nike, Adidas, and Reebok — spends millions of dollars sponsoring "grassroots" teams like the Playaz and other youth programs, hoping their teen sensations one day will become endorsement giants, à la Michael Jordan (Nike), Tracy McGrady (Adidas), and Allen Iverson (Reebok).

"The theory remains the same: we're all looking for the next Michael," says Sonny Vaccaro, who revolutionized the market by signing Jordan for Nike in 1984 and now serves as Reebok's senior director of grassroots basketball.

Dreams are made and dashed at national camps and tournaments like the Real Deal, where big-monied sneaker companies and college coaches often determine the future of the nation's most promising amateur athletes. It's a basketball meat market, and the stakes are enormous for everyone:

- company-sponsored recruiters like Gassnola, who have scoured gyms and playgrounds to deliver the best players they can enlist for the showcase;
- players like Sanders, whose futures can hinge on their brief auditions before the nation's top college coaches;
- colleges like BC, whose fortunes can rise or fall on the players in whom they decide to invest lucrative scholarships;
- companies like Adidas, whose bottom lines can be determined by how many of the players they sponsor make it big.

If the companies or their representatives play fast and loose in the process, they rarely answer for it, as team officials such as Gassnola operate in a subculture in which pioneers like Vaccaro and Nike executive George Raveling set the standards, for better or worse.

Raveling, who followed Vaccaro as head of Nike's grassroots program, has acknowledged giving $100 to Amare Stoudemire's mother, Carrie, in 2000 while she was jailed on theft charges. (Nike was wooing Amare before he turned pro.) Stoudemire has since signed endorsement deals with Nike worth an estimated $33 million.

Vaccaro acknowledges that as an Adidas executive in the 1990s he bought street clothes for NBA player Lamar Odom when Odom played for an Adidas-funded youth team. (Odom later signed with Nike.) Vaccaro also says in an interview near his multimillion-dollar home in Calabasas, California, that he has provided players money for expenses not directly related to basketball, which critics decry as improper preferential treatment and the NCAA could consider a violation of its rules on amateurism.

"I would do that, absolutely," Vaccaro says of regularly giving players money for food and other expenses unrelated to basketball. "There's no hard-line rule against it, and it would be asinine to put one in because you couldn't monitor it."

Vaccaro acknowledges the sneaker companies participate in a system that exploits amateur youths for financial gain.

"It's a cesspool," he said, "but everybody's involved in it: the sneaker companies, the NBA, the colleges, and the high schools."

Vaccaro, Gassnola, and others justify the practice in part by citing the profits that sneaker companies, colleges, professional teams, television networks, agents, and others make on teenagers, many of whom are poor.

"I live in a beautiful place and I'm pretty damn successful," Vaccaro says. "For a lot of these kids, it's a rough life."

A number of coaches whose players Gassnola tried to lure away see it differently.

"We don't want to be associated with street agents, and that's the best way I can think of to describe him," says Mike Crotty, director of the Belmont-based Middlesex Magic, whose players pay to participate.

Guiding Light

Sanders says he just wants to survive financially. He was eleven when his mother died in 2000. His sister, Nyisha, who was eighteen at the time, has since raised him and four other siblings at a low-income project in Pawtucket, Rhode Island. Sanders's basketball ability helped land him at St. Andrew's, a small private school with a strong basketball program, and he hopes his athletic skills carry him further.

"I just want to get into college and not have my sister have to pay for it," Sanders says after leading the Playaz to victory in their first two games of the Real Deal's seventeen-and-under division. "Making it through school for free, that would be the best thing for me."

Gassnola, who has lured away numerous players from summer teams in greater Boston, including the Nike-backed Boston Amateur Basketball Club, has reached into Rhode Island for Sanders and a point guard, Andrew Hanson, one of twelve children from a Narragansett family, who also attends St. Andrew's.

The Playaz have picked up a pair of six-foot-eight forwards from Springfield: Garrett Kissel, whom Gassnola helped enroll at St. Andrew's, and Travon Wilcher, whom Gassnola steered to Lee Academy in Maine. The team features two other talented guards: Sedale Jones, a prolific scorer from Pittsfield High School, and Dominique Price, a star for Holy Name in Worcester. Gassnola's second-leading scorer is six-foot-three Corey Bingham, a 2005 Globe All-Scholastic at Lynn Tech who joined Wilcher at Lee Academy.

Gassnola also helps some of his players choose colleges, as he did last year with former Lynn Tech star Antonio Anderson. With several top Division 1 teams pursuing him, Anderson selected Memphis, whose coach, John Calipari, Gassnola considers a close friend.

"I'd take a bullet for the guy," Gassnola says.

Calipari's assistant, Derek Kellogg, has been Gassnola's best friend since they attended Cathedral High School together in Springfield.

"I told Antonio, 'You need to go to a place where you're comfortable, with people I know, because I can't call [North Carolina coach] Roy Williams, but I can call Cal,'" Gassnola says. Calipari and Kellogg did not respond to interview requests.

So far this year, the ten-member Playaz squad has competed in New Jersey, Rhode Island, and Arkansas. Before the summer ends, they will play in Washington, D.C., Georgia, North Carolina, New York, Nevada, and California, with all their expenses paid.

Nearly every member of the Playaz appears poised to secure a Division 1 basketball scholarship, and most say they have joined the team to try to enhance their recruiting positions.

"TJ gets us out to the bigger tournaments," says Sanders, who joined Gassnola last year after playing for the Rhode Island Breakers since he was twelve. "He gives me a better chance to showcase my talents."

Bingham, who will spend two postgrad years at Lee Academy, credits Gassnola with helping him attract interest from his top choices: the University of Nevada at Las Vegas, St. John's, and Miami.

"You get way more exposure with the Playaz," Bingham says.

Wilcher, an athletic shot-blocker, already has generated interest from UMass, URI, and Wyoming. But his stock appears to climb during the Real Deal tournament as several recruiters, including one from UConn, ask Gassnola about him. (He verbally committed last week to UMass.)

Wilcher says he might not have made it out of Springfield if Gassnola had not helped him academically by guiding him from Central High School there toward Lee Academy.

"I probably wouldn't be qualified to play right now if it wasn't for TJ," Wilcher says. "Now I'm in the correct classes."

A new member of the Playaz, six-foot-seven Josh Herritt, commutes from Stamford, Connecticut, in the hope of gaining more recognition. Herritt plays for King & Low-Heywood Thomas, a small private school little noticed by college recruiters. He hopes to play for a Division 1 program, perhaps in the Ivy League.

"Unfortunately, in today's environment, it's all about exposure, and Josh needed to get some," says his father, Dave Herritt. "TJ came to watch him play, and it has worked out for all of us."

Overseeing Operation

Since NCAA rules bar individuals who have been charged with a felony from coaching in tournaments it certifies, Gassnola has not coached the Playaz since he formed them in 2004. (A jury found him not guilty in 1997 of felony assault and battery and unarmed burglary.) He has left the coaching first to Mike Jarvis II, now the head team manager at Duke, and since then to Shawn Bloom, who played at Salem State after starring at Minnechaug Regional High School in Wilbraham, Massachusetts.

While Bloom directs the team, Gassnola stands amid the college recruiters at one end of the court, alternately cheering and chastising his players. After the Playaz win their opening game in the tournament, Gassnola peels a $100 bill off a roll he pulls from his pocket and hands it to Hanson, instructing him to buy food for the team.

"Anything we need, TJ gets it for us," Bingham says.

The Playaz dine at local restaurants between games, sleep at the Quality Inn, and travel about town in a rented van. Before the summer ends, Gassnola will have spent several thousand dollars per player, each of whom is outfitted with a full line of Adidas gear, including two game uniforms, warm-ups, and sneakers.

Gassnola, who describes himself as a real estate entrepreneur, also supports a fifteen-and-under travel team, which has not traveled to Fayetteville. He says he funds the program with his own money as well as contributions from Springfield-area businessmen and three NBA players he declines to identify. He says the program costs about $100,000 a year.

"TJ does everything," Hanson says. "All he wants me to do is run the team [on the court], and he said he'll take care of me."

Adidas is pleased with Gassnola because the Playaz are wearing its brand in a national showcase, where more than 175 colleges and 40 recruiting services are represented, with television cameras recording much of the action.

Gassnola's goodwill ebbs, however, when the Playaz fail to over-come a lackluster start in their third game of the tournament and suffer a one-point loss to a team from Memphis.

"That's it," he says, fuming, to Bloom. "Take away their cell phones, their iPods, everything. I'm kicking [butt]."

Despite the sullen interlude, Gassnola gets plenty of attention from college recruiters, who recognize the influence he wields. When he first walks into the Boys and Girls Club, he exchanges a hug and handshake with Tennessee coach Bruce Pearl, who quickly hands his cell phone to Gassnola.

One of Pearl's assistants is curious about Kiwan Smith, a six-foot-eight star Gassnola brought to the tournament the previous year. Gassnola had pushed the seventeen-and-under age limit with Smith, who is twenty-one and was barred from another tournament last year because of his age. (Tournaments often permit limited age exceptions, which is how the BABC's fifteen-and-under team recently won AAU national, regional, and state championships with four players who are sixteen.)

As for Smith, questions also arose about his character: he pleaded guilty in 2004 in Schenectady (New York) County to a Class D felony of third-degree criminal possession of stolen property (an SUV) and was sentenced to five years' probation. But the more pressing matter seems to be that Smith, who attends Laurinburg Institute in North Carolina, has yet to meet NCAA academic eligibility requirements, diminishing Tennessee's interest.

Still, one coach after another, including Kansas State's Bob Huggins, makes a point of schmoozing with Gassnola. With dozens of major college prospects participating, organizers charge the coaches $250 each for team rosters (178 colleges are registered). And even though the NCAA bars the coaches from speaking with players — coaches may only observe the players but are allowed to speak with organizers like Gassnola — Huggins has turned out with many of his contemporaries, including Pearl, Williams, Calipari, Kentucky's Tubby Smith, and Michigan State's Tom Izzo.

In the past, Gassnola has helped at least one college recruiter break the rule barring communication with players. The *Record* of Bergen County, New Jersey, reported in 2002 that Gassnola, then an associate of the Playaz Basketball Club of Paterson, New Jersey, handed his cell phone to Demetris Nichols of Dorchester, whom Gassnola had enlisted with the Playaz, so Nichols could speak with a Syracuse recruiter who was standing in the same gym during a tournament.

When a *Record* reporter asked Gassnola whether the NCAA would ever be able to stop such prohibited communication, he replied, "They can't do a [expletive] thing about it."

Traveling Show

In Fayetteville, the Reebok-sponsored tournament has drawn 156 teams from coast to coast, despite Nike advising its teams to boycott the event because of its rival's sponsorship. Several Nike-sponsored teams, including the Illinois Warriors, who win the tournament, have ignored the company's ban, a measure of the event's significance on the recruiting calendar. An additional 83 teams that sought to pay the $450 entry fee were wait-listed.

Izzo said it's "imperative" for recruiters to attend such talent shows. One problem, he said, is the outsized influence many sneaker-company operatives have gained, sometimes for the worse.

"Some of the coaches are real good, like in high school," Izzo said, "but some of them are shady."

For Gassnola, it's just another stop on the road. His team travels more than nearly any in New England, including the BABC, Nike's premier program in the region. The Playaz and BABC rarely face each other, for several reasons, including their rival sponsorships and Gassnola being barred from AAU tournaments for failing to pay an estimated $2,500 in entry fees. Their premier teams also compete at different levels, Gassnola's in the seventeen-and-under division, Papile's at fifteen- or sixteen-and-under.

At the Providence Jam Fest, for example, which drew teams in April from as far as North Carolina, the New England Playaz won the seventeen-and-under title, with Sanders named the division's most valuable player, while the BABC captured the fifteen-and-under championship behind division MVP Erik Murphy.

The only team in New England that travels more than the Playaz is the Boston-based Junior Celtics, who receive sneakers, gym bags, and warm-ups from New Balance. (The company does not provide cash grants to youth basketball teams.) The Junior Celtics, the only other New England team to compete in the Real Deal tournament, are funded mostly by their coach, Craig Stockmal, and the players' parents, several of whom will donate frequent flyer and hotel points to help underwrite trips this year to New York, Rhode Island, Arkansas, Texas, Washington, D.C., Georgia, North Carolina, New Jersey, and Nevada.

Stockmal says Gassnola and the BABC's Leo Papile have tried to lure away a couple of his players, who include major college prospects such as six-foot-seven Andrew McCarthy of Buckingham Browne and Nichols and six-foot-three Jamal Turner of Thayer Academy. But Stockmal says the players and their parents are pleased with both the national exposure the Junior Celtics provide and the program's emphasis on team play, which sometimes is lost on star-studded summer squads.

Stockmal says he also values his freedom from the sneaker wars.

"The more you see it," he says, "the happier you are that you're a small, independent program."

The Junior Celtics, like the New England Playaz, win two of three games in their tournament pools before they are eliminated from the Real Deal. Soon, Stockmal will return to his sales job for a national printing firm. Sanders will be vacationing at Disney World. And Gassnola will be back prowling for the region's best young players, trying to deliver for Adidas.

Are You Kidding?

You've never heard of Joe Sharkey, a fourteen-year-old who just finished eighth grade at Brimmer and May, a small private day school in Chestnut Hill. But Adidas has.

Sharkey was twelve and ranked by a national scouting service among the top twenty sixth-grade players in the country when Adidas gave him his first free pair of basketball shoes and apparel. He was thirteen and rated the best player from New England at the company's invitation-only Jr. Phenom Camp when he received his second free pair of Adidas shoes and gear. And when he accepted his invitation this month to the Adidas Phenom 150 Camp for players entering ninth and tenth grade, he collected more free merchandise.

It has come to this in the sneaker wars. A generation after Nike revolutionized the marketing of athletic footwear by signing a twenty-one-year-old NBA rookie, Michael Jordan, to an endorsement deal, the sneaker giants — Nike, Adidas, and Reebok — have turned their multimillion-dollar hunt for the next Jordan into a struggle for the souls of middle schoolers.

The competition has become so fierce — Nike signed LeBron James to a $90 million contract before he received his high school diploma — that Hoop Scoop, a national scouting service, rates fifth-grade players and the sneaker companies are scrambling after prepubescent prospects.

"The whole thing has gotten out of control, and the shoe companies are driving the bus," said Hoop Scoop's Clark Francis.

As the young Sharkey sits before a bowl of chips and dip in the kitchen of his Norwood home, the notion of him one day becoming the face of a blockbuster marketing campaign for a multinational corporation may seem unfathomable.

Not to Adidas.

"He's one of our golden-child kids," said Joe Keller, who two years ago opened a new front in the sneaker wars by launching the invitation-only Adidas Jr. Phenom Camp for middle schoolers. "He should definitely be a Division 1 basketball player, and he has his head screwed on correctly."

All of this for a boy of fourteen. All of it in the hope that Sharkey or some other eighth-grade phenom — Ron Giplaye of Lowell, Rodney Beldo of Dorchester, and Nadir Tharpe of Worcester also rank among the state's best — beats astronomical odds and becomes a bankable marketing commodity as a professional basketball star.

All of it, too, to the possible detriment of the children's development, according to specialists in youth sports.

"In a word, it's obscene," said Bruce Svare, a child psychologist and executive director of the National Institute for Sports Reform. "I understand that they're trying to move billions of dollars' worth of sports apparel, but they're doing it by coddling these young kids into a sense of entitlement that could hurt the kids and work against the companies."

Low-Grade Fever

The sneaker giants forge ahead nonetheless. Sonny Vaccaro, Reebok's senior director of grassroots basketball, set the trend as an Adidas executive in 2003 when he invited four eighth-graders to his ABCD Camp in Teaneck, New Jersey, for the nation's elite high school players. The same year, Vaccaro dipped lower into the talent pool by creating Camp Next for children who had completed eighth or ninth grade. (Reebok now sponsors the program.)

"We're going to find them, expose them, and get them used to the grind at an earlier age," Vaccaro said. "I believe in that theory."

As a result, Vaccaro wasted no time last year establishing ties to Renardo Sidney, then a six-foot-nine-inch eighth-grader in Mississippi widely considered the nation's top prospect in the class of 2009. Vaccaro provided Sidney an all-expenses-paid trip to the ABCD camp and arranged for the sneaker company to sponsor Sidney's summer team.

Vaccaro also spoke last year with Cully Payne, then a fourteen-year-old eighth-grader in Chicago, about committing to a college team before he reached high school. Three weeks after Payne completed the eighth grade — and not long after his conversation with Vaccaro — the boy verbally accepted a nonbinding basketball scholarship offer from DePaul, a rarity for a child so young.

Vaccaro, who pays freelance scouts to help him target the nation's best young players, also took Juwan Moody, an eleven-year-old phenom from Detroit, to lunch two years ago at a Johnny Rocket's restaurant near Vaccaro's home in Calabasas, California.

"When I met him, he was five-foot-two, and it was hard explaining to him that at some point he will have to grow a little bit," Vaccaro said. "But I've maintained a friendship with him and his dad. I haven't seen him play, but he's supposed to really be a phenom."

In the next breath, however, Vaccaro shared a secret of the sneaker wars.

"The word 'phenom' is nothing more than a selling tool," he said. "It's a trick."

In New England, the most prominent company-sponsored youth teams — the Nike-backed Boston Amateur Basketball Club and Adidas-sponsored New England Playaz — have all but cornered the market of the region's middle school phenoms. BABC coach Leo Papile has stocked his program with so much young talent that he recently entered two fifteen-and-under teams in the state AAU tournament, with both teams advancing to the championship game. (They shared the trophy rather than play each other.)

"They are probably the best basketball team I've ever seen at that age category," said John Kottori, the AAU's chairman of youth basketball in southern New England.

Papile already has enlisted Sharkey to join a fifteen-and-under team next fall that is expected to include Giplaye and Beldo, both of whom are fifteen-year-olds entering ninth grade. Papile also picked up several of the region's best fifteen-year-olds entering tenth grade, including six-foot-seven Erik Murphy of St. Mark's and six-foot-six Dartaye Ruffin of St. Andrew's, though Ruffin recently jumped from the BABC to Thomas J. "TJ" Gassnola's New England Playaz. Murphy is the son of former Boston College star and NBA player Jay Murphy.

Papile also has a six-foot-eight phenom, Alex Oriakhi, who completed ninth grade at the Brooks School and who turned sixteen June 21.

Tharpe, who ranks with Sharkey among the region's best fourteen-year-olds, is considered such a dominant player that the New England Playaz built a new fifteen-and-under team around him. A speedy, five-foot-ten guard with exceptional passing and shooting skills, Tharpe played as an eighth-grader last season for the varsity team at St. Peter–Marian of Worcester and wasted little time turning heads as he scored twenty-four points against Worcester's Doherty High School and twenty-three against St. Bernard's of Fitchburg.

"He's one of those kids who comes along once in a lifetime," said Gassnola, who recruited Tharpe.

Just as Papile has helped many of his young players land scholarships to private schools, Gassnola has tried to do the same for Tharpe, recently taking him for a visit to St. Andrew's School, a small basketball power in Barrington, Rhode Island.

"He's the best I've seen come through Worcester in the last eight or nine years in his age bracket," St. Peter–Marian coach Tim Tibaud said. "We're hoping to keep him, but once the prep schools see him, it's going to be hard."

Five-Star Prospect

As for Sharkey, a six-foot-two sharpshooter, his basketball life took a dramatic turn in the summer after sixth grade. By making the all-star team at the elite Five-Star Basketball Camp while he competed against players who were two years older, Sharkey earned an invitation to the inaugural Adidas Jr. Phenom Camp and gained the top twenty rating from Hoop Scoop, all at age twelve.

"It was really exciting," he said, "because I never thought I could play that well against older kids."

Sharkey has done so ever since. In addition to playing in higher age brackets on the summer circuit, he created a stir at Brimmer and May two seasons ago when he became one of the only seventh-graders in state history to play varsity basketball. Blending his skills as a floor leader with his deft shooting touch, Sharkey played so well as a seventh-grader that in one game he led his senior-dominated team in scoring.

"He was the most advanced player in both basketball talent and knowledge of the game I've seen at that age level," said Daryn Freedman, the former Brimmer and May coach who suggested Sharkey apply to the school after spotting him at a Five-Star camp in Pennsylvania when Sharkey was eleven. Alumni of the Five-Star camp include dozens of NBA players, including Jordan, James, Vince Carter, and Carmelo Anthony.

Freedman, now an assistant coach at Duquesne University, said Sharkey was so skilled at age twelve that he once created an uproar among an opposing team's fans when he made a rare appearance with an injury-depleted thirteen-and-under summer team after playing in a seventeen-and-under division.

"I'm excited to see what happens in his career," Freedman said.

So are the sneaker companies, even as they hunt for more Joe Sharkeys.

"My job is to discover them before anybody knows who these kids are," said Keller, founder of the Adidas Jr. Phenom Camp. "Everybody wants to find out who the top players are at an earlier age."

Francis, the scouting analyst, has seen the competition between sneaker companies intensify as he travels the country to rate players at youth camps and tournaments. Nike last month signaled its commitment to competing with Adidas and Reebok for middle schoolers by launching a national tournament for sixth-, seventh-, and eighth-graders as part of its Memorial Day Classic in Nashville.

"The interest has skyrocketed because the shoe companies and colleges now realize that if they don't start going after kids in middle school, they're not going to get them," Francis said.

So it is that hundreds of college coaches subscribe to scouting services like Hoop Scoop. But even Vaccaro, who tracks middle schoolers as aggressively as any sneaker company operative, said adolescents can undergo so many physical, attitudinal, and social changes that trying to rate children as potential basketball stars as young as eleven may be foolhardy.

"You can't define players that young," Vaccaro said. "It's humanly impossible because there are so many intangibles. That's why somebody has to stand up and say, 'It's [b.s.].'"

Francis defended his rankings, to a degree.

"Quite honestly, I think our lists of sixth-, seventh-, and eighth-graders are really good," he said. "But I think our list of fifth-graders is a joke."

No New Englanders appear on Hoop Scoop's list of the nation's top fifth-, sixth-, and seventh-graders, but the list of the top three hundred eighth-graders includes Beldo (42), Sharkey (117), and two six-foot-five players from Waterbury, Connecticut: Josh Turner (55) and Cory Andrews (160).

Francis said he has yet to hear parents complain about their children appearing on such lists. He said he hears instead from parents who believe their children should be ranked higher.

"I tell them, 'Don't worry, we've got six more years to get it right,'" he said.

Disturbing Trend?

The best of the young phenoms are celebrated in teen-oriented magazines like *Slam*, which is thick with ads and features touting sneaker company apparel, camps, and tournaments.

Child prodigies also are tracked by websites such as New York–based metrohoops.com, whose stated mission is to provide "cutting-edge stories about the hottest grammar school players" as young as second-graders.

The trend troubles specialists like Peter Roby, who has captained Dartmouth's basketball team, coached Harvard's basketball team, served as Reebok's vice president of U.S. marketing, and now heads Northeastern's Center for the Study of Sport in Society.

"It sends a bad message to many of these kids that their basketball skills separate them from their peers in a way they don't deserve," Roby said. "It bothers me a lot because we already know we have issues with adult athletes who feel they have a special sense of entitlement because people are falling over them. If adult athletes have trouble keeping their perspective, imagine how difficult it can be for a sixth- or seventh-grader."

Fixing the problem may require the sneaker companies, perhaps with support from the NBA, to cooperatively fund a network of regional youth development programs that addresses the needs of both recreational players and elite college prospects, said Brian McCormick, author of *Cross Over: The New Model of Youth Basketball Development.*

McCormick said his plan is aimed in part at curbing the profit-driven competition between the sneaker companies and its harmful effect on young players.

"It may not be the perfect solution," he said, "but at least it will get people talking about the problem."

Vaccaro acknowledged the exploitative nature of the system, but he also defended it.

"We put these kids on pedestals, and when they bottom out, the entities that supported them and the people who rated them don't bottom out," he said. "We're wrong in this evaluation thing more than we're right, and no one sees our failures. But when we're right, it allows us to perpetuate the dream. There's nothing wrong with that."

Many youth coaches cringe, however, as they watch sneaker companies and college recruiters pursue ever-younger players.

"You see people drooling over ten-year-old kids, and you wonder, at what point is he no longer just a kid playing the game because it's fun and at what point does it tarnish him," said Carl Parker, who coaches a regional travel team from Maine and recently became the head coach at Lee Academy in Maine. "All that hype and exposure at such a young age, I'm not sure how good that is for the kids."

It hurt Demetrius Walker, who was twelve when he was featured on the front page of the *Los Angeles Times* and fourteen when he was trumpeted last year on the cover of *Sports Illustrated.* Walker, who will be a six-foot-four sophomore at Fontana (California) High School, got swept up in his hype and slipped, at least temporarily, from can't-miss to overrated.

Vaccaro blamed the media and Walker's handlers.

"That was the greatest miscarriage of justice I've ever seen, proclaiming the kid to be the greatest when he was in sixth grade," he said. "Demetrius is pretty good, but he's never going to be LeBron."

Keller, who coached Walker in his Adidas-sponsored summer program, acknowledged the boy "was hurt to some degree" by the booing he received when his game deteriorated after the hype.

"Anytime someone tells us we're the greatest in the world, we tend not to work as hard, and that happened to Demetrius," Keller said. "But this has brought him back to reality, and he's back in the gym five or six hours a day."

Unlike some sneaker-sponsored coaches who avidly publicize their players, others prefer to shield the youngsters from media exposure.

Only after some prodding, for example, did Craig Stockmal, coach of the Boston-based Junior Celtics' sixteen-and-under team, share the names of three of his players who were invited to this summer's Adidas 150 Phenom Camp: his twin sons, Cory and Kyle Stockmal, of Watertown High School, and Tucker Halpern, of Noble and Greenough. All three will be entering tenth grade.

"I don't want them to think they are that good at such a young age," Stockmal said. "If you keep telling them they are the best, they may not work hard enough to compete at the next level."

Sharkey said he considers himself an Adidas kid, though he expressed no reluctance about joining the Nike-sponsored BABC in the fall. He and his parents, Patrick and Denise, said they are keenly aware of the pitfalls of his youthful stardom and plan to avoid them.

As part of his development, Sharkey is leaning toward eventually transferring from Brimmer and May to Worcester Academy, which plays a more rigorous schedule but also has a strong academic program.

"It all depends on whether you keep everything in perspective," said Patrick Sharkey, a Boston trial lawyer. "You have to think, just because some guy says you're the twentieth-best player, who died and left him in charge?"

The truth is, the elder Sharkey said of many talented younger players, "they're all seeds, and you don't know who's going to blossom."

Still, the sneaker companies spend millions of dollars working the garden, searching for prize flowers. And no one seems able to control them, including watchdog agencies that have tried.

"There are groups that seem to invest a great deal of money in this," said Robert Kanaby, executive director of the National Federation of State High School Associations. "Until that changes, I think we're a long way from a solution."

SARA CORBETT

Baseball for Life

FROM THE NEW YORK TIMES PLAY MAGAZINE

> Remember the days when kids rode their bikes to the games and
> picked their own teams and didn't want or expect their parents to be
> anywhere near them? Long gone, for better and worse.
> — D.M.

JARROD PETREE HAS SPENT his whole life throwing. The first
things he threw, according to his mother, were assorted toys and a
fair amount of food from the highchair. Before long, he moved on
to throwing balls. Some babies, of course, are throwers. But from
the very start, Jarrod had an especially determined arm. At least
this is the view taken by his father, Tim, who played Division II baseball at the Florida Institute of Technology in the late '80s, graduating only a few years before his son was born: the kid basically arrived on earth wanting to throw.

Nowadays, Jarrod is five-foot-three and weighs 110 pounds. He is
a recent graduate of the sixth grade at Apopka Memorial Middle
School in suburban Orlando, and arguably as close to being a professional baseball player as a twelve-year-old can be. He has buzz-
cut blond hair, a solid tan, and what seems to be a perpetual rasp-
berry on his left arm — the product of diving, again and again,
headlong toward second base. He is also a dedicated sleepwalker,
piloted by his unconscious, especially on nights before a big game.
"We've found him out in the yard, in the garage," Tim says. "When
we're on the road, he'll wander around the motel. Usually it means
he's going to play well."

Along with twelve other boys his age, Jarrod plays for a traveling
baseball team called the Central Florida Express, one of the best

twelve-and-under teams in the country. The team's head coach, a coin-op laundry entrepreneur named Ben Nichols, started the Express four years ago, primarily so that his son, Brad, an exceptional second baseman who was then eight, could have some exceptional teammates. Someone told him about another eight-year-old playing in a local recreational league who fit the bill, and one afternoon Ben Nichols drove over to watch Jarrod Petree play. Tim Petree describes Ben as having rescued Jarrod from what he calls "rec-ball hell." Taking the field with children who were just learning to play — who couldn't field a zinging line drive or get their glove around a crisp throw from third base — had been troublesome. "He was going to end up hurting somebody," says Tim, who has been practicing baseball with Jarrod since he was two. "We couldn't get out of there fast enough."

Though he also plays shortstop and third base for the Express, Jarrod is primarily known for his role as a big-game pitcher — a precision right-hander whose fastball is somewhat less fast than those heaved by bigger kids who've hit puberty already, but which nonetheless tends to cross the plate with uncanny and merciless accuracy. At the end of last year, Jarrod was listed as one of the top players of his age in the country by a website called Travel Ball Select.

While his teammates will jabber on the field, ferociously chewing Dubble Bubble or handfuls of sunflower seeds, Jarrod seems tuned to a lower frequency, throwing his sliders and curveballs and changeups without so much as a glance toward the stands. When he strikes someone out, he reflexively clenches his right fist — a celebratory gesture so small you have to pay attention to see it. Tim, who is the team's pitching coach, sits on a bucket next to the dugout during games and signals to the catcher his choice for the next pitch and over which corner of the plate it should pass. Whatever his dad calls for, that's what Jarrod throws. "I've never seen a little boy go out there and hit spots like that all day long," says Joe Winker, an assistant coach for the Express. "It's pretty cool to watch."

Coached and financed by parents, with the help of a handful of local sponsors, the Express, which is based north of Orlando, plays what amounts to a ten-month season, taking time off at the end of August and again at Christmas. The players spend the rest of the year traveling to multiple states and slugging it out against other elite-level, baseball-obsessed kids in weekend tournaments where the winning teams are sometimes required to play up to eight games in a single forty-eight-hour stretch. Last year, the Express team had seventy wins and nine losses and won the coveted Amateur Athletic Union national championship in its age group for the third year in a row. Due largely to its reputation, the team now has players on its roster whose parents think nothing of driving an hour and a half each way from Tampa or Gainesville for the twice-weekly practices. One player, a freckled kid named Zac Ryan, even flies in from northern Indiana to play.

All this has made the Express a particularly alluring team to try to beat. "We're kind of like the Yankees," Jarrod explained one night in late April. He lay sprawled on the carpet in his family's living room, idly watching basketball highlights on ESPN and scratching the nose of the family's beagle, Zoey. "We have a target on our back all the time," he said. "People pretty much hate us."

In the next room, Jarrod's younger sisters, Analyse and Kaylie, were getting ready for bed. Analyse is eight and plays fast-pitch softball in a local Babe Ruth League. Kaylie is ten and isn't much interested in sports. ("We call her Fangirl," Tim joked. "She plays Barbies in the bleachers.")

Tim has negotiated for flextime at his job as a DNA analyzer for the state's crime lab so that he can coach and travel with the Express. Jarrod's mom, Lori, who is dark-haired and pretty with a wry sense of humor, runs a small day care center from the family's stucco home. There was a time when the Petrees liked to drive to the beach on weekends, but weekends are now all about Jarrod's baseball — and, to a lesser extent, Analyse's softball. Last summer, as a concession to leisure, the family had a heated pool put in behind the house. Tim recently sawed down two oak trees that stood in the narrow strip of remaining backyard to make room for the pitcher's mound that he intends to build out there. "Our bullpen," he called it.

While his parents say they understand that the odds are vastly against him, Jarrod has big plans for himself: playing for the Red Sox, his dad's favorite team. More specifically, he'll face his best friend and teammate on the Express, Jesse Winker, probably in a pitching duel and definitely in the run-up to the World Series. And Jesse will be playing for the Yankees, *his* dad's favorite team.

"But if I don't get drafted in an early round out of high school,

I'll go to college," Jarrod said, still playing with the dog. His backup plan, he explained, is to become a crime-lab scientist like his father, or possibly a phys ed teacher, but this is only if his arm fails him. And nobody wants that to happen. A moment later, Zoey started to gnaw playfully on a couple of Jarrod's lanky fingers. His mother, sitting on the couch nearby, instantly raised an alarm. "Pitching hand! Pitching hand!" she called, until her son quietly extracted his fingers from the dog's mouth. She said this lightheartedly — joking, but only a little.

Because of his arm, and because of his team, Jarrod has a list of things that he won't do, or can't do, by decree of his parents, who are usually thinking ahead to the next baseball game. He will not, for example, jump on a trampoline. When his friends from school hold their birthday parties at a rock-climbing facility, Jarrod does not go. He does not play pickup basketball at school, and if it is the week before a tournament, he sits out of gym class. If he goes swimming in the backyard pool, he's careful not to get sunburned or tired out. He is not allowed to skateboard or ride a scooter.

"Nothing with wheels," Tim told me one day, outlining the policy. "We don't even really let him ride his bike that much."

"He rides his bike," Lori interjected. "Just not a lot." Then she sighed, adding, "I know we sound psycho, but we're not."

There was a time when being a baseball parent meant little more than playing catch in the backyard and cheering through fifteen or so Little League games in the spring and summer. But by all accounts the level of play in youth baseball, as well as the degree of competitiveness and the investment of time and money required of parents, has escalated dramatically in the past ten years or so — primarily owing to the rising popularity of tournament-oriented travel teams. Today, there are an estimated thirty thousand teams playing travel ball, which is entirely separate from more long-standing youth organizations like Little League and Babe Ruth. The greatest concentration of travel-ball teams appears to be in sun-drenched states like Florida, Texas, and California, places rich with retired professional players who coach or offer private lessons, and where the weather allows for year-round play.

Phil Van Horn, a former reporter for ESPN's *Baseball Tonight*, coaches his twelve-year-old son's travel team in Glendale, California, and also gives lessons to players as young as six. The combination of high-level coaching and constant competition over the course of a never-ending season has resulted in children who are "far more accomplished," he says, than young baseball players in the past. "They're mentally understanding the game at a major league level." The best travel teams, according to Van Horn, turn out players who report to their first practice on a high school team more or less as "finished products." Whether this apparent abundance of elite-level prepubescents will have an eventual impact on major league play remains to be seen. "But the game of baseball is changing," he says. "It's definitely a new day."

For parents like the Petrees, the challenge is deciding at which point, and to what degree, to commit to a child's baseball career. It's a fundamental question, of course, that can be applied more broadly to all parents who want to see their children thrive: To what extent do you nurture your kid's talent? How far do you go to feed a dream? Van Horn is aware that gung-ho travel-ball families who shell out thousands of dollars for equipment, uniforms, tournament fees, and travel costs may appear extreme. Yet he suggests that it's simply a traditional model of athletic development — in which promising kids are basically isolated from "normal" childhood in order to refine their physical gifts — applied to a new game. The only catch is that baseball, more so than tennis, golf, swimming, or gymnastics, remains governed by the great American notion of sports democracy: any determined kid with a ball, a bat, and a sandlot to play in stands a chance of making it big.

"People have accepted that it's okay for a talented seven- or eight-year-old gymnast to go away and live with Bela in Houston and not see her family at all," says Van Horn. "But for a baseball player to do anything close to that, it's like, 'Oh, my God, that's terrible!'"

Most travel-ball players actually spend enormous amounts of time with their parents, who shuttle them to and from practices, sharing rooms at the Comfort Inn and meals at Denny's as they crisscross the country in search of the best competition. What's unfamiliar, at least to those who played youth baseball a generation ago, is the seriousness of it all. Elite baseball players do, in fact, start to resemble elite gymnasts — specializing early, training year-round, living a life in which purpose comes ahead of play. The difference is that in baseball, with more than two million kids competing on travel teams, the elite is also the mainstream.

While Little League still operates on populist principles — any player who signs up gets to play, and the children on a team are required to live within the same area — travel baseball uses a major league model. Teams hold annual tryouts, cut children who fail to live up to expectations, and seem to be on an endless mission to scout and recruit new players, unhindered by matters of geography. One thirteen-year-old player I spoke with, a manifestly gifted hitter named Bryce Harper, lives in Las Vegas but regularly boards a plane to play with various travel teams who recruit his services — and sometimes pay his expenses — for big games.

An early bloomer at six-foot-one and 185 pounds, Bryce Harper is what might be considered youth baseball's premier free agent. As a twelve-year-old last year, he played for teams from California, Colorado, Texas, Arizona, and Nevada. The arrangements are negotiated between the coaches and his dad, an ironworker named Ron Harper, who usually accompanies him. Bryce describes his experiences as uniformly "awesome," not just for the baseball but for the opportunities they afford him to savor the world beyond Nevada. Because of baseball, he has been to Atlanta. ("I love their gumbo down there. Their gumbo is awesome.") He's been to Boston. ("I love their steak and lobster.") And he's been to New York. ("I had their steak, and it's amazing.")

One afternoon earlier this spring, on a visit to Texas to play with the Houston Heat, Bryce found himself standing in front of Roger Clemens's house, squired by one of his temporary teammates, a kid called Boomer. For a boy who leaves home to play more than 120 baseball games a year — not far from a major leaguer's schedule, laid over the rigors of seventh grade — it was a heady glimpse of the sport's ultimate payoff. "He has four H2 Hummers," Bryce told me. "He has a workout dome in his backyard, and I heard he has a huge tree house and a batting cage, but I didn't see them. But there were pillars on the front of the house and the grass was all green and he had, like, deer and other animals carved from bushes and stuff."

Bryce has his eye on a career with the Oakland A's, and unlike many more measured parents I spoke with, his father is unabashed in his faith that his kid will get there. "A lot of people say it's not realistic to think this way," says Ron Harper. "But I've read Derek Jeter's book, and several other books by big-time ballplayers, and they all say they wanted to do it from the time they were young. So I say, Why not Bryce Harper?"

Twelve is something of a magical age in baseball, as it is in life. It is a kind of twilight, a last gulp of innocence before puberty arrives in full force and begins to wreak its usual havoc. It is also the last year kids play on the "little diamond" — a junior version of a baseball field, with shorter base paths and a pitcher's mound set closer to home plate. Players at twelve generally are experienced enough to pitch, hit, and work the infield with skill, but also without any loss of exuberance. There is still an unblemished sweetness to their game. You will see players cry when they strike out. They may hug their moms at the end of a long outing. Even on a serious team like the Central Florida Express, where the coaches are constantly talking about "getting to the next level" and what it will be like to play in high school, high school itself still feels a long way off.

I watched the Express practice one recent evening at a complex of public fields in Apopka, not far from where Jarrod lives. The late-day light fell richly over the field. A pesky wind caused the infield dirt to swirl. The players wore white team T-shirts with their numbers on the back and pristine white baseball pants. Parents were camped out in the parking lot, reading newspapers or talking on their cell phones. A couple dads drifted over to watch from the bleachers. Various batters took turns laying down perfect little base-line bunts, which dribbled cloyingly along the foul line every time. "You got it," the coaches would call, pacing around in sunglasses. "Atta boy there," they'd say.

Among his teammates, Jarrod Petree is no superstar but rather just another ringer in what appears to be a complete set. There is Gaby, Alexis, Peter, Gabe, Max, David, Jesse, Caleb, Brad, Zac, Derek, and Chris — each one of them plying his individual gifts but in the service of a mechanically efficient team. As two hours wore on, bats clanked, balls zipped, gloves popped. If you squinted, you might believe you were watching a group of unusually small college players.

Travel baseball is a fairly cerebral form of child's play. Recreational leagues often simplify the game by prohibiting players from leading off, but in travel ball it is a strategic cornerstone, a full expression of the mental war between a pitcher and the opposing base runners. Similarly, it is not uncommon in travel ball to find twelve-year-olds who can pitch — and hit — arching curveballs, outfielders who can handily throw to home plate, or a team capable of executing blindingly fast double plays. When he formed the Express four years ago, Ben Nichols, who played baseball at Newberry College in South Carolina in the early 1980s, compiled a forty-page playbook outlining complicated moves like double-cut relays and wheel rotations at second base. He handed out copies to the boys on the team, who were eight years old at the time. "I remember thinking, *Whoa, what are we getting into here?*" Tim Petree says. "But it's paid off. My son has a better understanding of baseball at twelve than I did when I was in college. Honestly."

What the onset of puberty will or won't do to these boys is, of course, the great unknown. They may shoot up three inches and pack on twenty pounds before they turn thirteen, adding more power to their swings, more giddyap — as their coaches like to say — to the balls they throw. Then again, they might not grow much at all, dwarfed suddenly by the kids around them. The distractions, too, may become oversize. Already, a couple of boys on the team have girlfriends. Already, some use their iPods to tune out their parents in the car on the way to games.

You can sense it in the parents, that universal, desperate wish to give a child everything — love, guidance, skill, opportunity — before suddenly he's carried off by the forces of his own maturation. To understand this, you need only visit the Winker family at the modest ranch house they own in Windermere, a thirty-minute drive from the field where Jesse and the other Express players practice. Joe Winker and his wife, Karen, bought the place two years ago, drawn by its expansive yard, and Joe immediately built a netted batting cage out back. "We hadn't even moved the couch in," says Joe, who makes a living customizing driveways and has three sons who play baseball. "But we got the cage right up."

At night, when there is no baseball game, or when the game ends early, all three Winker boys — Jesse, Ryan, and Joey — like to hit in the cage with their father pitching. They generally stay out there for hours, throwing and hitting, sometimes until nearly midnight. Jarrod, who has been Jesse's best friend since Jesse first joined the Express three years ago, frequently drives over with Tim to join in. Like Jarrod, Jesse was named one of the top eleven-year-old baseball players in the country last year. He is an accomplished outfielder and a boisterous pitcher, the purveyor of a hard fastball and the occasional intimidating wild throw. Where Jarrod wages war with a left-brained form of precision, Jesse hurls the ball with what feels like his whole heart. If you ask him, he will tell you that he has modeled his game on that of his oldest brother, Joey, who is seventeen and will soon be leaving on a baseball scholarship to Mercer University in Georgia.

On the day that I visited the Winker house, Joey's letter of intent from Mercer had just arrived in the mail and was sitting, freshly opened, on the kitchen counter. The idea of his big brother leaving home was so painful to Jesse that he had a hard time even talking about it. Joe, too, seemed a little stunned, if only because Joey's impending adulthood served as a reminder of how quickly the other Winker boys would also disappear. Even in the batting cage, Joey no longer needed his father. "It's done," said Joe, with more pride than resignation. "I don't offer him advice anymore, because he doesn't need it. All I can do now is throw the ball and get out of the way. I throw it and just duck."

Last July, the Central Florida Express beat a team called the Houston Banditos in a nail-biter of a playoff at the "Elite 24" World Series, one of travel ball's biggest national events, sponsored by the United States Specialty Sports Association (USSSA). The score was 4–3. Jesse Winker ably pitched five of the game's six innings, with Jarrod as his closer, and the whole team came away with championship rings. The final image of the tournament's televised coverage, aired on the College Sports TV network, shows Ray DeLeon, the Banditos' head coach, hunched in defeat, weeping openly.

One of the things parents, coaches, and even kids frequently say about youth baseball is that the adults tend to be far more competitive than the children. "The kids shake off a loss a lot quicker than we do," Ben Nichols says. "It stays with me for a week, but for them it's gone after ten minutes."

At a tournament south of Orlando, I stood next to Henry Ryan, a real-estate broker from northern Indiana, as he watched his son Zac — a willowy redhead who was just shy of his twelfth birthday — play for the Express. The team was winning, and Zac was having an excellent game. Henry explained that he contacted Ben Nichols last December, requesting a tryout for Zac. The playing season in Indiana was proving to be too short, and the competition up north wasn't up to snuff. Ben eventually offered him a spot on the team, specifying that the Ryans would have to cover their own commuting costs.

"Way to crush, dude!" Henry called as Zac drilled a line drive and ran to second base. "Since Zac could walk and talk, his ambition has been to play professional ball," Henry said. "And Florida is where you have to be if you want to play in the MLB."

He went on to detail his son's weekly schedule, which includes two hours of private batting instruction on Tuesdays and pitching lessons after school on Thursdays. Roughly every other Thursday, Zac and Henry catch a late flight out of Chicago to meet up with the Express, wherever they happen to be playing. He makes up his schoolwork around the edges. On weekends when the Express are idle, Zac plays for a travel team in Indiana. Since he started with travel ball as an eight-year-old, Zac has played about 120 baseball games a year — an experience that has cost the family between $15,000 and $30,000 annually. "Zac's the kind of kid who will play two or three games in a day, no problem," Henry told me. "If he wasn't that way, we'd quit. It's one of these things that when your kid's got that talent, you want to feed it."

But how does a kid quit baseball when it has become not only his life but his parents' life as well? Daniel Gould, who directs the Institute for the Study of Youth Sports at Michigan State, says that youth athletics can be a "tornado" for both parents and children — easy to get sucked into, difficult to get out of. "Behind a lot of great athletes is a parent who made tremendous sacrifices," he says. But he adds that a parent's investment often also translates into pressure on the child. "Kids realize the sacrifices their parents are making," he says, "and if they don't play well they feel like they're letting them down. It can be very subtle. They realize, boy, I get the bigger hug when I hit the home run than when I strike out. My dad walks a little taller when we win."

The following day, playing in the tournament quarterfinals against a local team called the Bomb Squad, neither Zac Ryan — the game's starting pitcher — nor the other Express players seemed in control of their game. On the mound, Zac appeared nervous, unsettled, taking a lot of time to gather himself between pitches.

Henry Ryan stood pressed up against the fence, clutching a camera. "Look at me, Z," he called. "Look at me. There's nobody better. Nobody better than you."

The game continued to deteriorate. Zac went to bat and struck out, stranding a runner on base. Henry stalked outside the dugout, his fatherly patience having departed. "You're not at the hotel," he screeched at his son. "You're at a game! You got the winning run at second base. You gotta drive that run in!"

This behavior might have been embarrassing, but Henry was not alone. A number of the Express dads were out that day, lined up in a row behind the dugout, barking corrections, throwing their hands in the air each time their kid failed to measure up. Afterward — after the team lost, 4–3, and the Bomb Squad all but skipped from the field — Ben Nichols gave a postgame speech to the players and their families, essentially blaming the adults for the loss. "They were tight as a drum," he told the group. "Bottom line is, as hard as it is as a parent, you have to let them play. Let us coach them." He then shook his head dejectedly. "You gotta cut the cord," he said.

Youth baseball bears little resemblance to the quaint, regional pastime it once was — a fact that has stoked not just a broader competitive fire but also an industry that exploits talent as much as it nurtures it. Little League's World Series is carried on ESPN and ABC, complete with commentators and postgame interviews. Last year, the *Dallas Morning News* counted twenty other baseball organizations that had enticed teams to play in "national championship" or "World Series" tournaments. One organization, the Super Series Corporation, holds both summer and winter nationals, involving 1,200 teams in ten age divisions, each one paying about $500 for the privilege of competing.

"There are people out there getting very, very rich off parents' need to see their little darlings win some sort of national title," says Bruce Lambin, a longtime youth coach in Texas who produces instructional coaching DVDs. He adds, "Heck, I have a lot of friends making nice six-figure incomes giving private lessons to ten-year-olds with delusional parents."

With the growth of Internet sites like Travel Ball Select, which is dedicated to scouting and ranking young players, children are assessed and compared at increasingly younger ages. And with so many kids playing travel ball, the measuring stick is impossibly long. A parent or young player who goes looking online will soon discover, for example, that Andre Real, twelve, of the SoCal Redwings, hit eight home runs in seven games in one recent weekend. Or that there's a thirteen-year-old named Michael Gill from Flower Mound, Texas, who can throw a fastball eighty-four miles per hour. "Now you've got daddies all over the country out in the park with their radar guns on a Sunday afternoon, trying to do better," Lambin laments. "Little Johnny's going to blow his arm out just hoping to make his daddy feel good."

Overuse injuries — particularly in the elbows and shoulders of young pitchers — are indeed becoming epidemic. Orthopedists often blame coaches and parents for failing to monitor how many pitches kids are throwing and for not giving them time to rest their arms. They also view breaking balls — particularly the curveball — as placing undue stress on the soft growth plates in the arm, which do not harden until a child reaches puberty. Glenn Fleisig, the research director of the American Sports Medicine Institute in Birmingham, Alabama, has studied pitching mechanics for more than ten years. He and his colleagues have come up with two basic recommendations, both of which are widely ignored across travel baseball: young players should take at least four months off per year, and nobody should throw a curveball before he's old enough to shave.

Dr. Timothy Kremchek, the medical director for the Cincinnati Reds, specializes in an elbow-ligament reconstruction procedure commonly known as Tommy John surgery, named for the Los Angeles Dodgers pitcher who first underwent it, in 1974. There was a time when the surgery was reserved for aging professional pitchers, says Kremchek, but today, with young players pitching more games over extended seasons, the average age of his patients is quickly lowering. "I'm seeing fifteen to thirty kids a year who are younger than eleven years old and in need of surgery," he says. "It's unheard of." He maintains that there is currently a shortage of skilled pitchers in Major League Baseball because too many promising young players have self-destructed "trying to get to the Hall of Fame when they were ten or eleven."

There is an obvious risk of mental burnout as well. "We're seeing the adult elite-athlete model dropping down to younger ages that aren't developmentally appropriate," says Gould, the director of the youth sports institute. "I worry that we're beginning to professionalize childhood."

Baseball America, a magazine devoted primarily to minor league, college, and high school baseball, has started publishing all-star lists of players as young as twelve years old. Certain "showcase" events, designed to allow high school–aged players to strut their stuff for college and pro scouts, are now open to thirteen-year-olds. Are the scouts actually paying attention? "Not really," says Alan Matthews, an editor at *Baseball America*, noting that most scouts don't bother to evaluate players who are younger than fifteen. "But I don't think it'd be a stretch to say there are some college recruiters who browse our lists and store those names in the back of their heads."

Tim Petree is hedging all his bets when it comes to Jarrod's exposure. He checks Travel Ball Select about twice a day, to get a sense of who's winning and who's losing and who the "high publicity guys" are on a given day. Sometimes it's his son. After the Express team dominated a tournament in Knoxville, Tennessee, in early May, Jarrod's picture sat atop the website's home page, which identified him as an "ace." "A lot of getting somewhere in this sport is promotion," Tim says. "It's gotten to where you have to be known and seen." He and Joe Winker are planning, over the next several years, to travel with Jarrod and Jesse to various college-sponsored camps and showcase events around the country so that the boys can play for an audience of college scouts and coaches.

Their longevity as pitchers is not at issue, Tim says, since both boys keep their arms in good shape and have learned what he believes to be proper pitching mechanics. Coaching for the Express, he uses a pitch-count clicker to keep track of how many pitches each player on the team throws. Most tournaments also enforce limits on innings pitched.

What remains controversial, though, is the curveball's prominence in travel ball. Little League is currently discussing the possibility of outlawing breaking balls altogether because of the link with injuries, but most agree that in travel ball, a rule like that would never stand. Curveballs, after all, give a kid the competitive edge, which is basically what travel ball is all about. Tim insists that Jarrod, who has been honing his curve since he was ten, throws a less taxing form of the pitch in which the curve originates from his wrist and not his elbow. But Dr. Kremchek, the Tommy John specialist, is adamant that any type of breaking ball puts "abnormal stress" on a young arm and that its use could be a death sentence to a promising career. "It may not bother a kid now, but it'll come back to bite you," he says. "If you really want your child to be Nolan Ryan or Roger Clemens, you don't do it when they're twelve years old."

One of Jarrod and Jesse's favorite things to do is to watch Jesse's big brother Joey play with his high school team. We went together one balmy evening in April to see Bishop Moore, the Catholic high school Joey attends, face a top-seeded Orlando public school called Boone. At dinner beforehand in a nearby strip mall, Jarrod had worked his way methodically through a sixteen-inch rack of ribs, while Jesse devoured a steak slathered in butter and blue cheese. Between them, they polished off two baskets of dinner rolls. Now they were primed for the game, taking seats side by side in the stands, each boy with a baseball glove resting in his lap.

High school baseball in Florida is a serious affair, especially in the months leading up to the major league draft in June. About fifteen scouts stood behind the fence at home plate that night, identifiable by their radar guns and notebooks, their plastic foam cups of coffee and emotionless faces. Every time Boone's pitcher, a stringbean kid with a ninety-mile-per-hour fastball, threw the ball, the scouts raised their guns, checked their readings, and made a note. A few got on their cell phones, presumably to relay information to some unseen, big-league power in a faraway place.

This was undoubtedly a vision of Jarrod and Jesse's future — the packed stands, the scouts, the row of giggly girlfriends perched high in the bleachers. Jesse treated everybody there like an old friend, cheering on the Bishop Moore players using their nicknames — Go, Sapp-Daddy! Get 'em, babeeee! — and punching fists with Jarrod whenever somebody, especially Joey, hit the ball.

Three innings into the game, however, the two boys slipped away. I assumed that they were going for a hot dog or to find the bathroom, but another inning passed and they still hadn't come back. When I asked Karen Winker, Jesse's mom, if she knew where they had gone, she didn't have to look. She just pointed backward, over the top of the bleachers toward a dark field beyond. "They do this every time," she said, smiling. It wasn't just Jarrod and Jesse out there but a whole collection of kids, barely visible in the light spilling out of the high school ballpark. Having scrounged a bat and tennis ball, they were playing their own impromptu game.

I thought back to an earlier conversation we'd had, as Jarrod and

Jesse tried to describe all the ways in which they were different from each other, despite being best friends.

"He likes rap and I don't."

"He's neat and I'm messy."

"I hate the Red Sox," Jesse announced.

"I hate the Yankees," Jarrod responded.

Jesse lifted his chin defiantly, "Someday I'm going to hit a home run off of you," he said.

"Ain't gonna happen," said Jarrod. Then both boys started to laugh.

I then asked them what they thought was the best part of playing elite baseball. Jarrod stared at the sky for a moment, appearing to think. Jesse looked sideways at Jarrod, as if seeking permission. "I'm gonna say it," Jesse said. Then he turned to face me. "It's about winning," he said. "But not just about winning — it's fun too. I want to do it for the rest of my life."

He paused and looked to his friend.

"Same as Jess," Jarrod said solemnly. He added, "Baseball for life."

Jesse understood this to be a pact. He looked back at Jarrod. "Baseball for life," he said.

ELI SASLOW

A New Game Plan

FROM THE WASHINGTON POST MAGAZINE

Third-and-seventeen and the QB calls play 686. From a bright young sportswriter, a timeless story of loss and recovery.
— D.M.

DREW HIXON SOMETIMES STOOD in front of his mirror in the morning and pretended to get dressed for a different job, the kind he'd expected to have after graduating from college. He imagined himself as an up-and-coming businessman, and that it was important to look nice. Everything he wore needed to coordinate, even his sunglasses. Drew removed his earrings and trimmed his thin mustache, lingering in front of the mirror until he looked completely professional. Then he went to work and took orders from teenagers.

Doctors called it miraculous that Drew, then twenty-three, held any job. But every time he walked into the Nike store where he worked, he thought: *Failure, plain and simple.* Not long ago, Drew had played college football, and Nike had provided him with its best merchandise for free. Not long ago, he'd interned for the Washington Redskins, where his father, Stan, is the wide receivers coach. Now he swiped shoes and shirts across a scanner at the Leesburg outlet mall.

Drew longed to tell everyone he met that he didn't belong at this store, that he had been on the verge of accomplishing great things before a crushing tackle in a Tennessee Tech football game knocked him first close to death, then back to infancy. He'd spent months recovering, but he still walked with a limp, slurred his speech, and struggled to retrieve words from a brain so badly bruised that it once looked like a peach hurled against a brick wall. Drew worried people would think he was a dummy.

Then, this past March, a woman and her daughter walked into the Nike store looking for shoes. Drew forced a smile and helped them find their sizes. The woman asked Drew how he liked working for Nike, and Drew explained that the job was temporary. He'd just graduated from college with a degree in finance, and he wanted to get a job at a bank.

"This could be a great coincidence," said Jill Aydelotte, a vice president at Citibank. She told Drew that the company wanted to hire one hundred personal bankers to staff new branches opening in the coming year.

Aydelotte gave Drew her business card and told him to e-mail her a résumé later in the week, but Drew wanted this opportunity too desperately to wait. He e-mailed his résumé that night. Then he stopped by Aydelotte's office the next day. Aydelotte liked his initiative, and she wanted to hire him. But there was one big catch, as Aydelotte discovered a few days later when she typed Drew's name into Google and found a news story about him. He was, she realized, eighteen months removed from a traumatic brain injury.

To become certified as a personal banker, Drew would have to pass three timed, multiple-choice financial-knowledge tests in two months, a challenge only about half of Citibank's applicants survive. Aydelotte called Drew and asked if his brain had recovered enough for him to tackle these tests. He paused before answering.

It was a stretch, Drew admitted, but what was the worst thing that could happen? "I've been to hell and back," Drew told her. "I don't think I have much more to lose."

Even before he started elementary school, Drew Hixon had built his life around football. His daddy coached, and Drew made sure everybody knew it. As Stan Hixon moved up the college coaching ladder as an offensive assistant, Drew stood by his side. At two, Drew dressed in yellow and posed for a football poster at Appalachian State University. At nine, Drew ran onto the field during games to pick up the kicking tee at the University of South Carolina. At eleven, Drew held Stan's headset cord on the sideline at Wake Forest University and sometimes ended up on TV.

Stan loved bringing his only son to summer camps, practices, and games. They were a team. "You knew he was getting so much enjoyment out of being there, and that's fun to watch," Stan says. "It was always great having him with me."

By the time Drew's mother, Rebecca, decided her son had grown big enough to join a team in the eighth grade, Drew had already learned that football, in his life, was more than a game. It shaped his relationship with his father, provided his family's sustenance, and gave the Hixons their identity.

School mattered less, at least to Drew. His parents fretted constantly about their son's academic indifference. Drew's typical pattern infuriated them. He would slack off until the last month of a grading term, then pile on extra credit during the final few weeks to make a C. His laziness resulted in some of the family's biggest fights.

But now, with the Citibank job on the line, Drew started studying hard for the first time in his life. Stan and Rebecca, both forty-nine, teased their son that maybe he finally would realize some of that untapped potential his teachers always talked about. That description, repeated in at least a dozen parent-teacher conferences, had always tormented Rebecca. Now she tried hard to suppress another worry: how much of Drew's potential was still there?

Rebecca, a former journalist, took one look at the Citibank preparatory books Drew was reading and knew she would need a translator to understand them. They were academic texts about state securities regulations, investments, and mutual funds. "To be honest," she says, "I don't think I could read those things for ten minutes."

Citibank highlights the pressure of its tests to discourage weak applicants. Its rules are basic and unforgiving: Fail a test once, and you must wait thirty days before trying a second time. Fail the same test again, and you're done at Citibank.

To prepare for the exams, Drew quit his job at Nike and began taking classes in Washington with eleven other aspiring personal bankers. Most days, Drew studied for at least ten hours. His classes at Citibank ran from about 9:00 A.M. to 5:00 P.M. Then he studied on his Metro ride home. Then he barricaded himself in his room and studied late into the night. He was driven by what he saw within his grasp, what he had long ago identified as the final goal of his recovery: landing a good job, the kind coveted by even top college graduates. Drew had already bragged to old friends about his new job and its starting salary.

"I'm not going to call my friends back," Drew vowed, "and tell them, 'Oh, yeah, that job I told you about? I don't have it now. I failed these tests and blew it.'"

To ease his commute to classes in Washington, Drew spent two weeks living with his aunt, Lynn Jones, in Silver Spring. Drew typically left her house at 6:00 A.M. and returned at 9:00 P.M. During twelve days in Silver Spring, Drew allowed himself two breaks. He cleared out an hour on two weeknights to watch *24*, his favorite TV show. Both times, he fell asleep during the first fifteen minutes.

Fatigue crushed Drew. His brain grew tired after even the simplest activities — such as driving or talking on the phone for twenty minutes — and studying for one-hundred-plus-question tests brought a new kind of exhaustion. Drew tried caffeine pills, but they changed nothing. He relied instead on a drug prescribed for him by his doctor called Provigil, often used by narcoleptics to curb excessive sleepiness.

Drew's aunt called Rebecca three times during Drew's stay because she was worried he might crumble if he didn't take a break. Jones told Rebecca she barely recognized her nephew anymore. The old Drew was self-assured and laid-back. This new Drew was almost the opposite. He was anxious and intense. Nothing came effortlessly anymore. Drew got lost taking the Metro from Jones's house twice, and he called his aunt distraught one night because he couldn't remember where he'd left his car in a parking lot.

"Slow down," Jones told him. "You're still recovering."

"I can't," Drew replied. "I don't have time to recover."

The entire Tennessee Tech team went to Golden Corral for breakfast on September 11, 2004, but Drew didn't order anything. Not hungry, he said. Kickoff loomed more than ten hours away, but already nerves had seized him.

Almost half a decade had passed since a football game mattered to Drew this much. At 7:00 P.M., he would walk onto the field of an NFL stadium in Tampa as a starting wide receiver for Tennessee Tech University, a Division I-AA school in Cookeville, Tennessee. If Drew, a senior, played his best — he needed to make at least seven catches and score a touchdown, he told friends — Tech had a slim chance to upset Division I South Florida. It would be the biggest win in school history.

Drew had already talked to his father about Tech's game plan:

pass liberally, take risks, and turn the game into an offensive shoot-out. Stan's own football schedule had prevented him from attending any of Drew's games, but he knew as much about the Tennessee Tech team as any season-ticket holder. He called Drew before and after each game. "Sometimes it made me worried," Rebecca says, "because they only talked about football."

Stan had never spent much time teaching Drew the intricacies of playing receiver, because he had never had to. Drew had absorbed the game's minutiae by spending hundreds of hours with his father at games and practices. When he started high school in Kennesaw, Georgia, he quickly blossomed into a star.

Drew's teammates at Harrison High found his athleticism impossible to quantify, because nothing about him stood out. At five-feet-ten-inches and 170 pounds, Drew usually fell to the ground with the first tackler. He had good but not exceptional speed, and he rarely faked his way around an opponent. Somehow, though, Drew's instincts always led him to the holes in a defense. He caught almost every pass within his reach, and led his high school team in receptions during his junior and senior years.

Drew joked with friends that he might take a football scholarship at some school far away, such as Boston College. But his teammates knew Drew would end up standing on a sideline next to Stan. Sure enough, when Stan took a coaching job at Louisiana State University, a Southeastern Conference powerhouse, during Drew's senior year, Drew committed to play there.

They arrived in Baton Rouge, they say now, with very different expectations. Drew thought he had NFL potential and would play immediately; Stan believed Drew could become a contributor only if he compensated for his athletic shortcomings with guts and hard work.

Regardless of how Drew performed, Stan vowed to never treat his son preferentially, because that would cost a coach the respect of his other players. He was hard on Drew, criticizing him for clumsy route running at team meetings in front of thirty people. He rarely sent Drew into games. And when Drew's confidence waned — when he began to reconcile his lofty self-perception with reality — Stan resisted the urge to hug Drew. "There are some things you can't do as a coach," Stan says. "I wanted to be there for him, but it was like I couldn't."

Drew rarely played during two seasons at LSU, and his football struggles echoed elsewhere. His grades slipped. He saw a doctor to talk about depression. For the first time in his life, he complained about being the coach's son.

"I found out pretty fast at LSU that the only reason I was there was because of who my dad is," Drew says. "The other players were faster, more prototypical. I knew that. I'm not stupid. It wasn't like I was mad at my dad, just sad. I felt like I had let him down."

After his second season at LSU, Drew told his dad that he wanted to transfer. Drew's decision violated Stan's principles, and he spent two weeks trying to dissuade his son. "You can't quit. You can't give up," Stan said. "Especially not in football." But Drew had made up his mind, and he fled to Tennessee Tech in January 2002. Stan wished his son luck, but the good-bye felt cold. It took several months — and consistent prodding from Rebecca — before Stan forgave Drew.

Tennessee Tech appealed to Drew less as a destination than as an escape route. He knew almost nothing about the school, which is eighty-two miles east of Nashville, or its football program. It had offered him a scholarship, and Drew accepted without so much as visiting the campus. He often regretted that hastiness during his first two seasons at Tech, when he rarely played on a team loaded with experienced receivers. But now, as he prepared to play South Florida, Drew believed he was on the verge of a breakthrough season.

Drew had played the best game of his life the week before, in the season opener against Gardner-Webb, grabbing nine passes and scoring the winning touchdown with less than two minutes left. He had felt so sore after the game that he skipped the parties in Cookeville that night, choosing instead to eat pizza rolls on the couch with his girlfriend, Terramani Collier. Drew told Collier that his aches felt good, almost satisfying. He called Stan, who had just taken a job with the Washington Redskins and was preparing to coach his first professional season opener. Stan listened as his son detailed all nine of his catches. "Don't get a big head," Stan teased. "You're not that special." Then Stan hung up the phone and called a friend to brag about Drew's breakout game.

Drew's performance against Gardner-Webb had legitimized him as one of Tech's senior leaders, so he tried hard to ignore his own nerves and calm his teammates in the Tampa locker room. At LSU, Drew had played with and against athletically superior players. He had experienced the thrill of a big crowd in an NFL stadium. "Don't worry about that stuff," he told his teammates before Tech took the field. "All that matters is we want this more. We can make this day memorable."

Quarterback Robert Kraft called the play in the huddle — "Okay. We're doing 686. That's 686. Let's get this" — and nodded at Drew. Tennessee Tech faced a third-and-seventeen early in the second quarter. The Golden Eagles trailed South Florida by seven points, and their offense had gained a total of four yards so far in the game. If Drew wanted to galvanize his team, this was the time.

Drew lined up near the left sideline, sprinted fifteen yards up the field, and turned hard to his right. An unsightly pass wobbled toward him, but Drew snatched it with outstretched hands and ran just beyond the first-down marker. After Drew had gained about nineteen yards, South Florida safety Javan Camon caught him from behind and wrapped up his legs. Drew started to fall forward, but halfway to the ground, South Florida cornerback Mike Jenkins, in a full sprint, lowered his head and chest and dived into Drew. Jenkins's facemask hit Drew in the chin strap, and both players ricocheted backward, their momentum reversed.

Rebecca Hixon, sitting in the lower level near the thirty-yard line, reacted to the play with the impulse of a football coach's wife. "Oh, no!" she screamed. "Drew fumbled!" But as Rebecca watched the ball roll out of her son's arms and land in the hands of teammates, she noticed another loose object on the field, bouncing almost ten yards ahead of Drew and his tacklers. *Wait. Oh, God. Drew's helmet.*

Kraft and Tech receiver Brent McNeal rushed to Drew and found him motionless on his back, his eyes closed. They waved at their sideline for help, and Tennessee Tech trainer David Green and team doctor Richard Williams jogged onto the field.

With forty years of combined football medical experience, neither Williams nor Green felt particularly alarmed by Drew's condition at first glance. He had been knocked unconscious, something the two men witnessed a few times each season. Usually, the player woke up in ten or fifteen seconds, left with nothing more than wooziness and a headache. Green tried hard to stimulate some sort of response from Drew. He pinched his leg. He shouted near his ear. Nothing.

Fifteen seconds.

Drew looked like a baby, peacefully sleeping, with no visible marks or bruises on his face. Williams guessed that Drew had suffered a neck injury, and the doctor checked his pocket to make sure he had brought his pen and knife onto the field. If a broken neck blocked Drew's airway, Williams was prepared to cut into Drew's chest and create a new one. Williams bent his ear over Drew's nose. A deep breath. So what the hell was wrong?

Forty seconds.

Rebecca stood on her seat, looked down at the field, and tried hard not to panic. She had seen Drew injured before. He'd had the wind knocked out of him once, and a mild concussion a few years earlier. Rebecca closed her eyes and prayed. Six of Stan's relatives from nearby Lakeland, Florida, had come to the game, and they urged Rebecca to make her way to the field. "No," Rebecca said. "Let them do their jobs. I won't help anything." But when Drew remained motionless, she hurried down to the edge of the sideline, where a security guard stopped her. "I'm his mother," Rebecca said. "Please let me through. I need to be with him."

Two minutes.

Williams and Green carefully strapped Drew to a backboard. They felt as though they were handling a cadaver. Drew's vital signs were normal, but he remained limp and unresponsive. His left eye looked dilated. Green suspected that Drew had a brain injury, maybe some sort of cranial bruising or bleeding. The trainer remembered the last time he had felt this confused and helpless. Four years earlier, a Tech defensive back named Preston Birdsong had collapsed during an informal jogging drill in the middle of August. Green had worked to resuscitate him for three minutes. Birdsong died.

Five minutes.

Doctors let Rebecca squeeze her son's limp hand, and then they wheeled Drew into the ambulance. They had almost loaded him in when — wham! — Drew's legs yanked up, and his arms jerked to his chest. He had started posturing, a reflex that usually indicates a traumatic brain injury. Chris Clifford, an assistant trainer, strapped Drew's arms and legs to a stretcher before the ambulance took off for a major trauma center located just one mile away.

Ten minutes.

In the emergency room at St. Joseph's Hospital in Tampa, doctors diagnosed a brain shear, an injury that occurs when a person stops moving or decelerates so suddenly that the brain jolts violently forward and then backward. An emergency room nurse connected an IV to Drew's arm and administered a sedative, which would medically maintain Drew's coma to reduce the risk of seizures and ease the strain on his bruised brain. The medical staff had shut Drew down, essentially, so his body could channel all of its energy into healing. Now he had to emerge from the coma himself.

An hour. A night. Forty days.

His family kept praying that Drew would wake up.

About a week before Drew takes his first Citibank test, he has a vivid nightmare for the first time in years. He dreams he's in the testing center when a bell goes off, signaling that he's out of time. Then he looks down at his test and sees that he still has forty questions left to answer.

As Drew studies, he worries more about his brain's processing speed than about the quality of its decisions. On the first test, he has to finish one hundred questions in two hours, fifteen minutes, and he's not practicing at anywhere near that pace. On practice tests, Drew sometimes has to read a question three or four times before he understands it. The questions are filled with jargon, and they're mathematically difficult.

Question: An individual has started investments of $100/month into a spread-load, periodic payment plan. What is the maximum sales charge that may be taken by the company over the first 48 months?

With the help of his calculator, Drew comes up with the answer — $768. But it takes him more than four minutes. To improve his speed, Drew takes several practice tests each week and memorizes different question formats. He's still terrified when, at 8:45 A.M. on April 14, he walks into the Prometric Testing Center on Lee Highway in Fairfax, a nondescript building that's outfitted a lot like a funeral home. Reproduced art hangs on whitewashed walls, and fake flowers sit on a coffee table.

Drew places his personal belongings in a locker. Then a proctor hands him two pencils, a calculator, and a pair of orange headphones designed to block out noise. Drew is already sweating when he walks by the sign that reads ABSOLUTELY NO UNAUTHORIZED ACCESS BEYOND THIS POINT and settles into a small cubicle with nothing but a chair and a computer.

Ten questions into the test, Drew knows he's going to pass. He has taken so many practice tests that he recognizes almost every question that appears on his screen. "I couldn't wait to get to the end and see my passing score," Drew says. He finishes in less than two hours, and he scores an 81. He walks out of his cubicle with his confidence soaring.

The Hixons go out that night to Ruby Tuesday to celebrate, and Drew talks about his future at Citibank as if it's a sure thing. Later in the week, he creates a spreadsheet on his computer to manage his own finances. He divides his much-anticipated Citibank salary into several allotments: food, housing, gas, and others. "I'll make enough to move into my own place," Drew says. "This could work out to be real nice."

Stan was enmeshed in final preparations for the 2004 Redskins' season opener when Rebecca called him from the hospital in Tampa at about 11:00 P.M. Stan listened to the story of Drew's injury and reassured his wife that Drew probably had suffered a concussion. Stan told Rebecca that he would fly to Florida the next afternoon, after coaching his first Redskins game. But when Rebecca called again Sunday morning to report that the doctors had decided to medically maintain Drew's coma, Stan packed his overnight bag and headed to the airport, with the encouragement of Redskins coach Joe Gibbs. His debut as an NFL coach could wait.

During their first few days at St. Joseph's, the Hixons struggled to make sense of what the doctors were telling them. Rebecca and Stan understood that Drew had a brain injury and that doctors had sedated him. They knew he was in a coma, but they imagined that Drew would wake up soon, say hello, and ask for a big plate of pasta.

They were optimists by nature, confident that their faith could lead them through a crisis. Even before the doctors had finished examining Drew, Rebecca had issued the first rule of his recovery: only prayer and positive thoughts would be tolerated. In the waiting room, she'd dug through her purse and pulled out pictures of a recent family vacation to Hawaii, laughing as she told her in-laws a story about Drew showing off his muscles at a hotel swimming pool. Rebecca and Stan told every well-wisher who called them during those first two days that their son would recover quickly.

On Tuesday morning, about sixty hours after Drew's accident,

St. Joseph's neurosurgeon Rakesh Kumar walked into the hospital waiting room to update Rebecca and Stan. Kumar said Drew's brain had continued to swell in at least three places and that doctors needed to put a probe in his brain to monitor the pressure. Drew's body temperature kept escalating, Kumar said, so nurses had wrapped him in a cooling blanket. Rebecca and Stan nodded back at Kumar, but nothing he said seemed to penetrate their optimism. The doctor worried that maybe the Hixons had fallen into denial, and he decided to shock them out of it.

"Your son could die," Kumar said. "He's fighting for his life."

Kumar walked out, and silence filled the room. Stan's cell phone rang, as it had maybe a hundred times during the last two days, and he answered it. Michael Haywood, an old friend and the offensive coordinator at Notre Dame, wanted to send his best wishes, and Stan began to give Haywood the same update he'd already recited dozens of times. *Yes, Drew's still in a coma. We need your prayers. He's going to come out of this.*

Then Stan started sobbing.

It was only the second time in twenty-seven years of marriage that Rebecca had seen her husband cry — the other was at his father's funeral — and she rushed to hug him. His breakdown lasted for maybe three minutes, but it jolted an entire family back to reality. Nothing felt the same after that. The Hixons remained relentlessly positive, but the scale of their expectations changed. They stopped anticipating instant improvement and prayed for small signs of progress. Stan and Rebecca bought clothes at Kmart, and they moved into a Tampa hotel room with Drew's two younger sisters, Avis and Adele.

Doctors took Drew off sedatives about seven days after his injury. For the next two weeks, the Hixons spent eighteen hours each day at Drew's bedside, trying to coax him out of his coma. A physical therapist visited for half an hour each day, and showed the Hixons how to stretch Drew's limbs and improve his range of motion. A speech pathologist suggested that Drew might respond to familiar sounds, so Rebecca, Stan, and Drew's sisters clapped and screamed like cheerleaders in his hospital room. They borrowed a boom box and played rap CDs, blasting the same kind of profane music that, eight years earlier, had prompted Rebecca to throw out her son's entire CD collection.

The hospital staff liked caring for Drew, because the smallest improvements thrilled his supporters. When Drew squeezed his girl-friend's hand, she ran into the hall jumping up and down, even though doctors guessed it was a simple muscle reflex. When Drew defecated in his bed, Rebecca fought back tears. "Thank God," she said, "that something in him is still working."

"In my time here at the hospital, I've never seen the staff get more attached to a family than we did with Drew's," says Will Darnall, St. Joseph's spokesman. "Here they were in the worst situation imaginable, and the only thing they could see was their son's improvement."

Rebecca wrote a note to Tennessee Tech's football team on the eve of its first game after the injury, and her words — *Drew loved playing, and he would want to play with you today* — caught in the head coach's throat when he read them to his team. How, Mike Hennigan wondered, could this family remain so optimistic? Drew's injury, coupled with the memory of Birdsong's death during Tech football practice four years earlier, had pushed the coach into a depression. He tried to relay updates about Drew's condition to his players at the beginning of each practice, but the news always came across as gloomy and discouraging.

"How can you get excited about the jerk of the left arm if you weren't there to see it?" Hennigan says. "Our guys couldn't understand that as progress. They wanted Drew back — the athletic guy, in the prime of his life, with a smile that just knocked the wind out of you. No update I had was going to give that to them."

Hennigan knew football was dangerous. At least fifty high school and college football players have died over the past ten years, according to the National Center for Catastrophic Sport Injury Research. But Hennigan, with three young sons of his own, hadn't become a football coach to guide players to injury and death. For a time, he says, he considered quitting.

The two South Florida players who collided with Drew also recoiled from the game. Cornerback Mike Jenkins told reporters he was holding back on the field. Safety Javan Camon, a notoriously hard hitter, also couldn't tackle with the same abandon. "I didn't want to be as aggressive," Camon explains, "because now I knew how many bad things could happen from a good hit."

Yet Stan and Rebecca never questioned the sport that had given their family so much — and threatened to take away so much more. At a hospital news conference a few days after the injury, a local reporter asked Rebecca what she would tell other football players in light of her son's experience. "Accidents can happen anywhere in life," she replied. "You could injure yourself walking down the sidewalk. I would say you should never go out onto the field feeling scared or timid."

For the Hixons, football had not put Drew on his deathbed. No, they said, just the opposite. The game had given Drew the tools to survive. "If Drew hadn't been in top shape from playing football, he might not have lived through the hit," Stan would say later. "And football taught Drew how to fight. He's a competitor now."

On a Monday night in Tampa, nine days after Drew's injury, Stan turned on the television in his son's hospital room and pulled a chair to the side of Drew's bed. He held his son's hand and provided a running play-by-play of the Redskins-Cowboys game. He told Drew what passes the Redskins offense would call, and why each one might work. His voice was soft and simple, almost nurturing. It sounded, said a hospital administrator who heard Stan's play-by-play that night, like a devoted father teaching his boy about a game he loved.

Drew drinks an iced tea in the basement lounge of the Citibank training center. He's scheduled to take the second test in two days, and he feels confident. He has studied less for this test, and his parents privately worry that he's underprepared. But Drew is relying on the momentum from his first test. "This one isn't going to be as hard," he predicts.

A classmate walks into the break room, and Drew makes small talk. He mentions that he's drained from studying but still has about 150 pages of the preparatory textbook to read. The conversation halts. The woman's eyebrows pop up, and her head jolts backward in disbelief.

"You *still* have 150 pages!" she says. "Are you sure you're going to be ready?"

Drew just shrugs in response, but he walks out of the room fuming. The woman has handed Drew a competitive trigger, the kind he always used on the football field. Over the next forty-eight hours, Drew imagines himself as an underdog with critics who scoff at his weaknesses. He heaps nineteen months of self-doubt onto a woman whose last name he can't remember. *What does she think? That I'm too dumb? Too slow? Too lazy?* When Drew walks into his cubicle at the testing center on April 27, he imagines what it will feel like to approach his doubter and wave a printed, passing test result in her face.

One hundred and fifty questions later, Drew feels more thankful than vengeful. The computer calculates Drew's score and finds that he answered 105 questions correctly for a score of exactly 70 percent. One more botched question would have resulted in failure.

Drew's knees feel weak as he walks out of the testing center and climbs into his Blazer. He sinks into the driver's seat and tosses the keys on the passenger chair beside him. For almost ten minutes, he sits in an emptying parking lot with his eyes closed. He prays.

"I guess I'm just thankful that God gave me that wake-up call without making me fail," Drew says. "A seventy. That's pretty lucky. But the bottom line is I passed, and now I know I can't stop working."

A month passed, and Stan returned to work, but Drew remained in a coma-like state in the hospital in Tampa. He opened his eyes — a development that elated his parents — but his progress stalled there. His mouth still hung eerily agape. He responded to almost nothing.

One glance at his MRI explained why, says Peter Patrick, a neuropsychologist who met Drew on October 6, 2004, after he was moved by air ambulance from St. Joseph's to Kluge Children's Rehabilitation Center in Charlottesville. Drew's brain looked, Patrick says, as if somebody had taken a Jell-O mold and shaken it fiercely. Shock waves had rippled through Drew's brain, tearing axons and stretching neurons. "It is one of the most dramatic MRIs I've ever seen in any kind of sports accident," Patrick says. "If you showed that MRI to any expert, he would think this was the result of an incredible car accident. There was just unbelievable impact."

Patrick theorized that Drew's unique injury demanded creative treatment. The doctor had experimented in clinical trials with Amantadine, an antiviral drug typically used to treat Parkinson's disease. Patrick believed the drug also helps activate certain tracks that connect the upper and lower centers of the brain, and he discussed it with the Hixons. He also discussed possible side effects, which included a spike in blood pressure and seizures. "It was kind of scary, because this was all on the cutting edge, and nobody knew exactly what worked and what didn't," says Rebecca, who was spending two and a half hours each morning driving from Leesburg to Charlottesville and then another two and a half hours returning home. "But at that point, we were looking at Drew and nothing was happening. What did we have to lose?"

The drug worked like magic dust, Rebecca says. In three days, it rekindled the life in Drew's eyes. He started to respond to his family and his girlfriend by nodding his head and giving them the thumbs-up sign.

Even Patrick was stunned by Drew's rapid improvement. The drug set off a wave of neural activity within his brain. "Drew was the best responder we had seen," Patrick says. "He helped us pioneer a new treatment." But for the Hixons, Drew's thrilling improvement also brought sobering awareness. Only after Drew began to respond could his family accurately survey the devastation of his injury. Nothing — *nothing* — came naturally to him anymore. To help Drew learn how to stand up, doctors strapped him into a machine that slowly raised him to a ninety-degree angle. At about sixty degrees, Drew heaved and vomited. His body no longer knew how to fight gravity.

At Kluge, Rebecca watched her son advance through all the stages of infant development for a second time. Drew spent two weeks learning how to sit up and balance his weight. It took a week for him to relearn how to swallow so he could eat solid food.

Drew's growth was simultaneously exhilarating and heartbreaking, because everything he did could be measured both as the progress of a coma patient and the deterioration of a college athlete. "We were so excited to see him doing all these things, but at the same time it was just weird to push your older brother around in a wheelchair while he was wearing a diaper," his twenty-two-year-old sister, Adele, says. "I was kind of always unsure whether this was how it was going to be forever, or what."

Drew spent five hours each day rotating through different kinds of therapy, and he sometimes felt as if he never made progress. Every exercise ended in physical and emotional aching. Drew thought movement would come to him naturally, but instead his body felt awkward and foreign. "It was like I had never moved my foot or my arm before," Drew says. "It felt like somebody else's body." He learned to take halting steps after a month at Kluge. He made his first facial expression a few weeks later, when Tennessee Tech quarterback Kraft visited, and Drew smiled at one of his jokes.

On a fall Saturday, Drew's girlfriend, Terramani Collier, heard her cell phone ring and recognized Stan Hixon's number. Since Drew's injury, she had carried her cell phone everywhere, waiting for Drew's first call. Before the injury, they'd talked three or four times each day. Now she hadn't talked to him on the phone in two months. She answered the call.

"Hello?"

"It's Drew. I love you."

Collier could barely find the composure to respond. Drew had slurred all five words together, and he'd spoken in a voice that barely rose above a raspy whisper. It reminded Collier of how someone with a severe cold might sound after answering the phone in the middle of a deep sleep. And it was, Collier told Drew, the most beautiful sound she'd ever heard.

Drew's memories of this period are hazy, leaving him only with snapshots of pain and frustration. He developed a severe hematoma in his left leg during his coma, and that agonized him during rehab. He slept in an enclosed bed, like a crib, so he wouldn't get up in the night and hurt himself. He had to page for a nurse to unzip the top of the bed cover if he wanted to get up and go to the bathroom. Occasionally, Drew found it easier to urinate on the corner of his bed.

At one point, he went on a field trip to a grocery store in Charlottesville to buy the ingredients to make cookies, and shopping for six items took him almost two hours. "We thought it was great he could shop, but Drew was devastated," Rebecca says. "He wanted to shop like a totally normal person. Just completing a task wasn't good enough."

One afternoon after a rehab session in a swimming pool, Stan and Drew walked through the Kluge gym. Stan picked up a basketball and passed it to Drew, suggesting that he shoot it. Drew caught the ball and lined up for a lay-up, expecting an easy swish. But he had lost thirty pounds of muscle and most of his natural coordination during the past two months, and his hardest heave left the ball two feet short of the rim.

It was dawning on him, he says, that there was "a new Drew and an old Drew, and they had a lot of differences. I wanted the old Drew back, but there wasn't anything I could do about it."

The accident had changed Drew's memory as drastically as anything else. Drew recalled nothing between the end of July and the middle of October. He remembered interning with the Redskins in Virginia during the summer; then he next remembered a nurse at Kluge telling him to slow down while he drank through a straw. Rebecca considered the memory loss something of a blessing. Her son would never be able to recall the most difficult months of his life.

Late in Drew's stay at Kluge, Patrick prescribed him another cutting-edge drug called Aricept, which is often used to fortify memory in Alzheimer's patients. Drew started to retain small things. Drew memorized the order of the seasons and months of the year. He spent ninety minutes each day with speech therapist Rebecca Epperly, and his vocabulary returned. Like a child, Drew relearned how to write. He developed his motor skills by connecting dots and then learned to draw large, basic letters that looked nothing like his old, tiny handwriting. He wrote and memorized a sentence explaining the circumstances of his life: *My name is Drew Hixon, and I was injured in a football accident on September 11, 2004.*

The doctors at Kluge cleared Drew to go home to Leesburg two days before Thanksgiving of 2004, and Drew hugged a dozen staff members before climbing into Stan's SUV. Stan pulled away from Kluge, and father and son talked briefly about the Redskins. Stan felt elated, as if he finally had his same old Drew back. The sensation lasted for only a minute.

"Wow, this is a really nice car," Drew told Stan. "When did you get it?"

"Drew, you drove this car at least ten times last summer," Stan said. "You really don't remember?"

Drew had only been home for a week when Stan asked his son to tag along to football practice again.

It was December 2, 2004, when father and son walked into the lobby at Redskins Park to greet dozens of well-wishers. Drew shook hands and caught up with players he'd met during his internship the previous summer. Stan watched proudly from a few yards away. "I had to take it all in," he says. "It was a great moment."

The visit felt more bittersweet for Drew. When he had last visited Redskins Park, he had identified with these players as his peer group: talented, self-assured athletes whom many people admired. Now, as players walked up to embrace Drew, he leaned heavily on a cane.

He still loved football — he turned on ESPN's *SportsCenter* every morning as he read the sports section of the newspaper — but seeing athletes sometimes made Drew melancholy. Once, he'd watched football players and identified with their abilities. Now, he watched and recognized his limitations. "I used to think, 'Oh, I can do that,'" Drew says. "Now it's like, 'Man, I wish I could still move like that.'"

Vinny Ceratto, the vice president of football operations, came by to see Drew during his visit to Redskins Park. Ceratto had supervised Drew's internship. At that time, Drew had talked about a future in football, maybe coaching or working in the front office for the same team as Stan. Ceratto asked Drew if he still had football at the center of his plans.

Drew hedged. Maybe, he said, but I might try finance first.

When Drew decided he would return to Tennessee Tech in the fall of 2005 to finish the two classes he needed to graduate, friends told him it would be the best social decision of his life. "Every girl on this campus loves you," declared James Roinson, Drew's roommate for two years. "You're a celebrity, and all these girls think you're so brave and amazing. They're going to flock to you."

The old Drew would have relished that type of attention. During his two years at Tech, Drew had earned a reputation as being comically conceited. Drew sometimes stood in front of the mirror in his apartment, flexing his muscles and announcing, "Man, I'm fine!" Once, when Drew walked across campus with Robinson, he stopped a random woman and asked her to decide which roommate was better-looking. She picked Drew.

Before the injury, Drew color-coordinated his outfits even on days when he pulled on sweatpants. He went to parties sporting a collared shirt, designer pants, and a Kenneth Cole watch. Drew liked to wear sunglasses, even indoors. When friends asked why, Drew explained that he aspired to be "the definition of cool."

The new Drew returned to Cookeville with none of that swagger. He walked with a halting limp, and his movements often appeared mechanical. Gone was the smooth talker who could interact comfortably in a room filled with fifty football boosters. Now Drew spoke laboriously, even in the company of friends. But he never apologized when conversations were stilted or awkward. He had to learn to live with the new Drew, he decided, and so did everyone around him.

Drew's best two remaining friends in Cookeville — teammates Robinson and Anton Thomison — searched hard for the Drew they remembered. Thomison and Robinson took Drew on the same simple outings the trio had enjoyed before: hanging out at Kmart or laughing at the line-dancers at the local country bar. No matter what they tried, Robinson and Thomison could never keep Drew awake past 9:30 P.M.

Hennigan invited Drew to attend football practices, but he came only once. "It was hard on him to be there, and it was hard on us," Hennigan says. "The last time he was at practice he was running around and making great plays, and now he was having a hard time shagging balls for the receiver coaches. Everybody thought it might be uplifting to have Drew there, but it was also a hard dose of reality. It hurt."

The former linchpins of Drew's life — his football coaches, his friends, his girlfriend — no longer understood him. Collier thought Drew's personality had flattened, as though someone had injected him with a tranquilizer. When the couple had visited Collier's family in California over the summer, Drew had stayed in the house. He'd slept a lot and kept to himself. Not long after that, the couple decided to break up. "It took me a while to accept the fact that he was always going to be different," Collier says. "That might have been one of the problems we had in the end."

The loss devastated Drew, but he rarely talked about it. When pressed, Drew told his friends that the breakup registered as just another severed tie between his old life and his new one. "I never cried or complained," Drew says, "because what's the point of that?"

Instead of mourning what he'd lost, Drew focused on what he wanted to become. He developed new interests to occupy himself and new goals to pursue. He sought out an internship at a local bank. He spent one night each week at a campus Bible study. Drew told Thomison and Robinson that he had a limited amount of energy, so he needed to devote all of it to his classes. He wanted to graduate, find a good job, and seize the second chance God had given him. "I committed myself," Drew says. "I was tired of doing just enough to get by."

Near the end of the semester, Drew hung around late after Bible study and talked with a friend, Joie Puckett, about the way the accident had transformed him. Yes, it had taken a lot away. He'd lost his athleticism and some of his affability, Drew said. But he was starting to appreciate what he'd gained. His work ethic had improved, he told Puckett, and he had a greater appreciation for his opportunities. "I'm more proud," Drew said, "of the person I am right now."

Later, he would go even further, saying: "I'm glad the injury happened. I've grown so much since the injury. So much. So much. Going through something like that, a life-changing event that 99.5 percent of the world will never go through, and then surviving it, and then not only surviving it but coming out a better person — I mean, what are the chances? That's nothing but God right there. How can you not be thankful?"

Before Drew leaves the house to take his third and final Citibank test on the morning of May 15, he turns to his parents and promises not to be crushed if he fails. He has overcome so much adversity in the past eighteen months, Drew says, that one more speed bump will not devastate him. It's a nice thing to say, but none of them believes it.

He walks into the testing center, and a man in a stiff black suit greets Drew and guides him to his cubicle. For the next seventy-one minutes, Drew endures a mental beating. Questions pop up on the computer screen in front of him, and none of them seems similar to the ones he saw on practice tests. He rushes through questions that he barely understands, because he's worried about the seventy-five-minute time limit. At the end of the test, he decides not to review his answers. What's the point, anyway? He only has three minutes left.

Drew clicks the submit button on his computer, and he spends the next two minutes imagining how he's going to tell his parents that he failed. He needs a 70 to pass, and he guesses he scored about 65. Drew closes his eyes and prays, then opens them to check his fate blinking on the screen.

In the coming months, Drew will begin working as a personal banker at Citibank's Reston branch. He'll start dating a pretty girl he met at church. He'll move out of his parents' house and into his own apartment in Leesburg. But no milestone will mean as much to him as the one on the testing center computer screen.

Congratulations! You scored 71.

Beads of sweat drip down Drew's forehead as he practically jogs back into the lobby. He pumps his right fist, high-fives the stiff man in the suit, and then struts out of the testing center. When Drew reaches his car, he stops at the driver's side window to check his image in the glass. He tugs up on the collar of his blue, buttoned-down shirt and loosens the knot on a checkered tie. Then he slips on his sunglasses and idles at the tinted window, smiling at himself.

His reflection has never looked so good.

ERIC NEEL

The Saturday Game

FROM ESPN.COM

Basketball forever? Eric Neel offers his bona fides as a core court
guy. Most of us can relate somehow. I came home early from my
honeymoon for a softball game.
— D.M.

I PLAYED BALL on my wedding day.

It was a closed game with friends who were in town for the festivi-
ties. We started at eight in the morning, in a middle-school gym in
Kalona, Iowa. It was late June and steam-bath hot; guys were swig-
ging Gatorade going up and down the floor, like runners hitting
checkpoints in a marathon. I had a terrible day, short-arming everything on my way to an 0-for-8, I think, and was positively abused
on the blocks by my old friend John. But still, it was beautiful.
There was no place I'd rather have been. In fact, I was a little late to
the ceremony after trying to squeeze in one more game that morning, and if you look closely, you can see I mucked up the pictures a
bit with a fresh sweat line around my collar and a blotchy boiled
pink in my cheeks.

This is the first thing I tell Dave, one of the Saturday Game originals, when we meet. The wedding day run is my most faithful gesture, my most devoted act. I offer it in tribute, and as a kind of shib-
boleth.

"Sounds like a near-perfect day to me," he says. "If only you'd hit
some shots. . . ."

Dave knows a thing or two about faith and devotion. He's sixty-
five years old, New York born and bred, and he has been playing in
the Saturday Game, in the same grade-school gymnasium in New
Rochelle, New York, just north of New York City, for thirty-five

years. The Saturday Game began in 1971, and it's continued, from Labor Day to Memorial Day, every year since. Dozens of guys have played in that time, many for twenty years or more, and two of them for the entire run of the game.

"A lot of guys moved in and out over the years, but a lot of us played for a long time," Dave says in a slightly hoarse Bronx accent. "Guys grew up and grew old in the game."

Sixty-five isn't young, but Dave still sports a baller's body: broad across the chest, upright, long in the leg. He's chief administrator of a Huntington's disease unit, but even in the halls of the hospital, he moves like a shooter, sliding into spots, never looking hurried.

In the beginning, the Saturday Game was Cuppy, Ripp, and Bob Edlitz. (I give you the names as the guys give them to me, as handles; some with nicknames, some with first names, some with last names, and some with both.) Ripp knew Elliott, and Elliott brought in Danny and Dave. Kenny, who's still playing, has been there almost from the start, along with Billy and Schiff. And Richie Glover too. Sid came in a few years later. The Commish came on board about twenty-eight years ago, through Sid, and Matty arrived soon after that. It evolved the way these things do: you'd invite a friend from the neighborhood or the job, or maybe you'd play pickup with a guy somewhere else, appreciated the way he played, and asked him to join in.

It was just a game in the early days, just ball, a little safe harbor at the end of the week. But over time, Saturday by Saturday, game by game, it became a way to live, rules to play by, truths discovered, a creed, a kind of religion. "We've all been enthralled by our experience in it," Cuppy says. "The game, how you play the game, the people you play with, that's who you are."

You Want Fifteen, and Only Fifteen

The Commish comes to the gym one Saturday in his first year, 1978, and there are only seven guys there. The Commish is not happy. "Are we playing, or are we not playing?" he thinks. "Because if we're playing, let's play, and if we're not, what are we doing here?" The Commish, five-feet-five worth of bedrock shoulders and drill-bit gaze, is not to be trifled with. He's gonna shape up the ship. He makes a list of names and numbers, and he works the phones all week to make sure they'll have fifteen come the next Saturday. And every Saturday after that.

"Sixteen's a mess," he says. "Fifteen is perfect: ten on the floor, and five waiting on winners." You want flow, you want to catch a blow between runs but not cool down, and you want everybody into it. Fifteen is what you want.

You can have a game without the list, but you cannot have the Saturday Game. The list is the shape and structure of the thing. The birth of the list is the moment when the game becomes an institution. The Saturday Game is not pickup, you see; it's plan, it's ritual, and a hallowed one at that. If you're on the list, you have a responsibility to lace up. If you're not on the list, you wait by the phone, high-tops on, hoping for the Commish to call and say, "We're short one this week."

A lot of the guys who play now once served time on the list. Jeff, the Commish's son, brought them in, one by one, over the years. "That call every week was make or break," says Amin, a forty-something regular with a bright, quick laugh who likes to roll off picks. "It was the difference between a good week and a bad week; it changed your whole outlook." Part of it is just the run, the sweat and bank shots leaching the workaday toxins from your system, but part of it is the belonging too. Being in a closed game is like knowing the secret handshake; there's some blush of pride that comes with it, some keepsake buzz.

You don't wander into the Saturday Game. Walk-ups get turned away. Shorthand phrases and familiar tendencies are the coins of the realm. You know guys. Guys know you. "There's a comfort in it," Dave says. "You do something together, you're not talking about it maybe, but you're together in it." I know what he's getting at. Although it doesn't sound like much, it's kind of everything. It's why I risked the ire of my beloved and organized the wedding-day game. It's why the Commish sounds like the height of rationality when he tells me about the time he ran.

Someone, Kenny thinks it must have been him but can't really remember, brought a friend, an extra, to the gym one Saturday. No call to the Commish the night before to check on numbers, no warning at all. So there they are, loaded down, out of whack, trying to fit sixteen pegs into fifteen holes come game time. I get the story at Chef Ho's on Second Avenue, waiting on the hot and sour soup. It has been years, but the Commish, a little pink rising from his col-

lar, smoothes out a wrinkle in the tablecloth like maybe a patch of
flush white linen will erase the pain when he says, "I walked out."
Jeff jumps in, laughing: "You didn't walk!" True enough. He ran.
Out of the gym, down the hall, off the school grounds, and down
the block. And down another block. And another. He kept running. He ran until the anger, the disgust, wound down, until he
thought he could breathe again without wanting to spit or shout
first. Thirteen miles he ran. Ran blindly. Ended up on some corner
somewhere he'd never seen before. Panting and fuming.

"That's the Commish, right there," Kenny says, shaking his head
in mock disbelief. Kenny's a lawyer, big-time firm in Manhattan. He
has a scrapper's body, short and wiry. Keeps his face quiet, doesn't
impress easily. And he's right about the Commish and the run: it's
extreme, it's the act of a madman, and we're all laughing about it
when the soup comes. But I'll tell you what, it's the act of just the
sort of madman you want on your club, in your game, and on your
side. The Commish had to give up playing last year — he's seventy-
one now, and his mobility ain't what it used to be — but he speaks
in the present tense when he looks at me straight, while the table's
still cracking up, and whispers, "What do you want? I live and die
for the game." I smile and nod; extremism in defense of the Saturday Game is no vice. ·

You Know a Man by His Game

Kenny bleeds Blue Devils blue and suits up most Saturdays in a
faded brown Cleveland Browns T, number 32. He's a hustling go-
to-spots guy, a ball hawk, a box-out boarder. Dave's a shooter, a
deadeye, unblockable, southpaw Silk Wilkes; looks like he's putting
his arms in the sleeves of a sport coat or scratching an itch on
the back of his neck, but he hits it, and if you're smart, you hit him
trailing on the break. Matty will tell you he doesn't have much
game and never did, but even at seventy-one, the same age as the
Commish, he runs. Constantly. Slowly. And in circles, like you're
the skinny-dipping prey and he's the menacing midnight shark.
Offense or defense, it makes no difference — Matty runs, and always with a devilish grin, like he can't believe he's out there, like he
has discovered the secret of life. Jeff and John are the engines,
pushing the ball up the floor. Jeff fancies the midrange outlet pass.

John gets to the bucket on quick crossovers and sports a steady stream of in-game chatter. Amin floats the perimeter. Chip works the midrange. Seth owns the base line. And young Omar, one of the twenty-something "babies" in the game, part of a recent influx of players who aren't, as Dave says, "a bunch of old, white guys," is all over the floor, a slasher in the modern vein. Cuppy, his broad shoulders and tree-trunk legs, used to set some shivering picks, the sort of picks you mark on the calendar — "Remember that one you laid on Sid that one time, Cupp?" The sort of picks that echo down through the years so guys, sitting in their Manhattan offices in suits and ties, fourteen floors up and ten years removed from the contact, rub their shoulders and wince when they talk about them. And Schiff, Schiff's an artist, and a retired architect — kind of looks like Pollock with the bald head and the sinewy hands — and he could really play. Every phase of the game he had. He saw the floor. He had a feel for space and pace. He could shoot and dish. He was the Saturday Game's J-Kidd, the guy who made it flow, made everyone around him better.

Everybody plays a role. It's pieces of a puzzle, chips in a mosaic. And your game is your calling card. Some of the core guys know each other going back to high school or even before, but the general protocol is your first name and your game. "You go, you play, you pat a guy on the shoulder and say, 'See you next week,'" Schiff says. "That's how you know guys."

Schiff, Kenny, and Billy would drive up from the city together every Saturday. Schiff had to pick up his coffee and doughnut along the way. Kenny and Billy would have their encyclopedic reminiscences about the old Holiday Festival tournament at the Garden, or their debates about whether Clyde or the Pearl was more important to the '73 Knicks. On the way home, they'd write backstories, imaginary lives for guys in the game. The guy who wears the green shirt all the time — Mike, right? — he works in a hardware store; his specialty is grass seed, weed and feed stuff; he's a whiz with the lawns. And the one who made the last shot today, that friend of Jeff's, who has been playing for a few weeks now, he washes high-rise windows for a living; he's that guy you see outside your office on that rig, the one you figure must be crazy to be up so high in the wind like that. One guy has quintuplets at home. Another's an ice cream taster. And we can't be sure, but we're thinking maybe one of the crew is using the game as part of his CIA cover. "We had no clue," Kenny says. "But we had a lot of fun with it."

Yet, "clueless" flights of fancy notwithstanding, the Saturday Game's also an intimate exercise. "It's the direct contact, the physical element," Schiff says. "The guy's right in front of you, he's trying to stop you, you're trying to do something to him. It's intense." And those confrontations run parallel to the game's collaborations. "You get familiar with the way guys move and how they react to situations. You know each other's games, and you know where to get the other guy the ball, and you have the experience of doing some good stuff together, some special stuff," Dave says. He says this last part, about "special stuff," with a short shrug and a curled lip, as if maybe he has said too much, as if he has put into words something better left unsaid. It's five in the afternoon, and we're in his office in the Terence Cardinal Cooke Health Care Center, way up on Fifth Avenue. There's a security guard in the lobby; the office door is closed; and cabs and buses buzz by outside the window. No one can hear us. But still, there's something illicit about what he has said, about the inarticulate but universal hoop truth he has hinted at. Which is just this: the game is a high. Even the most unassuming run on the most unremarkable Saturday, when it's going right, when you're in synch with guys whose games you know, can bring about the sort of bliss most of us only wish we got from sex, drugs, or rock 'n' roll.

I'm playing as a guest of the game one Saturday in March, and we're tied at six, game point, when a shot comes hard off the rim. John, probably the fittest guy in the bunch, the guy with a little rip on his frame, grabs the rebound and turns to run up court, and at the opposite free-throw line, he stops, feints right, and flicks the ball to his left, hitting Jeff right in stride for the winning lay-up. It looks choreographed. It looks perfect. John watches the ball fall through the net, then spins on the ball of his left foot, pumps his fist, and howls: "Au naturale, baby! Au naturale!"

And woe is he who kills that buzz. The Saturday Game has had its share of lawyers playing over the years, so there was always some debate, but the guys decided a long time ago that it would be an esprit de corps gig. The Commish set the lineups, mixing up the young and the old, the short and the tall, the got-game and the not-so-much. Games were to seven, call your own, play it straight. Keep disagreements short, handle them like the possession arrow: you get this one, we get the next one. And no smack. A brash guy, new to the game, hits a few shots over Bobby Edlitz, this was years ago now, and decides to tell him about it. He's chatting him up — "I own you," "You got nothing" — every time down, and when it's over, the Commish takes the guy aside and tells him it's *over*, privileges revoked, walking papers issued. "No —— holes, no bull ——," Dave says. "That's the rule, that's always been the rule."

Life's too short. There are too many good runs to be had. Play the game right. "When I was first bringing guys in and adding guys to the list, I had to tell them what the game was like," Jeff remembers. "Not just that there were older players who'd been at it a long time, but that there's a standard, or a quality, I guess, and some guys I knew couldn't handle it." Jeff's not as intense as the Commish, a little quicker to smile, a little more willing to just see how things play out, but he has known from the get-go, as though he inherited it from Pop right along with a head of prematurely white hair, that the spirit of the game was a real thing, a thing to be respected and cherished. The first player he invited, in fact, was not his best friend but his best friend's brother. "His brother was more level-headed. He got what we were about," he says, laughing at the memory of having tweaked his buddy a bit.

How deeply ingrained is the code after all these years? Jeff remembers Chip, one of the guys he invited many years back, voluntarily suspending himself for two Saturdays after he laid a pick on Matty he knew was cheap. "Nobody had to say a word," Jeff says. "He just disappeared for two weeks and got himself together."

And it works the other way too. If a man's a legit, fair-minded baller on the floor, if he makes the extra pass, owns up to touching the ball last as it flew out of bounds, and picks you up when you're down, then you know he's good people out in the world. Cuppy calls it a litmus test. One of the guys they played with for a while back in the '80s got snagged in a Giuliani insider-trading bust. He was a Goldman Sachs guy, escorted out of the building in cuffs, the whole deal. He was later exonerated. "I knew it was a bad rap all along," Cuppy says, with a quick clap of his hands. "There was no way. I played ball with him. I knew him. I knew he wouldn't do something like that. He was a ballplayer. That stuff they accused him of — that just wasn't his way." We hold these truths to be self-evident . . . that's how he says it, simple, declarative, like it's an article of faith. If the world is full of what you don't know and can't be sure of, you can be sure *he was a ballplayer.*

That can't be true, of course. I know about subterranean pathologies and the survival-instinct virtues of suspicion; I've seen *Blue Velvet*. But even if you know it's not enough, you gotta have something, some kind of measure. You gotta invest in something, gotta lean on something, gotta cloak yourself in some sort of cover against the coming of the chaos and the danger and the crap, don't you? And why not the game? Why not something with a collaborative heart, a democratic backbone, and a good soul-cleansing sweat to boot? Why not something you've lived and done and known every Saturday for ten, twenty, thirty-odd years? Why not adopt it as a worldview? "It's not that I can't work with somebody or have a civil conversation with somebody who doesn't play ball," Dave says. "It's just that I'm not sure I can trust him . . . I mean not all the way."

You Never Know

You get slightly different stories on Bobby Edlitz's last words.

Kenny thinks he said, "Oh s——." Sid remembers, "Oh, God." Schiff heard a drawn-out "Nooo." Dave doesn't think it was words at all, just some kind of eerie, deflated noise, "like 'oooooh.'"

Bobby had just come off the floor; his side had lost the last game. He was standing next to Dave. They were both breathing heavy, the way you do. They were looking out onto the court while the next game got rolling. They were talking some about the last run, or maybe they weren't — Dave can't remember.

Then came that word or that noise, and then he was down. He wasn't big — maybe six-foot, 180 — but he fell hard; a stagger and a thud, a sick, wrong sound. "Everybody stopped," Dave says. "We knew right away it was serious, that something had happened."

It was his heart. Someone called 911. Seth tried mouth-to-mouth. They circled around him, their own chests pounding, not sure what to do. They talked to him, told him to hold on.

The paramedics came and hurried him to the hospital, but he never regained consciousness.

Bobby was a core guy. He got the first gym permits way back when. He brought guys in, he boxed out, he hustled on D, he knew how to pass, and he loved to stick Dave, even though Dave was a better player. "He was a bulldog, very competitive, a terrific athlete, had great stamina," Schiff says. "He was the kind of guy who'd play on Saturday morning with us and then go out and play tennis or golf afterward." He was a stalwart. Then he was gone, like the flip of a switch.

Most Saturdays, the game breaks up and guys go their separate ways, back to their families and their routines. But the day Bobby died, they stayed together. After the hospital — "massive heart attack . . . he was dead by the time we got there," Kenny says — they ended up at a neighborhood Friendly's, in one of those red vinyl booths around a big Formica tabletop, talking, not talking, eating, not eating, and sitting there with the hurt, shoulder to shoulder. "We just didn't want to be alone with it," Dave says. "It was a terrible day, but it would have been even worse if we were alone."

At the funeral a few days later, Cuppy sat in the front row with his wife. "I'm not doing this again," she said. She looked him in the eye, then she turned her head and nodded in the direction of the casket. "I'm not doing *this*." Cuppy was fifty-nine years old and had been playing in the game for twenty-four years. Thanks to the infusion of some of Jeff's buddies, the game had gotten a little younger and quicker while he and some of the other originals had gotten a little older and slower. It didn't take much for her to picture him in Bobby's place. She didn't care that he felt strong. She didn't care that he'd grown up hauling boxes and crates up the stairs from the storage basement below his father's Washington Heights grocery. She didn't care that even at fifty-nine he was stronger than most of the guys he played with. "She was worried about the heart," Cuppy says. "And I didn't feel like I could just tell her not to worry; maybe I *was* pushing it." So he quit the Saturday Game. Eleven years ago. "I still feel I could run forever," he says, and makes a joke about maybe getting a note from his doctor to let him play again someday. He's halfway out of his office chair. The words come quickly. He has a barrel chest, his hands are strong, his legs are still solid. I believe him. "But I owed it to her and to our kids to stop; they were scared," he tells me. "It was the right decision." I believe that too, but I know from the way he's shifting in his seat, and from the way his eyes come alive when he tells me he "loved the game, loved the way it was played, loved the way we played it," that it's an article of faith he must rehearse and repeat to observe, to believe it himself.

The Commish will tell you a lot of guys thought about giving it up after Bobby died. "We were shaken," he says. "We weren't sure we should keep the game going at all for a while." In the end, for most, the antidote to fear and sorrow was more ball. "I couldn't imagine not playing. I couldn't imagine getting up on a Saturday and not heading to the gym," Kenny says. "I finally felt like he didn't die because he was playing basketball; it could have happened playing tennis the next day, or doing anything. The thing is, you never know, you can't predict, boom, you might as well do what you enjoy doing. You might as well play."

It was different when Billy died a couple of years ago. They saw it coming for a while.

He began missing appointments, at work, at the dentist. One Saturday, Kenny and Schiff showed up at his house — "I would pick him up every Saturday morning at quarter to eight," Kenny says — and Billy never came out the front door. Finally, his wife came out and said she thought he was still sleeping. "That was the tip-off something was really wrong," Kenny says. "In thirty years, that had never happened." Tests revealed a malignant brain tumor.

Between operations, some of the guys from the Saturday Game would occasionally meet other days of the week for dinners with Billy. "In the beginning, I think it made a difference," Kenny says. "We had fun, talking about the game, remembering things that had happened years before." Kenny and Schiff hadn't expected to find one of the great friendships of their lives when they started playing ball with Billy. (Schiff and Billy began playing when they were students at Cornell; Kenny met them both at a parks department gym in the late '60s, before the New Rochelle game began.) But for the three of them, hoops was a bridge, from the court to the car rides together, and to dinners out, and ball games, and phone calls, and eventually the weddings of each other's kids. "We became the best of friends," Kenny says. "Because we had basketball, and because that opened up other things for us."

They lost Mike, a friend of Jeff's, on 9/11. "He was a helluva player," Dave says. And that, in its way, is an obit unto itself, a summary statement, a testimony. There's no way to gauge the losses.

Schiff shows me a photograph of Billy he keeps pinned to the wall in his art studio. Billy's at a party, maybe, smiling broadly behind round wire-rim glasses, looking like no kind of ballplayer at all. "He would surprise you," Schiff says, with a proud chuckle.

Kenny tells me about Billy's Bill Sharman set shot and a patented fake move, slipping the ball up and under the defender's armpit and laying it off the glass when the guy turned to look for the ball. "His fakes would drive new players crazy," he says, delighted, as if he has told me everything there is to know. The real measure of it, the sense of what it must have been like for them to watch him sink into sickness, the hint of what it must be like for them to live without him now, is that when I ask them about the Saturday Game at all, about what it has been and meant over the years, they bring up Billy and Bobby straightaway. Everyone who has played does.

Even now, the Saturday Game doesn't exist independent of those who died in it; it's a living memorial. Every time Kenny or any of the other regulars laces up, it's an act of memory, a chance to feel the sting of losing those guys and at the same time to pay tribute to them. The game echoes with memory and the bittersweet richness of loss and love. There's no shortcut to that kind of thing. You can't anticipate it or design it. You never know it's there until it's there. You make your way to it game by game. Over time. Schiff hasn't played since his legs gave out six years ago, at age sixty, and he swears he doesn't reflect on the game, but in the same breath, with Billy's picture on the wall five feet from where he sits, he says, "These were your guys, you know. These were guys you spent a major portion of your life with."

You Can't Overestimate the Value of a Good Run

Dave tells me he loves the game, tells me I'm going to hear that a lot the more I talk to the guys, tells me simple love of the game is a big part of the story of the Saturday Game. More than anything, he thinks, it's what has kept guys coming back.

I ask him what he means by love, not expecting much; it's kind of an impossible question, actually.

Dave tells me everything.

His brother was a mathematician, and he was supposed to be a mathematician too, because that's what his parents wanted. He was smart, but it wasn't his thing, and he eventually gave it up. He wondered, as we all do, if he'd disappointed them, if they approved of the things he did instead. He carried the wondering with him over the years, he says, sometimes feeling unsure of himself, sometimes feeling alone . . . like any of us. He dropped in and out of college, suffered through the breakup of his first marriage, and struggled some to find a career, a relationship, and a version of himself he felt at home in.

He has a kind of peace about him now. I know that because he's brave enough to be candid with me. I know it because there's nothing fancy in his delivery, no romance or hyperbole. He's telling it plain. He's speaking his truth.

Blows me away. Listening to him, I wonder whether I'll ever have such handle, such calm consciousness and understanding of my own twists and turns.

He tells me it's the product of heavy lifting, of a whole lot of introspection. But he tells me, too, how it's a function of the game. For as long as he can remember, ball has been the antidote to all the other stuff going on with him, whatever it was. From the very beginning, he felt he was expressing something in playing, tapping some core element of his character, some hidden-even-to-himself longing, some outrageous alien confidence. Ball isn't just an escape for him, it's wish fulfillment, it's life-saving.

Ball makes him feel better about himself. Period. Without fail. You can't overestimate the value of a good run, he says. There's nothing like the way it burns the bad feeling out of you and replaces it with something good. The collaborative aspect is intoxicating, but Dave really revels in simply doing something well. He can pass and shoot, without hesitation. He has darting moves and a quick release. He can play. He could always play.

So this love isn't some casual or abstract affection. It isn't the way you feel about your favorite food or a special car. This is more akin to the feeling you have for your spouse and your children. This is ballast. This is the fabric.

"I tell you what it is," Dave says. "It's that I can't imagine my life without it. I can't imagine who I'd be or what I'd be like."

You Don't Shoot an Airball at Game Point

We're eating at Il Vagabondo on East Sixty-second Street, me and about twenty guys from the Saturday Game, past and present. Big long table in the back room, waiters in white shirts and aprons, antipasto to die for, and, I kid you not, a competitive bocce ball court downstairs. It's a set in a Scorsese picture. I'm sitting next to Amin, talking about Pitt Panthers hoops (Pittsburgh being his alma mater). The Commish is across from us, and he leans over our way, looking at me but pointing at Amin, and says, "Let me tell you a story about this guy." His delivery is entirely without affect, it's Walkenesque. Amin's arms fly into the air like he's riding a coaster on Coney Island, as he shouts, "Here we go! Again with this?! It was twenty years ago!"

Laughter erupts from the Commish's left. "God, I miss it! God, I miss the ball busting!" says Wittner, a longtime regular who hung it up last year, a guy so in love with the game and its roots he drives me out in the black of night to see the outdoor court, near the entrance to Fort Tryon Park, where a lot of the guys played growing up, just so I can soak up whatever silent secrets it holds.

It seems that on some Saturday in the past — Amin says it's ancient history, the Commish remembers it like it was yesterday — the team the two of them were playing on was locked in mortal combat with the opposition, the game tied 6–6, when Amin let fly from the top of the key . . . and got nothing for his trouble, no iron, no backboard, no net, no nothing. The Commish tells me this without so much as a smirk. Amin is laughing and hollering, "Come *on!* What about the shots I hit that day?! What about all the shots I've hit in all the games since?!" The Commish is resolute. He wants me to know the kind of dodgy character I'm dealing with. He wants me to enter into any and all conversations about Pitt Panthers hoops with my eyes open. He wants me to understand this isn't all fun and games. Yes, it's true they had a guy named Little Jay who played in pants and long-sleeved shirts for a while. And yes, it's true Kenny sports what his school-days buddy Larry Brown once called "the worst shot I've ever seen." But still, the ball is legit. The ball is serious. This is a New York game, after all. There are standards.

Richie Glover was a standard-bearer, a neighborhood legend coming up in Washington Heights. He played in the old citywide all-star game (players from Manhattan and the Bronx against guys from Queens, Brooklyn, and Staten Island) at Madison Square Garden when he was in high school. Best ballplayer in the Saturday Game, even after he'd gotten older and put on a few. Big guy — "like a rock," Schiff says — but quick on his feet. Could go left or right, could hit the J, knew how to defend, work the angles. Total package. Wittner remembers him, years past his prime, sitting on the courtside bench at the outdoor court up near Fort Tryon Park, reading his newspaper and smoking a pipe. "He looked like he was just a guy in the park," he says. "He'd have that paper up high so you couldn't see his face; the smoke from his pipe would kind of float up above his head." And then, after a while, somebody would be down one and somebody who knew him would say, "Hey, mister, wanna play?" and the other side would think it was about to rack up a couple of easy wins. "And Richie would just use them up," Wittner says. "They never had any idea what hit them."

Dave's a standard-bearer too. Like a lot of guys, he played the parks as a kid. He and his Bronx buddies, Danny and Elliott, used to play bragging-rights games with the rich kids from Riverdale. Danny was a terrific player, went on to play freshman ball at NYU. Dave played college ball at Baruch (a division of CCNY) in the early '60s, and years worth of competitive pickup ball after that, and all the while he drained that funky shot. "It came naturally to me; you'd never choose to shoot the way I do, behind the head and from the left," he says. "But whatever it was, it was just what I did." Whatever it was, it worked; still does most days.

Mel, who played in the Saturday Game for years, takes me aside at Il Vagabondo and says, "Make sure you get this: I've seen a lot of ball in my day; I've seen top college ball at the Garden, I've seen all the great Knicks teams; and Dave has the greatest shot I've ever seen. Bar none. I'm serious." Dave's take on his game is more modest — "I can't jump at all; I'm a middle-class Jewish kid from the Bronx!" — but he figures he was just good enough to know what true greatness was. "It was very satisfying to me to play as well as I played," he says. "But to see someone like Elgin Baylor, or Earl Monroe, do what they did and to know, in my bones, how much better they were than I could ever be, that blew my mind."

It isn't a Rucker Park run, but the Saturday Game guys, then and now, aren't hacks — they could always play. In the winter of '85, one of the guys in the game, a sports agent, got a few of the regulars hooked up in a weekly side game with players from the New York Mets. They played again for several weeks in 1986, just after the Mets won the Series. Howard Johnson played, Ron Darling, Darryl Strawberry, David Cone, Tim Teufel, and Lee Mazzilli too. "It was always us against them," Dave says. "Cone was very good, Strawberry was not nearly as good as he was supposed to be, but they were all friendly. It was fun, it was a competitive run, but nobody put on airs. If you didn't know who they were, it was just a bunch of guys playing some ball."

Although the present-day Knicks are a major exception — don't get Dave and Big Jay (Little Jay's shorts-and-T-shirt-wearing doppelgänger once upon a time) going on the ills of Starbury and Co. unless you have some time on your hands — the New York teams, and the whole NYC hoops scene, have been a model for these guys. "It's a culture," Kenny says. "It's something you're born into." In addition to tales from their days in the parks and the gyms of the city, most every guy in the game has stories about waiting in line for tickets to the Garden. The sixty-something guys saw Bill Bradley go heads-up with Cazzie Russell in 1965, and they wax poetic about the time Oscar Robertson dropped fifty-six on NYU back in the day. The forty-something guys, Jeff's crew, tell you about the times they witnessed Kenny Anderson's lights-out performances in high school and the great St. John's teams of the mid-'80s. And both groups revere the early-'70s Knickerbockers of Bradley, Willis Reed, Dave DeBusschere, and Walt Frazier. Those Knicks are like an enduring zeitgeist unto themselves, like some sort of Jungian archetype burned into every New York baller's consciousness. "There was nothing better than those guys," Kenny says with the proper hushed homage. "The way they moved the ball, so unselfish, so crisp, and such shooters, all of them." And it's not that you could be those guys, or play as they did, it's that you couldn't shake the impulse to try, to aspire, to mimic in your own way their impossible ideal. Not if you lived in New York. Not if you played in the Saturday Game. "Everybody, no matter what level you're at individually, knows what it's about," Kenny says.

And it ain't about airballs at game point, that's for damn sure.

"I swear, I've had a lot of good games since then," Amin protests. "And I've never done it again!"

"Keep it that way," the Commish says, and this time he cracks a grin.

You Get a Two-for-One Deal with Me, Sweetheart

Richie Glover goes hard to the basket, and Cuppy slides over to cover him. The ball goes up — they collide, arms entangled, sweat mingling, groans and gasps raised as one voice — and they go down. Cuppy, somehow, ends up on top of Richie, belly to belly, cheek to cheek. Formidable bellies. Sweaty cheeks. After the thunder of the fall, the room is quiet. Is either guy hurt? Is one of them pissed? Obviously concerned, Billy says, "Look, it's two elephants mating!" Everyone cracks up, including the elephants.

That's the Saturday Game.

Seth, a forty-something, sets a midkey pick and holds it, waiting for Matty, a seventy-something, to come rolling around from right to left, with a clear path to the bucket. Matty isn't one to create on offense, but if you get him the ball in space, and let him launch his favorite little left-hand hook shot, you get two rewards: the points, and the beaming smile on his face. Matty tracks his made baskets week by week: "One-for-one, that's a great week for me," he says. Seth and the others track them too. "If you can get Mattie a bucket, that's huge," he says.

That's the Saturday Game.

You ask Chip, the "hothead," the guy who had to suspend himself once upon a time, to recall a favorite memory from all the years he has played, and without skipping a beat, he says, "Every time I've run the pick-and-roll out there with my son. I can't even tell you what that feels like. It's an honor is what it is."

That's the Saturday Game.

Matty and the Commish go way back, to grade school. "They're like an old married couple," Schiff says. One tall, one short. One thin, one stout. Joined at the hip. So, anyway, when the Commish and his wife buy a new house years ago, after living outside New York for a short while, the Commish gives Matty a key. "I didn't even think about it," he says. He also didn't think to tell his wife. So Saturday morning comes, early, maybe a little before eight, and Matty heads over to the new house and lets himself in. It's game day; it's time to go. He walks in the front door, strolls through the living room, down the hall, and to the bedroom. He opens the door, walks in, and says, "It's Saturday, let's go!" The Commish and his wife are still in bed. She looks at Matty; she looks at the Commish; she looks, shall we say, incredulous. The Commish gets up out of bed, turns to her, and says, "You get a two-for-one deal with me, sweetheart."

And that, my friends, that moment when you wouldn't want to lay odds on who would get to keep his or her key if push came to shove, that moment when history is a passkey, for life, *that's* the Saturday Game.

You Reach a Point . . .

"I didn't know how bad I was getting until we started to bring our sons into it," Schiff says, reaching out with both hands to rub his knees a bit. "When you play against people your same age, you and the guy guarding you or going against you are getting worse, getting slower, at the same pace. But when the next generation came . . . then you knew how horrible you were."

The downside of playing in a game for years is the inevitable physical decline each guy goes through. "My legs just aren't moving like they used to," Dave says. You imagine yourself into spots you can't reach; you take shots only the younger you could pull off. There's a troubling, persistent dissonance. Socially, the game's everything it always was, but physically, it's ebbing from you. And you find yourself getting angry — not just the run-of-the-mill "I had a bad shooting day" frustration, but a real seething thing, like you're failing yourself, like something's failing you. There's a pride that comes from still being out there at fifty-five, sixty-five, seventy, and a tremendous boost when you prove you can still hold your own — "I hit five straight shots the other day," Dave says, "and man, I needed a game like that, just to know I still had something to do out there" — but some part of every week on the court means reckoning with loss.

"It would have been better if I'd never really had any game at all," Schiff says. "But there was a time I could play, and feel good about what I was doing, and then you reach a point where that's just not true anymore, and the whole game changes." And that's before we get to the nagging injuries, and the way they linger longer the older you get. . . .

So a lot of guys stepped away. Only Dave, Kenny, and Matty are left from the old-school crew. But there have been infusions over the years. Jeff and his gang — Chip, Seth, Amin, John, and his brother James — are the "new" blood, twenty-year vets with "only" forty-odd years on their biological clocks. And after them, there's a new "new" gang: Omar and his brother, plus some others looking to get in should spots open up. It's not the same tight ship it once was; there's the occasional day when they have sixteen or more. "I'm a little uncomfortable bossing people around like my father did," Jeff says, laughing. "But most of his rules are still basically how we run the game." And with the mix that has been brewing these past several years, there come different satisfactions. For the over-the-hill gang, it's the pleasure of surprising themselves and their younger, quicker opponents — Kenny keeps a mental list of blocked shots he tallies on the young turks. For the guys in their prime and the kids coming up, it has been the chance to temper their ball-above-all instincts in the interest of the relationships they've built. "The game's matured me," Jeff says. "When I was younger, I was really, really competitive, and in the Saturday Game, I learned how to play hard but still know the guy I was guarding was a friend."

And it's not just friends, it's fathers and sons. Three of Cuppy's boys have played in the Saturday Game. Schiff's son played. Kenny's too. Dave's son, John, plays now. Chip's son comes out when he can. And Jeff keeps the Commish's seat warm, of course. Nat, a high school hoops coach, and one of a handful of black players in the game these days, brings his daughters sometimes, just to show the guys how it's done. "The game's evolved," he says. "We're a more diverse group than we used to be." Beyond the arc of any of the individual lives in the game, the game has a life of its own. It's not a point so much as a continuum — it has generations, it has eras, it has a past and a future. Bobby's death, Schiff's failed ankles, they have counterpoints in whatever move Jeff put on Omar this week, in whatever baby hook Matty managed down low. "While it was happening for me, I never said, 'My God, this is something special,'" Cuppy says. "But looking back, and seeing it still go on now, I appreciate it. It's clear to me we've been a part of something."

Maybe that's what keeps Kenny, Dave, and Matty suiting up. In addition to their love of the game, and thanks to bodies that — knock on wood — have hung on a little longer than some, maybe it's the simple sense of being caught up in something bigger than themselves, something that commands them in some quiet, steady way. "I don't know how to say it," Kenny tells me. "It just is. It's like you have to do it. It goes without saying. It's the game."

You've Got a Game Too

Richie Glover's at the far end of the table at Il Vagabondo, leaning slightly against an aged photomural — an in-good-company shot of hat-wearing, mustachioed men who used to frequent the restaurant for the bocce and the veal parmigiana, a group that mirrors our own tonight in spirit if not costume. Richie's teasing Cuppy about the way he played defense: "It was more touch football than basketball," he says with a wink.

Next to him, Sid and Schiff are telling Cuppy's son Teddy about who it was that found the Ward School gym in the first place and about the places they played around the city before the game became the Saturday Game.

Across the table, Matty's sipping on a drink and the Commish is whispering something to him that makes him laugh.

Next to them, Wittner, Amin, and Kenny are measuring J. J. Redick for a draft-day suit and tie, assessing the way his jump-shot game will, or will not, translate to the big stage.

Up a bit from that group, John, who Jeff says is in the best shape of anyone in the game, is talking with Chip and Mel about a weekday morning game he has been playing in, "just to stay sharp for you guys!"

And across from them, Dave's showing Seth a photograph taken of him and his cabinmates in summer camp once upon a time. The young Dave cuts a handsome figure, no doubt, but the real interest in the picture is the guy behind him, the cabin counselor, who is none other than Sandy Koufax.

And so it goes, for three hours, between bites and courses. Guys move up and down the table to connect and reconnect. There is much hugging and hand shaking, reminiscing, and not a lick of shoptalk. The room is full of lawyers, financial advisers, agents, teachers, and hospital administrators, but those labels don't stick here. The connections and recognitions are deeper than that.

At some point, Dave comes to me and says — and we've had this conversation a few times before — "I still don't understand why you want to write about us. We tell you our stories, you meet us, you play with us, but what does it all add up to?"

I look out over the table, straining to hear someone retell the mating elephants story, catching a bit of Wittner remembering the time the Commish took him to the parking lot outside the gym and showed him all the expensive cars of his running mates, then pointed to Wittner's beater and said, "*That's* why I'm cutting you some slack on paying up for the court permit," and I think the Commish must be insane. Looking at these guys, I think: thirty-five years' worth of ball and the dozens of charming, quirky rituals that come with it. Looking at these guys, knowing each other the way they do, belonging together the way they do, come hell or high water, across time and distance. How do I *not* write about it?

"The game means something to us, sure; it's our game," Dave says. "But I don't see why it would be interesting to anyone else. Everyone's got a game."

We're taking a group picture at the end of the night, and the Commish tells me to hand the camera off to a guy at the next table and get in the shot. I'm hesitant at first: this is their crew, their night. But you don't say "no" to the Commish, and as I kneel down in front of the group and smile, I feel him reach out and put his hand on my shoulder. It sounds corny, but I do feel like one of them in that moment. And it hits me just then that Dave's right, that everyone *does* have a game, and that I'm also here because we used to hold weekend three-on-three tournaments, complete with burgers on the grill and drinks in the cooler, in my Long Beach, California, backyard, and because I was in a regular Sunday morning run at the Field House in Iowa City, Iowa, when I was in grad school, and because I know a group of guys who lace up every weekend at a high school gym in Coronado, California, and because I know there are guys all over this great land of ours who get up and play at 6:00 A.M., before the workday, two, maybe three, days a week. How do I *not* write about it?

The difference between the Saturday Game guys and the rest of us is a matter of degree. What they have, the connection they share to the game, to each other, isn't magical; it's just hard-won. Which is, of course, its magic. I'm sitting there at Il Vagabondo, twisting the stem of a wineglass, watching the guys talk, and I identify with them, but I envy them even more.

I'm not in a game now; my guys are scattered to the wind, busy, whatever, who knows . . . life has gotten in the way.

I try to explain this to Dave. He recalls our first conversation.

"You can write about us if you think there's something to say," he says. "But what you really ought to do is find a gym, and start calling the wedding-day guys."

Amen.

Playing 4 Keeps

FROM CHICAGO MAGAZINE

Just hanging out with Baby Ray and Calhoun and the guys for a few
pages has to put a wide smile on your face.
— D.M.

THERE'S NO MUSIC, but Baby Ray is dancing. No jitterbug or
jump-and-jive, but the kind of high strut that a man uses when he's
feeling it, say, when he's rolling a hot pair of dice or flipping pocket
aces or holding sway on a faded felt pool table through five games
of sloppy eight — and not just doing it, but telling you about it, the
way Baby Ray is right now. "Yow!" he says, stroking his cue, strutting
around the rectangle of green. "Looka' here." One after another,
balls clop into pockets. Racks fill. Baby Ray is seventy, but it doesn't
slow his two-step. "I came here to play pool today!" he crows. He is
wearing a yellow cap swung backwards and an old gray apron soiled
with the chalk and table-grime of a thousand games. He always
dons the apron before playing, using the pockets to stash cubes of
chalk and a small blue container of baby powder, which he bangs in
his hands before taking up his cue. The apron's front bears his
nickname — BABY-RAY — hand-inked in crooked blue letters. As
if it were needed, the name also ornaments the butt of his cue and
his cue case. "Get out of Baby Ray's way," he declares, as another
ball rolls across the green and thunks into a pocket.

Lucky Lazard, deep in a game of his own, looks up with wry
amusement. "Go ahead, Ray-Ray," the seventy-four-year-old says.
"Ain't nobody in your way." Ernest Calhoun, eighty-seven, who has
been dozing in a plastic chair against the wall, lifts a seamed face,
grumbles something about luck, sinks back into slumber. Lucky

and Ed Strong, shooting two tables over, look over at Baby Ray, then back at each other.

"What?" Strong says, eyebrows raised.

"Got my eye on you," Lucky volleys.

"I hope it's your good eye."

"Ahhh, getting sassy down here!"

"C'mon, someone rack them balls," Strong says. "Let me run this turkey off the table."

One by one, the old men have arrived — some by bus, some on foot, others by senior citizen van. They have come down the stairs, into the fluorescent shine of this large recreation room at Seventy-ninth and Cregier in the South Shore neighborhood. They've hung their jackets on little brass hooks, unfastened their small cylindrical cases, and settled into a routine as worn as the baize of the room's three overused tables. They come to shoot pool, Baby Ray and Lucky Lazard and Lefty, Jamaica Joe and Mississippi Willie, Calhoun and Rambo, Isaiah the Prophet, Frank Sparks, known as the "salsero," and a man who calls himself The Truth. Retired workers and widowers in their seventies and eighties, all African American, spry men in flannel shirts and jeans and pressed pants and polished Stacy Adams lace-ups, most getting by on small pensions earned in hardscrabble years of another era, pouring steel and pressing garments and cleaning stockyards and selling insurance, South Siders either by birth or by right — the non-natives having traveled to Chicago during the great migration to escape the poverty and hard bigotry of small towns in the Mississippi Delta and Arkansas and Louisiana. They come five days a week to trade gossip and insults, to compare aches and ailments, slowed only by doctor's orders or death.

"Who's hot?"

"He's hot."

"I'll cool him down."

Chalk squeaks. Balls roll. Racks drop.

"My name is Isaiah and I'm a prophet," says Isaiah.

"I predict you ain't going to make it," Jamaica Joe shoots back.

And now, Baby Ray jabs his pool cue fiercely, thrusting like a fencer. He sights his shot, and smacks the eight ball across the cloth toward a corner pocket. He's had the table too long now. The other men are growing annoyed. They're decent players, good, not great, and when someone gets on a run like this, it irritates, especially when that someone is dancing and talking like Baby Ray. The eight ball creeps toward the pocket, but slows as it nears the lip, teetering on the edge. The moment sends Baby Ray into a spasm of body English, his pool cue cradled like a dance partner waiting to be dipped. And the old men watch through ancient, amused eyes, readying whatever quip they need, make or miss, to needle Baby Ray and to keep alive the place that means so much more to them and their dwindling numbers than winning or losing.

Under a cone of light, Fast Eddie Felson and Minnesota Fats pounded whiskey and chain-smoked while they wagered thousands a game in the seedy, smoke-stained upstairs of Bennington's Billiard Hall in the novel *The Hustler.* Surly, sharp-eyed crowds skulked around the tables, dazzled into silence by the virtuosos. In this poolroom, there is no gambling. No gathering of pool sharks. There's no whiskey. No video games. No smoking. Just old men playing and waiting to play.

The Francis J. Atlas Regional Senior Center at 1767 East Seventy-ninth Street crouches along a faded thoroughfare of mom-and-pop shops, squeezed into a gap between stores like Buddie's Liquors and Wilma's Chateau of Beauty. Here, five days a week, these old-heads gather, each with his own brand of comic timing and wicked repartee. In the poolroom, after all, wit is the hustle; bragging rights, not bets, the spoils. It's part vaudeville, part sitcom — with the ability to cap, crack, rank, rib, diss, and snap as important as any fancy cue stick.

At the Atlas, the games are about getting the old bones — and the blood — moving. The playful putdowns — the kidding, jiving, and teasing — are about exercising the mind, not rattling an opponent. In another era, the practice was called "playing the dozens," a rich tradition in the African-American community of matching insults in a kind of workingman's duel. But the Atlas also provides the men with an escape from apartments that roast in the summer and chill in the winter. Most important, it furloughs them from houses left empty by children long gone and spouses now departed. For them, these hours, these games, heal body and soul better than any medicine, any doctor's prescription, certainly better than sitting home, alone with their years. The hours are, in a sense, life, youth, home.

*

Calhoun gets there first, followed closely by the other regulars. At eighty-seven, he moves with a ponderous but efficient shuffle that transforms into a skater's slide around the pool table, a swooping step that gives him an unlikely grace. He is soft-spoken, with a raspy voice dredged from the bottom of a box of gravel, and he has been coming to the Atlas Center for more than two decades. Cataracts, for which he has had two surgeries, coat his eyes and make them weepy, giving him a vaguely sad appearance. He was born Ernest Calhoun, but around here he's simply Calhoun. GET YOUR KICKS ON ROUTE 66, his blue cap declares.

" 'Morning, everybody!" he rasps, walking in with a cane, his cue satchel slung over his shoulder. It's raw outside, and he's bundled in a ski jacket and scarf and gloves.

"Don't go too hard on me. You know I can't see."

"Hey, Calhoun," says Ray. "You put on all the clothes you got?"

"Just the good ones," he says. "I got more."

You reach the poolroom by walking through the Atlas lobby, past the lunchroom, where men are required to remove their hats before eating the day's potluck, past several seniors lolling on benches and chairs, working on art projects or waiting for flu shots. The three tables form a row in the basement, under a low fiberboard ceiling, next to a glass-enclosed workout room, where some of the men toddle over to watch the older women stretch and scissor their way through their daily aerobics. Bid whist players crowd tables at one end, hurling insults as fast as the snap of the cards. The checkers crew commands a small alcove at the entrance, slapping the disks down and, if anything, strafing their fellow players with insults more caustic, more cutting, than those of their poolroom counterparts.

In the poolroom, the smell of menthol and balm fills the place, giving it the familiar, musty feel of a grandfather's favorite parlor. A TV murmurs at one end. In the summer it's tuned to White Sox games. The rest of the time, the screen flickers through those shows where smart-aleck judges scold trailer park divorcées, programs all but ignored until the Lotto numbers are announced. A bottle of talc dangles from a frayed string attached to the metal frame of the tile ceiling like a spider suspended on a thread of silk over the linoleum. House cues on a rack line one of the walls.

Within a few minutes, pool games bristle on each of the three four-and-a-half-foot tables. Like the men who play them, the tables show the wear of many years, gouged and scuffed, but still sturdy and dignified. Tape wraps the triangle racks, each of which has cracked from use. Blue chalk marks streak the felt, mingled with smudges of powder. A Band-Aid binds a fault line in one of the plastic pocket drops. But the tables work fine, the men will tell you. Just fine.

Except for the Chicago cop who occasionally sneaks in for a few games on his lunch hour, and the janitor who wanders by to talk a little pidgin Spanish, the men are old. Gray dusts their hair and beards. Some walk with canes; fine lines trace their hands like faint road maps. Anyone under sixty is automatically a "young blood."

"Now, see, that's a colossal miss," muses one of the players, after badly botching an easy corner pocket shot. "None of these penny-ante misses."

"Oh, no!" adds another player, who strands a striped ten ball just short of the pocket. "You didn't eat your damn Wheaties!"

"Wait a minute; I thought I had stripes," says his opponent.

"Well, senility comes in all ages," the other player observes.

The morning wears on, and the other regulars arrive. Leo "Lucky" Lazard, seventy-four, dapper, as always, dressed in creased black pants, polished wingtips, and a silver-and-black merino wool sweater. He is lean and fit-looking, with a salt-sprinkled goatee. Like many of the men, he was born in the South — New Orleans in his case — and came to Chicago in 1950 in search of more work and fewer racial hassles. He was unaware, he says, that his family was actually moving to one of the most segregated cities in the country at the time.

Indeed, when he arrived in Chicago, he found much more work than tolerance. "In New Orleans, because of the Creole, there wasn't as many problems," he says. "You couldn't tell who was black and who was white. When I first came here, blacks couldn't go over Drexel, couldn't go to the beach. There were white people sitting out on their porches and they would tell you."

He found work delivering medicine for a drugstore, then at a printing company, until he settled into what would be his trade for the next forty-one years — one reason he's always so natty — pressing lapels and sewing side seams for Hart Shaffner & Marx. He began coming to the Atlas about a decade ago after wandering by one day. "I didn't play pool for a long time," Lucky says. "I never used to play pool when I was younger. I bowled. I would sit up there [by the

door] watching. Finally, someone asked me and I said, 'Why not?'"
He picked up the game quickly, so quickly that the other players
began calling him "Lucky."

One of the men, James C. Wills, spent thirty months overseas, in
Casablanca and Corsica, during the Korean War, one of the many
veterans who frequent the poolroom. "Army buck sergeant was as
high as I got," he says. "It was rough being a soldier. Some fellas just
lost their minds." He says he was wounded three times in the war
and pulls out a gold Veterans of Foreign Wars card with his name
on it to confirm his status. "I'm not a lying guy," says Wills. "I don't
have to impress anybody." He used to play a lot — even entered the
citywide pool tournament for seniors. Now, he's content to watch.
"I don't need it anymore," he says. "I leave it to these youngsters.
But you know I could play."

"Baby" Ray Rayford was born in Arkansas, then moved to Kansas
City, Missouri, where he worked in a bowling alley. "There were six
or seven pool tables there," he recalls. "That's where I learned to
play better." He came to Chicago after four years stationed in Japan
during the Korean War. He worked in a packinghouse, for White
Castle and Sara Lee. He's here virtually every morning, dancing to
his own music.

"How are your eyes, Calhoun?" he asks.

"They're open," the old man says.

By noon, the room's three tables are full. The players on deck sit
on the plastic and metal chairs. "Skill and cunning, skill and cunning," Lucky is saying. His playing partner, a big man with a two-day
growth of silver-flecked beard, leans on the table to attempt a difficult cut shot. "Doggonit, I think you broke the table," Lucky says.

"How?" the other player asks.

"By putting your big booty up there!"

So it begins.

"Whoa, you shot already?" Strong asks at the next table over.

"It don't take me long to shoot."

"Don't take you too long to do anything."

"He doesn't do that much," says Lucky.

"It takes me all day to do what I used to do in one hour," another
man says.

"Hey, Baby Ray."

"What?"

"Baby Ray."

"What?"

"Baby Ray."

"What you want?"

"Where you from, Baby Ray?"

"California."

"California?"

"Twenty-sixth and California."

The room explodes with laughter.

"C'mon, Baby. Tell the truth. I thought you were from the Show-Me State."

"Did I show him?"

"You showed him."

"Then I guess it's the Show-Me State."

Hours pass. Tables click with the sound of balls hitting balls, balls slapping the back of pockets, racks busting open. And always, always, the talking, the rapid-fire chatter, the running commentary, the carping over bad rolls, the injustice of unlucky shots, the regret for poor play, the boasting, the big talk, the tall tales, the showboating; cursing the gods, the tables, each other; and laughter, always laughter.

"All right," says a player. "Let me win this game so I can leave."

"You're about to be late," says another.

"All I can say is I just sank seven balls on you."

"Six!"

"Seven," he says, bending over. "And here come eight!"

In the convivial swirl of the poolroom's wit and wordplay, serious topics rarely find voice. It's not that kind of place. When a woman occasionally shuffles by — usually Rose on her way to play cards — they display a gentleman's charm and politeness, nodding and stepping out of the way.

Nearly every man can lay claim to the hard knocks, the joy and loss, the regrets and triumphs that come with their longevity. In 2004, Calhoun lost his wife of sixty-two years, Helle; his bereavement still shows in a sort of resigned bemusement. The sparseness of his words in describing such loss speaks more poignantly than the tears that fill his ravaged eyes: "Sixty-two happy years," he says. "She was a good girl — she had to be to live with me."

Leonard Lucas, seventy-two, presides as the closest thing the poolroom has to a sage. Born in Vidalia, Louisiana, his life has traversed the disparate roles of the Renaissance man, from a poor southern boy who attended segregated schools to an athlete scouted by the Harlem Globetrotters to the holder of a master's degree in urban sociology to the author of three books of poetry. For more than three decades he has recited his work at colleges and penal institutions, churches and senior citizen centers. He came to Atlas six or seven years ago, he says, after a friend mentioned the poolroom. "For me, this is a place where old people can come to eliminate their stress — to touch their humanity," he says, then adds, laughing, "and their humility."

James Wills, like Calhoun, like Lucas, like so many of the men here, grew up in a Chicago that exists now only in sepia photographs and history books — and in the memories of men such as themselves. They recall streets clip-clopping with horses and brimming with streetcars, and neighborhoods where they knew not to venture. They reminisce about show palaces like the Savoy, Regal, and Metropolitan Theaters; the rise and slow decline of the "Black Metropolis" — areas like Bronzeville that once bustled with shops and restaurants only to slide into urban blight. "Segregation was everywhere," recalls Wills, who spent most of his career building diesel locomotives in La Grange. "We couldn't get into most places."

That doesn't mean some areas of the country weren't worse. One of the poolroom regulars tells the story of how he came to Chicago. "I was born in Little Rock," he says. "I remember walking with my father and he looked over at something. They had hung a man and had him down on the ground. My father told me to run all the way to the house. He put my sister and me on a train [to a relative's house in Chicago] and followed as soon as he could. But I don't have no regrets. I've had a nice life. Where I live, I keep clean and neat. Sometimes I go to Country Buffet. I wouldn't take nothing for it."

Some regulars have a second life. Frank Sparks, for one. By day, he is known as the thin, elegantly dressed sharpshooter with an unshakable grin and a quiver full of barbed insults. By night, he is the "salsero," dancing the evening away at clubs around town. Sparks, like the other men here, credits the poolroom with keeping him young, and indeed, the men seem to take on a new energy, move with newfound grace, around these tables, as if, for a moment, they forget how old they are, how their bodies no longer work as they once did.

As the afternoon wears on, one of the other regulars, Herman, beats Ed Strong, rousing Calhoun out of a doze. "C'mon, Calhoun, your turn," Herman says. As Calhoun shuffles to the table, Strong teases Herman: "The man is blind, a hundred years old, and he's still going to beat you." But Calhoun, despite playing well, doesn't win. "We're going to have to do something about this," Strong says. "I don't like what you did to Calhoun," he tells Herman. Baby Ray steps up, the next challenger to Herman. Strong looks at him. "Take off the mask, Baby Ray. Halloween was last month."

Baby Ray ignores him and sends the cue ball into the rack like a sledgehammer. The balls dance and swirl on the break, a solid falling in the corner.

"I thought you were a man of peace, not violence," Herman says.

"C'mon, don't do me like that!" Ray grouses at the table, finding himself snookered behind a clump of balls.

"Talk to it, Ray," Calhoun says. "Talk to it."

"That ain't an easy shot," Strong says.

"I'm gonna make it easy."

Just as life is apparent in this room, death lurks as a constant if unspoken presence. It's easy to forget, watching the men day after day. But sometimes, one of the regulars just stops showing up. One Tuesday night in October, Frank Sparks went to one of his favorite salsa haunts, Green Dolphin Street on North Ashland. His wife of forty-three years stayed home, as usual, having resigned herself long ago to Sparks's love of dance, just as she has learned to tolerate his love of pool. Like Lucky, Sparks dresses sharp, favoring open-collared silk shirts and, occasionally, a driver's cap tipped at an angle. Thin like Lucky, he wears a clean-shaven head and moves with the easy grace of someone who has danced many years. On this night, as ever, he waits for a song he likes, then picks a partner, then turns her and dips to the beat. But when he returns to the bar, something is wrong.

A few days later, the men arrive at the poolroom as they always do. Calhoun first. Baby Ray. Lucky. They don't notice at first that a newspaper clipping has been taped to one of the walls. "Longtime Salsa Dancer Died on the Dance Floor," the headline on the *Sun-*

Times obituary reads. "Did What He Loved Right Up to the End."
At the bar, Sparks collapsed and died of an apparent heart attack.

One by one, the men pause before the article, read, shake their
heads. Later, several stop by the funeral home for the service. Many
don't. Not for lack of caring, but perhaps because, for all the life
this room gives them, moments like this also remind them that it
won't go on forever. For them, coming to this place, playing a game
in Frank's honor, serves as an appropriate tribute. Still, the jibes
take on a softer edge. The room is quiet. But as the day proceeds,
the regulars loosen up. Once again, like balls bursting on a break,
the jokes and insults begin to fly. That seems right too. This place
accommodates many things, but sadness is not welcome. They are
old. One day, somebody here will be the one who doesn't show up.

It's late afternoon in the poolroom. The guys are done for the day.
Ed Strong twists his cue apart and tucks it into his satchel. "That's it
for me."

"Don't leave, Ed," Calhoun pleads.

"Oh, I know. You just want to whup me like everyone else."

"I'll play you," Baby Ray tells Calhoun. "I don't like what you did
to me yesterday."

It has been a difficult few weeks for Calhoun. Earlier this morning, he had yet another procedure on his eyes. They have been
bothering him all day — so much so that he has been wearing dark
glasses, hiding behind inky blue lenses. For as long as he has been
coming here, the balls on the table have held crisp edges under the
fluorescent lights. Now, they cast small shadows, blur when they are
hit very hard. Stripes and solids are no longer so easy to discern.
The pockets seem farther and farther away. He lifts his cue butt,
the way he always does, and strokes the cue ball gently. It rolls
across the felt and taps a ball in the corner. And Calhoun does his
skater's slide around the table to the other side.

Baby Ray watches and smiles. Of all the players here, Baby Ray
can be the most animated, one of the loudest — at times — and,
when he gets to strutting like a gamecock, one of the most exasper-
ating. But now Baby Ray holds a bottle of eye drops, tenderly leaning over Calhoun, who is sitting with his head tilted back. "Take it
easy, Cal," he says, gently. "Let's get these in there." The players
around take little notice as Ray puts in the drops as reverently as a
priest anointing a baby's forehead. Calhoun tilts his head back up,

blinks his ancient eyes, and nods. He's ready to play, ready to get back into the game, one more game. "I can see!" he says, with mock exultation.

The eight ball rolls and Baby Ray dances. Time slows down, as the ball seems to hang on the lip. In slow motion, it drops. The men roar. One stretches his arms skyward. Baby Ray jumps, then lands flat-footed and skips to the side, bellowing out, "Yow! That's what I'm talking about!" And as he dances his dance, his vanquished foe digs into the pockets and begins clopping the balls in the center, pulling out the triangle with the thick tape that covers its cracks. "All that dancing ain't going to help you, Baby Ray," he says.

"It already has," Ray shoots back. And he dances again, as the other men laugh, and turn back to their tables, their shots, their games, always ready for one more rack, one more shot, one more joke, until they grab their coats from the peg and head out for the day; until tomorrow, when Calhoun and Lucky and Baby Ray, and Ed Strong and Isaiah the Prophet and Jamaica Joe and Mississippi Willie will once again trudge down the stairs, back to the place they love, to see the men who are more than just foils, to do what keeps them, for a few hours at least, young.

L. JON WERTHEIM

The Ultimate Assist

FROM SI.COM

> Thought I knew the Shoe Bomber story, but missed this entirely. You figure at least the 196 other passengers on American Airlines flight 63, if not the entire nation, are rooting for Kwame James to make his run.
> — D.M.

THE IRONY WAS, in retrospect, striking. But if your life keeps turning on quirks of fate, eventually you take the world for one big funhouse mirror. So it was that Kwame James shrugged and didn't say a word when he — handsome, well spoken, well dressed — was yanked from the security line at Charles de Gaulle Airport outside Paris and given the full pat-down-and-wand treatment while an unkempt fellow passenger carrying only a backpack and muttering to himself in Arabic passed through the checkpoint without a problem.

James, a dual citizen of Canada and Trinidad and Tobago and a recent graduate of a college in the United States, has what he calls "an extreme dislike" of racial profiling. However, it was December 22, 2001, barely one hundred days into the "new reality" of life after the terrorist attacks of September 11, and if you were subjected to one of those exhaustive airport security searches, you smiled through clenched teeth and took one for the team. "I just figured, Oh well, my bad luck," James recalls.

At the time, James was a twenty-three-year-old center for A.S. Bondy, a pro basketball team in France's B League. After being frisked he boarded his flight to Miami, where he would meet his girlfriend, Jill Clements, and take her to his family's home in Trinidad for the holidays. When you're six-foot-eight and can only af-

ford coach class, international flights are brutal. James had deliber-
ately stayed up all night so that, after folding his frame into his seat
like so much origami, he would zonk out for the journey's duration. The flight, American Airlines 63, was packed, and there were
lots of screaming kids, but James went right to sleep.

Three hours later he was roused by a frantic flight attendant.
"We need your help in the back!" she said. "Now!"

The terror etched on the woman's face extinguished any notion
that James might be dreaming. Without hesitating he rushed back
to row 29, where he found other passengers struggling with that
scraggly-haired man who had breezed through the security line. A
flight attendant was tightly holding her own hand, stanching the
blood from a bite wound. The stench of sulfur filled the air. A
thickset Italian passenger had the unkempt man, who was screaming incomprehensibly in Arabic, in a headlock.

For years James's coaches had chided him for being insuf-
ficiently physical, for shying from contact. Now here he was, helping to wrestle a flailing man into submission. James's adrenaline,
surging far more than it ever had on a basketball court, spiked
when a flight attendant warned, "Careful, he's got a bomb in his
shoe!"

James looked down, saw a small Koran under the captive's seat,
and fixed his gaze on the wires poking out from the tongue of his
black boot. Six times, the man later identified as Richard Reid —
and universally called the "Shoe Bomber" — had tried to ignite the
wires with a match. With no air marshals on board to help, James
and a scrum of valiant passengers and flight attendants finally subdued Reid, who is six-foot-four, weighs more than two hundred
pounds, and, as James puts it, "was possessed, clearly willing to die."
Using belts and headphone cords, they tied Reid up, and two doctors on board injected Reid with a sedative.

"It was like in the movies," recalls Philippe Acas, a Parisian businessman who had wrested the matches from Reid's hands. "It was
just one of those cases where you don't think — you act."

James, the largest man on the plane, was asked by the captain to
stand sentry over Reid for the rest of the flight. For nearly four
hours, James sat on an armrest and pressed against Reid, gripping
him by his greasy ponytail. As a basketball player, James was a
lunch-pail type who, despite his mild nature, had always found it an
honor to guard the toughest guy on the opposing team. Now the

nastiest defensive assignment of his life had arrived at thirty-seven thousand feet.

In a remarkable display of restraint, no passenger tried to injure Reid, much less kill him, even though he had tried to turn a plane with 197 people on board into a cloud of atmospheric particles. James, who outweighed Reid by fifty pounds, could easily have snapped the guy's neck. "I didn't even let my mind go there," James says. "All those kids who had to witness the struggle already were terrified. Imagine the effect on them if something worse had happened."

For the rest of the flight, frightening thoughts cartwheeled through James's mind. He feared that the man he was holding had another bomb, in his checked luggage. He wondered whether Reid had a co-conspirator on board. When the captain announced that the flight was being diverted to Boston and would be escorted by F-15s, James panicked, recalling the conspiracy theory that United Flight 93 had actually been shot down by U.S. fighter jets on September 11. He said a prayer. He sang to himself. He reflected on his family, his girlfriend, his basketball career, and his friends scattered all over the world.

"Then I really got upset," he says. "I have Muslim friends. This guy is willing to kill 197 people he doesn't know? For what?"

Reckoning that in order to blow up a plane full of passengers, one first has to make them abstract, James tried to humanize himself to Reid. "So," he said, addressing his captive as if he were a widget salesman from Toledo, "what's your deal?"

Reid smiled. "You'll see," he said in a British accent.

"So did you really have a bomb?" James asked.

"You'll see. It will all happen the way it was meant to happen."

James is boundlessly social, one of those guys who, his friends lament, will go into a store and not emerge for half an hour because he stopped to chat up the cashier. "So," he persisted, "where are you from?"

"Jamaica," Reid replied.

James laughed. "Wrong answer," he said. "I'm from the Caribbean, and it's all about love and respect. No one from the Caribbean is going to blow up a plane. Where are you really from?"

Reid changed his answer: "I'm from everywhere." He then explained that he had recently been to Afghanistan, Belgium, the Netherlands, Pakistan, Turkey, and France.

"I knew right there," says James, "he was part of some serious terrorist network. A guy who looked like him wasn't traveling all over the world on his own dime. I stopped talking after that."

Finally, seven hours after it had taken off, the plane landed in Boston. The wheels had barely touched terra firma when a SWAT team stormed down the aisle to row 29. Before Reid was whisked away, he turned to James. Smiling, he asked in a pathetically soft voice, "What was your name again?"

Big Shoes to Fill

Kwame James was born in Canada, but when he was a small boy his family moved back home to Trinidad, where his father became a government economist and his mother worked for the United Nations. All the "Trinny" kids played soccer, none more fervently than Kwame's fraternal twin brother, Kwesi. Kwame, though, kept growing and, unable to find soccer cleats that fit, gravitated to basketball. He'd play for hours on the island's pocked asphalt courts, but he had no great hoops ambitions. It was just recreation.

"The big appeal of basketball," says James, "was that I had shoes that fit."

They came courtesy of his Aunt Pat, who lived in Indianapolis and had a contact with the Pacers. She had gotten him a pair of Dale Davis's game-worn size-16 Reeboks.

In 1994, when he was sixteen, Kwame spent the summer before his junior year of high school with Aunt Pat in Indiana. She thought it might be fun for Kwame, now six-foot-seven, to spend a few weeks at Bob Knight's basketball camp. Playing full-court — indoors! — for the first time, Kwame dominated the other campers. Late in the session Knight summoned Kwame to his office and explained that he wanted Kwame to play at Indiana. The hitch was that Kwame would have to finish high school in the States, get some coaching, and add some muscle to his lean physique.

Augustus and Carole James, both PhDs, had never heard of Bob Knight and wondered what cult their excited son had joined. Get your butt on a plane, Kwame, they effectively said. After much agonizing, however, Kwame decided to stay in Indiana with his aunt. It meant not getting to say good-bye in person to his parents, siblings, and friends. It meant adapting to a different culture. But it also meant a chance to go to college in the United States for free.

Aunt Pat's home was districted for Lawrence North High, an Indianapolis basketball powerhouse. The Indiana High School Athletic Association, suspicious because Kwame had transferred to the district without his parents, barred him from playing varsity his first year. He had to settle instead for the jayvee, but he didn't care.

"Keep in mind, I'm just this skinny Caribbean kid," he recalls. "Suddenly I have a uniform with my name on the back! I have my own shiny track suit! I spent that whole year in a state of awe."

As a senior he was a star on the varsity and made a recruiting visit to Bloomington to watch the Hoosiers practice. What he observed was how thoroughly Knight had drained the fun out of basketball. "Getting yelled at playing sports?" James says. "That was totally foreign to me. In Trinidad, sports are just fun. I'm thinking, I'm not signing up for four years of that."

Instead, James chose Evansville, whose basketball program, oddly enough, might be best known for the plane crash that killed the entire team in 1977. James turned out to be a good, not great college player, an undersized center who shot judiciously and was all too happy to sublimate his offense for the good of the team.

As a junior he was among the NCAA leaders in field-goal percentage, a factoid that once ran on the ESPN crawl. When he saw his name streaming on the television screen, his arms were covered with goose bumps. "Kwame was a humble guy but a real overachiever," says Marty Simmons, a former Evansville assistant and now the coach at Southern Illinois–Edwardsville. "He's one of those guys who, when a coach hears his name, he automatically smiles."

Ask James about his experience at Evansville, however, and he barely mentions basketball. He says the highlight of his four years there was befriending classmates from small-town America. "They'd say, 'Kwame, we've never met anyone from Trinidad before!'" he says. "I'm like, 'I've never met anyone from a town with no stoplights!'" His senior year he fell in love with Clements, a nursing student from such a town, Loogootee, Indiana, population 2,700.

James graduated in 2000 with a degree in international business. While he knew that the NBA wasn't in his future, he wasn't through playing basketball. He spent the next year pinballing among club teams in Switzerland, France, and Argentina. The pay was awful. The living conditions were too. The travel — fourteen-hour bus trips sometimes — was worse. James was thrilled. In Argentina he learned to speak Spanish. In France he spent hours as a tourist, walking the streets and alleys by himself. "I never lost the skinny-Caribbean-kid mentality," he says. "I was getting paid to play basketball, man. It was a privilege."

In the fall of 2001 James was playing for A. S. Bondy, averaging double figures in points and rebounds. Yet for reasons he couldn't fully grasp, basketball was losing its appeal to him. Late one night he was out with some Bondy teammates, including Marcus Wilson, who played with James at Evansville, and he unburdened himself. "I told him not to get down because we were losing, but he said it was bigger than that," Wilson recalls. "It's ironic that he was thinking of doing something bigger than basketball."

The next morning James boarded flight 63.

Close Call

James's instinct had been right. The Shoe Bomber hadn't been acting alone. Within hours of the plane's landing, details emerged. Reid, a petty criminal in Britain, had been born in South London, the son of an English mother and a Jamaican father. After discovering radical Islamism, he had attended an al-Qaeda training camp in Afghanistan and was, according to e-mails he'd sent, upset that he hadn't been asked to participate in the September 11 attacks.

When he had shown up at De Gaulle Airport on December 21, he had triggered security alerts: he'd paid for a one-way ticket to Miami in cash; he'd checked in no bag; and despite having traveled to seven countries in recent months, he had no fixed address or apparent employment. Authorities questioned Reid, causing him to miss his scheduled flight. But, apparently satisfied with his answers, officials put him up at a $280-a-night hotel and allowed him to board flight 63 the next day. Enough plastic explosive had been packed into his hollowed-out boot heels to blow up the plane. The explosive bore the palm prints of a well-known al-Qaeda bombmaker.

Fortunately, Reid had a lousy set of matches. "The fact is, if he had brought a lighter onto the plane instead, I wouldn't be here telling you this story," James says, an assertion that FBI officials confirm. "That will give me the chills for the rest of my life."

With the psychic wounds from September 11 still raw, the public in the United States was desperate for an inspiring story of good trumping evil, and the parable of flight 63 — a global coalition of passengers working together to thwart an al-Qaeda killer — quickly fell into the media's insatiable maw.

CNN, the *Today Show*, and the rest of the media applied the full-court press to James: you're going to be in the history books — don't you want your story told correctly? James was torn. He was proud of his role in Reid's capture but uncomfortable that so many other participants weren't being recognized, not least the five-foot-two flight attendant, Hermis Moutardier, who had first challenged Reid.

James tried his best to accommodate everyone, even staying an extra night in Miami to tape an interview. When he and Clements finally reached Trinidad, he was feted as a hero. "Keep in mind, I'm meeting his family for the first time," says Clements. "I guess at least we had an icebreaker."

When the holiday was over, James headed back to France to rejoin his team. He had reflected on how much he would miss basketball if he quit, and he'd be damned if terrorists were going to stop him from playing. "You stop doing what you enjoy, and they win," he told nervous family members. "You can't be scared."

Except that he was. In his first game back he barely concentrated on the action, he was so busy scanning the crowd for terrorists. That the A.S. Bondy players were housed in a Muslim enclave in Paris didn't help. He tried to quit after that first game, but his teammates convinced him to stay on. By month's end he'd handed in his jersey and returned to Evansville.

"My mind was just going haywire," he says. "Suddenly my name is all over the Internet and I'm thinking that people on the street are looking at me funny. It was too much."

Back in Indiana, James did some motivational speaking and stayed in shape. In time, the media found another cause célèbre, and the flood of interview requests slowed to a trickle. But then another slew of calls came in, this time from the FBI and the U.S. Attorney's Office in Boston, asking James to testify against Reid. Sure, James said, but he warned them that he wasn't a U.S. citizen. No longer in school, he might soon need a special visa to remain in the country. "No problem," an FBI official said, according to James. "We'll take care of you."

As it turned out, there would be no trial. On October 4, 2002, Reid pleaded guilty to eight charges, including attempted use of a weapon of mass destruction. Three months later he was sentenced to life in prison.

Scarred for Life

After the events on flight 63, the plane's passengers were offered free counseling from American Airlines. James declined. "I'm twenty-three," he recalls thinking. "I'm physically strong. I'm an athlete, and sports have given me the foundation to deal with life. What do I need that for?"

Once the shock had worn off — and the offer of free psychological help had expired — James began to suffer emotionally. At Reid's sentencing, the flight attendant Moutardier said, "We will never be the same. That horrendous moment will live in our lives forever." James knew how she felt.

One image in particular was burned into his mind's eye. A television segment on flight 63, speculating on what would have happened had Reid been successful, showed a computer rendering of the plane transformed into a fireball. James's emotions whipsawed between a carpe-diem optimism and a crippling fatalism. On the one hand, having cheated death, he was primed to live each day to the fullest. At the same time, as long as a madman with a bomb in his shoe could so easily wreak havoc, why bother?

It was a rough time for Clements too. Even before flight 63, her relationship with James had been difficult. Most girls from Loogootee don't date Afro-Caribbean basketball players who toil overseas. Her family had just begun to accept James when he came home both famous and psychologically burdened. "It put a lot of strain on our relationship," Clements says.

Compounding the stress, James's immigration status was in doubt. James claims that in exchange for testifying against Reid, the Justice Department offered him a work permit to remain in the United States. He accepted immediately: since high school he'd aspired to U.S. citizenship. But after Reid was sentenced in 2003, the Immigration and Naturalization Service (INS) told James that he would not receive the permit. (The agency denies knowledge of a prior arrangement.) Nearing the end of his visa, James was warned that he could be deported. "Plain and simple," he says, "they hung me out to dry."

The INS, while conceding that James had acted with valor on flight 63, was unwilling to make an exception for him. "We go by the laws as they're written," says Bill Strassberger, spokesman for the U.S. Citizenship and Immigration Services. "We need to be consistent and fair in application."

James still had a number of options. One was to marry Clements and apply for a green card. But their relationship was sagging under enough weight without her worrying that he was marrying her for reasons other than love. Another possibility was for James to find a job in the field of his college major, international business, entitling him to an H1B visa. James, however, didn't want to join Cubicle Nation; despite his departure from A.S. Bondy, he still wanted to play basketball.

Michael Wildes, an immigration lawyer in New York City, learned of James's situation and took on his case pro bono. "Is this the message you want to send to someone who looked down the face of terrorism?" says Wildes, who is also the mayor of Englewood, New Jersey. "It was a national disgrace."

With Wildes's help, James reached out to politicians, even venturing to Capitol Hill. A member of Congress could sponsor a bill giving James permanent-resident status, but while many pols had been all too happy to pose for photos alongside the "Shoe Bomber hero," none took up his cause. By mid-2003 James was overstaying his visa and was subject to deportation. "It was crunch time," he says.

On top of everything else, money was tight. Devoting all his energies to resolving his legal status, James couldn't hold down a job, and Clements was studying full-time for an advanced nursing degree. One month they were behind on the rent and were warned that they faced eviction. The next day a letter arrived miraculously from an anonymous airline pilot.

"You helped save 200 lives and a $30 million plane," the letter said. "I think you deserve more than a pat on the shoulder." Enclosed was a check for $200.

"We made rent," James recalls. "Of course, reading that letter, we also broke down and cried."

The Next Chapter

In the Hollywood version of the Kwame James story, he becomes an NBA All-Star, helps achieve world peace, and, of course, lives blissfully ever after. While the real-life plot hasn't followed quite that arc, perhaps it's headed toward a happy ending.

In the summer of 2003, having wearied of relying on others for help, James and Clements were married by a New York justice of the peace, making James a legal resident. He expects to receive his green card "any day now," he says, and he'll be eligible for full citizenship in three years.

His passion for basketball still burned for a while. He called minor league executives and was invited to play for the Gary Steelheads of the CBA and the Brooklyn Kings of the USBL. If he didn't turn heads with his play, he still made a good impression. He also found a balance between letting the teams market his story and not shamelessly "playing the hero card," as he puts it.

"Kwame's one of the classiest guys I've ever met," says Dan Liebman, a former owner and assistant coach of the Kings. "Unless you asked, you never would have known him as anything but a hardworking player."

In 2004, eager to exorcise memories of his previous, unhappy stint in Europe, James returned to France and signed on with BC Longwy, a B-league team near the Luxembourg border. He became the Kevin Garnett of Alsace-Lorraine, playing all three frontcourt positions, scoring twenty points a game (second highest in the league), and averaging nearly a triple double. He had no illusions about the caliber of the competition, but basketball had never been this much fun, this gratifying. After his last game of the season, mission accomplished, he retired from hoops.

Last July, James and Clements had a formal wedding ceremony that melded traditions of the Caribbean with those of small-town Indiana. "We were just determined to make [our relationship] work," she says. "No matter what got thrown in front of us, it wasn't going to stop us."

The newlyweds bought a modest two-bedroom apartment in Virginia, where Jill found a job as a registered nurse and Kwame is trying to break into pharmaceutical sales. His existence isn't completely back to normal, though, and he has slowly come to accept that it may never be. He still fears backlash from terrorist groups. (He asked *SI* not to name his city of residence.)

Plenty of times, banished thoughts and memories come echoing back to him, as they did in April when Zacarias Moussaoui, the so-called twentieth hijacker who belonged to the same London mosque as Reid, was sentenced to life in the same Colorado maximum-security prison as the Shoe Bomber. James would like to see the movie *Flight 93*, but he doubts he could make it through a screening.

Unable to abide his wife being the sole breadwinner, James waited tables for a time. Nowadays he offers personalized basketball workouts at local gyms. "I won't lie, it's been a struggle," he says. "People say to me all the time, 'Kwame, you're famous.' Let me tell you, I'd give it up in a second for this never to have happened."

James heaves a long, reflective sigh. As he replays the past five years, forces war within him. Finally, optimism wins. "You know how in the NBA, no matter how far down a team gets, you just know they're going to make a run? In my life, I've had my down period. I'm ready to make my run."

BRUCE WALLACE

In Iraq, Soccer Field Is No Longer a Refuge

FROM THE LOS ANGELES TIMES

Pat Tillman was killed by friendly fire. What words do you use to describe the fire that killed Manar Mudhafar? Another of the thousands of unintended consequences of war.
— D.M.

AT THE MOMENT he jumped to head a ball during afternoon practice on the second-to-last day of March, Manar Mudhafar was one of the best soccer players on the best team in Baghdad, an easy-smiling nineteen-year-old with speed, skills, and a toughness that made him a rising star.

By the time he hit the ground, he had a perplexed look on his face and a bullet in his throat. Mudhafar didn't say a word as he struggled to breathe and blood soaked his white jersey, staining its Canon logo and his number, 29.

He was dead in three minutes.

"He looked like he had been stung by an insect," recalled Haidar Mahmood, the captain of the Zawra team, who was standing beside his friend and teammate when he went down. "I got to him and I saw it was a bullet and I ran away, because I couldn't stand seeing my buddy dying on the ground."

It's hard to hide from the rain of bombs and bullets that brings danger to the streets, the homes, and even the mosques of Baghdad. But the bullet that killed Mudhafar invaded one place in Iraq that had been seen as a sanctuary: a soccer field, where the troubles

of this splintering society could be left behind for the simple pleasure of kicking a ball around.

Mudhafar's death, from what teammates accept was a stray bullet, possibly fired from a nearby police station, shattered that illu-
sion of immunity and brought a singular hurt to a city riddled with
individual tragedies.

"Our club is like a family because we train together, travel together, and play together," said Mahmood, a thirty-two-year-old veteran of Iraqi football, who once captained the national team under
the Saddam Hussein regime. "Sectarianism is affecting everything
in Iraq. But in football, it's the opposite. There is no sectarianism.
We are part of a team. Our soul is sport."

A look at player rosters from teams across Iraq suggests that his
words are more than just another sports cliché.

Sunnis play for the club in Najaf, a Shiite holy city, and Kurds
play for the team in Samarra, a town in the heart of the Sunni Triangle. Irbil and Dahuk, the top clubs in Iraq's heavily Kurdish
north, have recruited Shiite players from the talent-rich neighborhood of Baghdad's Sadr City.

Even Salahuddin, the local team for Hussein's overwhelmingly
Sunni hometown, Tikrit, has been signing Shiite players from the
south.

"Sport does not know the sectarian voice or the political voice,"
said Samarra coach Ayoub Younis, recalling the warm welcome his
team received when it played this year in the mostly Shiite city of
Nasiriya. "Football is the gathering point for the whole spectrum of
Iraq, and the best example of that is our Samarra team that has
Shia, Kurd, and Sunni players, all born in Samarra."

The same mix applies to Zawra, which has accumulated a host of
championships since it was formed in 1969. The Baghdad club,
once controlled by the Hussein family and its gangster associates, is
now run by a group of former athletes who took it over after the
war, when its facilities had been looted and it was left with nothing
but the grass on the field. They are rebuilding in a time of little
money, trying to keep sectarian politics at bay.

The team's mix of Shiites, Kurds, and Sunnis means they are not
a target for attacks when they travel, said Abdel Rhaman Rashid,
the club's Kurdish manager. "We don't take a guard when we travel,
and there is not a gun among us," he said.

This was the storied sports club Mudhafar joined when he was a kid, playing his way up through Zawra's youth teams and onto Iraq's national junior teams. Rashid had known him since Mudhafar was twelve, and remembers "a shy and very polite kid" who quit school in his teens but who never coasted on his talent.

"Our club's best players noticed how good he was when he was very young," Rashid said. "We are very careful in who we choose: we don't just take players off the street; we want players who are good people too. Who will be loyal."

Mudhafar's parents divorced when he was young — his mother remarried and moved to the United Arab Emirates — and he lived with his grandfather. But Zawra was his real home, Rashid said. The club's coaches were the ones who looked out for him, gave him money. "He was a son of the club." The manager said he never thought to ask Mudhafar whether he was a Sunni or a Shiite.

"When he died, people were puzzled," recalled a visibly shaken Rashid. "They said, 'Where do we bury him? A Shia cemetery? Or Sunni?' Until he died, no one knew what he was."

Paeans to sectarian harmony notwithstanding, soccer is hardly a beacon for some fantasy future Iraq with its communities happily at peace. Players and executives agree that their sport is in deep trouble.

In this soccer-mad country, where fans follow European leagues on satellite TV and many will shell out more than $300 — or about two months' wages — for a pay-TV subscription to watch next month's World Cup, the domestic league suffers from the same ills that beset the rest of Iraq: poor security and lousy economics.

"It's very hard to keep players in Iraq," said Rashid, citing the widespread violence and low salaries that make it tempting to play abroad. Zawra's players are paid $6,000 a year, good by Iraqi standards and higher than in most clubs, but a fraction of what teams in Qatar or Saudi Arabia can afford.

Soccer's free-market economics are tough in a country that once survived on government funding. Emerging corporate sponsorship and television revenues can't make up the shortfall in cash. Rashid said Iraqi TV paid only $300,000 for rights to broadcast the entire season, a sum that had to be divided among twenty-eight teams. And low ticket prices in a country with rampant unemployment mean modest gate receipts.

Team officials say attendance has dipped from prewar levels, mostly because of security worries and dilapidated stadiums. With few fans willing to congregate in public places that present a target for bombers, Baghdad teams have been the worst affected — Zawra is lucky to draw five thousand in its fifty-thousand-seat Shaab Stadium. Attendance is better outside the capital, with games in Basra or Irbil sometimes drawing ten thousand.

The obstacles frustrate players and owners, who see themselves as underappreciated heroes of the new Iraq. They complain that while billions of reconstruction dollars wash through the economy, they must struggle to sustain one of the country's few successful symbols of unity.

They are particularly bitter that the government failed to capitalize on the adrenaline kick for Iraqi national pride that came from the national soccer team's surprise fourth-place finish in the 2004 Athens Olympics.

"The Olympics was an unbelievable achievement, but the government never cared for the players who raised the flag for Iraq," said Zawra's Mahmood, who was left off the Olympic side. "I was a professional in Qatar when the war ended, but I came back because I was so optimistic after the fall of the regime.

"I had so many plans," he said. "Now I want to get out of this country."

Manar Mudhafar also wanted to leave Iraq.

"He was looking for opportunities," said Mahmood, who for nearly three years had driven the younger player to daily practice from their Baghdad neighborhood. Sitting in Mahmood's 1999 Ford Crown Victoria, a status car in Iraq, they would talk about soccer and girls. On the last day of his life, they talked about the Korean car that Mudhafar was planning to import now that he was in Zawra's starting lineup and had been picked for Iraq's national team.

Mudhafar's mother heard about her son's death on a satellite TV channel. It was an accident, according to all but his distraught immediate family and a few conspiracy theorists on the Internet.

"Manar was moving, jumping when he got shot," Mahmood said. "It would have been very hard [for a sniper] to hit him."

The bullet probably came from the police headquarters adjacent to Zawra's field, the team said. The station has been car-bombed, and mortar rounds are sometimes fired its way. Gunfire in the vicinity no longer turns heads.

At Mudhafar's funeral, weeping fans placed his bloodied jersey over the spot where he fell. His teammates carried his body through his neighborhood, kids tagging along, then on to the Sunni cemetery for burial.

His death received national attention. Iraq's sports channel aired a documentary in honor of the "martyr," showing clips of Mudhafar playing soccer as a child.

Mudhafar is not the first Iraqi athlete to die violently. Teams have mourned players killed during the U.S.-led invasion or slain by kidnappers.

But Mudhafar's talent gave him a chance to improve his odds. Two years ago, a team in the United Arab Emirates offered him a contract and dangled the prospect of Emirates citizenship if he would leave Iraq.

But he was not yet eighteen. And the Zawra club wouldn't release him.

"The team wasn't offering much money, and it wouldn't have been respectful to give up Iraqi citizenship," Rashid said. "Manar wanted to go, but we refused."

Besides, he said, there was more optimism back then, a belief that Iraq — and Iraqi soccer — was entering a better era.

"Maybe his family will come to us and say, 'Why didn't you let him go?'" Rashid said. "But we had plans for him. We wanted to give him a good future."

The manager fingered photographs of the funeral, pointing out players carrying Mudhafar's wooden coffin through the stadium where he died.

"*We* were his family," he said. "We are the ones who lost him."

STEVE FRIEDMAN

A Moment of Silence

FROM RUNNER'S WORLD

Everyone in the sporting world wants predictions. But who, Steve Friedman asks, can really predict what will happen to a man? This is the story of a runner, running from the horror of 9/11, through trauma, on to a new life.
— D.M.

HE WILL WAKE AT 4:00 A.M., as he does every weekday, except Monday. He'll wear shorts and a T-shirt, even in the rain, unless it's winter, when he might pull on a Gore-Tex jacket and pants. When it snows and the snow is heavy enough, he'll stretch thin rubber sandals with metal spikes over his running shoes. He'll grab a small canister of pepper spray. Three seasons out of the year, he'll lace up one of his six pairs of "active" size 13 Sauconys that he keeps in a closet underneath his one hundred hanging T-shirts, and in the winter he'll wear one of his half-dozen pairs of active Nikes from the same closet, because the layer of air in them doesn't seem to compress in cold weather as much as the foam in the Sauconys. He'll be out his front door at 4:15, back inside at 5:05. Then he'll shower, eat a bowl of instant oatmeal, make himself a lunch of a peanut butter and jelly sandwich or pack a cup of yogurt, and leave his house in Warwick, New York, at 6:10 to drive to the train station in Harriman for the 6:42 train to Hoboken, New Jersey. The trip will take a little over an hour, and in Hoboken he'll board a 7:55 underground train bound for Manhattan. Once there, he'll walk fifteen minutes to his office at an insurance company at Madison Avenue and Thirty-sixth Street.

John Moylan is a man of habit and routine and caution, and for much of his life attention to detail has served him well. Some mornings, when he's feeling adventurous or wild, he'll make a little extra noise between 4:00 A.M. and 4:15 A.M., just to see if his wife of thirty years, Holly, will wake up. She hasn't yet.

His running route starts outside his front door, and it hasn't varied for six years, since he and Holly and their two daughters moved from Crystal Lake, Illinois, when his then-employer, Kemper Insurance, transferred him to New York City. Down Kings Highway, through the small village, up a small hill, and by the time he passes the Mobil gasoline station at the end of the first mile, he'll know if the run will be easy or hard, and if it's hard, he'll remind himself to eat healthier that day, to make sure to get to sleep by 9:00 P.M. At one and a half miles, he might pass a gaggle of geese that like to waddle near the black granite memorial to the seven people from Warwick who died on September 11, 2001. He'll run past one dairy farm and its herd of cows, and he'll make mooing sounds and wonder why they never moo back. Later, he'll pass another dairy farm and moo at those cows, who always moo back. One of life's mysteries. He'll run past what's really no more than a giant puddle next to the road that he thinks of as the turtle pond, because he once saw a turtle waddling across the concrete toward the water. He'll run four to five miles, ten or twelve on Saturday, and on Sunday anywhere from ten to sixteen. Mondays, he rests.

Moylan is by nature conservative, by profession cautious. He has been in the insurance business for thirty-three years and has spent much of his life calculating risk, calibrating the costs of bad planning and devastating whim. Men who worry about the future can guard against the worst sorts of accidents. Men who look ahead can avoid life's greatest dangers. Even when running, even during the time of his life that is devoted to release and escape from daily tallies and concerns, he can't quite escape the principles that have guided him for so long.

"What do I think about?" he says. "God, just about everything. Am I on target for my marathon goal? How am I going to pay my daughters' college tuition? Do I have good retirement plans?"

Some days — one of life's mysteries — he thinks of that terrible morning five years ago.

The Simple Things

He and one of his coworkers, Jill Steidel, had just arrived at their office on the thirty-sixth floor of the north tower at the World Trade Center in downtown Manhattan. They were carrying coffee they had picked up from the Starbucks in the building's atrium. He had his usual — a grande-size cup of the breakfast blend, black. It was 8:46 A.M., and Moylan was standing at his window, looking west, gazing at the ferries on the Hudson River. It was one of his great pleasures, what he called "one of the simple things in life." That's when he felt the building shake and heard a loud "thwaaang." He had heard longtime employees talk about the 1993 bombing in the building's parking garage, and now he thought the building might be collapsing as a result of residual structural damage. Then he heard screaming. He was one of the fire marshals on his floor, so he rounded up his employees — there were about twenty-five of them — and herded them to the stairs. As a longtime runner, he checked his watch as the group entered the stairwell. It was 8:48 A.M.

The stairwell was packed, but orderly. He remembers two "nice, neat rows" of people, scared but polite. He remembers many breathing hard and sweating, wide-eyed. He remembers thinking that his experience as a runner helped him stay calm. "What was it?" someone asked. "It wasn't a bomb," someone else said.

The people in front of his group would sometimes stop suddenly, which made his group stop. That didn't make sense. Neither did the smell. Moylan had been in the Air Force as a young man, and it was a familiar odor. "I thought, *What the hell is jet fuel doing here?*"

It took twenty-eight minutes to get to the ground floor. Moylan left the building at 9:16 A.M. He turned to his right and looked east, just as two bodies hit the ground. He saw other bodies on the ground, realized that's why firefighters had kept people from exiting the doors in a constant flow. He saw greasy puddles of blazing jet fuel, huge chunks of twisted metal. He saw more bodies falling. (It's estimated that of the more than twenty-five hundred people who died in the twin towers, two hundred had jumped.)

He and the others were marshaled to the overpass that stretched over the West Side Highway and to the marina next to the Hudson River. At the marina, he looked back. People on the higher floors were waving pieces of clothing and curtains from the windows. There were helicopters — he thought there were eight or ten — circling. He could see that the helicopters couldn't get through the fire and smoke, and he knew that the people in the windows could see it too. He was used to synthesizing facts quickly, and it didn't take long to comprehend the horrible calculus confronting the people in the windows: be burned alive or jump. He wondered what he would have done.

Thousands of people were on the marina. Some stared upwards. Others walked north, toward Midtown. The Kemper employees for whom Moylan was responsible had all gotten out safely; now Moylan needed to get home. The subway was shut down, as was the underground train to New Jersey, so he boarded a ferry to Hoboken. When he got to Hoboken at 9:59, he looked back, and as he did so, the south tower, which had been hit at 9:02 A.M., crumbled. The north tower, his tower, would fall at 10:28 A.M.

In Hoboken he boarded a train for home, but first he tried to call Holly and his daughters, Meredith and Erin. He had left his cell phone in his office, so he borrowed one, but it wasn't working. Neither, he remembers, were the landlines.

He remembers the hourlong train ride to Harriman, and from there the drive to Warwick. He remembers with absolute clarity walking through his door at 4:00 P.M., covered in soot, smelling of fire and death. Five years later, the memory still troubles him.

"The home office had called, looking for me, which just scared my wife even more. My suit was ruined. I was reeking. I scared the living daylights out of them. My daughters especially were emotionally ruined, or disturbed. . . . When your family thinks you're dead and you walk in your house and surprise them . . ."

He stayed up all night, watching television. In the morning, he knew what he had to do. He rose from the bed where he had failed to sleep. "I wanted desperately to go out running," he says. He just couldn't get his shoes on.

Accidents Happen

Moylan knows better than most men how accidents can shape a life. He had been working in the East Norwich, Long Island, post office in the summer of 1970 when he learned he had drawn the eleventh spot in one of this country's last drafts. He had always thought how neat it would be to fly planes, so he enrolled in the U.S. Air Force. And that's how he got to Iceland.

There he was, in the summer of 1971, a cop's son from East Norwich, playing softball at midnight, soaking afterward in thermal hot springs, gorging on fresh salmon, drinking beer with pretty girls who spoke another language. Forget planning. He couldn't have dreamed that summer — "one of the best years of my life." Pure chance. Then another one of life's mysteries. Late one night, in April of 1972, there was a knock on his barrack's door. It was the chaplain. Moylan's father had died; he was only forty-six. After the funeral, Moylan asked his mother how she was going to hold on to the house. She told him not to worry, but he pressed. Did she need his help?

The Air Force gave him an honorable hardship discharge, and he went back to the post office, and he might still be there if his mother hadn't insisted that he go talk to one of the leaders of the church she attended. He was an insurance executive, and he was always looking for bright young men.

So in 1973, Moylan became a company man, a trainee for Crum & Forster, a salaried student of chance and fate. Every morning, he waited for the 7:00 A.M. Manhattan-bound train from the station in Syosset, Long Island, and every morning he stood in the same spot and walked through the same door and sat in the same seat. And every afternoon, he did the same thing at Pennsylvania Station, when the 5:06 eastbound train pulled in. Then one afternoon, the train stopped twenty feet short of its usual spot and people pushed and shoved and Moylan's seat was taken and he had no choice, there was only one empty seat left. He found himself sitting next to a pretty blond dress designer from Huntington. Her name was Holly.

Accidents happen, and it's one of life's mysteries the effect they'll have, and all you can do is try to control what's controllable. And that's how a young, married company man started running. It was 1979, and Moylan had gone from a lean, 180-pound military man to a 220-pound, twenty-eight-year-old, pudgy, listless suit. He needed to do something. He had read an article about Bill Rodgers and the New York City Marathon, and he decided that running sounded like fun.

Moylan is not a man to make a big deal out of things, and he doesn't make a big deal about that decision. But two years later, in the spring of 1981, he ran the Long Island Marathon. He ran it in just under four hours. In the fall, he ran the New York City Marathon, and did even better, finishing in 3:51.

He cut out junk food, started eating lean meats. He woke early, ran before the sun rose. He experimented with equipment and distance and learned "to not let my mind get in front of my body. I learned that patience is a virtue."

He wore his running shoes when he walked from the train to his office building, and he wore them when he took his midday forty-five-minute walks around Manhattan. He always worried that people thought he looked funny.

By 2001, by the time he was fifty, he had run fourteen marathons, many half-marathons, countless 10-Ks and 5-Ks. Running helped him reduce his blood pressure from 120/90 to 110/60, helped him reduce his weight from 220 to anywhere from 180 to 195, depending on where he was in his training cycle. His resting pulse is 50 now, and when he gives blood, Red Cross officials routinely question him to make sure he's not a fainter. Running helped him cope when his mother died in 1985 at age fifty-nine, with the birth of his daughters in 1982 and 1985, with the demands of being a middle-age father and husband and provider and company man. He ran because he didn't want to die young, as his parents had, and because it relaxed him and was part of his life. Accidents would happen, and there were some things a man couldn't do anything about, terrible things. But with discipline and attention and will, a man could carve out a safe place, a part of life that was predictable, calming in its sameness. Half an hour or so in the early morning stillness could help a man deal with almost anything.

It was Tuesday, five years ago, the week after Labor Day, and warm for that time of year, in that part of the country. A morning like this was rare and precious. It would be a good run. It felt like it would be a good day. At the Mobil station, Moylan picked up his pace.

He ran past the cows and the geese and the turtle pond. He thought about his retirement fund, even though he had many years to go before needing it. He worried about his daughters' college tuition, even though he had been saving for years. He wondered if he would run as swiftly as he wanted to in the New York

City Marathon, even though it was still two months away. He was back at home at 5:05 A.M., and showered and had his instant oatmeal and caught his train and met Jill Steidel at Starbucks, and they rode the elevator up to the thirty-sixth floor, and less than a minute later, he felt the building shake. And the next day, he couldn't get his running shoes on. He couldn't put them on the next day either. He woke at four each day, got out of bed, thought about running, got his shoes out of the closet, then put them back. Then he would sit on the couch and watch television and his mind would drift. He thought about a framed photograph he had left on his office desk. Holly had taken it, and it showed Moylan and Meredith and Erin at a Yankees game in July. It was cap day, and they were all wearing Yankees caps. He doubted he could ever find the negative. Then he thought about all the people who didn't get to say good-bye to their families.

Friday, September 14, was his twenty-sixth wedding anniversary, and on that morning he got dressed and he laced up his Sauconys, and he opened up his front door. He looked outside, into the darkness. Then he closed the door and went back inside.

The Funny Sense

It is late spring, nearly five years later, and he is looking at the space where the World Trade Center once stood. It is the first time he has been back here. He says he's surprised that the footprints of the two towers aren't more clearly marked. He's disappointed that the twisted cross of metal that became the focus of so many Christians is no longer on the site.

He gazes into the sky.

"When I came out," he says, "it was on this level. I had a view — right in this area, the bodies were already falling. I could look up and see the people hanging out the windows. The news footage, you just saw smoke. From down here, it was like looking up from the bottom of a grill. I remember seeing how ungodly hot it was — there was an orange glow."

Moylan is a handsome man, square-jawed, gray-haired, hazel-eyed. He is six feet, a solid 190, on his way, he says, back to 180. He wears a blue suit and a pin of the twin towers and an American flag, and he looks like a soap-opera actor or the Air Force pilot he might have been. If this were a different place, he might appear to be just a tourist searching the New York City skyline for wonders.

He turns from the ghost buildings and looks toward the bank of the river, at the benches where he used to unpack his peanut butter and jelly sandwiches or his yogurt cup. "This place was my luxury suite for lunch in the summertime. . . . I used to come out here on the bench and just dream."

In the weeks after the attack, Moylan studied a *New York Times* article about the sequence of events and realized that had he taken two or three minutes longer to get his coffee with Steidel at Starbucks, he still would have been in the elevator on the way to his office when the plane hit and he wouldn't have survived.

Moylan turns back east, away from the water. Reflection can be healing, but he has work to do. He needs to get back to his office, five miles north in Midtown. "The funny sense that I get being here," he says, "is, life goes on. It's continuing."

"I Don't Remember That"

It is early spring, dusk in Orange County, New York, and Moylan and Holly and their oldest daughter, Meredith, are driving the back roads of Warwick. Holly points out a place where George Washington slept. Meredith points out a dairy farm and creamery. We drive through the gaggle of geese and past the granite memorial to the people from Warwick who died on 9/11.

At dinner, we talk about past races, about what running meant to Moylan before 9/11. Meredith talks about watching her father finish one marathon on an ocean boardwalk, yelling, "That's my daddy and he loves me," and years later joining him in center field of San Francisco's Candlestick Park for the end of a 5-K run. Holly and Meredith talk about how they enjoy staying up watching *Gilmore Girls* and chatting when John goes to sleep. Holly wonders aloud why her husband — or any man — needs one hundred T-shirts, and Moylan speaks mournfully of the "boxes and boxes" of his T-shirts she donated to charity.

I ask Holly and Meredith how long it took for them to get over the shock of seeing Moylan walk in the door, how they dealt with the hours of uncertainty.

"I wasn't uncertain," Holly says. "When we were watching the coverage on television, I told Meredith, 'Dad will be fine. He's a runner and he'll run right out of there. Besides, he called us from Hoboken, before he got on the train.'"

Moylan blinks, shakes his head.

"No, I didn't call you. I didn't have my phone."

"You definitely called us," Holly says. "You borrowed a phone and called us to let us know you were coming home."

Moylan blinks again. "I don't remember that," he says.

"Yeah, Dad," Meredith says, "you called from Hoboken. To let us know you were all right."

Storytellers

Harold Kudler, MD, is an associate clinical professor of psychiatry at Duke University and a nationally recognized expert on post-traumatic stress disorder (PTSD). He hears part of John Moylan's post-9/11 story and says, "It's quite common for people in the middle of an acute stress response to have disassociative phenomena."

To Dr. Kudler, Moylan's elaborate memory of his family being traumatized as a result of not hearing from him makes psychological sense. "Sometimes," Dr. Kudler says, "the effort to create meaning and to create a meaningful narrative about what has happened to you actually becomes more important than the actual memory and might replace it. This story about coming home as a ghost and having everyone else scared might be a way to say, 'Boy, was I scared. I felt like a ghost in my own life. I wasn't even sure when I got home if I had survived that.'"

Moylan's responses during and after the attacks — his vivid recollection of details, his construction of false memories, his nightmares, his long avoidance of the WTC site, his difficulty running afterward — are entirely consistent with symptoms exhibited by people facing extreme trauma, even the most resilient people, according to Dr. Kudler.

"There's a tendency to medicalize or pathologize responses," Dr. Kudler says. "It might be better to think that here's someone who is faced with a new challenge that's so radically different than the one he faced a few days earlier.

"Think of it like mourning. When you're bereaved, you wouldn't be able to invest in yourself, because you'd feel overwhelmed, and you'd sort of lose your center. For a while you wouldn't be able to do the things that reminded you of who you were, of the thing you did for yourself."

And Moylan's inability to go for his normal run?

"Running for him was something he did for himself, was important to him, and he made a point of always doing this regardless of anything else. Great exercise, recreational, self-affirming. But in the context of the disaster, when people are overwhelmed and filled with doubt, it's easy to see why someone wouldn't do those self-affirming things.

"And if he was angry, that anger may have drowned out his capacity to enjoy a simple pleasure like running, and take that simple time for himself. That anger could have drowned out a lot of those normal, good impulses."

When I tell Moylan what Dr. Kudler said, he is silent for a few seconds.

"He nailed me," he says.

Perspective

He would wake in the middle of the night, certain that his house was under attack. He would dream that he was up in a tower and flames were licking at him. He would dream of having to make a terrible choice but not knowing what to do. He would dream of dying, "that I went through what those people went through." Noises startled him. "He was restless and jumpy and things would frighten him," Holly says. "If we were out somewhere and a child cried out, he'd jump, he'd be scared."

During the day, he thought of the people who had died. "I couldn't rationalize what had happened. People in the normal course of living, going to work, murdered. I thought about how they never got to say good-bye to anyone. I thought about my family, and about facing a decision to burn to death or to jump."

Every morning in the weeks after 9/11, he would get up and he would plan to run. But he never made it outside. He would make coffee, and sit on the couch, and sometimes watch television, and have his oatmeal, and when it was time to take his shower and catch his train, that's what he would do.

He couldn't stop thinking about chance, and fate, and wondering why he had survived.

At his company's insistence, he had two conversations with Red Cross officials, once in a group, once alone. He talked about how angry he was that there had been an attack. He talked about how angry he was that he had survived while others had died. He talked about how angry he was that he couldn't run. "And that about covers it," he says.

He reported for work on September 13, in Kemper's New Jersey office. The company assured Moylan and his coworkers that they would be reassigned to a building in midtown Manhattan, on a lower floor. The morning they reported for work there, on the tenth floor of Rockefeller Center, was the day authorities discovered an envelope filled with anthrax addressed to Tom Brokaw in the same building. Some of the Kemper employees left and never came back. Moylan stayed.

The nightmares continued. He kept jumping at the slightest noise. But Holly didn't say anything. "We had talked about counseling," she says, "and he just said, 'Let me see how things go.'" He knew that running would help him get over all his problems. So he got up every day, ready to run. But he couldn't do it.

Then one day, he could. Just like that. One of life's mysteries.

There were no grand pronouncements before he went to bed the night before, no stirring speeches at dinner. He was still angry. He was still scared. He still thought about the falling bodies. But on Columbus Day, almost exactly a month after the attack, he managed to get his shoes on, and to get out the door. He made it four miles, and every step was difficult. His legs were heavy. He had trouble breathing. But he made it.

His first race was a half-marathon in Pennsylvania the next April. It was a clear day, warm, "almost like September 11," he says. "I remember that for the first time in a long time, I smelled grass, could smell flowers."

A few months later, in October, at a half-marathon not far from his home, he happened to overhear one of the runners mention that he was a firefighter. Moylan approached him. "He said he wasn't there, but he knew people who were. I told him I was in tower one. We both had similar feelings . . . about losing people. It was the first time I had verification that I wasn't the only person who felt like I did."

He ran the New York City Marathon in 2002 and 2003. He ran more marathons, more half-marathons. The nightmares faded away, as did his preoccupation with death and the randomness of fate. (He still jumps at the slightest noise, something he never did before 9/11.) Three years ago, Todd Jennings, who lived near Moylan and who had just started running, spotted Moylan on the train "in his gray flannel suit and running shoes." Eventually, they started talking. About training regimens, and race strategy, and running in general. "No," Jennings says, "we never talked about 9/11."

Moylan and Jennings traveled to the Boilermaker 15-K in Utica, New York, in 2005, and the night before the race they went out for a pasta dinner. "He told me," Jennings says, " 'I want to be remembered on my tombstone as a runner. Running is who I am.'"

There are things you can't control, no matter how much you worry and plan. Terrible things happen, and there's nothing you can do to stop them. Those are lessons that will change a man. For better or for worse.

After eighteen years, Moylan left Kemper Insurance in 2002 to go to work for Greater New York Insurance. He doesn't worry about what others think about his blue suit/white running shoes combination in Midtown anymore. He ran a 3:22 marathon in 1982 and a 4:50 marathon in 2003. He still wants to get back to a four-hour time, "but I don't worry so much about time anymore." He is training for this fall's New York City Marathon. He still thinks about retirement and paying for his daughters' education, but it doesn't eat at him quite as much as it used to. He still calculates risk and calibrates the likelihood of disaster and does his best to protect himself and his family, but he knows there are some things beyond a man's control, and to worry about them is to waste precious energy.

When he finds himself irritated or impatient, he thinks of a terrible choice he never had to make, and he is grateful. Every morning, as he steps out his door, he is grateful.

"I told my wife, I should have a new birthday," Moylan says. "My new life started on 9/11. The fact that I survived is a gift. I know quite a few people who didn't. I made a promise to myself. I was going to live differently." He tries not to dwell on the past, or to look too very far into the future. But he has made one promise to himself. "Yeah, I'm going to go back to Iceland sometime. That's a plan now."

The Hills Beyond

Weekends, he treats himself. Friday and Saturday nights, he soaks a pot of steel-cut oats in water so he can have homemade oatmeal after his runs. He sleeps till 5:30, has a cup of coffee, "my luxury," and dawdles for a full hour before he heads out the door. September 11 falls on a Monday this year, so he won't run. But the day before, he'll step out of his front door just as the sun rises above Warwick. He'll pass the Mobil station and the silent cows and the mooing cows, but that day he'll go at least fifteen miles, so there will be other sights too. He'll run by the VFW hall where the old men always wave and the fire station in town where the guys always have a nice word to say. He might see a deer, or a porcupine, or even a bear. At mile seven, he'll run by a house where a snarling rottweiler is tied to a tree, and he'll grip his pepper spray a little more tightly.

Just past that house, Moylan will ascend a gentle hill, heading east, and no matter how hard the run, no matter how he slept the night before or how he's feeling, as he crests the little hill, he'll slow down. It's his favorite spot on the weekend run — his favorite spot of any of his runs. It's just a little hummock, but when a man reaches it, he can turn to the right and look south, and he can see an entire valley stretching before him, and beyond that valley, forests and hills all the way to the horizon. He will still have another seven miles to go, and then his homemade oatmeal, with the apples and bananas and raisins and cinnamon he allows himself on weekends. Then on Monday he'll think again about the day that changed his life, and on the day after that he'll catch the 6:42 train to Hoboken, and on the day after that he'll do it again. Or not. Who can really predict what will happen to a man, even a careful man, a man who takes precautions? That's another of life's mysteries.

Moylan will allow himself to walk a little bit on Sunday at the top of the gentle rise, to linger, to look at the valley and the forests and the looming hills beyond. He loves this spot.

"It's a nice place to get perspective," he says.

JOHN BRANT

Team Hoyt Starts Again

FROM RUNNER'S WORLD

Maybe it's time to subscribe to *Runner's World*. Another story that runs past the shoes and practice regimens and diets and takes us deep into the human heart.
— D.M.

RICK HOYT LIES awake but unmoving, watching clear winter sunlight spill into his bedroom. He often spends whole days watching light move across a room, or along the course of a road race — the pale April sunshine filtering through the bare trees along Route 135 in the early miles of the Boston Marathon, for instance, or the tropical sun lancing the clouds that shroud Mauna Loa volcano at the Hawaii Ironman.

He lies on his belly, his head turned to the right, alone in the apartment, in exactly the position that Naomi, his personal care attendant, left him at ten o'clock the night before. You would think that Rick's nights would seem endless, but the medication he takes to relax his chronically clenched muscles allows him to sleep soundly for twelve hours at a stretch. Unable to voluntarily move any part of his body but his head, and that just barely, Rick lies calmly, studying the morning light. By its slant and texture he reckons the time to be around ten.

The sunlight keeps filling the bedroom, like April in January. It must be warm out on the streets. The women would have shed their heavy coats. From the vantage point of his wheelchair, Rick regards women from an arresting, navel-level angle. His two brothers give him a hard time about that. They call it a perk of cerebral palsy.

He hears the key in the lock, and then a step in the hallway. Then, "Good morning, Rick."

At 8:00 A.M. on this Saturday morning, Dick Hoyt swings his van onto the Mass. Pike, heading east toward Boston, seventy-five miles away. He lowers the visor against the rising sun and turns the car radio to an all-news station. "I've driven this route so often all I gotta do is sort of point the van and it finds the apartment on its own," Dick jokes.

He yawns behind the wheel. It's been a crazy week. On Tuesday, he was in Florida to give a motivational speech to business executives. On Wednesday, he was in Texas giving another one. Thursday night he and Rick were honored at a dinner in Hopkinton, where the Boston Marathon starts every April. Now, on to Boston. He makes this ninety-minute drive to Rick's apartment, in the Brighton section, almost every Saturday morning. He'll pick up Rick, bathe and shave and feed him, and then they'll drive back together to Dick's house in Holland, a village on the Connecticut border. Most Sundays they'll rise at 5:00 A.M. to prepare for whatever 5-K, 10-K, marathon, or triathlon is coming up. They race forty times a year, in a manner that, over the past quarter-century, has become no less miraculous as it has become familiar: a short-legged, barrel-chested, sixty-five-year-old man with a rocklike jaw, running at an 8:30-per-mile pace pushing a slight, forty-four-year-old quadriplegic in a twenty-seven-pound wheelchair.

Seven miles into his drive Dick pulls off the Pike to make his ritual Starbucks stop. "I shoulda bought stock in this place ten years ago," he says with a grin. The barista starts Dick's drink the moment he steps in the door — a vente chai tea, extra hot. He has been careful with his diet ever since his heart attack three years ago. The scare caught the extremely fit Dick by total surprise, as have several other setbacks the Hoyts have faced of late. Last December, a gale raked New England, sending a tree through Dick's roof and into his living room. Days later the lift on Rick's specially designed van broke down, necessitating the purchase of a new rig. Then, just before Christmas, Dick needed arthroscopic surgery on his left knee to repair cartilage damage, the first serious injury of his twenty-nine-year running career. The knee is still healing, and has kept Dick from running for a month, his longest inactive stretch ever. The Boston Marathon is only three months away.

Dick's tea is ready, but just before he turns to head to the door, he spots the Starbucks manager and asks him if the store might contribute to the Easter Seals fund-raising drive he has launched in conjunction with the Boston Marathon. "We want to raise a million dollars," Dick tells him. The manager pledges his support. Smiling, Dick heads out the door, back to his van, and back on the Pike.

He's drinking his tea and talking about races and running while changing lanes frequently and making great time getting to Boston. By 10:00 A.M. he's steering off the expressway and threading through the streets near Boston University. He parks near Rick's building, takes an elevator up five floors, and moves down a long corridor to Rick's apartment. He puts a key in the lock and turns. He opens the door and steps into the hallway.

"Good morning, Rick!"

The athletic phenomenon that is known as Team Hoyt began one spring day in 1977. Rick was fifteen at the time and came home from school asking his dad if they could run a five-mile road race together in their town of Westfield, Massachusetts, to benefit a local college athlete who'd been paralyzed in an auto accident. It was a strange request considering Rick's situation.

Cerebral palsy is a debilitating condition often caused by complications during pregnancy or at birth. In Rick's case, the umbilical cord got tangled around his neck, cutting off the oxygen supply to his brain and causing irreparable damage. Aside from his head, the only other parts of his body he can voluntarily move even slightly are his knees. His muscles chronically contract, hence the need for muscle relaxants. He can't control his arms, which jerk and wave spasmodically. He has a "reverse tongue," meaning he drools and reflexively expels food and drink, so he can't eat on his own. His head is usually tilted, his smile lopsided, but genuine, accompanied by a mischievous glint. He can't speak at all, but because he can move his head, he can communicate with the help of a specially designed computer. As a cursor moves across a screen filled with rows of letters, Rick highlights which letter he wants by pressing his head against a narrow metal bar attached to the right side of the wheelchair. When he completes a word and then a thought — a tediously slow process — a voice synthesizer verbally produces it.

At the time Rick asked to run that race, Dick was a forty-year-old nonrunner. When he and Rick got to the event, organizers saw the wheelchair, the disabled son, and the middle-aged dad and gave them a look that said, "You two won't make it past the first corner." They didn't know Dick. It wasn't in his nature to quit a job he'd started. And besides, by that first corner, Rick was having too much fun. They ran the entire five miles, and didn't finish last. Afterward, a wild grin lit up Rick's face. Later he tapped out: "Dad, when I'm running, it feels like I'm not handicapped."

Dick had a slightly different reaction. "After that race I felt disabled — I was pissing blood for a week," he says. "But we knew we were on to something. Making Rick happy was the greatest feeling in the world."

Running made Dick happy too. A career Army guy, he felt like he was back in basic training again, breezing through a forced march while the other guys struggled and bitched. And, like the military, running was structured. If you followed the program, you got faster. Dick bought a pair of running shoes and researched a training schedule. Judy, Rick's mother, located an engineer in New Hampshire to build a wheelchair modified for running, with three bicycle wheels and a foam seat molded to Rick's body. The Hoyts' first running chair was produced for $35, and its basic design forms the template for all the racing chairs the men have subsequently used.

Since 1977, Rick and Dick Hoyt have completed more than nine hundred endurance events around the world, including sixty-four marathons and eight Ironman triathlons. They've run their home-town Boston Marathon twenty-four times, and plan to do their twenty-fifth on April 17. With a marathon PR of 2:40:47, and a 13:30 personal best for the Hawaii Ironman World Championship, they are the furthest things from charity cases. Just consider how they managed the 1999 Hawaii Ironman. After completing the 2.4-mile swim (for triathlons, Rick lies in an eight-foot Zodiac raft, Dick pulling him with a strap fastened around his waist), their brakes froze with 30 miles left in the 112-mile bike leg, and lacking a replacement part they had to wait more than an hour for the mechanic's truck. When the repair was finally completed, Dick asked the wind-blasted and sunburnt Rick if he wanted to continue. (Rick rides on a specially constructed seat that fits on the bike's handle-bars.) Rick instantly nodded yes. So they soldiered through the bike phase in last place, and then transitioned into the marathon, their strongest event. There seemed little hope of completing the run by midnight, the deadline for official finishers. But feeling stronger as the night wore on, Rick and Dick passed dozens of runners and powered across the finish line with forty-five minutes to spare. They had run the notoriously difficult marathon leg in a remarkable 3:30.

Over the course of their quarter-century-long career, the Hoyts' incredible athletic achievements have made them, arguably, the most famous distance runners in America. They've met Ronald Reagan and Rudolph Giuliani, appeared on *Oprah,* and been the subject of a full-length documentary. In 1996, during the Boston Marathon's centennial celebration, the Hoyts ranked tenth in a poll of the most influential runners in marathon history — a list that included such legends as Bill Rodgers and Joan Samuelson. Dick has become a sought-after motivational speaker, making fifty appearances a year before corporate groups. Inevitably, after such speeches, Dick will hear the same well-meaning questions: *How do you and Rick communicate during a race? What happens if Rick has to go to the bathroom?* And, of course, *How much longer can you do this?* When the questions come up, he replies readily and cheerfully. "We feel real good . . . we love what we're doing . . . we've got no plans for quitting." But the questions, and the implication that Team Hoyt's run has to end at some point, still rankle.

The fact is, Dick Hoyt can expect to keep hearing the questions, especially after the heart attack, the knee surgery, the missed training. All that, and Dick turns sixty-six in June. Twenty-four Bostons have passed. How many more are really likely?

People can keep asking that question, Dick insists, but if they do, it means they don't know what drives the distance runner.

A few minutes after arriving at Rick's apartment, Dick lifts his naked, 110-pound son off his bed as if he weighed no more than a case of beer and sits him on the toilet. Dick is built like a catcher, his position as a star high school baseball player (he had a tryout with the Yankees, who rejected him, ironically, because he was too slow a runner), with a stocky frame and heavy legs featuring such exceptional muscular definition that his physical therapist jokes that he ought to model for an anatomy class.

Rick has trained himself to use the bathroom just twice a day, upon rising and retiring, a boon to his father and personal care attendants. (Similarly, Rick doesn't ingest fluids during marathons or shorter road races; during triathlons, he drinks only at the transition areas.) Lifting Rick again, Dick places him in the steaming water of the bathtub, where he bathes and shaves him. The water feels good. Rick gives a crooked smile of pleasure. Although he looks childlike sitting in the tub, his shoulders are surprisingly broad. Dick explains that the chronic contraction caused by Rick's spastic condition, along with the stress and stimulation of his athletic career, have given him excellent muscle tone. Paradoxically, Rick emanates an air of health and well-being.

"The human performance lab at Boston Children's Hospital wants to study Rick," Dick says. "His life expectancy is the same as any other man his age."

As he works, Dick talks quietly about the weather, last night's Celtics game, and his recent visit to the physical therapist for a checkup on his knee. "Jackie says I'm ahead of schedule," he says, toweling Rick's close-cropped, gray-flecked hair.

Dick originally injured his left knee in San Diego last November. The two were running with students from an elementary school through a bumpy field when Dick twisted the knee, tearing cartilage. Then, a few weeks later, when the Hoyts were in Florida for a race, their hotel's fire alarm sounded in the middle of the night. It was almost certainly a false alarm and another man — even another father — might have turned over in bed and gone back to sleep. But Dick didn't have that luxury. He got Rick into his wheelchair and humped down a narrow fire escape. While making one of the tight turns, Dick again twisted his knee. There was no denying this injury, and three days before Christmas he underwent surgery. Thus the doctors' orders not to run for a month.

Dick lifts Rick into his wheelchair and guides him to the kitchen table. The walls are covered with running memorabilia, including a quilt stitched out of T-shirts from 1980s-vintage road races, and a photo of Rick and Dick being greeted by then-President Reagan. Dick pours orange juice into a tumbler and, for the next twenty minutes, feeds it sip by sip to Rick, palpitating his jaw and neck with a milking-like motion to assure the juice stays down. Each moment ministering to Rick requires exacting effort, but his father never seems to lose patience.

"I was never angry or resentful about the hand we were dealt,"

Dick says. "People assume that I work out my rage through running, but that's not the case."

Rick Hoyt is one of an estimated 760,000 Americans who suffer from cerebral palsy. Unlike such crippling conditions as spinal cord injuries or Parkinson's disease, cerebral palsy research currently offers little hope of a cure. Through technology, physical therapy, counseling, and prodigious work, however, the condition can be managed. Perhaps the best indicator that Rick has successfully dealt with his condition is that in 1993 he completed a special education degree from Boston University, though it was an arduous process. A PCA had to sit with him through every class, taking notes, and then reading assignments aloud to him. He had to communicate with professors through the voice synthesizer. With such impediments, he could only take two classes a semester and he needed nine years to complete the degree.

Still, a college degree was hardly what Judy and Dick Hoyt expected from their firstborn when he arrived in January 1962. One pediatrician told the couple that their new son, his condition classified as nonverbal spastic quadriplegia, would be a vegetable for the rest of his short and miserable life; place him in an institution, the doctor recommended, and, in effect, forget him. Judy and Dick adamantly refused, though the first weeks and months with their severely disabled boy were unquestionably hard ones.

Judy and Dick had met in high school in North Reading, a community fifteen miles north of downtown Boston. She was a cheerleader and he was captain of the football team. The sixth of ten children, Dick was always a demon for work. At the age of eight he was earning money by odd jobs, and at sixteen he was running a crop farm. He taught himself masonry and other construction skills. After high school he joined the National Guard. He loved basic training — the order, the challenge, the physical rigor — and decided to make the military his career. The army placed him in the Nike missile program, assigning him to posts around New England.

When Rick was on his way, two years after they had been married, the couple looked forward to having a boy who would grow up to play catcher like his old man and go fishing with his grandfather. Instead, when he arrived, he couldn't manage a newborn's cry. Judy was crushed, and fell into a deep depression. "I hated Dick, and I hated all the mothers in the hospital and all my friends who were mothers of babies that were not handicapped," Judy says in the Hoyts' biography, *It's Only a Mountain.* "My feelings kept see-sawing from hate to denial for months. . . . Rick couldn't suck, he couldn't even open his little clenched fists. He was tight, tight, tight. We had to force him to eat every two hours just to keep him alive. We would wake him up by pinching the bottom of his feet."

Judy soon recovered from the depressive bout, and insisted, along with Dick, on raising Rick at home. She started to fight for her son's rights and those of other disabled individuals. After earning a degree in special education, she helped establish a summer camp for children with disabilities, and she battled endlessly to enroll and keep Rick in Westfield's public schools. While an estimated two-thirds of people with cerebral palsy suffer some degree of mental retardation, Judy says she could tell just by looking at Rick's eyes as a baby that he had an active mind. "His eyes would follow me around the room. My son was intelligent. He was alive inside."

As Judy worked this front, Dick was busy with his military career, rising through the enlisted ranks to attend Officer Candidate School and eventually attain a rank of lieutenant colonel. Nights and weekends, to pay for Rick's wheelchairs and other necessities, he moonlighted on masonry jobs. But for all their varied activities, Judy and Dick tried to maintain a typical family life. Rick's two younger brothers, Rob and Russ, both healthy, were taught to treat their older brother as normal as possible. Rick played goalie in neighborhood hockey games. Dick or the brothers would tie the goalie stick to the boy, then steer him in his wheelchair as he tried to block shots in the crease. Rick would go wild with each blocked shot. There would also be family hiking trips. Dick would drape Rick over his shoulders and carry him up mountains.

Then came that race in Westfield in 1977, and the family's life changed forever. The epiphany of that first race fed a desire to do other races around New England. But just because the Hoyts wanted to run more didn't mean they were necessarily welcomed by the running community. At a 10-K in Springfield, Massachu-setts, Dick remembers getting snubbed by the other athletes. "They shied away from us as if they thought they were going to catch a dis-ease," Dick recalls. The race officials were even less hospitable. "The officials said they didn't fit because Dick was pushing him," Judy remembers in the Hoyts' biography. "Dick did it 'differently' than all the other runners. The wheelchair athletes didn't want them because Rick wasn't powering his own chair, and the able-bodied runners said, 'You're just going to get in the way. Why do you want to push this kid of yours who doesn't talk and just sits in the wheelchair?'"

Judy was there to watch the two at all their races, strongly supporting them through the early stages of their running career, when even some people questioned Dick's motives. "I got maybe twenty or twenty-five letters," Dick says. "Parents with disabled kids saw the stories about us, and they assumed that running was my idea, not Rick's. They thought I was using him to get publicity for myself."

Four years after their first race, Dick and Rick sought to run the 1981 Boston Marathon, but again met resistance. They were told that they needed to meet a qualifying time, just like any other runner officially entered in the race. There would be no exceptions, even for a guy pushing his kid in a wheelchair. "The Hoyts were proposing a nontraditional form of participation and, at the time, any change at Boston was a big deal," says Jack Fleming, spokesman for the Boston Athletic Association, organizers of the marathon. Fleming, who was not with the BAA at the time, adds, "It wasn't just Rick and Dick; the same thing had happened with women running for the first time, and then professionals."

Team Hoyt decided to run the 1981 race unofficially, as bandits, and clocked a remarkable debut marathon time of 3:18. They ran unofficially again in 1982, going under three hours for the first time (2:59), and then shaved another minute off in 1983. Still, no waiver came from the BAA. Finally, in October 1983, they went to Washington, D.C., to run the Marine Corps Marathon, looking to clock a 2:50, the time Boston required for runners in Rick's twenty-to-twenty-nine age group (even though Dick, who was doing all the running, was forty-three and would have qualified with a 3:10). On a cold, rainy morning, they ran 2:45:30. They officially raced the Boston Marathon the following spring and have run all but one since, becoming two of the event's most popular participants. "They personify the race as much as the elite athletes do," says Fleming. "Besides being inspirational role models, they are also quintessential New England guys. The crowds love them."

In those early years, Judy proudly watched as Rick and Dick's celebrity grew with each Boston or with their first Hawaii Ironman in 1989. Her pride, though, faded as Dick began assuming more responsibilities for their son and, over time, supplanted Judy as Rick's primary caregiver. Rob, the Hoyts' middle son, says he can understand how Judy must have hurt. "I think my mother had a hard time with all the attention that my father got through running," says Rob, forty-two, who lives in Holyoke, Massachusetts. "The accolades seemed to come much thicker and faster for him than they had with her. She had been everything for Rick. My mother got a nonspeaking spastic quadriplegic through high school and then through college, and now that role was taken by my father, and in a much more public manner."

Judy's frustration and alienation culminated in 1992, when Dick and Rick completed a 45-day, 3,753-mile, bike-and-run trek across the United States. Her men's interest in running had morphed into a time-consuming obsession. After thirty-four years of marriage, she and Dick divorced in 1994.

After so many years, Dick tries not to dwell on what happened to the couple's marriage. "I know that Rick's and my involvement in running and racing was hard on Judy," he says. "First, because of all the attention that got put on me, and second, because, for all the time she spent around the sport, she never understood distance running — why Rick would want to spend all that time on the road, and why I would insist on going to bed at nine o'clock on a Saturday evening so I would be fresh to race the next morning."

Today, Judy lives in Union, Connecticut, just a few miles from Dick's house, but she avoids contact with him. She visits Rick once every three months or so, but no longer attends Dick and Rick's races. Her animosity toward Dick is still fresh. "I fear that Dick is going to drop dead some day in the middle of a marathon, and I just pray that Rick doesn't go down with him," she says one recent afternoon while sitting in her kitchen. "Why should Rick suffer more, and put himself at risk, just to please his father?"

It's just about noon as Dick pushes Rick through the parking garage of his apartment building and over to Rick's new van. Dick had shopped carefully and found the slightly used vehicle, with a working lift, at a dealer near his house. Dick lowers the lift, eases Rick on to it, and then works the lever. Staring into a private middle distance, Rick rises into the van. Dick snaps the chair's wheels into the locks on the van floor and fastens the shoulder belts so that Rick will ride securely.

Still not totally familiar with how the van maneuvers, Dick spends the next several minutes hassling it out of the garage; the customized raised roof clears the garage ceiling only by a few inches. He must back up and pull forward repeatedly to get past a car that is parked illegally in the exit lane. Once out of the garage, he retraces his route to the Mass. Pike and points the van west, back toward Holland. In the back Rick listens to NBA scores on the radio.

As they get close to home, Dick stops at a Greek pizza joint to pick up a couple of oven-baked grinders. The shop owner is a friend of Dick's, and with the sandwiches he sends along a flagon of homemade ouzo.

Once inside the house and settled in the kitchen, Dick sets the ouzo aside. He purées Rick's grinder in a food processor and then spoons it into his mouth. In between spoonfuls, Dick takes bites out of his own sandwich, and talks about what's planned for the year ahead. After the Boston Marathon, he explains, he'll begin serious training for the Hawaii Ironman in October. He and Rick are both eager to vindicate themselves after what happened in the 2003 race, when they wiped out at the eighty-five-mile mark of the bike leg.

"The last thing I remember, we were gliding into a water stop," Dick says. "I still don't know what happened. Most likely we skidded on an empty water bottle. Anyway, when I came to, we were both on the road, and blood was gushing from Rick's forehead. An ambulance took him to the emergency room. The doctors there were concerned because of all the blood and the fact that Rick was a quadriplegic. I kept telling them he was okay, but they insisted on taking fifty-two X-rays. Later, I got a bill from the hospital for $6,000. I refused to pay it, of course."

Hawaii, though, is still nine months away. As always at this time of year, the two are focusing on Boston. Rick and Dick prepare for the marathon by running several half-marathons from January through March. Because Dick trains solo during the week, typically running about eight miles a day, he relies on the half-marathons for building upper-body strength, and adjusting to pushing Rick and the wheelchair. He frets over the missed training.

"I've put on seven pounds since my knee operation," Dick says.

"I'm heavier now than I've been in years, although the weight should come off pretty quickly once I start running again." He frowns at his grinder. Watching what he eats isn't always easy, as much as he has tried since the heart attack.

Midway through a half-marathon in the winter of 2003, as he and Rick prepared for that year's Boston, Dick felt an unfamiliar tickling sensation in his throat, along with an unusual build-up of saliva. The sensation passed, and they finished the race without difficulty. But the phenomenon recurred at races over the next few weeks. Dick consulted his doctor, who administered an EKG.

"A day later I'm driving to my gym when my cell phone rings," Dick recalls. "It's my doctor. She asks me, 'Where you going?' I tell her, 'I'm going to work out.' She says, 'No you're not. You're coming straight to the hospital for a stress test. The EKG showed that you had a heart attack.' My problem is strictly hereditary — high cholesterol. She said that if I wasn't in such good shape, I'd probably be dead by now." The stress test indicated he needed an angioplasty. That procedure was done just days before the Boston Marathon, and meant Team Hoyt would miss the race for the first time in twenty-two years.

While Dick tells the story, Rick listens intently. His eyes flicker and his right arm jerks in a slow, almost graceful fashion.

Word got out about Dick's heart attack, and then he began getting calls from around the country from people offering to push Rick in his place. One running club offered to bring in twenty-six people, and each would push the chair for a mile. "They said they would consider it an honor," Dick says. "I left the decision up to Rick. He said no. Team Hoyt was exactly that, a team. We would run, or not run, together."

Rick's decision echoed one his father had made many times before. Shortly after the pair began running — as soon as Dick's vast latent talent for the sport manifested — people suggested that he should launch a concurrent solo career. If Dick ran so fast pushing a 140-pound load, the reasoning went, imagine what he could do unencumbered. But Dick declined to compete without his son. "The only reason I race is Rick," he says. "I've got no desire to do this on my own."

Dave McGillivray, the race director of the Boston Marathon and a close friend of the Hoyts, thought that if Dick had competed solo, he could have become a world-class age-group runner. In fact, it was McGillivray who first suggested that Dick try triathlons. "Maybe Dick has been fooling us all these years," McGillivray says. "Maybe Rick has been his big advantage, and not his handicap. Look at Dick's stride when he's pushing the chair — it's amazingly clean, he's doing a minimum of pounding, and with both hands on the chair he's always well balanced. He's always leaning forward, even when he's climbing a hill. Of course, he's also pushing 140 pounds. If there were a real competitive advantage, you'd see hundreds of guys in marathons pushing baby joggers. But you don't see that. In fact, after twenty-five years, and all the publicity, only a few have ever tried."

And that's okay, because watching the Hoyts roll down Commonwealth Avenue in the final mile of the Boston Marathon can be a near mystical experience. The roars of the spectators reverberate off the brick buildings and swell behind the two men like a following wind. Dick bears down and begins to sprint. Rick writhes and jerks ecstatically, the screams of his fans shooting through him.

The event in Hopkinton in early January demonstrated the intense emotional bond that the Hoyts have forged with their fans. A local newspaper had gotten wind of their recent difficulties — Dick's knee surgery, the tree coming through the roof, Rick's van breaking down — and ran a story that seemed to suggest that the two had fallen on hard times. The Hopkinton Athletic Association started a funding drive and hundreds of people from around the country sent in checks — a poor old lady didn't buy a Christmas tree so she could send a few dollars, and an anonymous wealthy donor contributed $50,000.

When Dick learned about the size of the gift, his first impulse was to refuse it or funnel it into his Easter Seals drive. But ultimately, given the need for a new van and other things for Rick, he accepted the association's check for $90,000 and the accolades that came with it. He and Rick had sat quietly on the stage of the school auditorium and patiently listened to a series of speakers. There were tears and testimonials. The Hoyts were made honorary citizens of Hopkinton. A state senator read a proclamation. Bob Lobel, a popular Boston sportscaster, called Dick and Rick the greatest athletes in Boston over the last thirty years, greater than any of the Red Sox, Celtics, Patriots, or Bruins. "Rick and Dick are originals," Lobel told the crowd. "We will never see their likes again."

Twenty-four Bostons have passed. How many more are really likely?

"I can understand why people always wonder when I'm going to quit," Dick says, finally willing to offer more on this subject. "It's a natural question to ask a man my age. But I can honestly say that stopping never crossed my mind. And I know Rick feels the same way. What keeps us going is that we see how much good we're doing, and not just for disabled people. We have inspired a lot of able-bodied people to start running or try some other kind of exercise."

Like the Austin insurance executive who heard Dick speak at a company sales meeting. His talk on overcoming obstacles, whether physical or mental, so inspired her that she used not just his message but Dick himself to fight through a long marathon training run. "I've been sitting here brainstorming the past week and trying to come up with a way to show how much your presentation meant to all of us, not only in our professional lives, but personally," she later wrote Dick. "When I was running my longest prerace run, twenty-two miles, Saturday after the meeting, I kept picturing your face, and it truly helped keep me going." There are other stories like this, too many to count.

After finishing lunch, Dick wheels Rick into the living room and places him in his favorite spot by the bay window, where he can look out over the sloping lawn to the edge of Hamilton Reservoir. His father hooks him up to the computer and headpiece equipped with a mouse that rests just behind his right temple. Now it's Rick's turn to answer questions.

Letters appear on a small screen at Rick's eye level. He twitches his head to move the cursor through the letters, double-twitching when he wants to select one. Each twitch requires a concentrated effort. As he works, his arm waves spasmodically, occasionally getting caught in the computer wires.

He is asked, "Do you ever have a bad race?"

Rick considers for several moments, then sets to work. He scans down the letters, each twitch of his head accompanied by a small electronic beep, like a bird chirping. *Y*, he types. Then, three minutes later, *E*, and, after a similar interval, *S*.

The next question comes, but Rick isn't finished with the first one. *W* . . . three minutes . . . *H* . . . three minutes . . . *E* . . . three minutes, and so on for a half-hour. Rick communicates no sense of frustration or impatience. *"Yes, when the weather is too cold . . ."* finally appears on the screen. The reply is read aloud, but Rick still isn't finished. The twitches and chirps continue. And then the full reply sounds through the voice synthesizer. "Yes," the disembodied electronic voice says after several more long minutes, "when the weather is too cold and the women are too covered up."

Rick laughs, his face twisting into a grin, his shoulders shaking. Forty-five minutes after the first question, the next one comes.

"Do you ever regard running as an unhealthy obsession? Do you ever think you should stop or cut back?"

"No. By running we are actually educating the public."

"Do you think that not being able to speak gives you a special insight into people?"

"Yes. I understand them not in terms of running, but as far as general life."

"What do you do when you feel down or depressed?"

"I just think about the poor people in the world."

The final, two-part question comes as dusk falls and Rick's father quietly enters the room to turn on a lamp. Three hours have passed since the Q&A started, roughly how long it takes Team Hoyt to run a marathon.

"Was fate at work at the time of your birth, and on that day nearly thirty years ago when you told your parents that you wanted to run? And do you think fate chose you to live such a confined life, but also one so free?"

Rick doesn't need the computer to answer this one. His face lights up. His whole body says yes.

PAUL CULLUM

The Big Show by Little People

FROM THE LOS ANGELES TIMES MAGAZINE

It sounds Fellini-esque, but there is a universal truth at the core of this story, the same for the little cowboys as for any writer: they do it because it's a living.
— D.M.

WHAT WONDERS ARE CONJURED, what rough magic promised by the phrase "Mexican Midget Rodeo"? Let us pause to savor that more slowly: Mexican . . . Midget . . . Rodeo. That is to say, a touring troupe of little people, renowned in their native land but unheralded in our own, who face off against their equally diminutive bovine counterparts to ensuing mayhem.

At one such micro-spectacle staged several years ago at the Pico Rivera Sports Arena, deep in the sequined heart of southeastern Los Angeles, these genial ambassadors of human pathology, just by showing up for work in the morning, accomplished nothing short of a secular miracle. In one brief cultural elision, they managed to bring together an audience of Latino locals inured to that special strain of humor found on Spanish-language cable — men in bee costumes, baby diapers, and so on — and drunken Anglos who saw the afternoon as something akin to dwarf tossing with a spicy flavor. And who's to say they were wrong? In the simple act of attending an ecumenical carnival, our warring tribes were reunited, the neural clash of our Meltingpotamian origins quelled and the lurking schizophrenia of cultural miscegenation momentarily tamed — all through our common fear of and fascination with "the Other."

Now that very troupe is said to be planning its triumphal return to Pico Rivera this summer. For anyone who thinks of Los Angeles as a video mash-up of *The Day of the Locust* and *Freaks,* look no further: here is empirical proof.

I first got wind of this dust-choked pageant from a poster in the Ranch Market, the meat emporium at Sunset and Western where they sell hamburger for $1.85 a pound and I try not to ask questions. Above a giant photo of an *escaramuza* team, recalling the distaff equestrian display in the film *Y tu Mamá También,* was a notice for the "3rd Festival Charro de Independencia," a Mexican Independence Day rodeo. Amid a long afternoon of singers, mariachis, and comedians, there would appear the legendary Enanitos Toreros — the midget bullfighters of Mexico — like Sasquatch or Nessie, long-rumored in these parts, yet unsubstantiated. "La Entrada es Gratis! Gratis!" the poster gushed.

Bursting with intrepid zeal, I set out on the hourlong drive through East L.A. Yet arriving at Pico Rivera, off the 605 just west of Whittier, I was distressed to learn that *entrada* to the sports arena required a special ticket — and was certainly not "Gratis! Gratis!" by any stretch of the imagination. As I was kept waiting for forty-five minutes in the pitiless southern California sun, giant humorless gentlemen with walkie-talkies amply demonstrated the folly of attempting subterfuge in a second language, even as they allowed large families all the *entrada* they wanted.

Eventually, I was escorted to the office of Leo and Fernando Lopez, whose La Noria Entertainment manages the arena. Leonardo, the patriarch of the family business, had been a concert and rodeo promoter for more than three decades, yet he graciously allowed his son Fernando to set the agenda and do most of the talking.

"This is the Staples Center of Mexico," Fernando said. His family had booked Los Enanitos Toreros here for the last three years, and he agreed that between *Fear Factor* and extreme sports, their stature may indeed have been, well, growing. "They have a miniature bull," he lectured. "It's bred from one of those huge bulls they have in Spain that run in Pamplona, but it's miniature. It has the same blood and the same anger, and it goes out there mad. At the shows in Mexico, they have everything back there — ponies, little motorcycles. Today, they just brought the miniature bull and all their costumes and everything. But you're going to get a kick out of it. It's a hilarious show."

Leonardo looked on from one side, smiling. "A lot of white people come," he said. "It's good to see them."

And in fact, thanks to a promotion by an L.A. radio station, a small but vocal minority of Anglos had made the pilgrimage that day, although their focus appeared to be limited. An on-air personality with a big burnished-chrome voice had run a live mic over to the corner of the stadium where his raucous drive-time demographic was ensconced, and they seemed thrilled at the prospect of the broadcast media straying beyond consensus boundaries of comportment and taste. This created an odd dynamic, as dueling announcers attempted to commandeer the proceedings and work their respective crowds. I could only assume that the Spanish-language commentator made use of a shared history and cultural identity to narrate the feats of strength and cunning before us. The gringo, by contrast, waited a few minutes into each new act to lead a spontaneous chant of "Mid-gets! Mid-gets!"

But soon, such observations were rendered trivial, as I learned I'd been granted an audience with the little people. I was led through concrete corridors and cattle chutes to a small cinder-block dressing room where half a dozen athletic gentlemen between three and four feet tall — some with proper proportions, some with prominent heads and truncated limbs — struggled into tiny toreador pants and bolero jackets. There has been some controversy over the terms "midgets," "dwarfs," and "little people" (the preferred designation, according to their domestic lobby and appreciation society, the Little People of America), with each phasing in and out of fashion over the course of modern history. I vowed to resolve this and other controversies, and to document the will, stamina, and character required of this assembled crew to face their daily challenge.

Problem was — and I don't know why this hadn't occurred to me on the long drive out — they didn't speak a lick of *Inglés*. These gentlemen, while appearing affable and eager to please, as the entertainment arts dictate, didn't have a clue as to what I was asking them, and there was no one free to translate. From my observations, the performers fell into specialized categories: The bullfighters appeared to be in their twenties and in prime physical shape, although age among little people is deceptive. There were the actors — the show included a mock-Chippendale's number and a comedy skit involving a giant inflatable bottle of Corona — who overlapped with the bullfighters, although a hierarchy began to emerge, with the front line in the mad-cow bulwark perhaps better termed "fresh meat." From our limited back-and-forth, I could also glean that the bullfights would be done Portuguese style, i.e., the bull would be allowed to live (perhaps for fiscal as much as sentimental reasons), and that there is a rich heritage of midget rodeos throughout Spain, Mexico, and Central and South America. This troupe, Los Internacionales Enanitos Toreros de Aguascalientes, was apparently the first to tour the United States.

Later, distilling these findings into a coherent thesis, I decided it would not be an outright breach of my professional duties to perform a quick survey of the phenomenon on the Internet. Here I learned, for instance, that the Mexican Midget Rodeo tradition (according to documentary videotape) might feature flaming go-carts, female midgets — hot female midgets — dancing to "Baby Got Back," and, on occasion, a midget bullfighter being mounted by a vindictive bull. Through the use of a Spanish-to-English translation generator on the Los Enanitos Toreros de Torreon site, I was further able to determine the following:

"For more than 20 years, the Spectacle of the Enanitos Bull-fighters of Tower has been characterized for being an amusing and healthy event of entertainment designed for all the public, but with emphasis on it children and girls. . . . The show has evolved with the step of the years, being returned more elaborate and with better characteristics than it have added emotion and admiration on the part of the assistants. Nevertheless, the main elements of the spectacle continue being the Laughter and the Healthy Diversion." In conclusion, the website assured, "whether facing to brave bulls, amusing bullfighting tasks, carrying out corrupt lucks and of American detour, performing daring acrobacias or representing the artists of the moment, the Enanitos Bullfighters of Tower continue being the Number One."

But all of that paled before the spectacle itself, which indeed began with the gray-felt-skirted, broad-sombreroed women of the *escaramuza* (Spanish for "skirmish"), a competitive trick-riding sport akin to an elaborate equestrian ballet or Busby Berkeley choreography. As a palate cleanser between acts, a figure in a yellow chicken suit threw candy into the stands, the assembled children following him back and forth in tight arcs like a roulette ball being gamed by a croupier.

Suddenly the midgets took the field, wearing modified Dalmatian-print jumpsuits of the kind favored by male strippers, with their considerable guts jiggling. "Man tits! Man tits!" chanted the gringo parishioners, led by their on-air spiritual adviser. The midgets quickly stripped down to tiny pink Speedos, the contents of which briefly silenced their newfound fan base. This was followed by skits, musical numbers, musical numbers in drag, more synchronized stripping, and a host of jokes that left one quadrant of the audience notably mystified. Eventually, they released the bull, or whatever they were calling it. It wasn't really a bull — it teetered on spindly legs, and you could count its ribs from the upper deck — but it was a fair-sized calf, with six-inch horns and a problem disposition.

One by one, the mini-Manoletes engaged the baby bull in ritual public humiliation: roping and riding it backward, dancing with it upright, crawling underneath it (it summarily peed on them), and taunting it with a bright red capelet. After one or two good passes, the bull knocked down one of the *matadoritos*, and then, to add insult to injury, stood on his capelet. Two makeshift picadors swept in from the sides and diverted the would-be bull's attention with the aid of plastic hammers. I was put in mind of my favorite capsule review from Leonard Maltin's eponymous movie guide, for the David Cronenberg horror film *The Brood*: "[Samantha] Eggar eats her own afterbirth while midget clones beat grandparents and lovely young schoolteachers to death with mallets. It's a big, wide, wonderful world we live in."

Following each altercation, another midget limped from the arena, and the field risked disappearing through sheer attrition. Finally, one last defender unsheathed a plastic sword and squared off against the cartoon bull, now snorting and pawing the ground, expelling cartoon steam from its nostrils. For his trouble, he was butted a third of the way across the arena before being flipped over the bull's head. He called it off then and there and was rescued by one of the *charros*, the full-size career cowboys on horseback. This effectively ended the competition. Final score: Bull 6, Midgets 0.

What is the enduring appeal of the Mexican Midget Rodeo? Is it the outré, the extreme, the Other, marshaled in traditional contests of skill and daring? A parody of an insular macho culture, nurtured from within? The simulacrum of defenseless children thrust into unspeakable danger, as we sit and smile helplessly? Or is it something deeper, primal, the stuff of myth and fairy tales — Rumpelstiltskin assailing the Cretan Minotaur, Taurus the bull engaging the Lollipop Guild, leprechauns at the Augean stables impeding the twelve labors of Hercules? And if such spectacles are predicated on our fears, then why would these participants sanction them, validating them with their presence?

Such suppositions are raised in the incubator of privilege. They do it because it's a living.

And so I find myself winging south of the border toward Aguascalientes, Mexico, capital city of the state of Aguascalientes, where Los Enanitos Toreros live, work, train, love, and no doubt try to avoid just these sorts of intrusions, to find out what constitutes ordinary life for these figures of legend.

We meet at the impressive multi-tiered bullfighting ring that anchors one end of the Plaza de Toros San Marcos, the promenade of colonial architecture that dominates the center of this dusty city of nearly one million people. Beneath a statue of famed matador Fermín "Armillita" Espinosa, who trained future film director Budd Boetticher in the art of the Veronica and doubled for Tyrone Power in *Blood and Sand*, I am introduced to manager Alfredo Rocha, a translator, and seven of the eight working members of the troupe — five men and two women, ranging in age from nineteen to forty, all dressed in identical red T-shirts.

After a brief tour of the ring, replete with on-site infirmary and chapel — a contingency plan for both before and after — we pile into a van and drive several blocks to El Cortijo (The Farmhouse), a bar and restaurant frequented by the bullfighting crowd — or as the proprietor takes pains to elaborate, "the bar for bullfighters to make party." Out back is a private patio and a small bullring where the troupe practices, and where they will later insist on staging a minor exhibition as a gesture of hospitality for the distance I've traveled. But for now, with the morning light refracted through the colored glass set into the stone walls of the open-air cantina, an enormous cauldron of paella simmering in one corner, they gather over chilled orange sodas to try to articulate what it's like to be them.

Juan Lopez is the ranking elder, trained in all parts of the show — bullfighting, impersonations, comedy skits. He started as a clown in a children's circus at twenty-five and has been with the

Aguascalientes troupe, one of a handful operating in Mexico, since its inception in 1991. He appears sanguine about the attention, but admits that it comes at a price.

"When we do the shows, people come down afterward and want to take pictures with us," he says. "They're excited to see us. But outside the show, if we're walking down the street, for example, they might cross the street to avoid us. We get ridiculed by kids who have never seen someone like us — we look like them, but we're older. And the parents maybe even encourage them to make fun of us. 'Hey, look at the little midget.' It hurts when people do that."

"There are more of us now, so people don't look at us as much as they used to," adds Tomás "Tommy" Emmanuel, the barrel-chested master of ceremonies who also emcees local wrestling matches and once wrestled under the name "the Little Savage." "When someone does offend me, instead of getting mad, I try to explain to them how we feel. I tell them we're not just little people that they see on TV or in shows, and that the myths surrounding little people aren't true — even the silly ones, like we eat people, or eat each other."

Hector Miguel (aka "Chiquito"), Ricardo Reyes, and Audelio Miranda are known as the three bullfighters and seem to be in the best shape, although none of them claims to work out.

"It's genetic that we're like this," says Audelio. "We don't do much in terms of training."

"We just eat and sleep," says Erika Amescua-Flores, Audelio's wife. Erika is one of two female members of the troupe, along with Elizabeth Medina, both of whom perform impersonations of famous singers such as Ana Bárbara and Thalia.

The eighth member, José Chipa, will join us late from his second job at an orange juice concentrate cannery. About half the troupe carry a second job: Juan works at a restaurant, Ricardo stocks shelves at the Super XX grocery, and Audelio occasionally moonlights as a mechanic and electrician.

"At first, I lacked confidence," says Audelio, when pressed on his experiences. "I couldn't even look at my own kind. I was ashamed. They disgusted me. . . . I still don't like midgets, but I'm not ashamed of being one now. They've got a lot of attitude, and they're difficult to deal with. There's always some kind of drama happening. They're eccentric. Stubborn. They just seem to have a lot more problems to deal with."

"We're not all the same just because we're little people," counters Tommy. "It depends on how we were raised. Some of us aren't happy; some of us are happy all the time. We have good days and we have bad days. But it's not because we're little people."

For José, who has a family to support, the rodeo has provided security and even a certain stature, and he doesn't have ambitions beyond it. But most of the others still hold on to larger dreams. Ricardo would like to be a doctor. Juan would like to have his own restaurant. Audelio might return to being a mechanic full-time. Tommy is content in his career, but would like to have a family.

"I'd also like to have a family," says Elizabeth. "But I'd like to put on my own show."

"I'd like to be a teacher," says Erika. "As long as they were small kids."

Suddenly, trumpets ring out over the patio's loudspeakers. This is "Los Gallos" ("The Cockfight"), the mariachi ballad and official bullfighting theme of Aguascalientes. As we collectively make hardly a dent in the surfeit of paella, Alfredo and his helpers try to coax two recalcitrant bulls out of a trailer and their inimical adolescent funk and into the open arena. As they pass through chutes as confining as the streets of Pamplona, they dig in every few feet. At one point, a bull reverses field and makes a sudden rush for the backstage holding pen, narrowly missing one of the *charros*, who is just then relieving himself, scaring the . . . well, let's say suitably alarming him, much to the delight of a couple on the balcony just overhead.

Los Enanitos perform their stock moves, going through the motions yet again, until finally one bull wanders back into the holding pen and the other apparently goes dormant, standing immobile across the arena for a good ten minutes. I lean against the wood slats of the arena wall, arms resting on the eight-inch banister that serves as a makeshift countertop for a notebook and half-eaten plate of paella.

"The strength is in the neck," Audelio is explaining to me. "The legs are tiny, but the shoulders and neck are where all the power is."

As he moves to demonstrate, I see a blur over his left shoulder. The look on my face causes Audelio to spin around and, in the same motion, to step sideways into a foot-wide enclosure built into the arena wall for just this sort of eventuality. With no backup plan of its own, 140 pounds of infuriated veal slams headfirst into the wall I'm leaning on. I suddenly feel like a human tuning fork, as my bones and teeth absorb the shock wave of mass times speed. I am covered in a light mist of paella, and everything moves in excruciatingly slow motion, like something out of — well, out of *Raging Bull.* And I am finally granted the one clear revelation I came all this way to find:

Whatever these people are being paid, it's not enough.

BILL BUFORD

Talking Turkey

FROM THE NEW YORKER

> What starts with a white raccoon ends with a wild turkey. When you get
> down to the last line, that's how I felt about all of these stories.
> — D.M.

JOE HUTTO, who is sixty-one, has spent most of his waking life looking at wild turkeys. He may have looked at more of them than any
other living American, with the "possible exception" of Lovett E.
Williams Jr., a wildlife biologist, and the bird's principal, and probably only, lifelong authority. Hutto is a trained wildlife biologist
too. He is an archaeologist as well. He has also managed a zoo in
Panama City ("heavy on the reptiles") and a ranch in Wyoming (a
thousand head of cattle) and been an elk-hunting guide, a competitive springboard diver, a dog handler (Labradors), a horse trainer,
a landscape painter, an antiquities scuba diver, and a venomous-
snake catcher (three dollars a foot for rattlers, a dollar for water
moccasins). But mainly he has been a student of the wild, especially
birds, and has come up with some surprisingly unconventional
ways of conducting his studies.

Thirteen years ago, Hutto, who was living near the Panhandle
coast of Florida, heard that a tractor-driver, clearing some land,
kept finding wild-turkey eggs. All his life, Hutto had wanted to raise
his own wild turkeys. The process — in which you convince newborn animals that you are their parent — is known as imprinting,
named by Konrad Lorenz in 1935, after he had raised greylag geese
from wild eggs. Many zoologists believe that it was through imprinting, or something like it, that societies took once wild animals, like
the wolf, and domesticated them into household pets, like the dog.

Hutto first applied the practice (without knowing it was a "practice") when he was ten years old, having come upon a baby squirrel, its eyes closed, and fed it with a nursing bottle. "You figure into the physiology of the brain of the animal — no longer a cute, furry thing in the woods but a creature with its own psychology and way of seeing the world." Since then, Hutto has raised hawks, coyotes, owls (three kinds), crows, rats ("one of earth's great generalists, like the cockroach, the coyote, and the human" — meaning that their diet and habitat are not locale-specific but can be virtually anything and that they are therefore capable of surviving almost anywhere), mice, rabbits, opossums, foxes ("no creature more intense, more deliberate, or more uncompromising"), bobcats, black bears ("I still haven't raised a grizzly," he lamented, although he was almost killed by grizzlies several times, having been unable to contain his curiosity whenever he came upon one and compulsively giving chase, oblivious that he was pursuing a female, say, and that the smaller versions running alongside were cubs), elk, a stump-tailed macaque, deer (four kinds), and monkeys. Recently, he raised wood ducks. He'd been walking through a park — Hutto has a home next to the St. Mark's National Wildlife Refuge, about thirty miles from Tallahassee — spotted a nest that had been exposed and crushed in a storm, and swooped the ducklings up in his arms. ("A highly illegal act — you don't steal animals from a game reserve, even if the mother isn't there. I just thought, *I will never have this opportunity again.*") At home, he put them in a wire cage and lay down on the ground next to it, perching his head on a corner. The ducklings had huddled, terrified, on the far side. He continued to stare, not moving. After thirty minutes, they started staring back. ("It was my eyes, they'd become aware of my eyes, and found in them whatever they needed.") Then, in a mysteriously spontaneous rush, they streaked across the cage and huddled up against his face: imprinting had started.

Hutto's wild-turkey flock began when he found sixteen eggs on his doorstep left by the tractor-driver. Hutto knew how difficult the eggs were to come by: hens, once impregnated, walk until they discover a site out of the way enough to make a nest and don't leave it unless aggressively chased off by a predator. Five days later, the driver left thirteen more eggs — all together, an astonishing bounty. For most of the next week, Hutto tended his stash, keeping it warm, talking to it (variations on "*yelp, yelp,*" to begin the imprinting process), until the poults were hatched. ("Poults" are chicks; "jakes" are young males; "gobblers," adult males.) Then he raised them. Effectively, Hutto turned himself into a turkey. He walked like one. He went up into a tree like one. He learned to hunt for bugs like one. Without instruments or recordings, he learned also to talk like one, modulating his vocal cords to match the complex, almost musical notes that now surrounded him. "A language of not just thirteen basic sounds that some experts had identified but many subdivisions within those categories of sound, a vocabulary of at least fifty different kinds of verbal instruction. I spoke to them and they, in turn, talked to me too."

When Hutto told me this, we were sitting at a handmade table in his home, a cabin he'd constructed from scratch three years ago, his fourth. ("I don't know why, but every few years I find myself having to build myself a new home" — Hutto has been married three times.) An image rose up in my mind of a bird version of Mister Ed, the talking horse. Joe Hutto acts like a normal man, but normal people don't talk to animals and understand their replies.

"Not long ago, I gave a reading at the Museum of Florida," Hutto explained. He had kept a field journal of his time with the turkeys and wrote it up as a book, *Illumination in the Flatwoods*, which was published eleven years ago. The book was scarcely noticed nationally, and is now out of print, but it made its author into a local celebrity. (On Amazon, used copies start at $99.43.) "It was a fundraiser attended by everyone in Tallahassee high society, very formal, very stuffy, and I was very uncomfortable. At the end, I was asked to make a turkey sound. I did. I looked up and saw that the whole room, these men in dark suits, the women with their perfume, was staring at me very intently. I thought, *I'm a clown.*" He looked at me plaintively. The look said, I know this seems crazy, but I really have conversations with wild turkeys.

I asked to see his turkey walk.

"No." My question pained him. "Please don't make me do this."

I stood up, hoping Hutto would join me (which he did eventually, and reluctantly demonstrated what amounted to an inconspicuous stroll, hands behind the back, done at the turkey's walking pace — the idea was not to be the bird as such, just not so obviously not one), and I found myself surveying his hand-built home, Smokey Bear browns and greens on the outside, cedar and hardwood floors within. The living room had a fireplace, with a nineteenth-century Appalachian rifle hanging above it and a round woven rug on the floor in front. On the facing wall were mounts of a mule deer and an elk. In the back, in Hutto's workroom, were massive black fossils — a mandible of a mastodon, the size of a tombstone; a fetal mammoth's tooth; a jaw of a piggy tapir: he'd pulled them out of the rivers nearby, along with hundreds of the spear points that had probably killed the animals. ("The mastodons and mammoths had no reason to die out. They're extinct because, ten thousand years ago, they were overhunted" — just as overhunting had almost eliminated the wild turkey.) There were arrowheads (hundreds), seventeenth-century Spanish clay pipes (the bowls still charcoal-blackened), hand-blown port bottles, "feather-edged china" (the ordinary plates of the early settlers), and drawers full of preserved birds, "study skins" — no bones, just skin and feathers. In fourth grade, Hutto had sent away for a mail-order taxidermy course and was still applying its lessons. ("When I study a bird, I long for a precise, anatomically perfect understanding of where every feather is.") I held a blue-winged teal in my hand and thought, This is the Hardy Boys. This is the stuff and paraphernalia of adventure stories. Hutto is the first man in his sixties whom I would describe as boyish. He has a teenager's mustache, no gray hair, delicate shoulders, a small frame, and a light step. He reminded me of an antelope. For him, the world is still a treasure hunt. He made me think of Daniel Boone. Maybe he could talk turkey after all.

The wild turkey is the most famous indigenous fowl of North America. You can now find it, or one of its domesticated descendants, just about anywhere on the globe — the bird, which reproduces reliably and plentifully, is another "generalist," able to survive in almost all conditions — but it originated on our continent about twenty million years ago, according to Hutto, and has evolved into five different kinds, each corresponding to the region it comes from: Eastern, Florida, Rio Grande (Texas), Merriam's (the West), and the Mexican, usually called a Gould's, after the zoologist who first studied it. The turkey eaten at the first Thanksgiving, in 1621, in Plymouth, Massachusetts, would have been a wild one of the Eastern variety — if a turkey was actually eaten. The evidence is famously meager: a letter written on December 11 of that year by Edward Winslow, which was later included in his "Journal of the Pilgrims at Plymouth," and a history written by William Bradford, the governor of the colony. Bradford mentions wild turkeys; Winslow does not. Bradford was probably writing twenty years later, whereas Winslow's letter was probably two months after the event. (It is now accepted that a three-day outdoor feast, with 150 people, was never held in stark, leafless late-November New England: if it's too cold for baseball, it's not warm enough for a picnic and a pajama party.)

According to Winslow's letter, the original Thanksgiving included a week's worth of "fowl" and five deer. A wild turkey could have been among the fowl, except there is no mention of turkeys anywhere else in the Pilgrim journal. This is curious, because there were plenty of them about (turkeys were among the first animals noticed by William Hilton, a passenger on the *Fortune*, which arrived in November of that year), and because Winslow loved his birds. Days after he arrived, on November 16, 1620, he (or his cowriter, the journal sometimes seeming to be a collaborative effort) notes six partridges, plus geese and ducks. Two days later, he and his company bag three geese and six ducks. Soon afterward, he gets some more. In fact, I don't believe there was a bird shot in Plymouth or its environs that Winslow doesn't report on. February is a veritable feast: not only a fat goose but a fat crane as well. And this should make historians pause: a crane? The crane is a migratory bird. There were no *fat* cranes in Massachusetts in February. This was almost certainly a turkey, but Winslow — the country's primary witness to its sole national feast — had no idea what one looked like.

He was not alone. Most Europeans were confused by the turkey and understood only that it was one of several big, foreign-looking birds — guinea hens, peacocks, even cranes — and the word for one was often used interchangeably for the others. (*Pavo*, Spanish for turkey, meant "peacock," and throughout the sixteenth century, in England, a turkey-cock and a guinea-cock clearly refer to the same thing, whatever it was.) The mystery is why English settled on the word "turkey" for an animal that came not from the East but from the very far West. The answer might be in why Italian did the same, not with a North American bird but with a North American grain. Corn, sold in Venice at about the same time, was called *granturco*, a "Turkish grain." (Inexplicably, it still is.) In the sixteenth century, fashionable foods weren't from the New World (it would take a hundred years before Italians accepted that a tomato wasn't poisonous) but from the outreaches of the Ottoman Turkish Empire. To call something Turkish meant just that: a very faraway exotic thing.

In fact, the turkey had come from Mexico, conveyed to Europe no later than 1521, probably by Cortes, who had been introduced to it by the Aztecs, who had been domesticating it for centuries, probably by Joe Hutto's method of imprinting, followed by an accelerated version of Darwin's — a kind of unnatural selection. With each new hatching, you pick out the birds with the qualities you want to see more of (feather color, say, or meat quality, or temperament), and they become your breeders. The rest you eat. The process doesn't take very long. "There is enormous variation even in one flock of wild turkeys," Hutto told me. "The species is easy to manipulate." It was a kind of manipulation that English farmers excelled at.

The turkey arrived in England some time during the reign of Henry VIII, and by the mid-sixteenth century was being widely bred, especially in East Anglia, a barren, windswept, flat land, distinguished by its open sky and its miserable damp climate and its modest agriculture — beets, cabbage, and eels were regional delicacies. (The turkeys, being turkeys, thrived.) Within a generation, the bird had become a feature of the English diet. Shakespeare's plays have turkey jokes in them, and around the same time a ditty commemorated the century's radical changes:

> Turkey, Carps, Hoppes, Piccarel, and Beer,
> Came into England all in one year.

Many of today's so-called heritage breeds, like the Norfolk Black (or the various Whites and Bronzes), hark from this time, having been introduced to the United States from abroad. The turkey might be an all-American bird, but the one on your Thanksgiving table is almost certainly descended from Europe. What mystifies me is why people now buy these heritage birds, for as much as ten dollars a pound. Do they believe they're getting the real thing?

On my second day with Hutto, I accompanied him into the flatwoods in the late afternoon, hoping to come across some wild turkeys. We saw none. Turkeys walk fast, in unpredictable directions, roam for miles, and can be, therefore, very hard to come upon. Unless you're not looking for them, and then you see them all the time, of course, something that New England residents have recently observed. Sixty years ago, the bird was almost extinct: there were none in New York State; now there are a hundred thousand. No one is quite sure where they've come from, but the belief is that they crossed the state line from Pennsylvania, where zoologists have been reintroducing them since the forties. But, like Edward Winslow, many people still have trouble identifying the bird, which is nothing like the domesticated version: more reptile than fowl, with what looks like a hard shellacked black coat, a long unmodern neck, and an ugly pockmarked head. (A pediatrician of my acquaintance had to resort to the label of a famous bourbon to confirm the nature of the beast he'd discovered one day near his home.)

On my fourth day, Hutto proposed trying again after the sun came up. "I promise we'll see birds." The normal practice is to get out before dawn, in the vicinity of where you believe the turkeys may have roosted for the night (they sleep in trees), hoping that in the morning they'll land near where you're hiding. But Hutto intended to visit a meadow where they'd be feeding. "Let's get there after they arrive."

It was a sandy mile from his home, through vines and Spanish moss, longleaf pines and thick palmetto. We passed several ponds, including one with a floating island, where Hutto had found orchids and carnivorous plants. As we walked, he casually identified every piece of vegetation — "I know the name of everything that grows here" — not an unpleasant expertise to witness: I came away with a sense that there was an order in an environment that seemed otherwise crowded and overgrown and impenetrable. This was a peculiar corner of America, backed up into a steamy corner of the Gulf, largely untouched by developers. It was humid and hot, ponderously tropical ("a land that loves to be wet"), and I found myself feeling an abstract interconnectedness: the fossils, the memory of mammoths, estuaries everywhere, the history of hunters and gatherers, these elusive birds. In his book, Hutto describes the feeling, a hypnotic, heavy sense of harmony, everything coming together — insects, vegetation, animals — a bird snuggling up against him on a damp, oppressive afternoon. (He falls asleep, dreaming of Joseph Campbell, and misses the approach of a hawk, which swoops down and picks up a two-week-old poult, and, startled that its mother has a mustache, drops it, but not before it dies — the first predator-death in the flock.)

We reached the large meadow and looked out. There were no turkeys.

I was accustomed to not seeing them. I'd tried to hunt them. I'm not a good hunter. I started late, at thirty, an anti-hunter suddenly converted by the philosophic dictates of what I would now describe as my own private pantheism, newly armed, and dangerously venturing out by myself into a Florida hammock, several hours south of Hutto's refuge. I found no turkeys. I returned the following year, around Thanksgiving, determined to get a bird for a holiday supper, and this time saw one: a speck on the horizon, running away at an impressive speed. Finally, my third year, I spotted two jakes walking down a trail toward where I was hiding. I didn't move. I didn't breathe. But I'd got such an adrenaline rush at their appearance that my heart went crazy. It was so amped — for a second I feared coronary arrest — that I could hear nothing but its pounding. Evidently, the jakes heard it too, because they looked in my direction and were gone. ("A tiny flicker of motion fifty yards away gets their attention like a slap in the face," Hutto writes of his flock, astonished by a sensory ability that "borders on the supernatural" and regularly embarrassed by how dull and dumb he seems in comparison.)

The commonplace is that turkeys are ungainly, obese, slow, so stupid they raise their heads to drink when it rains and then drown. Hutto acknowledges the commonplace but insists that these qualities do not characterize wild birds, although you may see a lethargic stupor among the industrial domesticated ones: now, after four and a half centuries of unnatural selection, misshapen things, with pumped-up breasts and ineffectual legs, too fat and debilitated to reproduce naturally. (For years, the hens wore saddles and the toms were inserted in place; today, the hens are artificially inseminated.) These birds can still make for good eating, although the less industrial the better, and, in any case, no sensible person should ever seek out buttery beach balls or ones with pop-out red plastic timers. Even so, it was my knowledge of the turkey's historical disfigurement (starkly depicted by Karen Davis in *More Than a Meal* and on the website of United Poultry Concerns) that led me to take up hunting. If I eat meat, shouldn't I come face to face with killing an animal? And, if I'm going to eat an animal, shouldn't it be a healthy one that has lived in the wild?

In the spring, I attempted my first turkey call, a counter-intuitive piece of hunting logic: conventionally, predators surprise their prey — a pretty universal law. With a turkey, predators advertise their whereabouts and invite the prey to come on over. I went out early one morning, heavily camouflaged — shirt, trousers, hat, mask, gloves, not a millimeter of human flesh showing. Basically, I was dressed as a bush. I'd learned my lesson and wasn't about to blow my cover with a color that didn't look right in the woods. Turkeys respond powerfully to color, which Hutto discovered early on, by wearing a blue T-shirt during his first weeks with his poults. They concluded, therefore, that Hutto was blue. When he wore a different color, they went crazy, pecked at the shirt, and tried to remove it.

My turkey call was a piece of slate and a stick, which, when rubbed in circles, made a scrapy squeaky sound that was meant to imitate a hen yelping for a mate. I practiced a few times and listened: it was like fingernails on a chalkboard. No turkey was going to buy this. I entered the woods, not hopeful, and sat behind a big bush and considered the prospects: I was a big bush behind a big bush. I was trying to be invisible but noisy — that is, in a sexy, come-hither turkey kind of a way. I was not feeling confident. I was really not feeling sexy.

Scrape, scrape, scrape.

I waited. I repeated the sound. I waited. I repeated it again. Then I thought, *This is ridiculous.*

According to Hutto, only one sound drives turkeys away: the wrong call — a gobble, say, when they're expecting a yelp, or a yelp when they normally hear a *putt, putt.* (How could mine be anything but wrong?) Hutto's initial education in the language of turkeys included different ways of expressing alarm, the sound that would tell his flock to recognize a hawk or look for a snake. (Predators were Hutto's greatest concern, and he built a cage to protect his poults at night, but, once, put them in it during the day, and joined his wife, now his ex-wife, for a rare Sunday lunch, dashing "to the house, trying to ignore the pleading lost calls behind me." When he returned, the birds were in a corner: a gray rat snake had slipped in and an enormous lump in its midsection was preventing it from getting out again — the second predator-death in the flock.) Slowly, Hutto came to see that he could also tell the birds where to go, or what to look out for, or when to follow him home, until finally they reached a point where they had no "significant miscommunication." "I cannot distinguish all the subtle differences in the vocalizations," he writes, "but somehow the subtle meaning is conveyed to me." When the birds were surprised by a cottontail rabbit, for instance, they gathered around him for an explanation, and he told them to relax, it was just a bunny, which the birds found wholly unsatisfactory — what kind of answer is that? — and which they conveyed to him in no uncertain terms, making him feel "hopelessly obtuse." Later, a titmouse called out, Hutto responded, and engaged it in a conversation (being a "speaker of fluent titmouse"), and his turkeys got really irritated ("I see that all my companions seem to have little question marks over their heads"), and he had to stop.

I pressed on with my slate scratching, wondering how often I should be doing it (every five minutes? every five seconds?), recognizing the obvious — that I had no idea how a hen behaves — when I heard a deep slow trilling. A gobble. Lo and fucking behold. I peeked, ever so slowly, through the leaves of my bush and saw him. Whoa! A gobbler, puffed and tail spread, looking like the NBC logo. Wow! I'd called him in! I'd done it! What a gigantic freak of nature! But he was also too far away to shoot.

I repeated my scrape.

"*Gobble, gobble*," he replied. I was ecstatic; I wanted to call someone on my cell phone.

I scraped again. Come on, big fella. Come to Mommy.

"*Gobble, gobble*," he replied, charmingly. Even so, he wasn't moving.

Scrape, scrape. I was thinking how I'd prepare him (a very hot oven? slow-cooked? with foil?), never a good psychology. What's the saying? A bird in hand is worth two in the bush. But I was the bush, and had nothing in my hand, and was thinking about a dinner I hadn't caught.

"*Gobble, gobble.*"

He hadn't budged. He was talking to me, but I wasn't understanding what he was saying. (Probably "You sound like a hen but look like a bush, and I'm not coming an inch closer until you can show me that you're not a bush.")

Scrape, scrape.

"*Gobble, gobble.*" The exchange, my scraping, his gobbling, went on and on. The sun had just come up when we'd started; it was now blazing overhead. I was hot. Should I be playing hard to get? (I stopped; he walked away; I scraped; he came back.) Every now and then, I'd peek at him: still in four-color display — he wanted me — but he wasn't going to come and get me. I had to come out. How could I come out? I couldn't come out. But that's what I did: I stood up and stepped away from my bush. In an instant, he was gone: plumage tucked back under, puff gone, once again black and sleek, already a distant figure, sprinting, half a mile away, and not stopping anytime soon. "That bird," Hutto explained to me, "was an older gobbler. He'd lived through a spring. He'd learned doubt." And he'd understood himself much more than a younger jake: on the most elementary level, he knew he was a gobbler. Hutto then told me the story of Turkey Boy.

In Hutto's experiment, the aim was not to domesticate the birds but to raise them wild. They were always going to leave. When they were four months old, they showed their independence for the first time and decided not to return to the cage but flew up to the trees to spend the night. (Hutto called out to wish them good night; they answered.) But the birds, waiting for him in the morning, were ready to resume their daily routine together, foraging, eating berries and insects. (In his account, Hutto ceases to be a first-person observer. "We are fifteen now," he writes, summing up the numbers lost to predators and disease — "if I include myself.") Even so, the birds did not disobey him for another ten days — in itself an extraordinary achievement — when, disregarding his instructions, they walked too close to a house with dogs. ("I am very upset, actually in pain.")

They were now young adults, starting to separate according to gender, in anticipation of the mating season — which is also the hunting season. "That's when I worry," Hutto told me. "The jakes understand nothing. Their bodies are crazy with hormones. They're getting beaten up by older birds and don't know why, and they're so ready to be loved they believe everything." He feared that, answering to the calls of hunters, the jakes would be shot. Even today, Hutto goes out into the woods before the season starts and calls the jakes to him, leaping out at the last second and screaming, scaring the bejeebers out of the creatures. "I'm teaching them caution."

After the first year, all the turkeys had left, except one.

According to Hutto, Turkey Boy had become his best friend. "We were inseparable. I took advantage of every minute I could to be with him, because I knew he'd be dead soon." They had meals together, because Turkey Boy didn't recognize that Hutto was different, so whatever Hutto ate the turkey believed he was entitled to eat as well: Hutto's coffee, his turkey sandwich, his glass of wine. ("There would be a small deposit of gray sand in the bottom from Turkey Boy's gritty mouth.") Every day, they went into the woods, and Hutto found a log and rolled it over — so that Turkey Boy could eat the insects — and then he'd sit and wait for the bird to tell him things. "He'd hear stuff I couldn't hear. That there were turkeys coming in our direction, about a mile away. I'd be quiet and wait for them to appear. Or he'd hear a fox running down a creek and tell me to listen out for it. He could spot snakes, especially rattlers. It was as though he had X-ray vision."

But what was the relationship? In the turkey's eyes, was Hutto a man or a bird?

One day, in the early spring, Hutto was on his knees, struggling to pull out a root. He turned and noticed Turkey Boy: his head was engorged, and his plumage was swelling. "My behavior must have provoked him. I was on his level, on the ground, thrashing around." Hutto reached out his hand to comfort the bird, but it pecked him, drawing blood. Hutto got up to go inside, but the bird got to the door first and blocked his way. He eventually got inside. "I assumed the incident would pass." When he stepped out four hours later, the bird flew at his head. Hutto then understood: he was being seen as a rival. He thought he should simply surrender and be submissive — the attitude that male turkeys assume to concede their spot in a pecking order — and threw himself on the ground. The bird attacked his head, which Hutto tried to cover with his hands, shredding the skin. It didn't stop — "Turkey Boy's wrath was bottomless" — and Hutto got to his feet and sprinted for the door. The bird flew at him, stabbing him from behind, embedding his spurs into the muscles on either side of Hutto's spine. The next day, the bird was lying in wait and ambushed him, spurs aimed at his eye. Hutto had a problem. He broke off a heavy limb from a longleaf pine, squared off in front of the bird, and swung it like a baseball bat. He missed, lost his footing, and fell. The bird beat him up. Hutto got to his feet and swung again, hitting the bird squarely on the head. The bird looked at Hutto, turned, and ran. ("I was sick. My heart was broken.") It returned the next day, ready to resume the fight.

On the last morning of my visit, Hutto suggested we drive out to the sea. "There are always turkeys there. I'm sure we'll see some."

We drove to the town of Panacea and followed dirt roads until there was nowhere else to go, a characteristically impenetrable forest, thick hammock on both sides of us that suddenly opened out onto a vast, undisturbed estuary, shaped like so many fingers poking into the continent, two big hands in rubbery shiny gloves. We had a panoramic view. The water seemed to be boiling — with shrimp and red fish, wood storks and egrets, a thoroughfare of wildlife, unspoiled. But there were no turkeys.

Contributors' Notes

CHRIS BALLARD is a senior writer at *Sports Illustrated*. He is the author of two books, *Hoops Nation: A Guide to America's Best Pickup Basketball* and *The Butterfly Hunter: Adventures of People Who Found Their True Calling Way Off the Beaten Path*, and he has contributed features to the *New York Times Magazine*, among other publications. He graduated from Pomona College in Los Angeles, where he played both briefly and poorly for the basketball team, and now lives in Berkeley, California.

JOHN BRANT is a writer at large for *Runner's World* and author of *Duel in the Sun: Alberto Salazar, Dick Beardsley, and America's Greatest Marathon*. A resident of Portland, Oregon, Brant is a frequent contributor to *Inc, Play*, and many other publications.

LARRY BROWN was born in 1951 in Lafayette County, Mississippi, where he lived all his life. At the age of thirty, as a captain in the Oxford Fire Department, he decided to become a writer and worked toward that goal for seven years before publishing his first book, *Facing the Music*, a collection of stories, in 1988. With the publication of his first novel, *Dirty Work*, he quit the fire department in order to write full-time. Between then and his death in 2004, at the age of fifty-three, he published seven more books, many of which are considered enduring classics of southern literature. A final novel, *A Miracle of Catfish*, was published posthumously in 2007. The handwritten manuscript for "The White Coon" was found among Brown's papers shortly after his death; according to his notes, it was written in 1982 and was his first attempt at writing nonfiction.

BILL BUFORD was born in Baton Rouge, Louisiana, grew up in California, and was educated at the University of California at Berkeley and at Kings

College, Cambridge, where he was awarded a Marshall Scholarship for his work on Shakespeare's plays and sonnets. A staff writer for *The New Yorker*, Buford was the founding editor of *Granta* magazine and the publisher of Granta Books. He is the author of *Among the Thugs*, an account of crowd violence and British soccer hooliganism, and *Heat: An Amateur's Adventures as Kitchen Slave, Line Cook, Pasta-Maker, and Apprentice to a Dante-Quoting Butcher in Tuscany*. He lives in New York City.

OSCAR CASARES is the author of *Brownsville*, a collection of short stories set along the U.S.-Mexico border. His fiction has appeared in *Threepenny Review, Iowa Review, Colorado Review*, and *Northwest Review*. He has received grants from the National Endowment for the Arts and the James A. Michener–Copernicus Society of America. He teaches at the University of Texas and is working on his first novel.

SARA CORBETT is the author of *Venus to the Hoop: A Gold Medal Year in Women's Basketball* and a contributing editor to the *New York Times Magazine*. Her work has also appeared in *Esquire, New York, GQ*, and *Elle*.

DANIEL COYLE is the author of *Hardball: A Season in the Projects*, the novel *Waking Samuel*, and *Lance Armstrong's War: One Man's Battle Against Fate, Fame, Love, Death, and a Few Other Rivals on the Road to the Tour de France*. He is a longtime contributing editor at *Outside* magazine.

PAUL CULLUM is a freelance writer and coauthor of *Ain't It Cool?: Hollywood's Redheaded Stepchild Speaks Out*. He has written about film and culture for the *New York Times, Variety, L.A. Weekly*, and many other publications. He lives in Los Angeles.

WILLIAM FINNEGAN lives in New York City, where he was born in 1952. He graduated from the University of California at Santa Cruz in 1974 and is a staff writer for *The New Yorker*. His books include *Crossing the Line: A Year in the Land of Apartheid, Dateline Soweto: Travels with Black South African Reporters, A Complicated War: The Harrowing of Mozambique*, and *Cold New World: Growing Up in a Harder Country*.

IAN FRAZIER grew up in Hudson, Ohio, and attended Harvard University, where he was on the staff of the *Harvard Lampoon*. After working briefly as a magazine writer in Chicago, he moved to New York City and joined the staff of *The New Yorker*. He is the author of nine books, including *Great Plains, On the Rez*, and *Gone to New York: Adventures in the City*.

STEVE FRIEDMAN is writer-at-large for the Rodale Sports Group, and his stories have been published in many national publications and anthologies. His third book, *The Agony of Victory*, will be published in October 2007. A St. Louis native and graduate of Stanford University, Friedman lives in New York City. This is his sixth appearance in *The Best American Sports Writing*.

BOB HOHLER is a sports enterprise reporter for the *Boston Globe*. He previously served as the *Globe*'s beat writer for the Boston Red Sox and chronicled the team's 2004 championship season. He joined the sports department from the *Globe*'s Washington bureau, where he covered government and politics, including President Clinton's impeachment saga. He joined the *Globe* in 1987, after writing for two New Hampshire papers, the *Concord Monitor* and *Monadnock Ledger*. Hohler was honored by the Associated Press Sports Editors for the nation's best investigative reporting in 2005. He is the author of *I Touch the Future . . . The Story of Christa McAuliffe*.

ROBERT HUBER, features editor at *Philadelphia Magazine*, is currently writing a novel about the fall of manhood. His profile of Joe DiMaggio Jr. appeared in *The Best American Sports Writing 2000*.

DAVE HYDE is a columnist at the *South Florida Sun-Sentinel* and author of *Still Perfect: The Untold Story of the 1972 Miami Dolphins*. A graduate of Miami (Ohio) University, he also has worked for the *Miami Herald* and the *Iowa City Press-Citizen*.

SALLY JENKINS is a columnist for the *Washington Post* and also wrote for *Sports Illustrated*. She is the author and coauthor of many books, including Lance Armstrong's autobiography, *It's Not About the Bike: My Journey Back to Life*, *Reach for the Summit* with basketball coach Pat Summitt, *Funny Cide: How a Horse, a Trainer, a Jockey, and a Bunch of High School Buddies Took on the Sheiks and Bluebloods . . . and Won* with the Funny Cide Team, and, most recently, *The Real All Americans*, about a Native American football team that had a lasting impact on the game.

JOHN KLIMA is the national baseball writer for the *Los Angeles Daily News* and the Los Angeles Newspaper Group. In 2007 he was honored for column writing by the Associated Press sports editors. He is a member of the Baseball Writers Association of America and the Society of American Baseball Research.

MICHAEL LEWIS is the author of *The New New Thing: A Silicon Valley Story*, *Liar's Poker: Rising Through the Wreckage on Wall Street*, *Moneyball: The Art of Winning an Unfair Game*, *Coach: Lessons on the Game of Life*, and *The Blind Side: Evolution of a Game*. In 2006 he served as guest editor for *The Best American Sports Writing*.

JEFF MACGREGOR is a special contributor to *Sports Illustrated* and the award-winning author of *Sunday Money: Speed! Lust! Madness! Death! A Hot Lap Around America with NASCAR.*

ERIC NEEL is a contributing editor for ESPN.com and a writer for *ESPN The Magazine.* His E-Ticket profile of John Wooden, "Forever Coach," received an Emmy Award nomination in 2006. He has a PhD from the University of Iowa (in another life he wrote a dissertation on James Baldwin, John Coltrane, Allen Ginsberg, and such . . .), but he learned to love language and stories listening to Vin Scully on a transistor radio in his grandfather's kitchen. He lives in southern California with his wife, Gwen, and daughter, Tess.

WILLIAM C. RHODEN is a sports columnist for the *New York Times.* He attended Morgan State University in Baltimore, where he played defensive back on the football team. Before joining the *Times* in 1983, he served as an associate editor of *Ebony* and as a columnist with the *Baltimore Sun.* He is the author of *$40 Million Slaves: The Rise, Fall, and Redemption of the Black Athlete* and *Third and a Mile: The Trials and Triumph of the Black Quarterback.*

ELI SASLOW is a staff writer for the *Washington Post,* specializing in enterprise stories about sports. A 2004 graduate of Syracuse University, he interned at the *Buffalo News* and the *Star-Ledger* (New Jersey) before joining the *Post.* He lives in Washington with his girlfriend.

BRYAN SMITH is a senior editor and the primary feature writer at *Chicago Magazine.* A 1989 graduate of the University of Maryland School of Journalism, he previously worked as a feature writer for the *Oregonian* and the *Chicago Sun-Times.* During his career, Smith has won numerous national writing honors, including gold medals in profiles and feature writing from the National City and Regional Magazine Association. He has twice been a finalist for Writer of the Year from the same group. In addition to *The Best American Sports Writing,* his work has been published in the book anthologies *Best Newspaper Writing* and *Chicken Soup for the Couple's Soul.* He has written several original features for *Reader's Digest,* among other magazines. Smith is an adjunct professor in the magazine writing program at Columbia College Chicago.

MIMI SWARTZ is an executive editor of *Texas Monthly* and the author, with Sherron Watkins, of *Power Failure: The Inside Story of the Collapse of Enron.* She has been a staff writer at both *Talk* and *The New Yorker.* Before that time, she worked at *Texas Monthly* for thirteen years. Swartz has been a finalist for two National Magazine Awards and won the 2006 John Bartlow Martin Award for Public Interest Magazine Journalism. Her work has appeared in *Vanity Fair, Esquire, Slate, National Geographic,* the

New York Times op-ed page, and the *New York Times Sunday Magazine*. She has been a member of the Texas Institute of Letters since 1994. Swartz grew up in San Antonio, Texas, and graduated from Hampshire College in Amherst, Massachusetts. She now lives in Houston with her husband, John Wilburn, and son, Sam.

WRIGHT THOMPSON is a senior writer for ESPN.com and *ESPN The Magazine*. He and his wife, Sonia, live in Oxford, Mississippi.

BRUCE WALLACE is the Tokyo bureau chief of the *Los Angeles Times*. He has been a foreign correspondent for sixteen years, originally for Canada's *Maclean's* magazine, covering events in Europe, the Middle East, and Asia, from the Gulf War to the Asian tsunami. Eight years living in London gave him an appreciation for English football to match his Canadian obsession with hockey, and he has always managed to sneak away from foreign news duties to write about sports. He has covered three Winter Olympics and has written about baseball and sumo from Japan. He wrote the story about the death of Iraqi soccer player Manar Mudhafer during a three-week reporting tour in Baghdad.

A senior writer at *Sports Illustrated*, L. JON WERTHEIM is making his third appearance in *The Best American Sports Writing*. Chris Hunt was his editor on each story. Wertheim is the author of the book *Running the Table*, an account of pool hustler Kid Delicious, and is currently working on a book about ultimate fighting. He lives in Manhattan with his wife and two children.

MICHAEL WILBON joined the *Washington Post* in 1980 as a general assignment sports reporter and since 1990 has been a full-time sports columnist. A native of Chicago, Wilbon was an original cohost for ESPN's *Pardon the Interruption* and has made numerous appearances on ESPN's *Sports Reporters* and other programs. He is coauthor, with Charles Barkley, of *I May Be Wrong but I Doubt It* and *Who's Afraid of a Large Black Man?*

DEREK ZUMSTEG is the author of *The Cheater's Guide to Baseball* and one of the coauthors at U.S.S. Mariner, the largest independent Seattle Mariners website. He lives with his wife in Seattle.

Notable Sports Writing of 2006

SELECTED BY GLENN STOUT

THE BEST AMERICAN SHORT STORIES® 2007. STEPHEN KING, editor, HEIDI PITLOR, series editor. This year's most beloved short fiction anthology is edited by Stephen King, author of sixty books, including *Misery, The Green Mile, Cell,* and *Lisey's Story,* as well as about four hundred short stories, including "The Man in the Black Suit," which won the O. Henry Prize in 1996. The collection features stories by Richard Russo, Alice Munro, William Gay, T. C. Boyle, Ann Beattie, and others.

ISBN-13: 978-0-618-71347-9 • ISBN-10: 0-618-71347-6 $28.00 CL
ISBN-13: 978-0-618-71348-6 • ISBN-10: 0-618-71348-4 $14.00 PA

THE BEST AMERICAN NONREQUIRED READING™ 2007. DAVE EGGERS, editor, introduction by SUFJAN STEVENS. This collection boasts the best in fiction, nonfiction, alternative comics, screenplays, blogs, and "anything else that defies categorization" (*USA Today*). With an introduction by singer-songwriter Sufjan Stevens, this volume features writing from Alison Bechdel, Scott Carrier, Miranda July, Lee Klein, Matthew Klam, and others.

ISBN-13: 978-0-618-90276-7 • ISBN-10: 0-618-90276-7 $28.00 CL
ISBN-13: 978-0-618-90281-1 • ISBN-10: 0-618-90281-3 $14.00 PA

THE BEST AMERICAN COMICS™ 2007. CHRIS WARE, editor, ANNE ELIZABETH MOORE, series editor. The newest addition to the Best American series — "A genuine salute to comics" (*Houston Chronicle*) — returns with a set of both established and up-and-coming contributors. Edited by Chris Ware, author of *Jimmy Corrigan: The Smartest Kid on Earth,* this volume features pieces by Lynda Barry, R. and Aline Crumb, David Heatley, Gilbert Hernandez, Adrian Tomine, Lauren Weinstein, and others.

ISBN-13: 978-0-618-71876-4 • ISBN-10: 0-618-71876-1 $22.00 CL

THE BEST AMERICAN ESSAYS® 2007. DAVID FOSTER WALLACE, editor, ROBERT ATWAN, series editor. Since 1986, *The Best American Essays* has gathered outstanding nonfiction writing, establishing itself as the premier anthology of its kind. Edited by the acclaimed writer David Foster Wallace, this year's collection brings together "witty, diverse" (*San Antonio Express-News*) essays from such contributors as Jo Ann Beard, Malcolm Gladwell, Louis Menand, and Molly Peacock.

ISBN-13: 978-0-618-70926-7 • ISBN-10: 0-618-70926-6 $28.00 CL
ISBN-13: 978-0-618-70927-4 • ISBN-10: 0-618-70927-4 $14.00 PA

THE BEST AMERICAN MYSTERY STORIES™ 2007. CARL HIAASEN, editor, OTTO PENZLER, series editor. This perennially popular anthology is sure to appeal to mystery fans of every variety. The 2007 volume, edited by best-selling novelist Carl Hiaasen, features both mystery veterans and new talents. Contributors include Lawrence Block, James Lee Burke, Louise Erdrich, David Means, and John Sandford.

ISBN-13: 978-0-618-81263-9 • ISBN-10: 0-618-81263-6 $28.00 CL
ISBN-13: 978-0-618-81265-3 • ISBN-10: 0-618-81265-2 $14.00 PA

THE B·E·S·T AMERICAN SERIES®

THE BEST AMERICAN SPORTS WRITING™ 2007. DAVID MARANISS, editor, GLENN STOUT, series editor. "An ongoing centerpiece for all sports collections" (*Booklist*), this series stands in high regard for its extraordinary sports writing and topnotch editors. This year David Maraniss, author of the critically acclaimed biography *Clemente*, brings together pieces by, among others, Michael Lewis, Ian Frazier, Bill Buford, Daniel Coyle, and Mimi Swartz.

ISBN-13: 978-0-618-75115-0 • ISBN-10: 0-618-75115-7 $28.00 CL
ISBN-13: 978-0-618-75116-7 • ISBN-10: 0-618-75116-5 $14.00 PA

THE BEST AMERICAN TRAVEL WRITING™ 2007. SUSAN ORLEAN, editor, JASON WILSON, series editor. Edited by Susan Orlean, staff writer for *The New Yorker* and author of *The Orchid Thief*, this year's collection, like its predecessors, is "a perfect mix of exotic locale and elegant prose" (*Publishers Weekly*) and includes pieces by Elizabeth Gilbert, Ann Patchett, David Halberstam, Peter Hessler, and others.

ISBN-13: 978-0-618-58217-4 • ISBN-10: 0-618-58217-7 $28.00 CL
ISBN-13: 978-0-618-58218-1 • ISBN-10: 0-618-58218-5 $14.00 PA

THE BEST AMERICAN SCIENCE AND NATURE WRITING™ 2007. RICHARD PRESTON, editor, TIM FOLGER, series editor. This year's collection of the finest science and nature writing is edited by Richard Preston, a leading science writer and author of *The Hot Zone* and *The Wild Trees*. The 2007 edition features a mix of new voices and prize-winning writers, including James Gleick, Neil deGrasse Tyson, John Horgan, William Langewiesche, Heather Pringle, and others.

ISBN-13: 978-0-618-72224-2 • ISBN-10: 0-618-72224-6 $28.00 CL
ISBN-13: 978-0-618-72231-0 • ISBN-10: 0-618-72231-9 $14.00 PA

THE BEST AMERICAN SPIRITUAL WRITING™ 2007. PHILIP ZALESKI, editor, introduction by HARVEY COX. Featuring an introduction by Harvey Cox, author of the groundbreaking *Secular City*, this year's edition of this "excellent annual" (*America*) contains selections that gracefully probe the role of faith in modern life. Contributors include Robert Bly, Adam Gopnik, George Packer, Marilynne Robinson, John Updike, and others.

ISBN-13: 978-0-618-83333-7 • ISBN-10: 0-618-83333-1 $28.00 CL
ISBN-13: 978-0-618-83346-7 • ISBN-10: 0-618-83346-3 $14.00 PA

 HOUGHTON MIFFLIN COMPANY www.houghtonmifflinbooks.com